Y0-BEB-449

PRIVATE MATTERS
AND PUBLIC CULTURE
IN POST-REFORMATION
ENGLAND

Lena Cowen Orlin

Private Matters and Public Culture in Post-Reformation England

Cornell University Press

ITHACA AND LONDON

DA
320
.O74
1994

Copyright © 1994 by Cornell University

All rights reserved. Except for brief quotations in a review,
this book, or parts thereof, must not be reproduced in any
form without permission in writing from the publisher. For
information, address Cornell University Press, Sage House,
512 East State Street, Ithaca, New York 14850.

First published 1994 by Cornell University Press.

Library of Congress Cataloging-in-Publication Data

Orlin, Lena Cowen.
   Private matters and public culture in post-Reformation England /
Lena Cowen Orlin.
     p. cm.
   Includes bibliographical references and index.
   ISBN 0-8014-2858-0
   1. England—Social life and customs—16th century. 2. Domestic
drama, English—History and criticism. 3. Patriarchy—England—
History—16th century. 4. Property—England—History—16th
century. 5. Privacy—England—History—16th century.
6. Reformation—England. I. Title.
DA320.O74 1994
941.06—dc20   94-1035

Printed in the United States of America.

♾The paper in this book meets the minimum requirements
of the American National Standard for Information Sciences—
Permanence of Paper for Printed Library Materials, ANSI Z39.48-1984.

For Glenn

CONTENTS

LIST OF ILLUSTRATIONS   ix

ACKNOWLEDGMENTS   xi

A NOTE ON DOCUMENTATION AND EDITORIAL PRACTICE   xv

ABBREVIATIONS   xvii

Introduction   1

Chapter One   The Place of the Private   15
Coda One   *Alyce Ardern's Rapes*   79

Chapter Two   Patriarchalism and Its Discontents   85
Coda Two   *Patriarchalism in Practice*   131

Chapter Three   Virtue and Domestic Interest   137
Coda Three   *The Key and the Cogito*   182

Chapter Four   Domestic Abdications   191
Coda Four   *Impertinent Tragedies*   246

Conclusion   253

BIBLIOGRAPHY OF PUBLISHED SOURCES   271

INDEX   299

ILLUSTRATIONS

1   "Riding the Skimmington," a plaster frieze at Montacute House in Somerset   *6*

2   Woodcut illustration from the 1633 edition of *Arden of Feversham* depicting Thomas Arden's murder   *17*

3   Eighteenth-century engraving of Thomas Ardern's house   *34*

4   Photograph of the exterior of Thomas Ardern's house   *36*

5   Photograph of the interior of Thomas Ardern's house   *38*

6   Two manuscript pages from an eighteenth-century miscellany compiled by William Cook   *58*

7   Eighteenth-century printed illustration from the Cook miscellany depicting Thomas Arden's murder   *60*

8   Woodcut illustration of the zodiacal man from Thomas Bretnor's *New Almanac and Prognostication for . . . 1615*   *196*

9   Woodcut illustration of the zodiacal man from Richard Allestree's *Prognostication for . . . 1623*   *197*

10   Chart of the number twelve from Cornelius Agrippa's 1531 *De occulta philosophia*   *208–9*

11   Chart of the number twelve from a 1651 English translation of Cornelius Agrippa's *De occulta philosophia*   *210–11*

12   Photograph of the exterior of Walter Calverley's house   *231*

13   Chart of household goods from Randle Holme's 1649 *Academy of Armory*   *257*

ACKNOWLEDGMENTS

This book has had several lives, each of which I identify with one of its acute and generous readers. Alan Dessen oversaw the literary project upon which it is remotely based. Leeds Barroll discovered its second, more historical incarnation. Catherine Belsey inspired its final form. My gratitude to each cannot be diluted merely for being shared.

Alan first introduced me to the Folger Shakespeare Library and thus to the academic enterprise at its best. John F. Andrews, former Chairman of the Folger Institute, and Susan Zimmerman, former Associate Chairman, made possible my affiliation with this remarkable institution. This association has continued under the supportive administration of Werner Gundersheimer, Library Director, and Barbara Mowat, Director of Academic Programs.

I think back to the Folger's resident community of scholars who first welcomed me here as they have so many: Doris Adler, Joe Martin, Jeanne Roberts, Barbara Taft, and, again, Leeds Barroll. Thanks also to the Folger, I have had the opportunity to work closely with the Steering Committee of the Folger Institute Center for the History of British Political Thought: John Pocock, Lois Schwoerer, and Gordon Schochet. They have provided an ongoing education in academic endeavor undertaken with dedication, energy, humor, passion, and collegiality.

Through the Library I have met many others who have offered moral support and intellectual stimulation: Deborah Curren Aquino, David Bevington, Stuart Curran, Juliet Dusinberre, Andrew Gurr, Miranda Johnson-Haddad, Carol Hall, John Headley, Allie Howe, Linda

Merians, Gail Paster, David Rubin, Audrey Stanley, Homer Swander, Robert K. Turner, Jack Undank, Paul Werstine, and, most especially, Tom Greene, Mary McKinley, and Joe Price.

For their contributions to this particular project I owe much to two readers for Cornell University Press: Constance Jordan, who helped me find my disciplinary footing and an organizational strategy in Chapter 1, and Jean Howard, who knew how to sort out the concluding sections. Although there would have been no Chapter 2 without Gordon Schochet, David Harris Sacks also had a great deal to do with its final thesis. Sue Lanser and Nancy Hodge made me gifts of their concern and advice; they solved the problems that arose as the manuscript was in press.

I am also grateful to those who have read (or listened to) some of this material in its various early versions and who have offered encouragement: Susan Amussen, Ann Jennalie Cook, Natalie Zemon Davis, Arthur Kinney, Carole Levin, Nick Phillipson, Marie Plasse, Karen Robertson, Mihoko Suzuki, and the members of an N.E.H. Humanities Institute directed by Jean Howard and held at the Folger in the summer of 1992. David Cressy, Shirley Nelson Garner, and Betty Hageman gave me the opportunity to share three papers with Folger, Shakespeare Association of America, and Modern Language Association audiences (respectively). For specific conversations and suggestions, I am most grateful to Peter Blayney, Michael Bristol, Betty Jo Teeter Dobbs, John Guy, Terence Murphy, Linda Levy Peck, Lois Schwoerer, Alan Sinfield, and Bruce Smith. Harriet Cowen, King David Johnson, and Marion Trousdale made material contributions, as well.

Most of my research has been conducted at the Folger with the help of Reading Room Supervisor Betsy Walsh and staffers Rosalind Larry, Harold Batie, LuEllen DeHaven, Karen Greene, Camille Seerattan, and Kathleen Stewart. Former Folger Reference Librarian Nati Krivatsy, Manuscript Curator and Cataloguer Laetitia Yeandle, Cataloguer Monique Hulvey, and Photographer Julie Ainsworth offered special help. So did Georgianna Ziegler during her tenure as Curator of the Furness Collection at the University of Pennsylvania and more recently as Reference Librarian at the Folger. I also thank the staffs of the Houghton Library at Harvard, the Library of Congress, the British Library, the Shakespeare Center Library in Stratford-upon-Avon, and the Huntington Library. I worked at the last of these with a generous grant, for which I am particularly grateful to Martin Ridge, and I appreciate the hospitality and help extended by Virginia Renner, Elsa Sink, and Mary Wright. At a critical point I received wonderfully generous information and encouragement from Arthur Percival of the

Faversham Society in Kent. Charlotte Haslam sent me information on the Calverleys; Roy and Norma Pleasance shared Arden's house and an architectural survey of it.

Three research leaves made possible the completion of this book. From the National Endowment for the Humanities I received a summer stipend in 1986, a senior fellowship in 1989–90, and a travel-to-collections grant in 1991. Patricia E. Tatspaugh, who has been a good friend at the Folger and in London, made the year-long leave possible by undertaking the Executive Directorship of the Folger Institute for 1989–90.

The quality of my daily life has been largely and happily determined by the astonishingly accomplished, dedicated, and good-humored people who have worked with the Folger Institute: Program Administrator Kathleen Lynch and Program Assistants and Coordinators Pierrette Ashcroft, Greg Barz, Carol Brobeck, Amy Brooks, Ivy Gilbert, Andrea Harris, Pat Kelly, and Rebecca Willson. For her fierce commitment to this project, as to all advanced research, I owe very special thanks to Carol. The book has also benefited from the attention of our Folger colleague Mary Tonkinson and of Cornell editor Carol Betsch.

My most profound debt is that which I can least explain—at least in this forum. What I share with and owe to the dedicatee of this volume shall remain a private matter.

L. C. O.

A NOTE ON DOCUMENTATION
AND EDITORIAL PRACTICE

Spelling has been modernized and punctuation regularized in all quotations from early modern texts.

Footnotes give short references only and are keyed to the Bibliography, where complete publication information is provided. For works from the early modern period, place of publication is London except when otherwise noted.

For the reader's convenience I refer to modern editions of Renaissance texts whenever possible. The Bibliography listing for each text indicates the edition used, and all textual and footnote citations refer to the specified editions. When multiple editions have been consulted, the footnotes specify copytext.

ABBREVIATIONS

APC	*Acts of the Privy Council*, ed. John Roche Dasent
CPR	*Calendar of Patent Rolls: Edward VI*, ed. R. H. Brodie
CSPD	*Calendar of State Papers, Domestic Series*: Edward VI, Mary I, Elizabeth I, ed. Robert Lemon
CSPF	*Calendar of State Papers, Foreign Series*: Edward VI, Mary I, ed. William B. Turnbull
DNB	*Dictionary of National Biography*, ed. Sir Leslie Stephen and Sir Sidney Lee
House of Commons	*The History of Parliament: The House of Commons, 1509–1558*, ed. S. T. Bindoff
JBS	*Journal of British Studies*
L & P	*Letters and Papers, Foreign and Domestic of the Reign of Henry VIII*, ed. J. S. Brewer et al.
OED	*Oxford English Dictionary*
RCHM	*Royal Commission on Historic Manuscripts*
SEL	*Studies in English Literature*
STC	*A Short-Title Catalogue of Books Printed in England, Scotland, and Ireland, 1475–1640*, ed. A. W. Pollard and G. R. Redgrave; rev. ed., ed. Katherine Panzer et al.
Tilley	Morris Palmer Tilley, *A Dictionary of Proverbs in England in the Sixteenth and Seventeenth Centuries*
Wing STC	*A Short-Title Catalogue of Books Printed in England, Scotland, Ireland, Wales, and British America, 1641–1700*, ed. Donald Wing

INTRODUCTION

England, according to the pioneering historian of private life, Philippe Ariès, is "the birthplace of privacy." He advances one cause: the popularity of diaries in that country in the late sixteenth century. "In France," he asserts, "there is nothing comparable."

Against his thesis can be juxtaposed another distinction between England and France, one tied to English legal traditions and observed by Donald R. Kelley. Kelley particularizes English common law for its "property fetish," which, he suggests, significantly antedates the sixteenth century and can be traced back to Bracton: "The overriding issue in civil society, and especially, it would seem, in English civil society, was the acquisition of things . . . and of course their retention, use, and inheritance. . . . private property, in a complex feudal context, was the central question of English society and social thought."[1]

The correlation of Ariès and Kelley introduces my own working hypothesis about early modern England, which locates the private in property, both real and movable. In essence, I refer to the household (as "owned" by occupance in addition to or in place of legal title) and to its accoutrements (including implements necessary to its operation as well as goods more indulgent of self-expression). The comparison at issue here is less nationalistic—that is, whether or not England in fact pioneered the private—than it is periodic, for my notion is that the medieval property fetish achieved its full and comprehensive measure in England in the sixteenth century. With the Reformation was inaugu-

1. Philippe Ariès, Introduction to *Passions of the Renaissance* (1986), p. 5; Donald R. Kelley, *Human Measure* (1990), pp. 167–71.

rated a glorification of the individual household, and this had consequences for the history of private matters.

During the sixteenth century, for example, the phrase "A man's house is his castle" became proverbial.[2] Even as the era of ambitious church and monastic construction ended, England also celebrated the decay of the old architectural form of the feudal lord's fortress: "At this present," William Harrison wrote in 1577, "there are very few or no castles at all maintained within England." Those remaining, built and maintained by the crown, stood in border areas vulnerable to foreign invasion. Like the dissolution of the monasteries, the decline of the castle was the occasion for Tudor propaganda, while the central monarchy's deracination of the feudal system and of its rival nuclei of political, economic, and military authority was mythologized instead as the introduction to an era of internal peace and security. After all, the apologist Harrison concluded, "it is not the nature of a good Englishman . . . to be caged up as in a coop and hedged in with stone walls."[3]

Of more importance here is the consequence that the perceived decline of the castle as a functional architectural form released it to the realms of proverb, of metaphor, and even of legal pronouncement; as Edward Coke put it in a report from the King's Bench, "the house of every one is to him his castle and fortress, as well for defense against injury and violence, as for his repose."[4] If every man's house could be his castle, then every house could be a little world sufficient unto itself, resistant of intrusion, still amenable to the nation-state but finally, as Coke suggests, protective of individual privacy.

The material effects of the Reformation were also necessary to the realization of the proverbial conceit. Vast monastic acreages dispossessed by the crown found their way for the first time into private ownership; the stone, lead, tin, and tile of razed abbey buildings were reused in domestic construction to give new senses of permanence, fashion, and competitive status; householders displayed ecclesiastical plate and valuables on their cupboard shelves; and each beneficiary of this redistribution of once inalienable resources discovered his sense of individual identity enlarged in his possessions. With this was coupled a thriving merchant economy, which imported a cornucopia of goods to

2. See Tilley, M473: "A Man's house is his castle."

3. William Harrison, *Description of England* (1587), pp. 221–23. See also John Leland as cited by Charles W. C. Oman, *Castles* (1926), p. 23; Philip Julius, "Diary" (1602), pp. 37–39; and William Westerman, *Sword of Maintenance* (1600), sig. C1^{v}. Like Harrison, Westerman purveys the national myth: "our castles, bearing only the ancient titles of war, are become for the most part ruinous by long peace."

4. Edward Coke, Report on Semayne's Case (1605), translated into English in *Reports of Sir Edward Coke* (1658), sig. Pp3^{r}. For Coke's legal precedents, see Chapter 2, note 38.

higher standards, in greater variety, and for unprecedented availability. There were, too, the new avenues to wealth and to the purchase of lands and chattels, through trade and through the offices of an expanding central government. These phenomena brought the aristocratic experience of the self-contained and self-celebrating castle within the reach of householders of non-aristocratic classes.

The builders of Renaissance great houses may have ornamented their structures with the decorative crenellations and gatehouses that recalled the most common castellar forms, but neither they nor less wealthy men actually built fortresses. Meanwhile, those who inherited fortified houses pierced the defensive walls with windows, and those who lived within ancient moats drained, infilled, and planted them. As the proverb emblematizes and as must be self-evident, the universal castle was an ideational construct, not a physical reality. This book primarily addresses the conceptual consequences of the Reformation. In doing so, it comprehends the social, economic, administrative, architectural, and material records of the period; by these counterdisciplinary means the history of property is linked with the history of privacy.

In the decades following the Reformation, the state and its attendant institutions reformulated ideas of social order, ideas adapted to the religious upheaval launched by the crown. The state designated the individual household, in the absence of the old authoritarian church and of a national police, as the primary unit of social control. It identified the householder as responsible for the maintenance of moral order in his immediate sphere but to macrocosmic benefit. And it reinforced the preexistent patriarchal hierarchy to further empower him politically and also to ensure his accountability. As a result the householder enjoyed a sense of individual agency that devolved from his hegemonic authorization.

Hegemonic synthesis is not my aim here. Rather, I introduce notional ideals for household relationships as the precondition for an apprehension of real stresses on those relationships, whether they are those easily (or in theory easily) dichotomized as husband and wife, father and son, brother and sister, and master and servant, or whether they are the more vexed and ambiguous ones of host and guest, mother and son, and mistress and servant. Because, in contemporary tracts, domestic relationships were primarily defined and negotiated in terms of household responsibilities, these responsibilities are a center of interest throughout this book. A recurrent crux involves the global accountability of the householder (in his various roles as husband, father, brother, master, and host) for not only the well-being but also the actions of wife, son, sister, servant, and guest. A social history would reveal that these domestic roles and duties were contested in practice, but in this conceptual history I find that they were often irresolute in theory, too. Such irresolutions indicate that the history of the private was contentious and motile.

For this study of ways in which the cultural phenomena associated with what we call "private life" changed in the wake of the Reformation, then, I identify "the private," for all practical purposes, with the household. While my argument must have some grounding in social history, my aim is a cultural history of the house: its notional structures, prescribed activities, prevailing aspirations, and persistent conflicts. My particular interest is not in how post-Reformation men and women conducted their private lives but, rather, in how they conceptualized their private lives and, especially, in their own awareness of how these conceptualizations both served and sometimes failed the community. This awareness informs four images of the early modern household which I present as emblems of my argument concerning contemporary notions of privacy. As a group, they introduce representative contradictions. The last of the four deals, as does much of this book, with the social function of the Elizabethan and Jacobean drama.

My first emblem, from Sir John Harington's "Praise of Private Life," demonstrates how the castle metaphor served the early modern exaltation of the household.[5] Harington declares that "the solitary man in his house exerciseth himself daily in prayer and godly contemplation, wherewith he useth the study of philosophy, both divine and human." In this, he says, the solitary man "shunneth the snares of Satan and, assisted with God's aid, repulseth all his assaults. So living securely, he inhabiteth a castle inexpugnable." But the following passage interrupts the logical sequence of this moral discourse; it is an intervening celebration of the self-definition achievable by the solitary man only, or so it is implied, in his own impregnable house-castle: "There, are no princes whom he need to please: there, is no body to abuse him; there, may he speak truly without disguising; there, is he subject to no commandment but his whose sight pierceth the darkest desert. There, is no poison of the body nor corrupting of the mind. There, is he not forced to flatter the people nor admire the magistrates. There, needeth he not bow his knee to betters nor adore any but God above."

Admittedly, this treatise is an exercise in translation, largely from Petrarch's *De vita solitaria*, and it is conventional in its depiction of the *beatus vir* and its opposition of country and court. But the passage is

5. John Harington, "Praise of Private Life"; see especially pp. 341–42.

also one in which Harington freely interpolates particulars for the English gentry: such "domestical exercises" of the private estate as music, conversation with friends, hawking, hunting, fishing, and fowling. Harington is or would like to believe himself to be a subscriber to the native promise of the universal castle, and he would like to read the castle metaphor in its guise as the purveyor of a vision of the secure and uncontested authority and "repose" of the individual English householder.

My second emblem is the contrasting vision of an anonymous plasterworker. The castle form that infused post-Reformation attitudes was one of thick stone walls penetrated only by the narrow slits of machicolations designed for launching missiles, never by windows vulnerable to attack. The image bears no relationship to that of the paradigmatic private house outlined in plaster relief in figure 1. This frieze ornaments one wall of the great hall at Montacute House, which was built in Somerset in the 1590s. At the center of its first section is the house. Inside, a man holds an infant while drawing a beer. His wife knocks him on the head, perhaps for his inattention to the child. Meanwhile, outside the house stands a second man directing our attention to this inversion of patriarchal authority. In the second section, the battered husband is mocked by his neighbors and townsmen, who parade him through the community astride a pole, subjecting him to a skimmington ride.[6]

Such communal rites of humiliation have been much commented on in recent years. But my immediate interest is in neither the corrective uses of carnival nor the normative gender hierarchy thereby reinforced; rather, I wish to attend to the plastic schematization of the house seen in the foreground. It stands in stark contrast to a building in the far distance, which presents itself as a closed planar surface with peaked roof. It is even more unlike the church, with its density of form, the detail of its crenellated steeple and portico, and, in defiance of even rudimentary perspective, the gated, wraparound walls of its yard. The house of the battered husband is indicated merely by two posts, a single brace, the fold of a roof—and entirely transparent walls.

In part this last is artistic license to permit our own view of the disordered household. But with regard to the watchful neighbor, it is also a fond symbolization of the prescribed social practice recorded by

6. For variations on this ritual of humiliation, see Natalie Zemon Davis, "Reasons of Misrule" (1971) and "Women on Top" (1975); Daniel Fabre, "Families" (1986), p. 536; Buchanan Sharp, *In Contempt of All Authority* (1980), pp. 104–5; and E. P. Thompson, "Rough Music" (1972). See also Karen Newman, "Renaissance Family Politics" (1986), and Michael D. Bristol, *Carnival and Theater* (1985), especially pp. 164–67.

FIGURE 1. The plaster frieze "Riding the Skimmington" from Montacute House, built in Somerset in the 1590s. Photograph © National Trust 1992 and reproduced by permission.

a foreign visitor in 1602: "In England every citizen is bound by oath to keep a sharp eye at his neighbor's house, as to whether the married people live in harmony." Lawrence Stone has concluded that the "gigantic flood" of complaints brought before the church courts during the early modern period demonstrates that this mandate for public vigilance was widely exercised.[7] Social regulation of this sort militated against privacy; in fact, it engendered a suspicion of the private. In other words, the cultural ambition to champion each householder as lord of his own castle conflicted with the compulsion to manage him through communal surveillance of his personal affairs.

My third emblem, which incorporates a set of reports from the Essex affair of 1600–1601, presents us with a variation on this suspicion of the private; it is political rather than domestic. William Harrison had helped to keep alive the tradition of representing political insurrection in terms of a rebellious lord's castle. Harrison describes King Stephen as having "live[d] in perpetual fear of those houses and the rebellion of his lords upon every light occasion conceived, who then were full so strong as he if not more strong." King Henry II, according to Harrison, learned by this example to raze castles.[8] From this perspective it is hardly remarkable that a variety of Elizabethan records exploit the symbol of the private fortress to chart both an earl's rebellion and the queen's response.

In December 1599, when Essex returned from Ireland, Elizabeth "dispersed" his household, a potential army of 160, requiring "every man to seek a new fortune," except for a few who would be permitted to attend Essex "where it will be her Majesty's will to send him." A year later came this ominous report: "The Earl of Essex is now returned to London, and it is much noted how his doors are set open to all comers," including "many captains, men of broken fortunes, discontented persons." Within a month the lord treasurer sent his eldest son to Essex with the complaints against him that he permitted "base captains and rascals . . . to have free access unto him" and that "his house was open to all new comers . . . whereby he discovered himself to affect popularity." Another month passed, and a delegation of nobles required Essex to "disperse his disordered company in his house." At his arraignment ten days later, "the only matter objected were his practice to surprise the Court, his coming in arms into London to raise rebellion, and the defending his house against the Queen's forces."[9]

---

7. Philip Julius, p. 65; Lawrence Stone, *Family, Sex, and Marriage* (1977), p. 6.
8. Harrison, p. 221.
9. Compiled by G. B. Harrison in *Last Elizabethan Journal* (1933), pp. 56–57, 132, and 140–41, from sources including the Penshurst Papers and Camden's history of Elizabeth.

These reports from several sources in fact evoke two competing images. The first is Harrison's antimonarchic castle, here defended against Elizabeth I. As in Harrison, however, the "castle" both threatens the state and serves the state: threatens because it is defended against Elizabeth, and serves because it provides a ready, universally comprehensible, and persuasive articulation of the danger Essex represents. At the same time, the reports introduce a new, second, and paradoxical anxiety concerning the residence that is too *un*like the fortress. This is the fear of a house that is too open, penetrable by and hospitable to any number of disorderly and masterless men, analogized implicitly with the female body in its stubborn resistance of male control.

The stone walls of the castle versus the transparent walls of the Montacute frieze, Harington's refuge versus communal observation, the defended doors of Essex House versus its open doors: these are synecdoches for a schizophrenic public policy. The state relied on the private household and also distrusted its internal activities; it authorized the householder and also deployed the larger community to monitor his domestic conduct; it felt itself endangered by the castle and also exploited the castle for its own propagandistic purposes. Such contradictions played out at the individual level, as well. The householder who aspired to enjoy the personal liberty celebrated by Sir John Harington would nonetheless have identified with the townsman in the Montacute frieze, who looks outward to establish a bond of sympathy with his viewer even while pointing into a troubled house. The social warrant to monitor neighboring households would, in short, have been compounded by native curiosity, and both phenomena together would have worked at cross-purposes with developing ambitions for personal privacy.

My fourth emblem looks to a dramatic genre to document the existence in the post-Reformation period of what I have termed a "curiosity" about the domestic affairs of others. The plays of the Elizabethan and Jacobean public theater satisfy the desires to which the Montacute frieze also caters: to see through walls, to discover the intimate secrets of conjugal relationships, to identify disorder and to imagine that in this way it is mastered, to participate in a communal restoration of the preferred order of domestic things. In serving these desires, the drama always, regardless of historically specific staging configurations, associates its audience with a fourth wall. In the first chapter I contend that the anonymous *Arden of Feversham* invented a dramatic genre to satisfy these voyeuristic desires in their domestic strain, a genre since labeled "domestic tragedy." By representing a criminal investigation, during which townsmen trace rushes found in a murdered householder's shoes to his own parlor floor and then discover a bloodstain on his accustomed seat, the play embodies a house yielding up its secrets to observers. Curiosity about the private lives of others surely accounts in some part for the fact that the next examples of the new genre were also based on historical incidents: in 1599 *A Warning for Fair Women* and *Two Lamentable Tragedies* followed *Arden* in dramatizing notorious sixteenth-century domestic crimes.

In this book I pursue the genre as an avenue into the idea of the private. In 1831 John Payne Collier first recognized this variant form of Elizabethan tragedy as "domestic." Undoubtedly he borrowed the term from Denis Diderot, who had announced for the French eighteenth-century stage a new dramatic kind, a "tragédie domestique et bourgeoise." The distinguishing characteristic of the Elizabethan variety was that, unlike orthodox tragedy, it featured protagonists who were neither royal nor noble.[10] Collier's successors easily succumbed to the influence of loose association and characterized the plays in Diderot's companion term, as bourgeois or, alternatively, as middle-class—even though those terms, with their implication of class consciousness, are inapplicable in any unmediated form to the Renaissance.

The word *domestic*, however, remains truer to its modern sense. For example: in Thomas Heywood's 1624 play *The Captives*, a character asks if the "strange news" received in a letter is "foreign," learns that it is instead "domestic," and then is told (in a play on the alternative meaning of domestic) that "'Tis household business all."[11] According with my own emphasis on "household business," the term *domestic tragedy* is for me a happy anachronism. The plays materialize the house in all its associations: first, as the primary social and economic unit of early modern English culture; second, as a construction delimiting a world-in-little and accommodating its occupants' most basic physical needs for shelter and sustenance as well as their psychological needs for beauty and perdurability; and finally, as an ideological construct receptive to the superimposition of political models and moral regulations.

This emphasis on the household is also true to the generic form, I maintain, because the protagonists of the plays generally categorized as "domestic" tragedies are property owners, householders, and most often gentlemen. Henry Hitch Adams's statement that "the lowly social station of the tragic protagonist" is "the one invariable characteristic of

10. John Payne Collier, *History of English Dramatic Poetry* (1831), p. 49; Denis Diderot, "Second Entretien" (1757), p. 119. The authoritative critical text is Henry Hitch Adams, *English Domestic or, Homiletic Tragedy* (1943).
11. Thomas Heywood, *The Captives* (1624), 3.1.51–54.

the genre" is therefore an exaggeration: these characters are admittedly not royal and clearly not noble, but neither are they lowly.[12] Property defined privilege in the early modern period, and its ownership placed the protagonists of the domestic tragedies in putative positions of status as well as of social accountability, as "kings" of their respective castles.[13]

To assert the significance of the domestic tragedy for a history of the private is to advance a specific argument about the role of literature in cultural history, to extend and invert the premise of Hayden White and Natalie Zemon Davis (among others) that archives can be fiction.[14] White and Davis propose that historical records suffer a narrative construct and submit to the inflection of interpretation. In the first chapter I initially press a distinction between the two forms, preferring the path of the documentary archive to that of the fictionalized chronicle in order to construct my own narrative of an English domestic scandal at least as notorious in its way as that of Martin Guerre. But this is a methodological convenience adopted to serve that particular argument. Elsewhere I rely on the ellision of source materials which White and Davis have effected and pursue an objective that is complementary to theirs: to demonstrate that, just as archives can be fiction, fiction, too, can be an archive. In this case, the domestic tragedy can be a resource for understanding the private matters of its period. The thesis is put to its most rigorous test in the third chapter, where I read a playscript of 1603 as a key text in the contemporary discourse of moral philosophy.

The historiographic principle is particularly useful in discussions of the post-Reformation period. Early modern ideals of order were constructed hierarchically, but they were conveyed analogically. The rage for analogy explains the permeability during the English Renaissance of discourses that today seem categorically distinct. It is important for us to continue to distinguish these discourses, because it is when issues transcend form or take multiple forms that they most convey their urgency and should command our particular attention. I see significance in the intersections of genres, in the defiance of taxonomy, in instances when the nature and function of the household become a

12. Adams, p. 1. On this subject, see also my "Man's House as His Castle in *Arden of Feversham*" (1985).

13. Susan D. Amussen emphasizes that sermons and manuals for household administration addressed themselves to "independent, property-holding households" (*Ordered Society* [1988], p. 67). The relationship of these genres to playtexts of the period is of relevance to my argument.

14. See Hayden White, "Value of Narrativity" (1981), and Natalie Zemon Davis, *Fiction in the Archives* (1987).

concern of architectural history, common proverb, national myth, legal thought, economic change, social prescription, folk ritual, local litigation, political event, and theatrical innovation. I have added to the castle proverb, Harrison's apologetic, and the Coke report the emblematic examples of the Harington translation, the Montacute frieze, the Essex rebellion, and the *Arden* playscript not only to illustrate domestic ideas and ideals in competition but also to demonstrate the prevalence of the theme through its appearance in a variety of sources and conventional disciplines.

The early modern literary forms that most directly address private matters include conduct books, household manuals, and sermons. I generally refer to their interests as "oeconomic." This is the taxonomic term of choice in the Renaissance, and it embraces such topics as the structure and governance of the household, the relationship of husband and wife, the education of children, and the supervision of servants. I prefer *oeconomic* because the word has not survived in common usage and is thus uncompromised by any modern association. For all its appearances to the contrary, the term *private* is not transparent, and in my first chapter I deliberately problematize our understanding of it.

At the same time, the oeconomic discourse is so much of its time that it inevitably has practical handicaps. Because oeconomic literary forms were thoroughly inflected by their role in advancing a larger hegemonic project, they must be examined in relation to such other contemporary texts as those in political thought (see Chapter 2), moral philosophy (see Chapter 3), and the occult sciences (see Chapter 4). The circulation and interpenetrability of these discourses determined the character of oeconomic conceptualization as much as—and for us far more revealingly than—did the oeconomic discourse proper. All contributed to the cultural construction of what in the third chapter I call a "domestic ethic."

The taxonomic permeability of thought in the early modern period engendered permutations of thought. As discussed in the second chapter, the discourse of political obligation included among its constituent philosophies patriarchalism, which in turn had two branches. The older, the more thoroughly established, and the more cogently argued was domestic patriarchalism; it traced to Aristotle its postulate of the father's absolute authority in his household. The second branch was political patriarchalism, which in the late sixteenth century first analogized the household's structures of authority with those of the state and then adapted domestic strictures to impose political obligation. The political branch cannibalized domestic ideology in order to advance the doctrine of royal absolutism. The translation of a domestic philosophy into political ideology testified to the former's effective power. But, once turned to this ideological purpose, the domestic began to be depreciated and eventually to be viewed as a mere service philosophy, a lesser adumbration of a larger order. By this means analogy came to "perform" hierarchy.

Having inherited this clearly stratified world order for state and household, we cannot readily intuit the place of the private in the early modern period—nor can we fully appreciate the conceptual underpinnings of one symptom of oeconomic thought in the period, the domestic tragedy. Among other things, the domestic tragedy seems to have borrowed political language and structures to validate its generic innovations on traditional tragic forms. Of course, theater was no more immune to the shifting of order than were other spheres. The synthesis of political and domestic which authorized the playtexts on which this book focuses and which allowed them to signify more largely than we can easily imagine eventually disintegrated along with a comprehensive patriarchal philosophy. We are the inheritors of a comparable literary hierarchy, as well, one that values state tragedies over domestic tragedies and that has neglected this rich resource for cultural history.

The playtexts I examine are in some sense vehicles merely, mechanisms of expediency, because they establish limits for a topic that otherwise defies limits. At the same time, my aim is not a tidy argument. One strategy for both acknowledging the artificiality and resisting the constraints of my generic framework is to append to each chapter a complementary "coda." In each I pursue a thesis that is related to material in the preceding chapter but that in some respect proceeds on a tangent from it and withstands incorporation within its structure. Often, these codas are more speculative than the main chapters. But they are not afterthoughts or lesser thoughts. On occasion I use them to position myself in relation to matters discussed in the accompanying chapters, to take up feminist issues with regard to social practice, say, or postmodern understandings of subjectivity.

My emphasis on playtexts should not disguise the fact that my first interest remains cultural history. The specific issues are how the private established its claims on public consciousness, how domestic patriarchalism was exploited by political discourse and was then reconstructed by it, how friendship and marriage were redefined in the wake of the Reformation, and how the householder celebrated and also resisted his hegemonic authorization. I approach the plays as principal witnesses to the struggle of early modern English men and women to fix their relationships with family members and household fellows and to impose a human logic on their immediate environment.

I read these plays as bearers of cultural value, as barers of counter-cultural uncertainty, and thus as engenderers of cultural meaning. In Thomas Kyd's English translation of Torquato Tasso's *Householder's Philosophy*, we find that "the form or fashion of the world is none other than an order" and that, "comparing little things with great, . . . the form of a house is the order, and the reformation of the house or family, none other than a second setting it in order."[15] But even if its end, too, is the restoration of order, the first business of drama is the setting in train of disorder. The texts I treat here serve as a public laboratory for intellectual investigation of disorders in the private sphere. They explore the nature of women, acknowledge ambiguities in the inscription of domestic rule, test the practical application of abstract philosophies of rule and order, register the competing pulls of political and economic interests in the household, expose the obsolescence of received ideas of virtue and ideals of friendship and benefice, and eventually discover that masculine authority can be an unwelcome burden. To the same extent that the cultural meaning revealed in them is complex and imperfectly orthodox, these plays participate in the construction of their culture's ideology.

In this they illustrate J. G. A. Pocock's thesis that every text is an "event." Texts, he says, "act upon the languages in which they are performed: as they perform they inform, injecting new words, facts, perceptions, and rules of the game; and, whether gradually or catastrophically, the language matrix becomes modified by the acts performed in it."[16] For most of this book I take texts as cultural and historiographic events. But in the first chapter I work an inversion on Pocock, too, making a text out of an event in order to introduce the claim of the private on public culture in the immediate post-Reformation period.

15. Torquato Tasso, *Householder's Philosophy* (1588), sig. F2^r.
16. J. G. A. Pocock, "Texts as Events" (1987), p. 29.

Chapter One

THE PLACE OF THE PRIVATE

Thomas Arden, known in his own time as Ardern, a gentleman of Faversham in Kent, was murdered in 1551. According to the Faversham Wardmote Book, his killers included his wife, Alyce; her lover, Thomas Morsby; and eight other conspirators. The crime became widely known outside Faversham when this official verdict, much amplified, was transmitted in two other contemporary records: Holinshed's 1577 *Chronicles of England, Scotland, and Ireland* and an anonymous play of 1592 based on Holinshed and titled *The Lamentable and True Tragedy of Master Arden of Feversham in Kent. Who was most wickedly murdered, by the means of his disloyal and wanton wife* (see figure 2). To reopen an investigation into this murder is to operate for the most part independently of—and in many respects against the grain of—the received tradition of chronicle and playscript. But these two redactions of the story remain crucial to the ways in which Ardern's case history advances my thesis concerning the place of the private in early modern England.

The murder of Thomas Ardern placed on the public agenda issues of private contention and consequence, in this way contributing to the reconceptualization of what we would call "private life" in the wake of the Reformation. One public site was the 1592 theatricalization of the story. The other and inaugural site was Ardern's incorporation into Holinshed's narrative, even despite the chronicler's evident unease about interrupting a history of matters of state for an account that is "but a private matter":

About this time there was at Feversham in Kent a gentleman named
Arden, most cruelly murdered and slain by the procurement of his own
wife. The which murder, for the horribleness thereof, although otherwise it may seem to be *but a private matter, and therefore as it were impertinent
to this history*, I have thought good to set it forth somewhat at large, having
the instructions delivered to me by them, that have used some diligence
to gather the true understanding of the circumstances.[1]

Even as the chronicle admits of the private, its apology for doing so
reifies the traditional hierarchical distinction between the public and
domestic spheres. Holinshed's special pleading for Ardern's story reminds us of how problematic the history of the private was in the early
modern period and of why we so often confront the historiographic
intractability of the private. Nonetheless, in this signal instance Ardern's story violates the conventional boundaries of decorum and the
understood disposition of significances. And it does so to the extent of
nearly five two-column folio pages, an extent described in the chronicle
itself as "large." More significantly, the inclusion by Holinshed of Ardern's story generates its own authorizing undertow, not only creating a
space for successor histories that similarly engage contested domestic
relationships and issues but also eventuating in what reads as an explicit denial of Holinshed's decorous misgivings. In his 1635 report concerning another homicidal wife, Puritan minister Henry Goodcole remarks: "I will only remember you of Mistress Arden, who caused her
husband to be murdered in her own house at Feversham in Kent, the
memorable circumstances thereof *deserving places* in a most approved
chronicle, may be very well spared in this short discourse."[2] The movement from Holinshed's hesitation to Goodcole's assurance, with Ardern's story marking the trajectory, traces one revolution in the early
modern place of the private.

The story of Ardern's murder also foregrounds the periodizing part
of my title, intersected as the story is by the wide-ranging phenomena
that followed from the English Reformation. These include the break
with Rome and with papal authority, the assertion of royal supremacy,
and the incipience of the doctrine of divine right; the mobilization of
faction at court, a readjustment of the relationship between king and
parliament, and a (much-argued) "revolution" in the administration of
government; the conduct of a national propaganda campaign, the imposition on all citizens of an oath of the king's supremacy, and multiple

1. Raphael Holinshed, *Chronicles* (1577), p. 148, emphasis added.
2. Henry Goodcole, *Adultress's Funeral Day* (1635), sig. B1ʳ, emphasis added. This reference to Alice Arden has gone previously unremarked.

FIGURE 2. A woodcut illustrating Thomas Arden's murder from the 1633 (third) quarto edition of *Arden of Feversham*. Reproduced by permission of the Folger Shakespeare Library.

executions for treason and rebellion; the advancement of humanism, private access to scripture, and an impetus toward print culture; the dissolution of the monasteries, the plundering of their treasuries and building materials, and the dispossession of their occupants; the redistribution of national wealth through the transfer of properties from the church to the crown and from the crown to members of the aristocracy and gentry; the use of revenues seized from the church to conduct foreign policy and to subsidize such central government operations as the royal household and administrative offices; the rise of evangelism, the placing on the national agenda of alternative strategies for poor relief and social reform, and a secularized redefinition of charity; the growth of a national identity and sense of history; the reinvention of the household as a unit of social control, the empowerment of the householder as defender of political order, and, finally, the promulgation of an enabling ideology of domestic patriarchalism.

In later chapters, I narrow my focus to the last of these phenomena, the post-Reformation consolidation of the householder's patriarchal authority. In the wake of the Reformation more men and men of a broader range of social classes were able to acquire property and were encouraged to assume the responsibilities and enjoy the perquisites of the householder. Ardern's story, which at one level I have shaped as a murder investigation, at another level reads as the narrative of how an unpropertied Englishman found himself a home. Of course, the story's conclusion in murder means that the loss of that home must be the end of this alternative domestic narrative. Ardern's case nonetheless remains paradigmatic for the present project: the Reformation was the occasion of his domiciliary opportunity. It offered him a home in all the senses in which the period understood the term: a material extension, through his physical house; a social seat, in the larger community; an economic center, for his business pursuits; a political body, of his co-occupant family and servants; a psychological structure, in the sense of place and belonging; and a moral force, as a restraining ethical influence.

One outcome of my reinvestigation of Ardern's case is a new narrative, one that suggests that the political, economic, and religious anxieties provoked by the myriad changes associated with the Reformation not only made it possible for Ardern to become a prominent householder but eventually conspired in his dispossession. Awareness of the interpretive intervention that instead memorialized the story as what Catherine Belsey calls "Alice Arden's crime" takes my argument to its next register, the political conceptualization of the post-Reformation household. For now, however, I am concerned primarily to develop that critical awareness of the apparent scapegoating of Alyce. Only with a thorough understanding of the profound historical themes represented in the life story of Thomas Ardern can we recognize the implications of the fact that reports of the murder of Thomas *Arden* focus on the threats of the desiring woman and of domestic disorder, on the private rather than the public.

To show how the private life of "Arden" was constructed, I compile available records of how the private life of Ardern was conducted, reinforcing the distinction between the two by the selective use of multiple orthographies throughout. These are conduct versus construct, archives versus fiction,[3] and Wardmote Book versus chronicle and play: Ardern versus Arden, Alyce versus Alice, Morsby versus Mosby, Faversham versus Feversham. Because Ardern's story survives in both historical and fictional texts, it illustrates as few other narratives can my argument that "private life" is a conceptual construct.

The ideological construct with which we are most familiar is that transacted in what the sixteenth and seventeenth centuries knew as "oeconomics," printed tracts that we usually identify as conduct literature or domestic manuals. Because these represent an early modern oeconomic discourse shaped in the interest of a prescriptive project, however, we must also consider alternative sources of post-Reformation perspectives on "private" life. The intersection of these

---

3. Cf. Natalie Zemon Davis, *Fiction in the Archives* (1987). For the moment I reify a distinction that she was concerned in certain respects to dissolve.

other discourses exposes the character and complexity of oeconomic conceptualization far more revealingly than do the oeconomics alone. Of these alternative sources, the least attended to is undoubtedly the dramatic. In fact, my analysis of the place of "private" life in the early modern period is also an exploration of the place of dramatic literature in the modern practice of history and an attempt to exploit drama for cultural history.

Ardern's story charts a diagnostic course in a culture burdening the private sphere with new social and moral accountabilities; reshaping cultural ideals of domestic conduct; selectively identifying the symptoms and agents of defaults from those ideals; struggling to verbalize its oeconomic anxieties; and finally, with the anonymous *Arden of Feversham*, inventing a theatrical genre that institutionalizes the meanings of domestic order and the sources of domestic disorder. If *Arden of Feversham* enacts the conservative cultural project of reconfirming the householder's patriarchal authority, as I argue it does, the later plays for which it paved a way do less predictable cultural work. They betray the fact that early moderns, too, recognized some incapacities in their operative belief system. This notion returns me to a methodological through-line of the book: to the extent that the cultural meanings in these plays are complex and imperfectly orthodox, the plays participate in the construction of cultural meaning and, I believe, secure a consequent historiographic purchase.

Finally, a word is required on my method in this chapter, in which I pursue what Gilbert Ryle and Clifford Geertz have termed "thick description."[4] At the first level, this strategy for cultural investigation effects an immediate immersion into a remote society—and early modern England, while deceptively familiar, preserves its remoteness from us. Because the early modern meanings of the "private" are peculiarly fugitive, the method is particularly apt. As part of the immersion process, the method aims for a rich texturing of the social fabric and so is predicated on the accretion of considerable archival detail. This level of particularity will be unsurprising to historians but may be less comfortable for those trained in literary studies.

It is important to recognize that detail in this case serves interests other than the method and is not method-driven. Rather, it plays to a question that has guided my research: if we began only with the information that the historical Thomas Ardern had been murdered, if we did not have contemporary narratives that tell us that his wife was the principal murderer among ten, if in the archives we pursued a

4. Gilbert Ryle, cited by Clifford Geertz, *Interpretation of Cultures* (1973), pp. 6–10.

criminal investigation independent of those fictionalized accounts—accumulating the available evidence about Ardern's life, activities, habits, places of resort, known associates, and possible enemies—would the trail lead us to indict Alyce Ardern?

My answer is that it would not. The fact is that Alyce Ardern scarcely exists in the archives, as is true for many women and especially early modern women, and so she cannot play a part in an archival reconstruction of Ardern's murder. Because the surviving evidence relates to Ardern's public life, his life of making a career, building an estate, and participating in town government, we must seek a motive for murder there, in the records of his public dealings. And, in fact, seduced by the nature of the documents and following the archival project to its end, I do propose an eleventh conspirator in the murder, a candidate from the public sphere. My goal is not an indictment of a historical personage, however. Rather, it is an indictment of historical research, which is always distorted by the absence of those records lost in the passage of time; which must always reach incomplete and provisional conclusions; which discovers the new endings generated by the very process of constructing a new narrative; and which can never be sufficiently aware of the social constructions of even those records that survive. My investigation of Ardern's murder offers an allegory for research, or perhaps a parody of it, and is in part intended to place in skeptical perspective all that follows.

The alternative conclusion to which the archival evidence leads was one available in Ardern's period as well, and this conclusion could just as easily have formed that period's accounts of the murder. Holinshed could have taken the life of Thomas Arden as an object lesson in the unsettling changes of his time. The chronicle could have obsessed about the new professions of an expanding central government, the unprecedented redistribution of land and wealth following the dissolution of the monasteries, the movement from an economy based on barter and the exchange of services to one fueled by cash, the readjustment of ecclesiastical administration and liturgical practice in the wake of the Reformation—and any of these concerns would have seemed more decorous in the context of his history of state. Instead, however, Holinshed and all the redactions of the Arden story closed in upon, worried over, broke generic precedent for, and totemized the murdered man's relationship with his wife. To recognize the early modern historicization of Ardern as a process that domesticated his murder is thus to open one window on the place in which his culture held the "private."

Thomas Ardern's Place

A deposition in the Consistory Court of Canterbury for 13 November 1548 refers to Thomas Ardern as forty years old, born, in other words, around 1508.[5] This newly discovered record supersedes the oral tradition, datable to the eighteenth century, that he was born in 1485 or 1486. That tradition in its own way fed the historicizing process, for it seemed to legitimate Alice Arden's presumed disaffection for her husband by vesting it in the considerable disparity between their ages; it had Arden as fifty-six when he settled in Feversham and Alice exactly half of that. Those who sought such a theme could have found some pretext for it in Holinshed, where Alice is described not only as "tall and well favored" but also as "young." But we can now be certain that the historical Thomas Ardern was younger than the historicized Arden.

As for his place of birth, eighteenth-century manuscript notes give it as Wye in Kent. By contrast, a variant of Holinshed's account of Arden's murder, which survives in manuscript in the hand of John Stow, describes Arden's aged mother as living in Norwich. P. G. M. Hyde has discovered archival confirmation that Ardern may indeed have been born in Norwich.[6] It now seems safe to say that Ardern was native neither to Faversham nor to Kent.

Ardern commenced his professional life in London, as clerk to Sir Edward North, and his patronage by North generally opens twentieth-century versions of his story.[7] This, too, is a tradition I hope to modify by demonstrating that Ardern had a second mentor of at least equal import, Sir Thomas Cheyney, and that, unlike North, Cheyney had the ties to Kent which can account for Ardern's eventual establishment in that county. Because Ardern's geographic, professional, and domestic "establishment" is my subject here, I begin with his relationship to the

---

5. Consistory Court of Canterbury deposition register, X.10.3, fol. 83ʳ. I rely insofar as possible on primary sources. I do not mean to slight necessary debts to my predecessors C. E. Donne (1873), Lionel Cust (1920), and M. L. Wine (1973), but the greatest debts are to Arthur Percival, Honorary Director of the Fleur de Lis Heritage Centre, and to P. G. M. Hyde, Faversham's archivist, who made it possible for me to approach the life of Ardern afresh.

6. For the manuscript notes, see "Was *Arden of Feversham* Written by Shakespeare?" (August 1881, p. 303); summarized by Wine, p. xxxvii. Stow's hand in "The History of a Most Horrible Murder Committed at Feversham in Kent" (BL Harley MS 542) has been identified by Folger Curator of Manuscripts Laetitia Yeandle; the manuscript is hereafter cited as "Stow." I am grateful to Hyde for sharing her research in private correspondence.

7. Peter Clark (mis?)identifies Ardern as a London merchant in *English Provincial Society* (1977), p. 82, and in "Reformation and Radicalism" (1979), p. 126. See also an "Arden', Tho[mas], cit[izen] and clothw[or]k[e]r," who registered a will in London in 1550 (*Index to Testamentary Records* [1974], p. 9).

two men who promoted it. Some sense of these two men is also important to my discussion of Ardern's murder in this respect: if I ask who
might have been expected to take offense at his injury—in particular,
what powerful allies might have been angered by his murder—then the
other side to the coin of North's and Cheyney's promotion of Ardern
must presumably be their protection of him.

Edward North modeled for his clerk the life of a "new" man, a rising
professional in Tudor society.[8] A lawyer educated in part at Cambridge
and admitted to Lincoln's Inn in 1522, he was clerk of the Council of
the City of London when in 1528 or 1529 he advanced his economic
position by wedding Alice, née Squier, the widow and heir first of John
Brigandine and then of Edward Murfyn. North was made clerk of
Parliament in 1531, a position he still held in 1537 when Ardern's
name appears in the documentary record as his assistant. Having at-
tracted the favor of Thomas Cromwell at Parliament, North went on to
achieve the treasurership of the Court of Augmentations in 1540 and
then the chancellorship of the Augmentations in 1544.[9] Meanwhile, in
1542 he was knighted, nominated high sheriff of Cambridge and
Huntington, and elected to represent Cambridge in Parliament. With
Edward VI's accession in 1547, he was appointed to the Privy Council,
although he was soon forced to relinquish the chancellorship of the
Augmentations to a Somerset protégé.[10] Mary retained him on her
Council and, in 1554, despite his support of Jane Grey, created him
Lord North of Kirtling. While he did not inspire great trust or affec-
tion in either of Henry VIII's daughters, North possessed a stature that
neither could ignore. He was among those who escorted Philip II from
Southampton to the royal wedding in Winchester, and he accompanied
Elizabeth from Hatfield to London on her accession, hosting her at his
own London Charterhouse for some days before she removed to the
Tower in preparation for her coronation.[11]

In fact it was in terms of wealth and status—not of political power—

---

8. On North, see Dudley North, *Some Notes Concerning the Life of Edward Lord North*
(1682); Lady Frances Bushby, *Three Men of the Tudor Time* (1911); the *DNB*; and *House of
Commons*.

9. The Augmentations seemed to operate through formally overlapping appointments.
Thus, North and Sir John Williams were briefly joint treasurers before Williams was named to
fill that position "*vice*" North; then Rich and North were joint chancellors before, on 4 March
1544, North had the office "*vice*" Rich. See *L & P*, vol. 19, pt. 1, nos. 1036.29–31, and Walter C.
Richardson, *History of the Court of Augmentations* (1961), pp. 65–66.

10. North's successor assumed the debt of £2,000 still remaining from North's treasurership, and North was further given £1,540 14s. 8d. "for certain considerations of service"—
probably, says Richardson, the consideration of resignation (pp. 189–90). North continued as a
member of the Privy Council.

11. Elizabeth's stay at Charterhouse is reported by both Stow, *A Summary of English Chronicles* (1565), sig. Gg6ʳ, and Holinshed, vol. 2, sig. Rrrr5ʳ.

that North was most successful, shrewdly exploiting his alliances and offices for personal gain. Alice Murfyn's inheritances enabled him to establish himself on the estate of Kirtling, where in 1536 he razed and began to rebuild his country seat; his London residence, a former monastic property, was acquired through the Court of Augmentations.[12] By the time North surrendered the treasurership of the Augmentations in 1544, he owed the crown nearly £25,000 in Augmentations funds, some of which he had clearly used to accumulate other properties. He paid in £22,000; summoned personally to account by Henry VIII, he traded some lands with the crown to its advantage. When he was replaced as chancellor in 1548 he was forgiven a remaining debt of £2,000. It would be misleading to term such practices corrupt, since it was customary for the king's officers to retain state revenues until they were called for, and it was generally understood that these officers would supplement their notoriously inadequate salaries with some portion of the monies that they received in the crown's name. By comparison, North's predecessor as treasurer, Thomas Pope, had left office with a debt of nearly £8,000, more than £500 of which was finally forgiven. Neither Pope nor North suffered any disgrace as a result of borrowing state funds.[13] North was able to negotiate advantageous marriages for his four children. His daughter Christian wed William Somerset, third earl of Worcester, and his daughter Mary wed Henry, ninth Lord Scrope of Bolton. North's elder son, Roger, strengthened a useful alliance by marrying the widowed daughter of Richard Rich, by then lord chancellor of England. The younger son and translator of Plutarch, Sir Thomas North, also enhanced the connection between the North and Rich families in his marriage.

For Ardern, North represented an ally at the Augmentations and on the Privy Council. But he also offered a pattern for advancement: first, through office; second, through exploitation of the newly available monastic lands; third, through the manipulation of large cash resources; fourth, through impatience with niceties of accounting; and,

12. North bought Kirtling on 1 January 1533, lost it in a title suit in 1534, and recovered it by an act of Henry VIII in 1536. The London Charterhouse was described by John Strype as "a very large and goodly mansion, beautified with very spacious gardens, walks, orchards, and other pleasures" (quoted by Bushby, p. 14).

13. On North's debt of £24,925 13s. 10-13/16d., see Richardson, pp. 331 and 189–90; on Pope's debt of £7,801 17s. 2d. (£534 of which was forgiven), see pp. 330–31. On official tolerance of these practices, see Richardson, pp. 230–32, and Robert C. Braddock, "Rewards of Office-Holding" (1975), p. 30. Ten years after North resigned from the Augmentations, the crown sued for £2,000 lost in an exchange of lead (North was absolved when the loss was attributed to a corrupt clerk; see Richardson, p. 238). For the other side of the coin to North's use of crown funds, see Richardson, p. 347, who notes that in 1541 the Privy Council ordered the Augmentations to pay out £4,000, that there were only £3,000 in the treasury, and that North contributed £1,000 from his personal funds.

fifth, through opportune marriage. Ardern's clerkship with North positioned him to demonstrate his mastery of the uses of office, of property purchases, of financial liquidity, and of inventive bookkeeping. As for benefit through marriage, he reportedly wed North's stepdaughter, Alyce (the daughter of the late Edward Murfyn, who had been named for her mother).[14] He thus wove himself into North's own influential kinship network.

The principal record of Ardern's clerkship with North survives from 12 July 1537, when Richard Rich and John Onley, since 24 April 1536 chancellor and attorney, respectively, of the newly formed Court of Augmentations, authorized Thomas Pope, treasurer of the Augmentations, to pay Ardern £6 13s. 4d. (that is, ten marks) "in recompense of such pains as he and his fellows have taken in and about the writing and making of certain books of Acts of Parliament for the King's Highness concerning as well the suppressed lands as the King's Highness' purchased lands."[15] As Parliament did not convene in 1537, the acts here referred to were undoubtedly among the last considered by the "Reformation Parliament," which met for its eighth and final session from 4 February until 14 April 1536. Having authorized the statute dissolving the "lesser" monasteries (those with an annual income below £200), Parliament then received and passed another bill establishing a "Court of the Augmentations of the Revenues of the King's Crown" to administer both the confiscated estates and all other lands newly acquired by the king.

The authorship of that bill has been variously attributed: the Augmentations was certainly conceived by Cromwell, and he may have written the preamble to the bill creating it; an anonymous Elizabethan chronicle identifies the authors as Lord Chancellor Sir Thomas Audley and Rich (the latter of whom had begun organizing the Augmentations well before his formal appointment as its chancellor); but Thomas Ardern, too, evidently played a supporting part in what has been called Cromwell's administrative "revolution." The size of Ardern's role can be inferred from the list of rewards distributed by the king to the officers of Parliament soon after its dissolution: Audley received an annuity of £300 and a dissolved priory; the speaker, £100; two chief

14. Canon W. Telfer states without documentation that Alyce was Ardern's second wife; that Ardern's (unnamed) first wife had died in 1548–49; and that Ardern's heir, Margaret (thirteen years and four months old at his death, according to the *inquisition post mortem*) was his daughter by the earlier marriage. Telfer also refers to a grandson, but neither Ardern's will nor the inquisition mentions one, and the will includes alternatives "if she happen to die without issue of her body." See "Faversham's Court of Orphans" (1966), pp. 194–96.

15. *RCHM, Eighth Report*, app., pt. 2, p. 22. For dates, personnel, and history of the Court of Augmentations, see Richardson, especially pp. 9, 30–33, and 70; and Stanford E. Lehmberg, *Reformation Parliament* (1970), especially pp. 225–29 and 247.

justices, £40 and 40 marks, respectively; Rich and the king's attorney, 40 marks each; other officials, 30 marks each; and Ardern, a principal share in 20 marks divided among the assistants of Edward North and some "others."[16]

In fact the profit was to be far greater. Ardern gained an insider's knowledge of the workings of the Court of Augmentations and an acquaintance with its powerful personnel. Most important, he was among the first in England to learn that the crown intended to alienate some of its newly acquired lands, a fact revealed in the statute,[17] and Ardern soon—perhaps as early as 1539—began to exploit his connections to broker other men's purchases of properties that had fallen under the jurisdiction of the Augmentations.[18] His brokerage fees were among the incomes that eventually enabled him to make purchases of his own, also of dissolved monastic properties, almost all of which were in Kent. This was to inaugurate his later career. When North resigned his clerkship of Parliament to succeed Pope as treasurer of the Augmentations on 17 March 1540, Ardern did not follow him. Perhaps as early as 1538, certainly by 1540, Ardern had instead settled in the county in which he was to negotiate so many property transactions.

Here Sir Thomas Cheyney enters the narrative. According to a previously unremarked record, Cheyney gave Ardern a foothold in Kent no later than 1541 by appointing him steward of his manor at Hothfield.[19] Cheyney was more mentor than model. Knighted by 1513, he served Henry VIII between 1514 and 1526 on several military and diplomatic missions on the Continent and two brief and effective embassages to France; by 1515, he was squire of the body to the king, and, when Henry reformed his Household in 1526, Cheyney was one of six gentlemen of the Privy Chamber. A number of administrative appointments outside London culminated in his succeeding George Boleyn, Viscount Rochford, as Lord Warden of the Cinque Ports on 17 May 1536 (the day of Rochford's execution for treason). The Cinque Ports, a coalition of port towns in Kent and Sussex which were stategically located between the English capital and the Continent, shared certain

16. Lehmberg speculates on Cromwell's authorship of the preamble, cites the anonymous chronicle, pp. 225 and 229, and lists parliamentary rewards, p. 247. See also Richardson on Rich's unofficial role in the creation of the Augmentations, p. 70. G. R. Elton's thesis that Cromwell introduced a "revolution in government" has come under attack; see John Guy, *Tudor England* (1988), pp. 156–64.

17. See also Joyce Youings, *Sixteenth-Century England* (1984), p. 160.

18. *L & P*, vol. 14, pt. 2, no. 236.3 (29 September 1539), lists a Thomas Ardern as a purchaser of crown lands, but this buyer may have been a Warwickshire justice of the peace with the same name.

19. *L & P*, add., vol. 1, pt. 2, no. 1514. For Cheyney, see the *DNB* and *House of Commons*.

ancient liberties and privileges from the crown because they were considered vital to national security. The lord wardenship established
Cheyney as their central administrator and the king's representative.[20]

Cheyney's own appointments and rewards continued from this influential office and demonstrate the insularity of privilege in the period.
For example, on 28 June 1541 he was simultaneously made constable
of Saltwood Castle; keeper of the mansion of Westenhanger; chief
steward of Allington and Chilham manors; bailiff and woodward of
Chilham manor; keeper of the parks of Westenhanger, Allington, and
Saltwood; and master of the deer in Lyminge park.[21] On 9 March 1539
he was made treasurer of the king's Household and a member of the
Privy Council, powerful positions he retained under Edward, Mary,
and, briefly, Elizabeth. On 23 April 1539 he was elected a Knight of the
Garter. He continued to serve the crown in the national defense and in
foreign courts, and in 1540 he both received Anne of Cleves at Dover
and manned the commission that informed her of the king's determination to divorce her. Cheyney, like North, amassed wealth and lands
as the perquisites of his positions: in September 1546, for example, he
was forgiven debts to the crown for rent on royal lands and for the
"first fruits" or incomes of a grange in the Isle of Harty (near his own
principal seat on the Isle of Sheppey); in 1550 and again in 1553 he was
granted ex-monastic lands at quantifiably bargain rates. Because of
Kent's vital location, the crown tended to reward its servants there
generously, and by the mid-1550s Cheyney was second only to the
archbishop of Canterbury in holdings of former crown lands in Kent.[22]

Cheyney's jurisdiction as lord warden included the river town of
Faversham. In exchange for loans and exemption from taxes, the five
ports of Hastings, Romney, Hythe, Dover, and Sandwich were expected to maintain in readiness fifty-seven fully staffed ships to serve as
a royal navy. As expenses grew burdensome for the original Cinque
Ports, they admitted to their membership other towns that could help
to underwrite ship service. In 1229 Faversham agreed to provide one of
the twenty-one ships for which Dover and its associates were responsible; in return it shared Cinque Ports liberties and privileges.[23]

20. See K. M. E. Murray, *Constitutional History of the Cinque Ports* (1935), especially pp. 50–
51, 77, and 207–25; Edward Hasted, *History and Topographical Survey* (1782), vol. 2, pp. 707–8;
Francis F. Giraud and Charles E. Donne, *Visitor's Guide* (1876), p. 17; and Frank W. Jessup,
History of Kent (1958), pp. 83–85.

21. *L & P*, vol. 16, no. 1500.33b.

22. *L & P*, vol. 21, pt. 2, no. 200.10. The purchase price of land was usually fixed at some
multiple of its annual rental value. At a time when the standard multiple was twenty-four years,
Cheyney purchased property at only twenty years' value, according to Michael L. Zell, "Mid-
Tudor Market" (1981), p. 62. On Cheyney's extensive holdings, see Zell, p. 63.

23. See Hasted, vol. 2, pp. 707–8; Giraud and Donne, pp. 17 and 21; Herbert Dane, "Story
of a Thousand Years" (1968), pp. 4, 5, and 11.

Faversham also enjoyed royal associations dating back to 811, when a charter of Cunewulf identified it as the "King's town of Fafresham." Domesday, too, listed it as one of the king's lands. In 1147 Stephen founded a Benedictine Abbey there in which he, his queen, and his son Eustace were to be buried. With a clear annual income of nearly £287, this abbey was numbered among the larger monastic institutions in England and thus was not suppressed until 8 July 1538, during the second wave of the dissolution. The site of the monastery was then leased to a John Wheeler, but almost at once, on 16 March 1540 and for a fee of £283 15s. 10d. (which included payment for marshland elsewhere in Kent and some land in London), the reversion went to Cheyney.[24] Cheyney may have been commissioned to preside over the razing of the monastic buildings and the salvage of their stone for use in the fortifications at Ambleteuse and Calais; keen concern for the decay of the latter had been evidenced in a parliamentary bill of 1536.[25]

Cheyney's major contribution to Ardern's early career was probably an introduction to the opportunities presented him in Faversham. Until the seventeenth century, when domestic trade patterns changed, Faversham's economic health was assured by its pivotal function as both a supplier of grain to London and a conduit for London merchandise to the rest of Kent. William Lambard assessed the prosperity of Kentish gentry "not so much by the quantity of their possessions, or by the fertility of their soil, as by the benefit of the situation of the country itself"; it was the richest county in England. According to a census taken in 1565, some twenty-five years after Ardern's arrival, Faversham numbered 380 houses, neither too small for opportunity nor too large for an ambitious newcomer to make an impact.[26] Settled there by 1540, Thomas Ardern became the king's customer, the collector of customs levied on merchandise both imported and exported.[27]

This highly desirable office could have been attained only through patronage or purchase. It has generally been assumed that North secured the position for Ardern,[28] but the more likely benefactor in this case was Cheyney; at the least, the lord warden would have had to

24. See "Domesday Survey," pp. 208–9. On the abbey's income of £286 12s. 6-3/4d., see Hasted, vol. 2, p. 703. For the dissolution, see *L & P*, vol. 13, pt. 1, nos. 1339–40 (8 July 1538); for Cheyney's grant, *L & P*, vol. 15, no. 436.44, and vol. 21, pt. 2, no. 200.24.

25. Cust notes demolition recorded in a 10 May 1539 indenture (p. 130). In "Faversham Abbey" (1965), Telfer suggests that Cheyney was commissioned to harvest the stone for Calais, pp. v-vi; Arthur Percival observes (in correspondence) that it was also used in Ambleteuse. For the bill, see Lehmberg, p. 240.

26. On trade in Faversham, see Peter Clark and Paul Slack, Introduction to *Crisis and Order* (1972), p. 13. For Kent's comparative wealth, see W. G. Hoskins, *Age of Plunder* (1976), especially pp. 23 and 26. Lambard is quoted by Gordon Batho in "Landlords in England" (1967), p. 292. The survey is reported by Dane, p. vii.

27. *RCHM, Sixth Report and Appendix*, pt. 1, p. 500.

28. Cust (p. 102) and Telfer ("Orphans," p. 194) both credit North but without sources.

approve the appointment. The appeal of the office lay in the wealth that could be and inevitably was skimmed off customs transactions and in the tax revenues that the customer (like the treasurer of the Augmentations) held until they were requested of him—and could meanwhile put to private use.[29] Sometime before November 1546 Ardern was also appointed the king's comptroller of Sandwich Port (that is, he maintained a counter-roll to check the records of the customer there).[30] This, too, was a lucrative position for anyone not overscrupulous about strict accounting, and the fact is that customs officials were uniformly not overscrupulous. Although a greater tinge of corruption would undoubtedly have attached to his profits than did to North's, Ardern would have been foolish not to benefit from his position. His increasing wealth proves that Ardern was no fool.

Primarily through his customership and comptrollership, additionally through fees for land brokerage, and gradually through rents, fines, and uses from his own properties, Ardern achieved the liquidity that enabled him to take advantage of the land market that had exploded in 1536 and concerning which he had privileged knowledge. The crown's distribution of former monastic property proceeded at what might seem a surprisingly slow pace, continuing after the death of Henry VIII through the reigns of all of his children, for there were few men with enough ready cash to make purchases that were often payable in half a year.[31] Ardern was one of the exceptions, a man who succeeded in making himself "new."

As I have indicated, he began as a broker. On 5 June 1540 a group of properties which had belonged to the late priory in Huntingdon was granted to Ardern and Sir Richard Long, with the note that the "remainder" would go "to the heirs and assigns of Sir Richard," a signal that Ardern was negotiating the purchase for Long and thus collecting a reward either in kind or in fee for services rendered.[32] Eighteen months later Ardern again joined Long in selling the granted property to a Philip Campe and his wife; for procurement of the king's license to alienate he would again have been rewarded. (Long was so well placed,

29. See *L & P*, vol. 14, pt. 2, no. 231: in 1539 John Bryganden proposed to sell land worth £14 or £15 a year to purchase the customership of Sandwich; his preference of office over property is suggestive.

30. *L & P*, vol. 21, pt. 2, no. 475. The appointment was renewed by Edward VI on 8 June 1550: *CPR*, Edward VI, vol. 5 (1547–53), app. 1, p. 346.

31. See Youings: purchases were at first payable within six months and later within three (*Dissolution of the Monasteries* [1971], p. 128). See also Zell, p. 67.

32. *L & P*, vol. 15, no. 831.17; I am grateful to John Guy for helping me to interpret these and other records. Youings notes that fees for such services were "routine" (*Dissolution*, p. 116); Braddock asserts that this was "a society in which no one expected favors to be done for nothing" (p. 42).

as steward to Henry's Household, that Ardern's familiarity with properties in Kent may have been of more value in this instance than was his ability to prefer requests through his connection with North.)[33] On 5 September 1543 Ardern received a grant in fee of nearby lands that had belonged to Faversham Abbey which, on 3 October 1543, he alienated to a John Nedam and his wife. On that date he also brokered a purchase of Kentish marshes for a merchant tailor of London, Henry Cooke; and on 5 May 1544, a purchase of a manor and lands for a William Walter.[34]

The pattern revealed by these negotiations suggests both that Ardern understood the power that devolved from consolidation of lands and that his intention was to establish himself as a principal man in Faversham. Notably, the 1540 grant to Long included a purchase in Ardern's name alone of four messuages (dwelling houses with their outbuildings and immediate lands) and a green in the town proper, as well as the site of the late Carmelite friary in Sandwich. From the Nedam grant in 1543, Ardern also reserved to himself a tenement (dwelling house), a shop, and a garden in Faversham.[35] His greatest success was achieved on 16 December 1544, when Cheyney received a license to alienate "the house and site, &c. of the late mon[astery] of Faversham, Kent," a grant confirmed to Ardern on 24 March 1545 for a fee of £117 3s. 4d. Included were twenty-five messuages, two corner tenements, two shops, a cottage, a storehouse, seven gardens, lands including the abbey site and another one-half-acre parcel, and "all other lands of Faversham mon[astery] in Faversham" itself—a substantial purchase on influence in Faversham.[36]

The records of Ardern's property transactions are most detailed and accessible when crown lands are involved, but he made other purchases and sales as well, as revealed by holdings listed in the *inquisition post mortem* taken at his death and in another surviving postmortem document, "Master Ardern's Evidences Searched." He bought from Robert Brokilsbye and Nicholas Girlyngton a house in Canterbury and a former abbey property called Flood Mill, from Clement Sisley and John Leeds some Faversham tenements, and from a Master Bellowe some

33. *L & P*, vol. 17, January 1542, no. 48. For Long, see *House of Commons*. The bulk of his purchases (worth £510 annually at his death) were in Cambridgeshire. Youings notes, however, that even those in "high places" did not always receive property they requested or did not receive it expeditiously (*Dissolution*, p. 118).

34. *L & P*, vol. 18, pt. 2, no. 241.7 and no. 327.7; *L & P*, vol. 19, pt. 1, no. 610.14.

35. Youings notes the significance of a compact estate for social and political status (*Sixteenth-Century England*, p. 166).

36. For the license to alienate, see *L & P*, vol. 19, pt. 2, no. 800.36; for the catalogue of properties, *L & P*, vol. 20, pt. 1, no. 465.79 (March 1545). Monastic holdings included endowments of lands and town properties in addition to the monastic grounds and buildings proper.

regional properties including the Surrenden Croft. He held tenure from Sir Anthony Aucher (another Kentish gentleman) of properties so extensive that his annual payment to Aucher was twenty marks; he leased the London parsonage of St. Michaels for an annual rent of four marks; he leased another parsonage in Canterbury for £32; he owned a manor called Epworth in Lincoln.[37]

The inquisition declares Ardern's annual income from property rental in Kent alone to be nearly £50. Although this sum was sufficient to make him a wealthy man, it was only a fraction of his total annual worth. For one thing, inquisition estimates were notoriously low.[38] For another, Ardern held some revenue-producing lands that did not enter the inquisition because, in the absence of a male heir, they reverted to the crown at his death (the manor of Lamberts Land is an example). Most important of all, there were the additional regular incomes of his offices, fines, and fees.

As a few examples serve to demonstrate, Ardern also earned irregular but highly lucrative profits from rewards, uses, and sales. His early reward for work on the Augmentations was matched by a November 1546 bonus associated with his comptrollership in Sandwich and made in the form of "the moiety of a forfeiture of cheese" valued at 104-1/2 marks—just short of £70. The uses of his lands produced incomes other than rent as early as 8 October 1546, when he was granted the right to harvest and sell oak from a wood known as "Faversham Blene" or "Boughton Blene."[39] The dispatch of Faversham Abbey stone to Ambleteuse and Calais evidently did not exhaust the supply, for the Wardmote Book of Faversham is sprinkled with Ardern's sales of stone to the town: 220 loads one year, 80 the next, and so on. He also charged the town for the temporary use of his abbey lands as fairgrounds—an

37. For Ardern's holdings of former crown lands, see: (1) the patent rolls calendared in *L & P* and *CPR* and cited individually; (2) *List of the Lands of Dissolved Religious Houses*; (3) the inquisition post mortem taken at Bexley, Kent, on 7 October 1551; (4) "Master Ardern's Evidences Searched," BL Harleian MS 58 H 18, which P. G. M. Hyde kindly transcribed for me; and (5) Ardern's will, transcribed in the inquisition and in the Faversham Wardmote Book. For the grant to Brokilsbye and Girlyngton (7 December 1546), see: (1) *L & P*, vol. 21, pt. 2, no. 648.22; (3); and (4). For the grant to Sisley and Leeds see: (1) *CPR*, Edward VI, vol. 2 (1548–49), pp. 23–24 (11 July 1548); and (4), as well as *Kent Obit and Lamp Rents*, p. 50. For Surrenden Croft, see (3) and (4). For leases from Aucher and of the London and Canterbury parsonages, as well as annual fees payable to the Augmentations, see (4).

38. Cromwell aimed to proscribe merchants from purchasing land worth more than £40 a year, "which was a sizeable estate" (Youings, *Sixteenth-Century England*, pp. 157–58). See also Braddock, who observes that the income of country gentlemen rarely exceeded £100 cash, "and many did not receive more than £50" (p. 36). On the undervaluations in inquisitions, see Batho, p. 278.

39. On the award of cheese worth £69 13s. 4d., see *L & P*, vol. 21, pt. 2, no. 475.8. On Faversham Blene, see *L & P*, vol. 21, pt. 1, no. 1546.68: some oaks were reserved to the crown, the lease was for twenty-one years only, and the land reverted to the crown on Ardern's death (and in 1553 was granted in fee to Pembroke; see *CPR*, Edward VI, vol. 5 [1547–53], p. 178).

important element in the Arden construct and one to which I will return. Finally, there were resales. A surviving indenture reveals that in August 1545 Ardern sold a fraction of his Faversham holdings—a messuage, a barn, a stable, a garden, three pieces of pasture and marsh—to yeoman Thomas Dunkyn. For this relatively small portion of the properties the whole of which had cost him slightly over £117, Ardern received from Dunkyn the handsome price of £90. The indenture also indicates that Ardern got another 30 shillings as a fee for delivering a royal license for the alienation—which, through his connections, he was of course able to do. He concluded other sales, like that of a Preston Street property to Sir John Baker in 1548, presumably also at substantial profit.[40]

From the first, Ardern was recognizably a king's man in Faversham; as early as 3 September 1542, not long after his arrival there, he was commissioned with a John Anthony to gather wheat for the crown, probably for the provision of English troops in Scotland.[41] Even before his massive acquisition of town property in 1545, in other words, Ardern's presence made itself felt. In 1540 he received the freedom of the borough, the first step toward participation in municipal government, and, as the Wardmote Book notes, that freedom was "given him" by the town heads without the payment of the 6s. 8d. fee that was charged to others that year. In 1543 Ardern was elected one of the town's twenty-four common councillors, twelve of whom were chosen by the mayor and jurats (or aldermen) and twelve of whom were chosen by the freemen. In 1545 he was advanced to the select body of twelve jurats from whose membership the mayor was annually picked. In 1544 townsmen offered Ardern a fee of £20 plus expenses if he could secure Faversham a new charter of incorporation.[42]

Because Ardern was eventually to betray the guiding principles of the contract he negotiated, an understanding of this charter is important here. By the mid-fifteenth century, according to Peter Clark and Paul Slack, incorporation as a self-governing collective had become the highest ambition of English towns.[43] In the case of Faversham, this

40. For the indenture, see Cust, app. 1; for the transfer of property, see L & P, vol. 20, pt. 2, no. 266 (24 August 1545). Percival notes the sale of property to John Baker in correspondence.

41. APC, N.S.1 (1542–47), p. 28. English troops in Scotland were defeated in August 1542; the Scots were not routed until 23 November 1542. Clark notes that Ardern was the crown's chief man in Faversham under Edward VI (English Provincial Society, p. 82).

42. The Faversham Wardmote Book contains records of Ardern's admission to freedom, the loss to the town of its usual fee for freedom, the process of electing the common councillors, Ardern's progress in town government, and the contract for the charter of incorporation. For these references, as for all those to the manuscript Wardmote Book, I am grateful to Arthur Percival, who shared with me photocopies of this crucial source.

43. Clark and Slack, English Towns (1976), p. 6.

ambition was consistent with a long desire for self-rule which had been frustrated by Stephen's 1147 creation of the abbey as the town's manorial overlord. Affiliation with the Cinque Ports had, in fact, been undertaken as a powerful civic counter to ecclesiastical authority. The abbot enjoyed rents; reliefs; profits from fair, market, and manorial court; services such as transportation of his corn to London; and the right to appoint certain town officials, including the mayor, who was sworn in by the abbot with an oath "to do true service to the King and the monastery." This last privilege had been contested as early as 1255, when the townsmen first called their leading citizen a "mayor" (for which the abbot accused them before the king of "conspiracy"); in 1257 they won the right to nominate three persons from whom the abbot chose one as mayor; by the end of that century, the townsmen exploited the abbey's financial distress to establish a new system, in which a mayor was elected outright and then presented to the abbot for approval. But the manorial relationship continued to rankle for another two hundred years; in 1511 mayor-elect Laurence Stransham refused to appear before Abbot John Caslock to take his oath of office and of service to the monastery, and Caslock successfully impeached him before Star Chamber.[44] With the dissolution of Faversham Abbey in 1538, controversy was reopened. The former steward of the abbey alerted Sir Richard Rich of "a doubt arisen"; in turn, Rich consulted Cromwell, noting that the liberty of mayoral approval had come with the monastery into the Court of Augmentations and asking whether that liberty should be reserved to the king, to Cromwell, or to himself as Augmentations chancellor.[45]

The issue was finally settled on 27 January 1546, when Faversham received its eighth charter of incorporation, listing the then mayor, the twelve jurats, and the freemen to whom civic administration was thereby delegated. It granted the right for the mayor and jurats annually to nominate two jurats from whom the freemen were to elect a mayor. Other rights included those to buy and sell land; to hold a borough court each weekday; to establish standards for bread and other foods; to hold a market thrice weekly, two annual fairs, and a court of piepowders to administer justice among itinerant tradesmen during

44. On the abbey as lord of the manor of Faversham, see Telfer, "Faversham Abbey," p. 1, and Dane, p. 3; on the town's membership of the Cinque Ports, Murray, p. 50; on the rights of the abbot, Murray, p. 51; for the mayor's oath of office, *L & P*, vol. 13, pt. 2, no. 274; on mayoral elections, Dane, p. 4, and Giraud and Donne, pp. 18 and 20; on the Stransham case, Telfer, "Faversham Abbey," p. 8, and Giraud and Donne, p. 24.

45. *L & P*, vol. 13, pt. 2, nos. 274 and 290 (3 and 6 September 1538). These records continue to refer to the nomination of three candidates for the abbot's selection, despite the change in practice.

fairs and markets; to establish a jail; to admit freemen; and "to make laws for the government of the town as the mayors, jurats, and commonalty of Sandwich do."[46] The reference to a town with which Ardern had considerable familiarity, through his comptrollership, is telling. So, too, is the fact that the incorporation was "subscribed by the Chancellor of the Augmentations," that is, Sir Edward North. In response to the 1538 petition, the Augmentations had evidently claimed its interest in mayoral approval, as the townsmen who commissioned Ardern would have known. Further, the first mayor installed under the new incorporation, John Sethe, took an oath of office administered in Westminster by the lord warden, that is, Sir Thomas Cheyney. To Ardern's reward for negotiating the incorporation the sum of £13 8s. 6d. was added to reimburse expenses he had incurred.[47]

By 8 November 1547, the jurats had selected Ardern to serve as church warden. On 26 March 1548, the "new" man was elected mayor. Annual elections were generally held on 30 September, but the death in office of Simon Auncell required this emergency vote. Although wardmote records indicate that the intention in March 1548 was for Ardern to serve an extended term until September 1549, an election was nonetheless held in September 1548 and Ardern was succeeded as mayor.[48] In only six months, however, he oversaw a legislative revolution that was unmatched even in any full-length term during the early Tudor period. The Ardern administration enlarged the powers of the mayoral office, extended the regulatory purview of town government, augmented the income of the corporation, and applied that income to town improvement.

Over Ardern's signature, for example, survives a "Statute for Making of Laws" that restricts wardmote meetings to the mayor, jurats, and commonalty "except [others] be called thither by the Mayor for special causes." Further, noting that for "time whereof no man's mind" (that is, time out of mind) the parish church had employed two clerks and a sexton but arguing that their "travails . . . be decreased and diminished," Ardern presided over the decision to maintain only one clerk,

46. *L & P*, vol. 21, pt. 1, no. 149.33 (January 1546). For more on the town's liberties, see Giraud and Donne, p. 27.

47. On North's subscription, see *L & P*, vol. 21, pt. 1, no. 148.30. On Cheyney's administration of the oath, see Dane, p. 8. Ardern's reimbursement is recorded in the Wardmote Book.

48. On the church wardenship, see *APC*, N.S.2 (1547–50), p. 520. For the mayoral election, see the Faversham Wardmote Book setting Ardern's term of office until the "last day of September then next following." An early modern hand has added "1549" next to the official entry; I am not the only reader, in other words, who has reached this interpretation of his originally projected tenure. If there was indeed a change of plan, it is unexplained. See Clark on the political appeal of "new men with wider, extra-city interests," "Reformation," p. 119.

FIGURE 3. Engraving made from an anonymous eighteenth-century drawing of Thomas Ardern's house, showing the outer gate of Faversham Abbey. From the second volume of Francis Grose's 1774 *Antiquities of England and Wales*. Illustration in the collection of the author.

and that one at a lower salary than previously.[49] The salary reserved to the superannuated clerk was allocated instead to the appointment of a "common carrier and avoider of all the mire, dung, and other contagious filths and refuse within every street of the said town or their liberties." Considerable attention was devoted to the problem of hogs and swine running loose in the town, as well. Each parishioner was to be assessed for clerk, sexton, and carrier salaries, and the mayor was empowered to jail all those derelict in payment. Ardern also supervised passage of "An Act for Orphan's Goods," reserving to the mayor and jurats the authority to appoint a guardian for any orphan not disposed in guardianship by his own father.[50]

Other decisions reached during Ardern's mayoralty benefited him more directly. For example, the town enlarged its tax base by requiring residents other than property owners to pay 3s. 4d. (or one-quarter mark) for each pound paid in fines to a landlord. This measure either relieved the burden of property owners, among whom Ardern was certainly to be counted, or it obviated the need to assess them at a higher rate. Also during Ardern's administration the first paving of town streets, including West Street, Preston Street, and Quay Lane, was undertaken and charged to those whose houses fronted on them.[51] Again, much of the stone for paving was provided—at a price—by Ardern himself. And there is some evidence, in the record of a payment to him "for spreading of the same stone," that he subcontracted for the labor involved.

Ardern may also have left his imprint on Faversham by renovating one of the few unrazed monastic buildings, which stood at the dissolved abbey's outer gate at what was then the northern extreme of the town (see figure 3). Unlike Ardern's other properties, this building was not already contracted to a tenant, because it had been used by the abbot as a guest house. Built to the highest late-fifteenth-century standards of luxury, the guest house had been added to the existing thirteenth-century gate during the abbacy of Walter Gore (1458–99). Caslock, Gore's successor and the last abbot, evidently considered the quarters to be suitable for entertaining Wolsey in 1516, 1527, and 1528, and perhaps Henry VIII in 1520.[52]

49. The statute is also excerpted by Giraud in "Parish Clerks and Sexton" (1893), pp. 208–9. Ardern's appointment as church warden would have given him direct experience of the clerk's work; see a 1531 order for church administration in Edward Jacob, *History of the Town and Port of Faversham* (1774), app. 5, pp. 166–71.

50. For more on this statute, see Telfer, "Orphans," p. 194.

51. Lessees were chargeable for paving if they held unexpired tenure of more than thirty years; otherwise, freehold owners were liable.

52. Brian Philp, *Excavations at Faversham* (1968), pp. vii, 30–31. For Gore and Caslock, see Telfer, "Faversham Abbey," pp. 6 and 9, and Giraud and Donne, pp. 24–25. Benedictine organizations typically built guest houses near their outer gates, and many modernized their

FIGURE 4. Exterior of Thomas Ardern's house. In the foreground is the upper-level jetty of the detached cottage that was once the service wing of Thomas Ardern's house. Photographed by the author with permission of the owners.

Ambitious rebuilding undertaken in the early sixteenth century may well be attributable to Thomas Ardern.[53] A large U- or H-shaped hall-house was attached to the guest house, its main section (the bar of the U or H) dominated by a communal great hall, with a cross-wing at one extreme housing the "high-end" family rooms of solar and parlor, and a second cross-wing at the opposite extreme containing the "service" rooms for food preparation and storage. Although the central hall block does not survive today, its form can be guessed, for it was characteristic of "new" men to substantiate their stature by recreating the medieval great hall that had for centuries symbolized wealth and power. A fraction of Ardern's service cross-wing remains as an independent two-storied structure, now called a "cottage" and stripped of its former association with pantry and buttery. Only the northernmost cross-wing still stands in any approximation of its form as Ardern knew it, and even it is foreshortened by the nearly complete loss of the gate to which it was attached and by the demolition of its lengthy extension in rooms bridging the road and in tenements across the road.

This surviving north wing is, however, the most interesting portion of the building archaeologically, since it incorporates older abbey structures on the site (see figure 4). The earliest portion, to the rear, preserves the stone and flint of one load-bearing wall of the medieval gate and marks the outer limit of former abbey lands. In front of it, attached to it, and constructed on town property is a second, half-timbered section with domestic rooms in three jettied stories and the close-studded exterior that signaled wealth in the Weald. The small scale and low ceilings of these interior spaces as well as the successive projections of the exterior jetties are characteristic of urban architecture of the late medieval and early modern period. From this section a third with a smoothly plastered exterior extends; also on town grounds, it originally functioned as a bridge between the old gatehouse and the new great hall. This last section, with only two stories and one large room on each level, a pair of bay windows originally framing the fireplace in both, was built on the scale of the Tudor manor or country house. The lower parlor has a ten-foot-high ceiling, and the upper solar—big as a hall itself—has a stunning open crown-post roof as well as an infilled door-

domestic buildings ca. 1500—conveniently for post-Reformation owners (Margaret Wood, *English Mediaeval House* [1965], p. 23).

53. For this speculative "reconstruction" of Ardern's house, I am grateful to Roy and Norma Pleasance, who conducted me on a personal tour of the house and shared with me an extremely helpful unpublished dissertation by Linda Rogers, "An Architectural Study of Arden's House in Faversham, Kent" (1990). See also Christopher Hussey, "Setting of a Notorious Murder" (1966), pp. 76–79; and Anthony Swaine, *Faversham* (1970), p. 62.

FIGURE 5. The solar of Thomas Ardern's house. Note the crown-post roof and, behind the piano, the doorway, now filled in, which once led to the main wing of the house. Photographed by the author with permission of the owners.

frame marking its connection to a now-vanished neighboring space in the hall block (see figure 5).

We have no way of knowing whether the building that Thomas Southouse in 1671 termed the "great house near the Abbey gate east-ward," "the scene where that fatal tragedy was really acted by Alice Ardern," was Ardern's whole or some variant on the fragment we now see. We know only that the gate with its road-spanning rooms was not demolished until 1772. Despite such uncertainties, it is telling that for a survey of former abbey properties Southouse recorded Ardern's house as renting at the highest annual value of £3, while one other house in town rented for £1 13s. 4d., a third for £1 6s. 8d., and a fourth for £1; the rest ranged from 16s. 8d. down to 4d.[54] Liminal in location, hybrid in structure, ambitious in design, Ardern's house simultaneously and totemically looked backward to the monastic source of his opportunity to establish himself in Faversham, forward to his civic aspirations, and outward as a proclamation of his wealth and status.

As for the fashion in which Ardern furnished his house, we have four hints. First, the linenfold panelling of the solar survives, although in another location. Second, three exquisitely detailed panels originally belonging to the abbey are preserved, also in another venue. These represent portrait medallions of the patron, King Stephen, and his queen, Matilda; their royal badges; the heraldic arms of England; and two monks ringing handbells. Third, in an Ardern window the North coat of arms was displayed as a proud declaration of affiliation, report-edly lasting there into the nineteenth century.[55] And finally and of related significance, an inventory of goods was compiled at the death of Alyce Ardern, indicating by its roster of controlled fabrics and bright colors that Alyce was not only housed but also clothed as a gentlewo-man. She had at least five "frocks," including one of tawny damask and valued at £4 16s. 4d., one of gold trimmed with lace and worth £5 16s. 4d., one of black satin trimmed with velvet and worth £6 13s. 4d., and two of worsted trimmed with velvet, worth £2 and £1, respectively; a cloak edged with velvet, valued at £1; numerous pairs of sleeves made of velvet, satin, or lace; a French hood valued at £1; two face masks, one of crimson damask worth over 13s. and one of black taffeta worth nearly 7s.; a red petticoat; a "chain of gold for a gentlewoman's neck" worth £3 14s. 9d.; and "two bracelets of gold" worth £3 5s.[56]

54. Thomas Southouse, *Monasticon favershamiense* (1671), pp. 59–64.

55. On the panelling, see Cust, p. 134. Jacob includes an illustration of "The Arms of Sir Edward North in a Window of Ardern's House," pl. 15; see also A. H. Bullen, Introduction to *Arden of Feversham* (1887), p. v.

56. The inventory of goods is preserved with records of the suit by Ardern's daughter Margaret to reclaim them; see *Monthly Journal of the Faversham Institute* 13 (September 1902), 565–67.

I mean to suggest that Alyce, as much as the multiwinged house, was a badge of Ardern's success. Her presence not only authorized the baronial coat of arms on Ardern's window; it also instituted a household in political subjection to him and augured a continuation of his line. From the time Ardern arrived in Faversham as its customer until the time he was settled as the holder of the great house, was established as a man of property and influence, and was elected as the town's mayor fewer than ten years had passed.

If a man's career can serve as an indication of his character, and inasmuch as investigative convention assumes that knowledge of a man's character is essential to understanding the motivation for his murder, then a summation of Ardern's career to this point is important. One way into the issue is provided by Wallace T. MacCaffrey, who remarks the material opportunity open to stewards in the early modern period: they presided over manor courts and enforced court decisions, granted leases and collected fines, and in many other ways, in his words, "regulated" and "controlled" the lives of manor tenants. Their rewards, he asserts, depended only on their "inventiveness" and "lack of scruple."[57] This observation characterizes not only Ardern's stewardship of Cheyney's Hothfield but also his customership of Faversham, his comptrollership of Sandwich, and, one suspects, his civic service in Faversham as well. Does constant and repeated proximity to such opportunity encourage its creative exploitation and engender a flexibility of ethics? In the face of Ardern's modestly meteoric career alone, even disburdened of the arguments and antagonisms that trailed him and to which I now turn, it is difficult to believe otherwise.

Thomas Ardern's Murder

To recover Ardern's reputation, resignify his local disputes, recognize his provincial allies, and identify his antagonists—and to do so with some skepticism toward the chronicles—are my aims in this section. The process of distinguishing archive from fiction is at its most complicated here and, because it bears so directly on his murder, at its most significant.

According to Holinshed, for example, Alice Arden advised her lover that "there was not any that would care for [Arden's] death, nor make any great inquiry for them that should dispatch him." Stow's manuscript version has it that Alice asserted, somewhat more memorably,

---

57. Wallace T. MacCaffrey, "Place and Patronage" (1961), p. 124.

that her husband was "so evil beloved" in Feversham "that no man would make inquiry after his death."[58] My introductory caveat regarding the credibility of the chronicle(s) is pertinent here, where omniscient narrators purport to recount a private conversation between an adulterous woman and her lover, both long dead. The notion that the exchange may serve a hortatory purpose, rather than a strictly reportorial one, may be confirmed by the marginal annotation that it provoked in the second (1587) edition of Holinshed: "O importunate and bloody minded strumpet!" In modern redactions, however, it is the image not of Alice but of Arden which lingers: Arden the "evil beloved."

The question is whether the archives bear her out, and the answer is that they do. One documentary touchstone is a record in the Faversham Wardmote Book which notes that on 22 December 1550 (not long after completing his term as mayor and just two months before his murder) Thomas Ardern was disenfranchised by his fellow jurats: "Thomas Ardern, by cause he being jurat and sworn to maintain the franchises, liberties, and freedoms of the said town, hath contrary to his oath in that behalf gone about and labored by divers ways and means to the uttermost of his power to infringe and undo the said franchises, liberties, and freedoms. That therefore the said Thomas Ardern shall be deposed from the bench, and no more to be jurat of the said town, but from henceforth to be utterly disfranchised for ever."[59] Arthur Percival plausibly suggests that Ardern may have refused to pay a cess (assessment) levied the previous year, the enforcement of which had been specifically addressed by the jurats one month earlier, on 21 November 1550, in Ardern's absence from the Wardmote.[60] Ardern was immediately preceded in disenfranchisement by another absentee from the November session, Thomas Dunkyn.

The town controversy that has usually been linked to the disenfranchisement, that on which the Holinshed and Stow chronicles instead focus, has to do with Faversham's annual Valentine's Day fair. By tradition, rents and profits from this week-long fair, which opened on 14 February, had gone to the town. A second annual fair, which opened on 1 August (Lammas Day), had been granted to the abbey by Henry II and was held on the abbey's three-and-a-half-acre green, with rents and

---

58. Holinshed, p. 154; Stow, fol. 36ʳ.
59. Anita Holt, who also transcribes the disenfranchisement in "*Arden of Feversham*" (1970), attributes it to Ardern's relocation of Faversham's Valentine's Day fair (pp. 2 and 3).
60. In correspondence. The Wardmote Book record of Ardern's disenfranchisement is followed by a list of jurats which includes Ardern; Wine accordingly suggests that Ardern was restored to juracy before his death. But Percival demonstrates both that the folio pages are not in chronological sequence and that the list is dated *before* the disenfranchisement.

profits going to the abbey.[61] The 1546 town charter Ardern had negotiated detailed that both fairs were now to be held at an unspecified
"place in the town" to the benefit of the corporation. According to the
chronicles, however, Arden arranged ("for his own private lucre and
covetous gain") for the Valentine's Day fair "to be wholly kept within
the abbey ground which he had purchased, and so reaping all the gains
to himself, and bereaving the town of that portion which was wont to
come to the inhabitants, got many a bitter curse."[62] In other words, by
relocating the 1550 Valentine's Day fair to the (Lammas Day) green
over which he held rights to ground rental, Arden purportedly used
his municipal standing for his personal profit.

The Wardmote Book records payments of 5s. to Ardern for use of
his land at "the time of Saint Valentine's fair" for the two years previous
to 1550. While relocation of the fair may have caused some local resentment, it patently was not, as the chronicles suggest, an innovation of
"this present year." Further, "all the gains," or profits, would have
amounted to considerably more than the 5s. rent, but 5s. is the only
figure about which there is any documented hint of controversy. That
hint survives in the will Ardern made on 20 December 1550, just two
days before his disenfranchisement, leaving to his daughter "A Rent of
5s. due to me from [the] mayor, jurats, and commonalty of Faversham
for liberty upon the upper green to keep Valentine [fair]."[63] Nearly ten
months had elapsed since the fair, and as this is the only debt registered
in Ardern's will, it is reasonable to suspect some disagreement concerning its payment—if not precisely on the scale suggested by the
chronicles.

It is possible to reconcile the evidence of the will and that of the
disenfranchisement by speculating that Ardern refused to pay the
town its cess to protest the nonpayment of his ground rent. And perhaps Ardern's companion in disenfranchisement, Thomas Dunkyn,
was also involved in the relocation controversy. The property that Dunkyn had purchased from Ardern in 1545 included a "small piece and
parcel of pastureland lying in the upper green." Put together the facts
that Dunkyn may have first established himself in Faversham with Ardern's 1545 sale of property to him (a record locates Dunkyn in
Cranbrook as late as 1542), that he was elected to the body of jurats
simultaneously with Ardern, and that he was disenfranchised concur-

61. See Giraud and Donne, p. 67; for a description of the outer courtyard, see Philp,
pp. 31–32; for a plan of the abbey grounds, see Telfer, "Faversham Abbey," p. iv.
62. Holinshed, p. 157; compare Stow, fol. 36ᵛ.
63. In correspondence, Percival notes that St. Valentine's Fair income was £2 5s. in 1550,
£3 3s. 4d. in 1551, and £3 12s. 2d. in 1552. The year after Ardern's death, the town again paid
5s. "to set the fair upon the upper green," this time making payment to Thomas Stransham.

rently with him, and we may, moreover, suspect some sympathy of action or intention.[64] Of course, we may also speculate that one man was implicated in an action that the other had initiated—and that the result in disempowerment was a bitter one for the unwilling accomplice.

Still, this suggestion of even a temporary alliance between Ardern and another local is notable. Only one other thread of possible affiliation can be documented: Adam Fowle first appears in the Wardmote Book among the names of the civic "twenty-four" in a group chosen "by the Mayor and Jurats" during the year of Ardern's mayoralty, and Ardern lists Fowle as his sole legatee outside his wife and daughter. The chronicles, whatever their reliability, deny Arden this association as well, for they represent Fowle as a go-between for Alice and her lover. Even were Fowle a loyal Ardern confederate, however, he, like Dunkyn, was not Ardern's social equal. There may be significance in the fact that the texts give no hint of an allegiance with other local gentry. The opacity of received information on the subject is so complete that the play *Arden of Feversham* was finally compelled for dramatic purposes to invent a friend for Arden. That "friend," Franklin, is *Arden*'s only addition to its cast of historical characters.

By contrast, the record of Ardern's antagonists in Faversham is spectacularly full; some are identifiable by name, and others can be deduced by implication. Ardern's career followed a pattern that was repeated throughout England by men reaping the material rewards of the Reformation. It was not unique to Ardern, in other words, but it was nonetheless experienced as unique by his fellows in Faversham.

Even the town's long chafing at monastic overlordship by no means ensured that the "new" man who assumed control of so much of the abbey's town property was received with sanguine expectation. Ardern's precipitant wealth and prominence would have collided with entrenched interests in such a way as to engender widespread envy and enmity. Cultural anthropologist F. G. Bailey has described in modern India a phenomenon that undoubtedly occurred in sixteenth-century England as well, that in the closed society of a small town, the notion of anything other than a zero-sum situation is counterintuitive. As Bailey puts it: "The amount to be shared out is fixed: if one gets more, then another man must get less. . . . Any change in relative command over

64. For Dunkyn in Cranbrook, see "Kent Contributors" (1877), p. 400. Percival first noted the simultaneous election of Ardern and Dunkyn, as well as Dunkyn's disenfranchisement (which is recorded first and with greater prominence in the Wardmote Book). Dunkyn had been elected mayor in 1546, two years before Ardern. Both Holinshed (p. 154) and Stow (fol. 36ʳ) say that Ardern called at Dunkyn's house just before returning home on the evening of his murder.

material wealth by definition means that the gainer has inflicted harm upon the loser."[65]

Ardern's 1545 purchases made him landlord to some of the most substantial and established of Faversham residents, and, as William Wentworth later observed to his son, "notwithstanding all their fawning and flattery, [tenants] seldom love their landlord in their hearts."[66] Ardern's tenants included John Sethe (mayor at the time of Faversham's 1546 incorporation as well as in 1537, 1539, and 1552), four men who were then jurats (Richard Dryland, Robert Colwell, William Marshall, and Simon Auncell), and five who were freemen (Antony Love, John Dryland, Jr., Thomas Oldfeld, Edward Gayle, and Thomas Bargrove). Descended from one of the most ancient families in Kent, Richard Dryland served as mayor of Faversham eight times between 1515 and 1541; John Dryland, Jr., held the same office in 1553 and 1555. William Norton was undoubtedly related to several Nortons who were elected mayors: Richard, in 1494 and 1498; John, in 1499, 1500, and 1502; another William, in 1512 and 1527; and the vicar Clement, in 1536. Also among Ardern's tenants were five other past or future mayors of Faversham: Simon Auncell (1548), John Bringborne (1535, 1542, and 1544), John Davy (1528), William Marshall (1551), and John Webb (1556). Robert Colwell was the son of a former mayor, Richard Colwell, who died in office in 1534; the "widow Lambert" was probably the relict of 1538 mayor Thomas Lambert.[67]

Most revelatory of the dramatic shift in power relationships that accompanied the dissolution of the abbey and Ardern's acquisition of its properties was the fact that he became landlord to the man who from 1499 until 1538 had been the town's overlord, the abbot before whom so many mayors had taken their oath of office and to whom so many town residents had returned rents and services. John Caslock converted the abbey brewhouse, with its attached "great garden," into his personal residence, paid Ardern £5 6s. 8d. yearly, and also shared tenure of an apple orchard with one of his former monks, John Taylor. Such transitions occasion uncertainties and conflicting loyalties of the

65. F. G. Bailey, *Stratagems and Spoils* (1969), p. 148. Bailey usefully describes "a small hitherto relatively self-contained political arena" that "is being progressively encapsulated within a larger arena" (p. 142); the post-Reformation story in England is one of progressive nationalization. I am grateful to David Harris Sacks for referring me to Bailey.

66. William Wentworth, "Advice to his son" (1604), p. 18.

67. For those listed in the charter of incorporation, see *L & P*, vol. 21, pt. 1, no. 149.33 (January 1546); Jacob lists all mayors, app. 1, pp. 117–29. Tenants are identified in the grants to Ardern in the calendared patent rolls and the inquisition post mortem. On the Drylands and the Colwells, see Edward Hasted, "Parish and Town" (1969), p. 12; and P. G. M. Hyde, "Henry Hatch" (1985), p. 116, nn. 26 and 30. The comparative wealth of Richard Dryland, Antony Love, John Davy, John Bringborne, John Sethe, and William Marshall is also suggested in the loans charged to them by the king's commission of 1542 (cited in note 64).

sort aptly analogized by Bailey: "who is going to help me get a gun licence: the old chief or the party agent? And how much will he want?"[68]

Less than a year after Robert Colwell learned that his landlord was not Faversham Abbey but Thomas Ardern, he also saw his father's legacy of marshlands on the Isle of Harty transformed from Faversham Abbey endowment to Thomas Cheyney's private property. Other kinsmen and friends of past residents similarly saw charitable bequests turned to Ardern's profit. Townsmen particularly decried the disintegration of a 1527 gift of 317 acres of land intended by its donor, Dr. John Cole, to endow a grammar school. They immediately appealed to Henry VIII to re-endow the school, but without success; meanwhile, much of the property was redistributed, with Ardern, for example, holding a seven-acre piece of it, Surrenden Croft. Just how long such memories of undone charity survived is indicated when, nearly fifty years later, the town petitioned Elizabeth that any of Cole's lands remaining among crown holdings might be restored "to the purpose and intention of Dr. Cole," and a grammar school was finally re-established.[69]

Holinshed and Stow, accusing Arden of "extortiousness" as a landholder, report that he unfairly evicted both John Greene, whom they identify as Sir Anthony Aucher's man, and a Widow Cook, who they say later married a mariner named Richard Read. The documentary record does not immediately substantiate the chronicles, although related names do surface and supportive conjectures can be mooted. It is true, for example, that there are three Cooks listed as tenants in an abbey rental of 1532 (Thomas, William, and "Coke the butcher"); that Ardern's 1545 grant of former monastic properties includes "a corner tenement late in tenure of John Cook and now of Joan Staple in Northstreet West"; that there was an Edward Cooke listed as a freeman in the town charter of 1546 and as a jurat in 1550; that a Richard Read received the freedom of the borough in Faversham during Ardern's mayoralty in 1549; and that, while there is no mention of a woman named Cook or a woman named Read, there might well have been such a woman obscured in legal documents by her successive marriages, a *femme covert*.[70] Meanwhile, although John Greene does not appear in

---

68. On Caslock, see the *RHMC, Sixth Report and Appendix*, pt. 1, p. 500. Bailey, pp. 154–55.

69. On Colwell, see Telfer, "Faversham Abbey," p. 9; Hasted, vol. 2, p. 713; and Hasted, "Parish and Town," pp. 13–14 and 25–26. For Cheyney's purchase, see *L & P*, vol. 21, pt. 2, no. 200.10 (September 1546). On the grammar school and its endowment of £14 10s., see Hasted, vol. 2, p. 714, and W. K. Jordan, *Social Institutions in Kent* (1961), p. 72. The Surrenden Croft is listed in Ardern's inquisition post mortem. Hasted discusses the reinstitution of the grammar school.

70. Holinshed, pp. 149 and 159; Stow, fols. 34ᵛ and 37ᵛ. Read's freedom is reported in the Wardmote Book, according to Percival.

any record of those holding property either of the abbey or of Ardern, he is listed among Faversham's freemen in 1546; the property that Ardern leased from Aucher might conceivably have been some of the former abbey land that Aucher was granted in 1544; as Aucher's man Greene certainly might have resided on or worked some of Aucher's property under a tenancy at will; and Ardern, assuming tenure of the property as a less sympathetic landlord to Greene than Aucher had been, might well have evicted him.[71]

Less speculative and particularly revealing, however, is the remarkable turnover of tenancies in the six years between Ardern's major acquisition of town property and the inquisition post mortem: of the roughly thirty-seven tenants listed, fourteen are peculiar to the grants, sixteen are peculiar to the inquisition, and only seven are common to both, reflecting continuous tenure.[72] Even if Ardern did not illegally evict tenants and increase customary rents (as some new landowners undoubtedly did), each turnover gave him the opportunity to raise the entry fine that was payable at the establishment or renewal of tenancies. William Harrison was but one of many who complained of entry fines being multiplied by as many as seven times during this period.[73]

In fact, Ardern's practices could have been unimpeachable—and still he would have suffered from the distrust that is adumbrated in the chronicles and that was in fact pandemic among those who did not benefit from the disposition of crown properties after the dissolution of the monasteries. The anonymous author of the 1555 *Institution of a Gentleman* complains of gentlemen who "get lands . . . purchased by certain dark augmentation practices. . . . such intruders, such unworthy worshipful men, have chiefly flourished since the putting down of abbeys."[74] Given Ardern's obsession with establishing himself— through powerful central-government connections, through extensive holdings in town property, through a principal residence within the civic limits, through local positions that gave him a voice in every aspect

71. See the grants calendared in *L & P*, especially *L & P*, vol. 20, pt. 1, no. 465.79 (March 1545), for Ardern, and *L & P*, vol. 19, pt. 1, no. 812.48 (13 June 1544), for Aucher; the 1546 charter of incorporation; "Master Ardern's Evidences Searched," which records the lease from Aucher; and the Faversham record of an abbey rental from 1532, a transcription of which was kindly sent me by Percival.

72. The data base consists of Ardern's grants of crown lands only. I assume that, e.g., the "Simon Auncell" listed as a tenant of property granted Ardern in 1545 and the "Elizabeth Anselm, widow" listed in the inquisition comprise an instance of continuous tenure; if not, there may be even fewer instances of continuous tenure.

73. Harrison is cited by Batho, p. 294. Some landlords even negotiated fictitious sales for the sake of the fines at transfer (Youings, *Sixteenth-Century England*, pp. 56, 174, and 50). See also Batho, pp. 347 and 293, and John Bayker, Letter to Henry VIII.

74. *Institution of a Gentleman* (1555), sigs. D2^r and D3^r. See also W. R. D. Jones on the "wonderful hate against gentlemen" (here quoting Protector Somerset) that seemed rife in 1549 and 1550 (*Tudor Commonwealth* [1970], pp. 90–91).

of town life, even through his indispensable efficacy in negotiating the town's 1546 incorporation—the irony is that he cannot but have remained in Faversham an "intruder." He evidently represented himself as concerned for the good of the town: he passed the statutes for street cleaning and the control of swine, and he left Faversham a bequest of property to endow a sermon to be preached in his own name annually. But his fellows in Faversham were unlikely to have taken such "civic spirit" at face value. Thomas Heywood in 1636 voiced the sort of suspicion that Ardern's charity may have engendered: "If he prove so rich as to raise an hospital out of his private usury, it is not for any virtue, but rather vainglory, as being only built for such as he hath before beggar'd."[75] Ardern's success was too sudden and dramatic to be attributable by townsmen to anything other than singular self-interest.

There were, moreover, individual quarrels. Peter Clark has suggested that there may have been a "dispute" between Ardern and Sir Anthony Aucher, for example. Not only is John Greene, convicted collaborator in Ardern's murder, named in the Holinshed and Stow chronicles as Aucher's man, but the storehouse in which two of Arden's assassins, Black Will and Shakebag, hid "by Greene's appointment" is there identified as Aucher's as well. Holinshed and Stow insist that the controversy was specifically between Arden and Greene, the two men on site in Feversham and concerned with property in Feversham; Alice, they say further, knew "that Greene hated her husband."[76] But Aucher could have involved himself in any presumed injury to his man. And the paths of Aucher and Ardern undoubtedly crossed—perhaps not happily—on many occasions besides that of the land lease they had negotiated.

Aucher was Cromwell's man by 1536, paymaster of the king's works in Dover from 1537, auditor and surveyor of the manors of Christ Church in Canterbury from 1539, receiver for the Augmentations in Kent from 1544, master of the King's Jewels from 1545, and surveyor at Boulogne from 1547, among other royal appointments. He is one of the men whose careers have been cited by those who would characterize Edward VI's administration as corrupt. In 1546 the accounts of the king's jewels were audited in anticipation of his malfeasance. In January 1551 Aucher was found to be nearly £2,456 in arrears in his payments to the crown from his receivership; while some monies were later discharged as having been legitimately expended to fulfill his responsibilities, he was still bound to repay £300 per year for six years.[77]

75. Thomas Heywood, *True Discourse* (1636), sig. B2ᵛ.
76. Clark, *English Provincial Society*, pp. 83–84. Holinshed, p. 149; compare Stow, fol. 34ᵛ.
77. Clark suggests Aucher's affiliation with Cromwell by 1536; see *English Provincial Society*, pp. 50 and 81. See also *L & P*, vol. 14, pts. 1, no. 1041, and 2, nos. 65, 299, 453, and 782, for

Aucher also made enemies readily. The record of his conflicts includes the 1538 complaint of a widow concerning her son's dispossession despite a grant in his behalf from Cromwell; the 1540 petition of a Dover ironworker protesting that "the paymaster is displeased with me without any cause"; and the impatient request of the bishop of Winchester, Stephen Gardiner, that the king's chief secretary, William Paget, require "Mr. Ager to serve like a man or else sue to be discharged." As receiver in Kent, Aucher had some purview over former abbey properties of interest to Ardern, in addition to those he leased to Ardern directly. In 1541 Aucher gained custody of a Faversham messuage during the minority of three orphaned girls, surfacing as a presence in town just as Ardern was establishing himself there. And a letter of 8 February 1549 reveals that Aucher involved himself in town matters. Issued by the Privy Council to the mayor of Faversham, the letter required "the sending to the Lords [of] one Asherst, to answer to the things objected to him in the letter of Mr. Aucher." While there were other wealthy and influential men in Faversham, Aucher was undoubtedly Ardern's principal local rival for central-government connections.[78]

Clark has also outlined Ardern's role in Faversham's religious controversies. Vicar from 1539 to 1554, Clement Norton opposed the reading of scripture in the vernacular, would not preach against the pope, and continued to follow traditional liturgical practices. His strong base of conservative neighboring clerics, county magistrates, and old landed families began to erode in the 1540s, however, simultaneously with the arrival in town of the reformist Ardern. In 1548 Ardern's name headed the list of nine who deposed against Norton in a church court; two years later, Norton was officially silenced.[79] From this perspective, Ar-

correspondence between and concerning Aucher and Cromwell in 1539. And see *L & P*, vol. 19, pt. 1, no. 1036.17. On Aucher's reputation, see especially A. F. Pollard, *England under Protector Somerset* (1900), p. 268. Richardson notes Aucher's arrearage of £2,455 19s. 6d. on p. 230; on evidence that the audits suggest keen suspicion, see p. 188. He realistically suggests that such debts as Aucher's were pursued because they would otherwise have "restricted the opportunities open to that infinitely more important officer, the Treasurer of the Augmentations." The January 1551 accounting would have dealt only in cash monies, but the receiver also collected easily saleable monastic valuables and presided over the stripping of lead from monastic roofs. Batho notes a reform bill of 1552–53 which observes that receivers were retaining Crown revenues (p. 264).

78. For the widow Jane Rooper, see *L & P*, vol. 13, pt. 2, no. 857. For the ironworker John Owen, see *L & P*, vol. 15, no. 193. For Gardiner, see *L & P*, vol. 20, pt. 2, no. 610. For Aucher's custody of the orphans' messuage, see *L & P*, vol. 16, no. 1056.21 (23 June 1541). For the Privy Council letter, see *APC*, N.S.2 (1547–50), p. 389. Accusations of corruption against receivers, Richardson suggests, may have proceeded primarily from resentment of their power (p. 8).

79. Clark, "Reformation," pp. 125–26. This controversy should be considered in the context of concern about heresy and Anabaptism in Kent; Cranmer headed an investigatory commission formed on 12 April 1549. See W. K. Jordan, *Edward VI* (1968), p. 228.

dern's involvement in the reduction of the number of church clerks in 1549 can be seen as part of a concerted campaign against Norton and Roman practice, for the responsibilities of the clerks that had been agreed upon in 1531 had included liturgical duties that a protestant would have numbered among the "travails" that had been "decreased and diminished" by the Reformation.

In addition, Ardern may have quarrelled with Simon Auncell, his predecessor as mayor. A letter from the Privy Council dated 8 November 1547 directs Auncell "to deliver, all excuses set apart, into the hands of Thomas Ardern, warden of the church of Faversham, the piece of silver by him of late taken from the church which was given thither by one Hatch deceased and had there continued by the space of twelve years and more." Early fears that the crown would dissolve the parish churches (as well as the abbeys) had resulted in the plundering of their treasuries; in 1545, with the Chantries Act, Henry VIII had recognized that men were similarly reclaiming property that their ancestors had given to endow masses for their souls; the very month of the Faversham controversy saw passage of a second, Edwardian, Chantries Act.[80] Auncell may have personally reclaimed a family member's donation (his wife Elizabeth was the sister of Hatch's widow, Joan); he may have acted, as mayor, on behalf of the town to enrich its treasury; or he may merely have been called upon by the Council in his official capacity to retrieve the silver from another townsman who had taken it. Because the church warden's purview included the church treasury, Ardern presumably acted in his own official and proper capacity in attempting to restore the appropriated silver.

As with Norton, however, there was a polarizing principle at issue in this dispute. The exact nature of the controversy is of less interest than is the involvement of the Privy Council. It is difficult not to suspect that Ardern himself had taken the matter to his patrons on the Council, North and Cheyney, in order to obtain official warrant for his own actions. It is also tempting to speculate that Ardern had reported his fellows at least once before, in 1544, when a "Petition to the King and his Council by the town of Faversham" requested an inquiry into the departure for Flushing of three boats loaded with grain, "contrary to the proclamation of restraint" and, it is imputed, "probably with the

80. For the letter to Auncell, see *APC*, N.S.2 (1547–50), p. 520. On chantries, see Arthur Hussey, ed., *Kent Chantries* (1936), pp. ii–iii. On "wholesale" losses of church plate, see Frederick George Emmison, *Elizabethan Life: Morals* (1973), p. 255. For popular sentiment, see also *L & P*, vol. 14, pt. 1, no. 1073: in 1539 one John Russell was reported to Cheyney for stating that "'the king of England hath pulled down all the abbeys in England, and he will pull down all the parish churches also'; and further that the King had caused 20 cartloads of gold and silver to be carried from Canterbury to London."

connivance of the searchers." Because customs searchers counter-checked the customer's receipts, controversy between customer Ardern and the town searchers was not unlikely.[81] If Ardern was the author of one or both of these complaints, his action reveals a graceless and provoking inclination to leapfrog local authority and flaunt his formidable connections. Such a procedure was in fact a violation in spirit (and in some towns also a violation in law) of the right of self-government established in the charter of incorporation that Ardern himself had negotiated.

Bailey writes that because "the essence of the role is to keep a foot in both camps," the middleman is inevitably "despised—and by those at both ends of his transactions. His fellow-villagers think of him as a liar and a cheat and a hypocrite, a man who has made a fortune (albeit a modest one) out of their predicaments with the administrators, a renegade who pretends to serve his fellow villagers but in fact serves no-one but himself." He is commonly regarded as "an unprincipled man on the make"—which he in fact "often" is. At the same time, "officials and politicians see him as a villager with ambitions far above his education and his abilities, an unreliable man, at the behest of the highest bidder."[82] The probability is that Thomas Ardern was all the more resented the more indispensable he made himself to both center and locality.

If, to return to my initial frame for this discussion, we were just now, at this conclusion of a review of Ardern's career, to learn that Ardern had been murdered—and no more—our analysis of the probable circumstance of that murder would look quite different to us from that which informed the official verdict. Despite his remarkable attainments, Ardern was in a precarious position: the probable antagonisms he had aroused were many, his powerful patrons were geographically removed, and his few possible allies on site were men of a lower status and ambiguous loyalty. In the months immediately preceding his murder on 15 February 1551, townsmen accustomed to attending the Wardmote were excluded from it, a clerk of the church lost his job, another suffered a reduction in wages, Ardern's mayoral term was aborted, the men of consequence in Faversham found cause to disenfranchise Ardern, his sometime ally Thomas Dunkyn was similarly humiliated, Clement Norton was silenced, and Anthony Aucher both levied public charges requiring the intervention of the Faversham jurats and was

81. *L & P,* vol. 19, pt. 2, no. 803. One of the accused boatowners was William Caslock, brother of the former abbot and probable representative of pre-Reformation structures of power. See also Norman Scott Brien Gras, *Early English Customs System* (1918), p. 97.

82. Bailey, pp. 167–73.

found delinquent in his receivership—these were, in other words, months when anxieties and hostilities involving Ardern reached a peak.

Even if any of these individual motives seems insufficient for murder, all nonetheless establish patterns in the victim's life and behavior that were eventually capable of finding sufficiency. At the time of Ardern's murder the mayor of Faversham and presumed superintendent of the homicide investigation was one William Marshall, a man who had held tenure of the abbey's "Apple Garden" when it was transferred to Ardern but whose name was notably absent from the post mortem list of Ardern's tenants. One suspects that there were many in Faversham who concluded, as did Charles Gibbon of an "ungodly" magistrate in another town, that "the town hath a happy turn by his death."[83] The murder of Thomas Ardern may well have enacted the spiteful desires of an entire community.

An archivally based list of suspects bears almost no relationship to that of the official indictment. My scenario matches the judgment of record in the sheer size of the cast of possible murderers; it is just that, with the exception of John Greene, the cast is an entirely different one. The town determined that Alyce Ardern "procured her said husband's death to the intent to have married with the said Morsby" and that she enlisted, besides Morsby, Morsby's sister Cislye Ponder, Ardern's servants Mighell Saunderson and Elsabeth Stafford, masterless men and hired assassins Blackwyll and George Losebagg, and Faversham residents John Greene, George Bradshaw, and William Blackborne.[84] On 5 March 1551 the justice of the peace in Kent was commissioned by the Privy Council to hang Bradshaw in chains in Canterbury; to hang Cislye Ponder and Thomas Morsby in Smithfield; to burn Alyce Ardern at Canterbury and Elsabeth Stafford in Faversham; and to hang, draw, and quarter Mighell Saunderson in Faversham. (The style of death for the last three was mandated for their particular crime of petty treason.) Among City of Canterbury accounts appears a record of 43s. paid "for the charges of burning Mistress Ardern and execution of George Bradshaw."[85] I will return to the fates of John Greene and Blackwyll.

Three indexes of contemporary dissatisfaction with the official in-

83. Charles Gibbon, *Praise of a Good Name* (1594), sig. C3v.

84. The Wardmote Book entry is excerpted by Wine, app. 3.

85. Privy Council members wrote to the mayor of Canterbury regarding Alyce and Bradshaw and to the sheriffs of London regarding Ponder and Morsby; see *APC*, N.S.3 (1550–52), pp. 229–31. On the charges for execution, see the *RCHM, Ninth Report*, pt. 1, report and app., p. 154. The statute of treasons adopted in 1352 and not abolished until 1828 held that "when a servant slayeth his master, or a wife her husband," the crime was petty treason. See W. S. Holdsworth, *History of English Law*, vol. 2, pp. 449–50.

vestigation survive. Principal among them is a protest of Bradshaw's innocence, preserved in the chronicles. The Wardmote Book confidently numbers him among the conspirators who endeavored by "earnest suit, appointment, and confederacy"—in other words, with premeditation—to summon Blackwyll from Calyce [Calais]. According to the chronicles, however, Bradshaw, who had met Black Will during the siege of Boulogne but who was "unwilling to renew [the] acquaintance," did no more than offer Greene the friendly warning, when the two crossed paths with Black Will en route to Gravesend, that the masterless man was a shameless ruffian and heinous murderer. Greene then, as Holinshed and Stow reconstruct it, took these characterizations as recommendations for his own recruitment of Black Will to the conspiracy. Bradshaw, described in the chronicles as a "very honest man," intersected the plot at only one other point, when he agreed to deliver a letter from Greene to Alice. For all his (purported) ignorance of the contents and innocence of its implications, Bradshaw was to be condemned by Greene's letter, which read: "We have got a man for our purpose, we may thank my brother Bradshaw."[86]

In a second shortcoming of the official verdict, one documented collaborator went unindicted. After the murder Greene escaped successfully to Cornwall—until word came from a London jail that a prisoner named Bate had "conveyed away one Greene of Faversham after the murder was there done" and had knowledge of Greene's whereabouts. In an apparent approximation of plea bargaining, Bate proposed that he would "bring such Greene again if he may have liberty." The members of the Privy Council agreed on 28 May 1551, "providing that he take sufficient sureties either to become prisoner again or else to bring forth the said Greene," and they authorized Bate's jailer to release him. Three Privy Council letters followed on 20 July, one liberating the captured Greene from a London jail for transportation to Faversham, another authorizing payment of twenty marks to those who had apprehended Greene and who would convey him to Faversham, and the last directing the mayor of Faversham "to see him hanged in chains."[87]

Third and finally, according to Stow the Kentish knight Sir Thomas Moyle, like Aucher a receiver for the Court of Augmentations, briefly its chancellor, and subsequently Speaker of the House, attempted to extend once again the circle of conspiracy. Mosby implicated Adam

86. Holinshed, pp. 150–51; compare Stow, fol. 35ʳ. In the chronicles, Bradshaw says that he was acquainted with Black Will at Boulogne. The savagery of the 1547 act against vagrancy has been attributed to the return from Boulogne of 48,000 masterless men (Jones, p. 131).
87. APC, N.S.3 (1550–52), pp. 285 and 319.

Fowle as a go-between, and "at this saying, Sir Thomas Moyle [and], after, Petit and Hawkens of the guard, being papists [and] hating Adam Fowle for the gospel, sent Hawkens to apprehend him, and carried him up to London with his legs bound under his horse's belly, and left him at the Marshalsey [jail]." In this instance, the chronicle has some documentary corroboration in the record of a letter sent on 3 March 1551 by the Privy Council to "Christopher Roper, William Webbe, understeward of Faversham, and Hawkens of the Guard, to apprehend one Adam Fowle, and to send him thither with all surety and diligence."[88] Fowle was subsequently cleared by Morsby, but in this anecdote of action taken by papist Moyle against reformist Fowle, only out of "hate for the gospel," can be recognized both a tantalizing echo of the religious rivalry of Ardern and Clement Norton and an impulse to widen the scope of complicity beyond the strictly domestic.

As should be apparent, I am sympathetic with the notion of extra-domestic hostilities at work in the murder of Thomas Ardern. But, from my reading of the records, the story does not end even with these fissures and inconclusions. Rather, they are symptomatic of yet another network of conspiracy that did not enter the formal indictment. In best murder-mystery fashion, the head of that network is on the surface of things he who might least be suspected, for he entered the narrative not among the large cast of those with grudges against Ardern but instead as one of Ardern's putative protectors. Bailey provided the first hint of this suspicion in his paradigm for the middleman, a man despised by those at "both ends of his transactions," central administrators as well as fellow villagers.

Both North and Cheyney reenter Ardern's story at its end. As a member of the Privy Council (confirmed present at their meeting of 5 March 1551), Sir Edward North joined the decision condemning his reported stepdaughter Alyce Ardern. One is reminded of Thomas Boleyn, presiding at the conviction of his daughter for treason. In this case, though, there is less probability of emotional conflict: Alyce was a stepdaughter, after all; we cannot know how much his wife's possible affection for her daughter may have weighed with him; and North had revealed how he valued Alyce when he disposed her in marriage as a reward to a lesser follower rather than, as with his natural daughters, a bearer of his dynastic ambitions.

The eighteenth-century tradition goes so far as to speculate that Alyce's marriage was arranged because she had had "familiarities" with

88. Stow, fol. 37ᵛ; compare Holinshed, p. 159. See also *APC*, N.S.3 (1550–52), p. 227; for Moyle, see the *DNB*. Clark notes this attempt by Moyle and other Catholics "to exploit the murder for their ends" in *English Provincial Society*, p. 84.

her stepfather's steward, Morsby, while still living in North's house. The
sense of family disgrace is apparent as late as 1655, when a descendant
came to write a biography of the founder of the North family by "per-
usal of the old and almost worn-out papers remaining at Kirtling." He
stated that Alice Murfyn had brought to her marriage to North two
"sons" by her previous marriages. This is of a piece with North's ob-
fuscatory translation, in the play *Arden of Feversham*, to a "Lord Clifford." It is not surprising that Alyce Ardern's probable kinship ties were
suppressed from the public record, but it is telling that she was apparently effaced from the family record as well.[89] Despite North's too intimate connections with Alyce and with Ardern, however, no record has
surfaced to offer any hint that he conspired in the crime.

That hint does survive for Sir Thomas Cheyney. As lord warden,
Cheyney had the power to overrule disenfranchisements taken in towns
under his authority; this was a privilege that Faversham, still seeking to
consolidate self-rule, challenged some fifty years later, in 1599, when
the town "indignantly asserted their right to disjurat and disfranchise
at their own will and pleasure without showing any cause to the warden."[90] Significantly, there is no evidence that Cheyney intervened in
his former protégé's behalf, at least during the short months between
Ardern's disenfranchisement and his death. The omission inspires a
search for other signs of Cheyney's disaffection.

By all accounts, Cheyney was a man with a less highly developed
sense of shame than was North. To moot a charge of his complicity—
one suggested to me, against expectation, by the records—I must begin with a controversy nearly ten years past at the time of Ardern's
murder. In 1541 a Walter Morleyn complained to Cheyney of a conspiracy on the part of Master Thomas Ardern and Nicholas Sole, respectively steward and farmer of Cheyney's manor of Hothfield, with
Thomas White, clerk in the commissary's court at Canterbury. Morleyn
accused the three of seeking "to get from him his lands in Benenden,
Kent." Sole had died with the charge still pending, leaving Ardern the
principal defendant. Ardern pleaded innocence, saying that after the
death of Morleyn's father, Morleyn had in fact offered to sell the lands
either to Cheyney or to one Master Poulested, acting for Cromwell.
Cheyney decided for Ardern and his allies, but not before there had

89. North asked to be buried beside Alice Murfyn rather than his second wife, but Alice
was the mother of his heir. The suggestion that Alyce's affair with Morsby predated her
marriage is from otherwise unreliable eighteenth-century manuscript notes transcribed in
"Was *Arden of Feversham* Written by Shakespeare?" p. 303. For the family biography, see Dudley
North (cited in note 8, above), p. 2.
90. Murray, p. 95. The issue recurred in 1657, when a town disenfranchisement was
overridden by the lord warden. See *Calendar of the White and Black Books* (1966), p. 501.

been read into the record testimony that Sole had been troubled that "all the country spake evil of them for the deceiving of the said Morlen of his said lands" and that Ardern had retorted, "Hold thy peace, fool, I would we had such an other bargain in hand." (This is the only direct quotation of Ardern which survives in the archives, but its credibility may be negated by its self-interest.) It is clear that Morleyn was both undependable and a troublemaker, occupied with so many complaints against others that it was an easy and entirely defensible matter for Cheyney to order him, "as a common brawler, barrator, and disturber of the peace, bound over to keep the peace."[91]

In this one instance, however, Ardern's nature and practice is less at issue than is Cheyney's. The implication that Cromwell and Cheyney may have been in competition for the land in Benenden is a particularly important one, and it is not unique in suggesting opposition between the two. On 20 November 1539 a Cromwell servant appealed to his master for the release of the mayor of Rye, a "sound man," from imprisonment by the lord warden of the Cinque Ports; as G. R. Elton observes, "behind the obscurity of this report there may lurk some very serious power struggles at Court." If Cheyney and Cromwell were political enemies, then Cheyney would have relished his 23 June 1540 commission to preside, with "all the King's archers," over the inventory and seizure of Cromwell's goods following his removal to the Tower under charge of treason.[92]

Cheyney was patently not shy of controversy. In July 1528 he had quarrelled with a fellow gentleman of the Privy Chamber, Sir John Russell, over Russell's suit to Wolsey for the wardship of Russell's own younger stepdaughter (Cheyney's interest was revealed later, when he married the elder stepdaughter, also a ward); in the course of the dispute, Cheyney denounced Wolsey, too. Henry VIII, among whose injunctions to his gentlemen was the order that "all six must always be loving one with another," exiled Cheyney from the Chamber, reportedly calling him "proud and full of opprobrious words, little esteeming his friends that did much for him." Cheyney was restored to favor only with the aid of Anne Boleyn, a distant relative who had better cause than kinship to seize an opportunity to best Wolsey.[93]

Cheyney's feuds continued. On 26 November 1541 his fellows on the Privy Council recorded that Cheyney's elder son had accused him

91. PRO SP 1/243. And see *L & P*, add. 1, pt. 2, no. 1514.
92. G. R. Elton, *Policy and Police* (1972), p. 169. On the seizure of Cromwell's goods, see *L & P*, vol. 15, no. 804.
93. Gladys Scott Thomson, *Two Centuries* (1930), pp. 155–56; J. H. Wiffen, *Historical Memoirs* (1833), vol. 1, pp. 309–10; and Diane Willen, *John Russell* (1981), p. 16. Willen notes that in fact the wardships were the king's, not Wolsey's.

of treason for iconolatry; because the accusation seemed to reflect "rather of pride than of any just matter," young John Cheyney was, presumably without objection by his father, committed to the Tower. In January 1543 Richard Cavendish, comptroller of Dover, "alleged certain matters against Sir Thomas Cheyney" before the Privy Council but, unable to prove his accusations, was constrained to ask forgiveness and to depart. In July 1545 Edmund Finche, a minstrel, was pilloried in Cranbrook and Dartford for using "slanderous words of the King's Counsel," namely Cheyney. On 12 November 1546 the members of the Privy Council, who had backed Cheyney against his own son, against Cavendish, and against Finche, were faced with a more delicate controversy. Cranmer, who had complained of Cheyney's religious conservatism some nine years earlier, now reported his "often suit" to Cheyney "for the matter of the wreck[age] depending in variance betwixt him and him"; the Council urged Cheyney to dispatch some books necessary for resolution, "whereunto they were the rather moved for that they would be very loathe the matter should grow to any further extremity between them," the two most powerful men in Kent. Thus, at one extreme Cheyney had quarrelled with Wolsey, Cromwell, and Cranmer; at the other, with his heir and also, it is hinted on 27 July 1558, with his second wife. Evidently he had evicted her, for Mary I herself wrote to Cheyney when the couple reconciled, commending him "for receiving his wife again, and continuing in house with her, lovingly."[94]

The long list of Cheyney's controversies reveals him to have been a man of quick temper, unapologetic self-interest, and uncertain loyalty. We may suspect that from his point of view Ardern had mismanaged the Morleyn affair by allowing it to proceed so far and to implicate himself so publicly. We may infer that the man who was capable of jailing his own son was equally capable of turning on a protégé. We may remark that in Faversham's religious disputes it was likely that Cheyney, a fierce conservative and accused iconolator, would have sympathized with Clement Norton rather than with Norton's accuser, the active reformer Thomas Ardern. We may suppose that Cheyney's opposition to Cromwell would have aligned him both with Greene's master, Sir Anthony Aucher, and against Ardern's father-in-law, Sir Edward North. We must note that Richard Cavendish was among Cheyney's most open antagonists, a fact to which I shortly return. And we may further remark that Cheyney's men were evidently caught up in their master's

94. On John Cheyney, see L & P, vol. 16, no. 1375. On Cavendish, see APC, N.S.1 (1542–47), pp. 73–74, and L & P, vol. 18, pt. 1, no. 18. On Finche, see L & P, vol. 20, pt. 1, nos. 1083 and 1140. On Cranmer, see APC, N.S.1 (1542–47), pp. 549–50. On Mary, see CSPD, vol. 13 (1547–80), no. 43.

quarrels, that they observed and reproduced his fractiousness, or that he may even have cultivated their contentiousness: on 12 June 1554 Henry Machyn in his *Diary* noted a "great fray between the lord warden's servants of Kent" and men of Gray's Inn and Lincoln's Inn, during which there were "some slain and hurt."[95]

These men, or some of their fellows, were implicated in the fate of the hired assassin Blackwyll. On 12 May 1553 (more than two years after the murder), the Privy Council informed their new agent in Flanders, Sir Philip Hoby, of the residence there of "one Blackwyll, who of long times has been a notable murderer, and one of the most wretched and vile persons that lives . . . and although there be many divers causes that of conscience more than require that he be sent over to be punished, yet one special case there is, the shameful murder of one Ardern, of Faversham in Kent, which much enforces them to require earnestly that he be sent over." The Council copied to Hoby letters they had already issued to the bailiff and other magistrates of the Flanders port of Flushing, requesting Blackwyll's extradition, and they directed Hoby to speak to Mary of Hungary, Regent of Flanders, "for her commands to the officers of that town, to deliver the culprit to those who shall be appointed to convey him to England." On 19 May Hoby reported to the Council that in his audience with the regent, she had bid farewell to English ambassador Sir Thomas Chamberlain, had welcomed Hoby as his successor, and had also allowed that "although contrary to the laws of Flanders, Blackwyll is to be delivered up, it being a pity so abominable a murderer should escape unpunished."[96] Hoby may have been rather too eager to advise the Privy Council of his diplomatic prowess, for the Wardmote Book, the Stow manuscript, Holinshed, *Arden of Feversham*, and Henry Machyn all insist—the last most persuasively—that Blackwyll was not returned to England after all but was for "divers" other murders burned to death in Flushing.

The extradition negotiations expose two intriguing elements of Ardern's story. One is the level of interest taken by the central government in this murder, perhaps the less surprising for the presence on the Council of North and Cheyney. The other is an unsettling implication about Blackwyll's escape. On 15 June 1551 the Privy Council had written to thank Sir William Godolphin, justice of the peace in Cornwall, "for his diligence in the apprehension of Blackwyll" and to request Godolphin "to send [Blackwyll] in safe guard," presumably to London.

95. Henry Machyn, *Diary*, p. 65.
96. *CSPF*, vol. 1547–53, nos. 679 and 684. On relations between Flanders and England, see Jane de Iongh, *Mary of Hungary* (1958). According to John Bellamy, the crown was not shy of seeking extradition but had greater success with men described to foreign princes as mere felons (*Tudor Law of Treason* [1979], pp. 88–91). Hoby continued as ambassador to Flanders until August 1553, when Cheyney was sent to recall him.

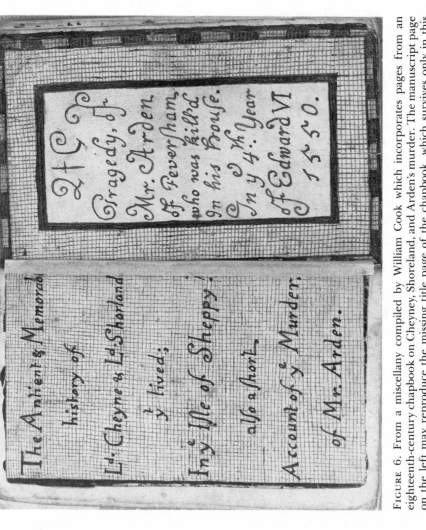

The Antient's Memorable
history of
Ld. Cheyne & Ld. Shorland
&c. lived;
In ye Isle of Sheppy.
also a short
Account of ye Murder,
of Mr. Arden.

A
Tragedy, of
Mr. Arden,
of Feversham,
who was kill'd
in his House.
In ye 4.th Year
of Edward VI
1550.

FIGURE 6. From a miscellany compiled by William Cook which incorporates pages from an eighteenth-century chapbook on Cheyney, Shoreland, and Arden's murder. The manuscript page on the left may reproduce the missing title page of the chapbook, which survives only in this incomplete copy. To the right is a page introducing an abbreviated version of the play *Arden of Feversham*. Reproduced by permission of the Folger Shakespeare Library.

But either en route to or after his arrival in London, Blackwyll had once again successfully evaded English justice, this time escaping to Flanders. It is unlikely that he could have done so without assistance. The 12 May 1553 letter to Hoby specifies that Blackwyll was at that time "stayed at Flushing, by the procurement of certain servants of the Treasurer of his Majesty's household"—that is, by Sir Thomas Cheyney's men.[97]

In this context *stayed* is a radically ambiguous verb. The word may have been intended to indicate that Blackwyll had been detained (pending extradition) by the treasurer's men. But *stayed* can equally denote that Blackwyll was supported by the treasurer's fractious men, perhaps abetted in escape as well as sustained in exile. The very letter that specifies that Blackwyll was stayed by Cheyney's men requests official Flemish intervention to "deliver" him instead "to those who shall be appointed to convey him to England"; Cheyney's men were evidently not to be entrusted with that assignment. If *stayed* means "sustained," then Cheyney is directly implicated in the murder of his former steward and Cinque Ports official. And even if *stayed* means "detained," Cheyney's long-lived interest in the assassin's fate smacks somewhat of a desire to contain and control a potential source of his own exposure.

Had Blackwyll been capable of incriminating Cheyney, his execution in Flushing, out of range of English inquisition, would have served Cheyney's purpose far better than extradition. Evidences are that Blackwyll was in fact not extradited from Flanders. Something or someone intervened between Hoby's diplomatic success and its promised end, and Blackwyll was executed at a safe and silent distance from London. The agents of last record with control of Blackwyll are Thomas Cheyney's men.

Meanwhile, Cheyney and Ardern were married to history by a chapbook printed in the eighteenth century, the only surviving copy of which is bound, along with an abbreviated manuscript version of the play *Arden of Feversham*, into the miscellany of one William Cook (see figures 6 and 7). Cook has removed the title page of the chapbook, but a leaf in his hand suggests that the pamphlet was titled *The Ancient and Memorable History of Lord Cheyne and Lord Shorland that lived in the Isle of Sheppy, also a Short Account of the Murder of Master Arden.* The text identifies Lord Shorland as Cheyney's heir, and its report of Cheyney and Shorland is followed by a catalogue of "The Characters of the Persons

97. *APC*, N.S.3 (1550–52), p. 306. The Council's interest in Blackwyll was consistent with both Tudor theory and general practice. See William Baldwin in *Mirror for Magistrates*: "what soever prince desireth to live quietly without rebellion, must do his subjects right in all things" (quoted in Jones, p. 49).

FIGURE 7. William Cook pasted this eighteenth-century illustration of the murder of Thomas Arden into his miscellany. Compare the earlier version in figure 2; neither was contemporary to the murder and this is the more polite. Reproduced by permission of the Folger Shakespeare Library.

concerned in the Tragedy of Arden" and an "Account" of the murder that is, despite its title, a lengthy one.[98] Similarly, the play *Arden*, which makes brief reference to North only as "Lord Clifford," features an appearance by Cheyney that is unprecedented in its chronicle source. In scene 9, Cheyney encounters Arden on his return home from London and recognizes Black Will waiting in ambush. Cheyney thus prevents one murder attempt, but he also sets up another attack by inviting Arden to travel to the Isle of Sheppey the next day. The play portrays Cheyney as obliged to protect Black Will, who calls himself Cheyney's "beadsman" (in another reminder of the religious difference between Cheyney and Ardern) and whom Cheyney rewards with a coin.[99]

The play also reminds us that Cheyney served at the siege of Boulogne, where he may have first become acquainted with Blackwyll.[100] If so, then Alyce could have learned of Blackwyll from Cheyney as readily as from Bradshaw. By passing on information about Blackwyll, even as innocently as Bradshaw is reported to have done, Cheyney could have been an unwitting abettor of Ardern's murder. But to see Cheyney as unwitting is to deny the evidence of his character and career; active collaboration was a hallmark of his style, and his own enlistment of Blackwyll to the cause is far from inconceivable.

The theory that Cheyney colluded in Ardern's murder finds some corroboration in the incrimination of George Bradshaw. Holinshed gratuitously (and all the more credibly for that) identifies Bradshaw as formerly "Sir Richard Cavendish's man," that is, an ally of Cheyney's old and doubtless unforgiven accuser before the Privy Council and one who happened to be on site in Faversham. If Bradshaw was as innocent as the chronicles allege, he would have made an ideal scapegoat, a blind for Cheyney's own complicity in procuring Blackwyll. After all, Bradshaw's guilt was evidently established solely by John Greene's letter to Alyce Ardern. And Greene, like Blackwyll, escaped after the murder to Cornwall, probably by the same network of assistance as Blackwyll, perhaps with the aid of the same Cheynean followers who two years later "stayed" their master's "beadsman" in Flushing.

Finally, as lord warden, Cheyney was in a position to know how the residents of Faversham viewed Thomas Ardern and how they would react to his murder. In the months following the crime, the town seized

98. Folger Library MS. D.a.6.
99. For this suggestion, I am indebted to Wine, p. 89. The play reveals some local knowledge independent of Holinshed: it mentions the nearby Boughton-on-Blene and interpolates the otherwise unrecorded story of Jack Fitten's theft of plate.
100. His elder son died in the battle, according to W. L. Rutton, "Cheney of Shurland" (1900).

the goods and jewels of all the local conspirators: Alyce Ardern, Thomas Morsby, Cislye Ponder, George Bradshaw, and John Greene. The goods alone sold for £184 10s. 4-1/2d., of which over one-third, £63 15s. 7d., went to the "accomptants or sellers of the aforesaid goods." Some townsmen, in other words, may have realized an immediate profit on the murder. Ardern's will, the probate of which the town was constrained to pay, left the corporation two tenements in Cooksditch, two gardens, the pillory in the marketplace, and a St. Nicholas Chapel and its lands, endowing both gifts for the poor and an annual sermon preached in Ardern's name to "provoke" others "to give the like." But the town sold some of these properties to meet other fiscal obligations, and nearly twenty years later his daughter sued to recover the value of the properties as well as the seized goods—with some success.[101] Although the annual sermon was apparently delivered into the nineteenth century, no monument was raised to Ardern in the Faversham church where he had served as warden—at least John Weever records none in his 1631 compilation *Ancient Funeral Monuments*, and none survives today. This omission alone speaks volumes.[102]

And what of the town's attitude toward Cheyney? First, it was in the town's Wardmote Book that George Bradshaw was judged guilty of conspiracy—without any of the doubts that plague other narratives, without any suggestion that others besides Bradshaw had possible connection with Blackwyll from Boulogne, and without any awareness that others could have recognized his qualifications for an assignment of murder. Second, Cheyney, who had not exerted himself on Ardern's behalf in the matter of his disenfranchisement, did act the lord warden locally later that same year. As was only appropriate in the wake of so dramatic a disruption of order in Faversham, he visited the town, or so a record in the Wardmote Book implies. Along with the accounts that report the profit to the corporation from receipt of the convicted murderers' goods is recorded the expenditure of town funds in the amount of 22s., again as was only proper, "for presents to my lord warden."

The Place of Ardern's Murder

The versions of Ardern's story that were told in the Renaissance—and there were many of them—are largely innocent of such implica-

101. Records of the receipt of conspirators' goods and of the probate of Ardern's will appear in the Wardmote Book. On the subsequent disposition of Ardern's property, see Cust, pp. 102–4; and Telfer, "Orphans," pp. 193–96.

102. John Weever, *Ancient Funeral Monuments* (1631). Percival remarks how striking is the omission in a church with "scores and scores" of monuments to townspeople far less distinguished than Ardern.

tions of a conspiracy centered on Ardern's public life. To expose the full measure of their reductivism is, after all, the main point of this exercise in biography. The themes that we now recognize as being of profound cultural consequence are precisely those that did not surface in the sixteenth- and seventeenth-century tellings: the reconfiguration of the local power structures that accompanied the redistribution of monastic property and wealth; persistent inabilities to reconcile fully religious tradition and reform, continuing hostilities between those who resisted the new theology and those who embraced it; the methods of town administration in practice, the motivations of local self-governance as an ideal, the manners in which localities negotiated their evolving relationship with the center; the unhappy twinship of patronage and corruption, the direct and indirect benefits of office, the uncertain ethics of the new professions; court faction as a microcosm for the circulation of contention, the way in which individual rivalries contaminated others, the easy communicability of such contagion in a comparatively small world; unprecedented material, commercial, and capitalist aspirations in the age of the "Great Rebuilding" (as W. G. Hoskins has termed it),[103] with new standards of housing accessible to a new range of men and with an influx of goods and furnishings disseminated from the dissolved monasteries and imported from the Continent; the surging numbers of "masterless men," the dispossession of those whom the monasteries had fed and housed, the requisite rise of civic virtue, private charity, and poor relief; the fact that opportunity for a few meant for many others old understandings betrayed, old accommodations violated, new anxieties generated, new envies engaged; the need for revised formulations and inculcations of the sources, agents, and enterprises of disorder.

Only this last phenomenon resonates in sixteenth- and seventeenth-century versions of Ardern's story. Their theme, my subject in this section, is encapsulated in the full title of the 1592 stage play, *The Lamentable and True Tragedy of Master Arden of Feversham in Kent. Who was most wickedly murdered, by the means of his disloyal and wanton wife, who for the love she bore to one Mosby, hired two desperate ruffians, Blackwill and Shakebag, to kill him. Wherein is showed the great malice and dissimulation of a wicked woman, the unsatiable desire of filthy lust, and the shameful end of all murderers.* That is, the story was moralized, as would have been expected of the genre, and domesticated, as certainly would not have been.

The Arden of the play is not even a "new" man; he is an established "gentleman of blood" (which William Harrison glosses as "defined to

103. W. G. Hoskins, "Rebuilding of Rural England" (1953). But see also R. Machin, "Great Rebuilding: A Reassessment" (1977).

descend of three descents of nobleness") and entirely nobler of character than his historical prototype.[104] Any hypothetically antecedent interest in advancement and business is at once eclipsed by Arden's more immediate obsession with his wife's suspected infidelity. In the opening scene, his friend Franklin triumphantly delivers royal letters patent, the title to the abbey lands. But Arden is indifferent to them, preoccupied instead with Alice's love letters to Mosby and with her presumed violation of another title, which is Arden's "mandate" to her in marriage.[105] Business is Arden's pretext for a trip to London, but in truth he goes of purpose to give her time to amend her behavior. Charges against him of greed and corruption, like the more preposterous ones of miserliness, whoredom, and intended uxoricide, enter the play almost exclusively as unsubstantiated accusations by self-interested collaborators in his murder. Alice tells Mosby that "my saving husband hoards up bags of gold" (1.220) to remind him of Arden's wealth, which she assures him will devolve to him if their plans succeed. And she pursues a similarly inflammatory strategy when she dismisses the tenure complaints of Greene, confirming that Arden legally controls the land in question—but only for the length of his life.

It is important to recognize that the refusal of the play to engage the professional life of Thomas Ardern, the insistence instead on the narrow domesticity of his murder, the strictness of focus on Alice Arden's crime, is not an invention of this text. The chronicles, too, were already substantially focused on domestic catastrophe. An alternative history does intrude itself in Holinshed, through references to Ardern's "extortiousness," but in the play these are identified as interpretive distractions and are digested to serve what is recognizably the prevailing myth of its source. In *Arden of Feversham* is thus completed a four-decade process of purging the story of its extradomestic elements.[106]

104. William Harrison, *Description of England* (1587), p. 110. Arden's anger with Mosby is an ennobling prerogative of position, as is his contempt for Mosby as a "servile," "fawning," and "injurious ribald" (1.28, 37). Arden also inspires—in addition to Franklin's loyal friendship—Alice's admission of "how dearly Arden lovèd me" (8.61) and Michael's testimony that he is "harmless," "gentle," doer of "many good turns," giver of "kindly love," owner of "liberal hand" (3.195–97, 176).

105. Although many modern editors of the play add to line 6, "Here are the deeds," the stage direction "*He hands them*" (or some variation thereof), the text suggests that Arden does not take them. In line 12 Arden calls them "foul objects" and speaks of them not as "these" at hand but as "those" still in Franklin's hands. Franklin may offer the papers a second time with "Read them" (line 8)—again, perhaps, to theatrically marked disinterest.

106. For the known redactions of the story, see bibliographic entries for the following, here listed chronologically insofar as possible: Henry Machyn, *Diary* (1551), p. 4; *Breviat Chronicle* (1552); John Stow, "History of a Most Horrible Murder Committed at Feversham" (n.d.); Stow, *Two London Chronicles* (n.d.), p. 22; Stow, *A Summary of English Chronicles* (1565), sigs. Dd4ᵛ– Dd5ʳ; Stow, *The Summary of English Chronicles* (1566), sigs. X6ʳ⁻ᵛ; Raphael Holinshed, *Chronicles* (1577); Stow, *Chronicles* (1580), sig. Uuu1ᵛ (in later editions entitled *Annals*); *Arden of Feversham*

Three instances drawn from the Wardmote Book, the *Breviat Chronicle*, and the Stow manuscript witness the ways in which the Arden texts fashioned themselves to this end. For my own interpretive purposes, I earlier placed the first report of the murder, that of the Wardmote Book, in the category of archive rather than fiction. But one result of the preceding murder investigation—of an acceptance, for example, of George Bradshaw's possible innocence despite that report's impenetrable conviction of his guilt—should be an awareness that we must also read this text critically. To do so is to note the particular care that has been taken to domesticate the murder by locating it in the Ardern house:

> . . . he was most shamefully murdered as is foresaid, as he was playing at tables friendly with the said Morsby. For suddenly came out of a dark house adjoining to the said parlor the foresaid Blackwyll, whom she and her accomplices had bestowed privily before, and came with a napkin in his hand, and suddenly came behind the said Ardern's back, threw the said napkin over his head and face, and strangled him. And forthwith the said Morsby stepped to him and struck him with a tailor's great pressing iron upon the head to the brain and immediately drew out his dagger, which was great and broad, and therewith cut the said Ardern's throat. Being at the death of him: the said Alyce his wife, Mighell Saunderson, and Elsabeth Stafford. And after that he was thus murdered, he was carried out of the said parlor into the foresaid dark house. . . . The said Cislye Ponder went to the said Ardern's and did help to bear the dead corpse out into a meadow there, commonly called the Amery Croft, on the backside of the said Ardern's garden. And about eleven of the clock the said Sunday night, the said Ardern was found where they had laid him, in the said meadow. Whereupon the said Ardern's house was searched, and thereupon his blood was found, that it was manifest and well approved that he was slain in his own house.[107]

Meanwhile, the second textualization of the event, the 1552 (first) edition of *A Breviat Chronicle Containing all the Kings from Brute to this Day, and Many Notable Acts unto the Year [1552]* interposes a second domestic construct. It translates the date of the murder from the Ward-

---

(1592); *World of Wonders* (1595), sig. F1ᵛ; Thomas Beard, *Theatre of God's Judgments* (1597), pp. 270–71; Thomas Heywood, *Troia Britannica* (1609), p. 462; John Rainolds, *Defence of the Judgment* (1609), sigs. N1ʳ and K2ᵛ; John Taylor, *Unnatural Father* (1621); "Complaint and Lamentation of Mistress Arden" (1633); Henry Goodcole, *Adultress's Funeral Day* (1635), sig. B1ʳ; Thomas Taylor, *Second Part of the Theatre of God's Judgment* (1642), pp. 94–95; Richard Baker, *Chronicle* (1643), sigs. Lll3ʳ⁻ᵛ. Many of these publications went through multiple editions.
107. See Wine, app. 3, p. 161.

mote Book's 15 February to St. Valentine's Day, the festival of lovers, the day when birds were anciently supposed to choose their mates and when human lovers in folk custom did, too, either by lottery or by the first encounter of the day. For Ardern's story as I have told it, the date had some significance in initiating the Faversham fair and rekindling whatever civic argument there was about his ground rental. For Arden's story as the Renaissance told it, however, the date colludes in a distant way in the notion that the murder represented a perverse celebration for Alice and Mosby of their adulterous love affair.

Third and most tellingly, the Stow version of Arden's story opens with a lengthy report that "this Arden had a mother dwelling in Norwich, who went a begging, but he assayed all means possible to keep her from it," principally and ineffectually by sending her financial support. The shame of it was that she did not beg for need but for pleasure; at one point she was discovered to have £60 in her possession, "tied up in several little cloutes not above ten groats in one cloute." After Arden's death, Norwich townsmen succeeded in controlling her as he had not, "notwithstanding she never enjoyed after she was restrained from her begging, and died within half a year."[108] Stow's preface, whether or not it is apocryphal, serves both to heighten its readers' impression of a man disgraced by a dysfunctional private life and to clarify our perception of a narrativizing investment in domestic dishonor.

One feature that remained popular in contemporary recountings of the story was the long catalogue of Alyce's collaborators. Such a catalogue appears in the earliest representation of the story outside Faversham, the *Breviat Chronicle*: "This year on S[aint] Valentine's day at Feversham in Kent was committed a shameful murder, for one Arden a gentleman was by the consent of his wife murdered, wherefore she was burned at Canterbury, and there was one hanged in chains for that murder, and at Feversham was [two] hanged in chains, and a woman burned, and in Smithfelde was hanged one Mosby and his sister for the same murder also." The sheer number of convicted collaborators seems also to have been the source of diarist Henry Machyn's interest in the matter: "The fourteenth day of March was hanged, in Smithfield, one John Mosbe and his sister, for the death of a gentleman of Feyversham, one Master Arden the customer, and his own wife was decaul . . . , and she was burned at Canterbury, and her servant hanged there, and two at Feyversham and one at Hospryng, and another in the

---

108. Stow, fol. 34^r. The widow who hoarded her funds and the widow who begged were frequent stereotypes, but see an analysis of inventories post mortem from Bedfordshire, which reveals that those with substantial amounts of cash were often widows ("Jacobean Household Inventories," p. 41).

high way to Canterbury, for the death of Master Arden of Feyversham." According to Machyn's modern editor, the diarist returned
some time later to add the line "and at Flusshyng was burned Blake
Tome [that is, Blackwyll] for the same death of Master Arden," further
to increase the terrible count of assassins and executions.

A thematic echo of this superflux of conspirators can be heard in the
chronicles' report that the murder of 15 February 1551 succeeded only
after a long series of failed attempts at assassination: poisoned milk, an
assault in St. Paul's Churchyard in London, murder in the night in
Arden's London residence, attacks on the road from London to Feversham and from Feversham to the ferry to Cheyney's Isle of Sheppey,
a quarrel at Feversham's St. Valentine's fair. The play, which finds its
structure, locates its tone, and builds its suspense in this sequence of
frustrations, adds abortive plots with a poisoned crucifix and a poisoned portrait. Together with the catalogue of conspirators, that of
their many miscarriages interjects the touch of psychological reassurance that provides a necessary counterbalance to the enactment of
its audience's deepest fears: Arden was hard to kill.

Because Ardern's body was discovered on the nearby abbey grounds,
the Wardmote Book's emphasis that he "was heinously murdered in his
own parlor" required its trail of evidence to link the household residents to the murder. The chronicles, too, detail the tracing of foot-
prints between house and field in a convenient snow, the recognition of
household rushes in Arden's slippers, the discovery of a bloody knife
and cloth in a tub beside the Arden well, and the identification of blood
on Mosby's clothes. This evidentiary process was subsequently recalled
by Thomas Beard, who, in his 1597 collection of notable murders,
Theatre of God's Judgments, emphasized that "as the murder of a gentleman in Kent called master Arden of Feversham was most execrable, so
the wonderful discovery thereof was exceeding rare." The difficulty of
the discovery, paired with its end in multiple executions, happily sub-
stantiated another cherished conviction of the period: murder will out.

Chroniclers Holinshed and Stow further reported that "in the place
where [the murdered Arden] was laid, being dead, all the proportion
of his body might be seen two years after and more, so plain as could
be, for the grass did not grow where his body had touched, but between
his legs, between his arms, and about the hollowness of his neck, and
round about his body, and where his legs, arms, head, or any other part
of his body had touched, no grass growed at all of all that time." The
purported cause of this phenomenon was a curse uttered by a tenant
dispossessed of the very field where Arden's body was laid. The report
might be assumed to have inflated the appeal of the story, were it not

primarily an afterthought on the chronicles' part. The play recounts the "miracle" only in an epilogue so disjunct in tone from the rest as to suggest another hand. And surprisingly enough, only one other chronicler, Richard Baker, pursues the theme, concluding in 1643 that "thus the divine justice even in this world oftentimes works miracles upon offenders, for a merciful warning to men, if they would be so wise to take it." Baker's "warning" seems rather to serve a general moral than to revive the suppressed story of Arden's "extortiousness." The relative infrequency with which this spectacular event is mentioned suggests that, instead of contributing to the level of interest in the murder story, it paid its own form of tribute to the intrinsic power of that story.

The number of conspirators, the many attempts at assassination, the exercise of investigative technique, the miracle of the blighted grass— all these represent the sensational, the curious, the particular about the Arden story. They help explain why this murder—rather than some other instance of mariticide—assumed an almost totemic significance in early modern culture. As the majority of references to the murder make clear, however, there remained one chief cause that Holinshed overcame the inhibitions of decorum, one element that resonated most deeply with contemporary anxieties, one fear that early moderns seemed compelled to revisit, one reason that the murder came to be used in a system of rhetorical notation as a symbol of the most extreme form of domestic evil—even a hundred years after the event. At the center was the agency of Alice. Alice served the cultural function of giving definition to the shape of domestic evil by marking its extreme.

Alice Arden was elevated to mythical stature as early as 1609 by John Rainolds, reader in Greek at Oxford and a principal among the translators of the King James Bible. His posthumously printed tract on the right of divorce is dense with citations from Greek and Latin authors, the Old and New Testaments, biblical commentators, and Continental humanists. References to only three near-contemporary events interrupt this display of humanist learning. The first is the assassination of the French king, Henry III, in 1589; the second is the defeat of the Spanish Armada in 1588; and the third (to a modern eye the most antipathetic to its context) is the murder committed by Alice Arden in 1551. Discussing the dangers of adultery, Rainolds suggests that the husband of an adulteress can "but live still in fear and anguish of mind, lest she add drunkenness to thirst and murder to adultery: I mean lest she serve him as Clytemnestra did Agamemnon, as Livia did Drusus, as Mistress Arden did her husband." An anonymous contemporary in 1596 explains, "neither was Clitemnestra so cruel unto her husband because she was a woman, but because she was a most wicked and unnatural woman."[109]

From Holinshed's emphasis that Arden was murdered "by the procurement of his own wife" forward, this is the note that authors strike most frequently. Thomas Heywood's epic poem of 1609, *Troia Britannica*, includes in a stanza for 1551: "At Feversham was murdered by his Wife / Arden, by help of Mosby and Black-Will" (and continues, in the hapless juxtapositions of its rapid verse form, "The trade with Muscovy did now first grow rife . . ."). Thomas Taylor's 1642 *Second Part of the Theatre of God's Judgments* numbers first among murders of "these latter times . . . committed through Lust" that of "Master Arden of Feversham slain by his wife and her adulterous companion." A highly anecdotal and ephemeral collection titled *A World of Wonders, A Mass of Murders, A Covy of Cosenages* summarizes, "in the [fifth] year of King Edward the sixth, Master Arden of Feversham in Kent was murdered by the consent of his own wife, for which fact she was burned at Canterbury." In 1633 Alice received her own ballad, "The Complaint and Lamentation of Mistress Arden of Feversham in Kent." In 1635 Henry Goodcole "remembered" his readers "of Mistress Arden, who caused her husband to be murdered in her own house at Feversham in Kent." Finally, the fact that John Taylor (the Water Poet) mentions the murder of Arden in tandem with that of a Master Page of Plymouth, which in 1599 also inspired a (lost) stage play, suggests that he was thinking of *Arden of Feversham* when he wrote that "both [these] murders are fresh in memory, and the fearful ends of their wives and their aiders in those bloody actions will never be forgotten."[110]

In the interest of a final clarification of the contemporary appeal of Arden's story, I offer a digression on the comparative life story of John Thynne. Nephew to Henry VIII's chief clerk of the Kitchens, Thynne advanced from a royal kitchen clerkship to the stewardship of the Household of Edward Seymour, earl of Hertford.[111] He thus attached himself to a man who served as a member of Henry's Privy Chamber and then on his Privy Council; who received a number of important

109. M. B., *Trial of True Friendship* (1596), sig. E1ᵛ. Nearly 300 years later, John Addington Symonds called Alice Arden "the bourgeois Clytemnestra" (p. 451)—as have Lionel Cust, Willard Thorp, E. H. C. Oliphant, Louis Gillet, Felix E. Schelling, and others.

110. Plays rather than pamphlets probably kept the memories "fresh" for Taylor. For *Arden of Feversham*'s extensive history of production and revision, see A. F. Hopkinson's introduction to his edition of the play as well as Wine, pp. xlv–lvii. Narrative versions of the story include: "A tragic fact, of 1550" (1804); "Alice Arden, Murderess," by Abel H. Coppinger (1897); and *Feversham*, by Diane Davidson (1969).

111. For Thynne and Seymour, see the *DNB; House of Commons;* David Burnett, *Longleat* (1978); and Mark Girouard, *Robert Smythson* (1983).

royal appointments; who amassed an estate with the astonishing annual value of £7,400; who pursued rivalries with Northumberland, Cromwell, Norfolk, Surrey, Wriothesley, and Warwick; and who on the death of Henry VIII seized the protectorate of England and, with the further title of duke of Somerset, stated arrogantly that he was "caused by Providence to rule." His patron's influence enabled Thynne, too, to accumulate properties in London, Wiltshire, and several other counties, most notably the former priory of Longleat. Thynne was also appointed packer of London, that is, collector of fees for skins and pewter packed for exportation. In 1547, wounded in battle during Somerset's expedition to Scotland, Thynne was knighted. In 1549 his career was further advanced by a lucrative marriage to Christian Gresham, heir to a lord mayor of London.

On 22 July 1549 Somerset ally William Paget warned that "Master Thynne has shown himself so dishonest and covetous," that "the covetous disposition of this man may do his Grace [Somerset] hurt," and that there was "nothing his Grace requires so much to take heed of as that man's proceedings."[112] Paget himself subsequently abetted Somerset's enemies in dispatching him to the Tower on 11 October 1549. On 14 January 1550 Somerset was deposed from the protectorate and deprived of his offices and lands; by 18 February he was pardoned and reinstated on the Privy Council; but on 16 October 1551 his rivals returned him to the Tower, where, although a charge of treason failed, he was convicted of felony and on 22 January 1552 beheaded. Thynne, too, was imprisoned in the Tower on 13 October 1549, pardoned in August 1550, and rearrested on 16 October 1551; ultimately, however, he was freed with a fine and the loss of his packership. Thynne recovered to serve as comptroller of Elizabeth's Household, as a member of Parliament, and as a justice of the peace in Wiltshire. In 1567, as a widower, he married a second lord mayor's daughter. And between 1567 and 1579 he built at a cost of some £9,000 a lasting memorial in Longleat, the facade of which survives as the first great English house in the Renaissance style. There, Thynne displayed on the walls of a gallery above his great hall the arms of Cecil, Suffolk, and Somerset.

Thomas Ardern's ambition, useful affiliation, advancement through office and marriage, accumulation of land, alleged corruption and political disgrace, and ongoing quest for place and status were, in other words, scarcely unique for his time; nor were they as dramatic as, for just one example, John Thynne's. On the occasion of Thynne's second imprisonment, however, his wife Christian pled his case before the

112. *CSPF*, vol. 1547–1553, p. 45, no. 192 (22 July 1549).

assembled Privy Council; what distinguished Ardern's story was his betrayal by his own wife and murder at her instigation.

While the histories of both men are supercharged with social, economic, political, and legal significances, only Ardern's exposes his vexed and irregular private life to public attention. And "Arden's" story pulses insistently through the pages of Holinshed, Stow, Machyn, Heywood, Beard, Thomas Taylor, Goodcole, John Taylor, and Rainolds—while Thynne's does not, in Goodcole's words, "deserve a place" in contemporary chronicles. To credit the cause simply to a sensationalistic interest in murder is inadequate. To suggest that Arden's story permitted a displacement of the multiple anxieties of the post-Reformation period onto a "disloyal," "wanton," and "wicked" woman is at best incomplete. To argue instead that "Alice Arden's crime" was a cultural phenomenon coequal with the others that I have listed is nearer to my sense of its import and, in fact, to the significance conferred upon it by the analogical thought of the Renaissance.

In short, the period discovered through Arden's murder its own way into and past the intransigence of the private. At the beginning of this chapter, I remarked the distinction between the conduct of Ardern's life and the construct of Arden's story. The significance of Ardern's life was that it lent itself to the construct. And it was this construct that was necessary to his culture's self-definition.

A Place for the Private

To conclude this part of my investigation of ways in which the "private" functioned in the sixteenth and seventeenth centuries, I present five apparent contradictions. First, even if my speculations concerning the role of Ardern's public life in his murder are valid, I suggest that the textualizations that insisted on the domesticity of that murder may nonetheless have been truer to fact than modern readers can immediately perceive. To make this case, I must undo the taxonomy by which I earlier associated patrons, townsmen, and tenants with administrative, financial, ecclesiastical, and jurisdictional motivations while implicitly identifying members of his household and their allies with domestic, sexual, testamentary, and personal motivations. The "public" personalities, I now argue, are easily as implicated in "private" matters.

A Renaissance commonplace held that no man is "fit to govern anywhere, or to bear authority that cannot govern his own house."[113] The

113. See Thomas Floyd, *Picture of a Perfect Commonwealth* (1600), sig. E12ʳ; and compare John Dod and Robert Cleaver, *Godly Form of Household Government* (1598): "none will think or

Wardmote Book specifies Ardern's domestic mismanagement in detail of extraordinary substance and emotion for so abbreviated an official account: "Alyce the said Morsby did not only carnally keep in her own house here in this town, but also fed [him] with delicate meats and sumptuous apparel, all which things *the said Thomas Ardern did well know and willfully did permit and suffered the same*." The Stow manuscript similarly stresses Arden's appalling tolerance of his own shame: "Master Arden perceiving right well their mutual familiarity . . . was yet so greatly given to seek his advantage, and cared so little how he came by it, that in hope of attaining some benefit of the Lord North by means of this Mosby who could do much with him, he winked at that shameful disorder and both permitted and also invited him very often to be in his house." Holinshed diverges from Stow in suggesting that Arden was more concerned to keep Alice's approval and influence than Mosby's, but he otherwise concurs that Arden was notoriously and culpably permissive. In both chronicles, the discovery of Arden's murder at once occasions suspicion of Alice, so well known was "her evil behavior in times past."[114]

The stigma of willing cuckoldry (wittolry) was so strong in the period that *Arden of Feversham*, in a significant departure from Holinshed and in a gesture at tragic convention, struggled to redeem its protagonist from the charge. The case was not easy: only two sorts of characters, both contemptible, would seem to permit of the long sequence of murder attempts that constituted the received plot, either a wittol or an uxorious fool. *Arden*'s inventive alternative gives us a protagonist who is wise enough to suspect his wife's infidelity, honorable enough to be enraged by it, true enough to grieve for it, but deterred from acting on his own instincts and from aborting Holinshed's plot by the advice of his "honest" and optimistic friend Franklin. The play's sole addition to the cast of historical characters thus serves to reconcile what would otherwise be two conflicting impulses: Arden's tragic stature and the sequential storyline. (That said, it must be added that this balancing act was difficult to sustain. Halfway through, the play quits the attempt, allows Franklin to realize Alice's betrayal, abandons Arden to rash and willful uxoriousness, and goes some way toward making his murder aesthetically palatable—if still not ethically justifiable.)

The philosophical basis for the symbiosis of public and private governance dates back to Aristotle, who in the *Nicomachean Ethics* had written that "the family is an older and more necessary thing than the state"

---

believe that he is able to be ruler, or to keep peace and quietness in the town or city, who cannot live peaceably in his own house" (sig. N1^r).

114. Emphasis added in Wardmote passage. Stow, fols. 34^r and 36^v; Holinshed, pp. 149 and 157.

and that "analogies and (as it were) patterns of [political constitution] can be found in the household." For Thomas Bilson, writing in 1576, the "private family . . . is both a part and a pattern of the commonwealth," part, in that the commonwealth is made up of a number of households, but also pattern, in that the household is the ancient example of order upon which contemporary government is based.[115] While there was historical import in an understanding of the "pattern," there was also contemporary urgency in the notion of the "part," for the larger political order was perceived to be dependent on order in each of its domestic elements.

The Arden texts do not pursue the consequences of Arden's behavior beyond his household because they do not acknowledge his public career. But Thomas Ardern was customer, church warden, jurat, and sometime mayor; and if the chronicles are correct that he was also a wittol, then that last was equally a matter of public moment. As Cornelius Agrippa von Nettesheim put it: "How shall he rule a city that hath not learned to rule a house? How shall he govern a commonwealth, that never knew his private and familiar business?"[116] So entrenched was the association between proper governance in micro- and macrocosms that Ardern's private failures may have motivated his public disenfranchisement more profoundly than any land-use fee or cess quarrel—and may even have required his murder. This is my first paradox: that in the early modern period, the private was, after all, public in consequence.[117]

Having said that, I suppose that my second paradox must be summed up in the notion that the public was private. Here, too, I must appear to undo some of my earlier arguments about Thomas Ardern's murder. Forget for the moment that Ardern's public career was a hazardous one; take the story as the Wardmote Book, the chronicles, and the play give it to us. Assume, that is, that his murder was simply Alice Arden's crime. Even if this was the case, the fact remains that all those with whom Ardern crossed paths in his public life, and especially his

---

115. Aristotle, *Ethics*, trans. Thomson, pp. 280 and 276; Thomas Bilson, *True Difference* (1585), sig. S5ʳ. Jean Bodin, in *Six Bookes of a Commonweale* (1576; translated into English, 1606), writes similarly that a family "is the true seminary and beginning of every commonweal, as also a principal member thereof" (sig. B4ᵛ).

116. Henricus Cornelius Agrippa von Nettesheim, *Commendation of Matrimony* (1526; translated into English, 1540), sig. C7ᵛ.

117. Gordon J. Schochet notes an "implicit failure to distinguish between the political and social realms of human experience" in *Patriarchalism in Political Thought* (1975), p. 54. See also Susan D. Amussen, "Gender, Family" (1985), and her *Ordered Society* (1988), p. 2. There *was* distinction, but the terms of distinction were different: Pierre Ayrault's warning that there should not be "one authority public, another private and domestic" encapsulates both the recognition of difference and the impulse to blur it (*Discourse for Parents' Honor* [translated into English, 1614], sig. B8ᵛ).

fellow townsmen, would have considered themselves to be personally, that is "privately," implicated in his death.

Richard Cooke, though writing nearly eight decades after Ardern's murder, helps us to apprehend both the intimate social bonds of early modern culture and the emotional reverberations these bonds would have generated among the witnesses to Ardern's shame and Alyce's crime:

> . . . what satisfaction can you make to this place and parish, where you lived of late—and a little too long? What dishonor have you done us, in bringing this disgrace and casting this aspersion on us? What favors have you had successively amongst us? How often have you been invited to our public feastings? How usually called to our counsels and meetings? How preferred to several places of offices with us? And after all this, to reward us thus, to cast this filth in our faces, to leave this stink behind you is base ingratitude. It must needs be a bad bird that thus defiles her own nest; we can count you no better, you have used us so badly. We shall be willing to pray for your well doing elsewhere, but not for your dwelling here, till you be a little sweeter.

Cooke concludes rhetorically, "Shall I tell you in a word or two, how you may make all well?"[118] In the case of Thomas Ardern, there was no making well except through civic justice. In their insistence on the innocence of Bradshaw, however, the chronicles betray the fact that so serious a rupture of the public order could not find closure easily. And what seems to us to be something akin to superstition in this community-wide sense of incrimination, even among those innocent of direct involvement, was in fact borne out: according to Holinshed, "many hundreds of people" came to the site of Arden's murder "wondering about him"; the name of the town was inextricably linked in the public record and imagination with the crime; and every townsman experienced the onus of association. That sense of personal complicity was undoubtedly compounded, in Ardern's case, among the many who had cherished privately their (civic, legal, economic—public) resentments of him.

The notoriety of the event informs my third paradox. Rosalie L. Colie has written that "experience can be seen as searching for its own form."[119] The pressure upon literature of an event like the Ardern murder accounts for the generic novelty that *Arden of Feversham* represents. For by dramatizing its story as "The Lamentable and True *Trag-*

118. Richard Cooke, *White Sheet* (1629), sigs. F2^{r-v}.
119. Rosalie L. Colie, *Resources of Kind* (1973), p. 30.

edy of Master Arden of Feversham in Kent," the play violates the ancient parameters of a highly theorized genre. An echo of Holinshed's anxiety concerning his inclusion of "a private matter," one "therefore as it were impertinent to this history," is relevant here. As a self-contained artifact, the play cannot by definition be "impertinent" in Holinshed's sense—that is, irrelevant to a larger literary purpose. But it is "impertinent" in another contemporary sense of that word—that is, unsuitable—and perhaps even in a more modern one—that is, presumptuous.[120]

In a formula that summarizes the operative notion of genre in the Renaissance, the fourth-century grammarian Diomedes defined comedy and tragedy in rigorous dichotomy: "The fortunes involved in comedy are those of little streets and unimportant households, not as in tragedy of princes and men of state. . . . The distinctions between comedy and tragedy are these: the characters of tragedy are semidivine, leaders of the state, kings; those of comedy are unimportant and private persons." At the same time, "the subjects of tragedy are woes, exiles, deaths; of comedy, love affairs and seductions. . . . Hence comedy and tragedy are by definition distinct: the one a full cycle of harmless incident, the other a reversal of great fortunes." Philip Sidney's *Apology for Poetry*, arguing that comedy deals with "our private and domestical matters" and tragedy with kings and tyrants, complaining of the "mongrel" plays that mingle the two, gives us every evidence that early moderns recognized the force of Diomedes' distinctions.[121] The story of Thomas Arden blurs those distinctions, with a comic hero (a private person), a comic setting (an "unimportant" household), and comic action (love affairs and seductions) achieving a tragic denouement (death and reversal). By its impertinence, *Arden of Feversham* altered the landscape of generic possibility in English drama.[122]

While sixteenth-century England received no classical warrant for a "domestic" tragedy, it perhaps imported contemporary theoretical precedent with Giraldi Cinthio's verse prologue to his *Altile*, printed in 1583 and here summarized in part by Bernard Weinberg: "The laws of poetry are not immutable, but change with the times (*l'età*), with audi-

120. *OED.* See Shakespeare's *Tempest*: "I'll bring thee to the present business which now's upon's, without the which, this story were most impertinent."
121. Diomedes, *Ars Grammatica*, excerpted by J. V. Cunningham, *Woe or Wonder* (1951), p. 43. Philip Sidney, *Apology for Poetry* (1595), pp. 117 and 135.
122. John Payne Collier labelled the genre "domestic tragedy" and included *Arden of Feversham*, *A Warning for Fair Women*, *Two Lamentable Tragedies*, *The Fair Maid of Bristow*, and *A Yorkshire Tragedy* (*History of English Dramatic Poetry* [1831], p. 49). John Addington Symonds notably added *A Woman Killed with Kindness* and *The Witch of Edmonton* (*Shakspere's Predecessors* [1884], p. 418). *Arden* may, of course, have been anticipated by a play now lost; remarks about its impertinence would apply equally to any predecessor.

ences, with the wishes of the patrons who order them, and with the subject matters (*la materia*) that are different from age to age." In a 1543 letter to Ercole II (also published in 1583), Cinthio declares further that

> if in certain respects I have departed from the rules that Aristotle gives, in order to conform to the customs of our times, I did so following the example of the ancients; for we see that Euripides began his plots differently from Sophocles, and that . . . the Romans arranged their plots in another way than the Greeks. And besides, Aristotle himself permitted me to do so; he does not at all forbid us to depart somewhat—when so required by the place or the time or the quality of the things that are being handled—from that art which he has reduced to the precepts that he gave us.[123]

Cinthio thus hints that the impulse to generic impertinence (among other innovations) is to be found in the "customs" and interests of the time that produce it. In an analysis of the dramatic process that is cagily less passive than Colie's and that is, paradoxically, equally true to the production of *Arden of Feversham*, Cinthio contradicts her with the suggestion that the form can be seen as searching for its own experience. The appetite of the English form was fed by two burgeoning institutions of the period: print culture and public theater.

This is my closing acknowledgment of the power of the Arden story and a first tribute to the achievement of the Arden play. *Arden of Feversham* proceeded from the early modern principles that, Diomedes to the contrary, there was no unimportant household and that, by virtue of analogy, Alice Arden's crime achieved notional parity with the opening of trade with Muscovy, the defeat of the Spanish Armada, and, most especially, the assassination of an anointed king. It established the precedent that found private matters fit for dramatic representation and institutionalized in a new medium an operative domestic ethic. It thus authorized a body of material that in its richness was capable of nourishing complexities and contradictions and that by its nature could anatomize contemporary ideology as the prescriptive vehicles of ideology could not.

I have suggested that Arden's story was constructed by its culture. In a fourth paradox that returns to the idea of Arden's story as a point of access to issues of consequence, I want also to propose that the story

---

123. Translations are from Bernard Weinberg, *History of Literary Criticism* (1961), vol. 1, pp. 210 and 913–14. For the Italian, see *Altile* (1583), "Prologo," sigs. A4^r–A5^v. I am grateful to Leeds Barroll for the reference.

constructed its culture. An anonymous pamphleteer of 1595 formulated a pandemic for domestic anxieties that never mentions the name Thomas Arden. But without the example of Arden, would he or could he have conceptualized his anxieties in quite this way?

> The son, desiring his father's living and to be great before his time, murdereth him; the friend, his dearest friend; the wife, the husband; and the husband, the wife; brother against sister and sister, the brother. Whereby the world is grown to such a pass, that no friend dare commit any secret to his most nearest and dearest friend, without some jealousy of his truth and faithfulness. If he have money, he feareth to reveal it to his wife, his servants, his children, his friend, or any, doubting lest the knowledge thereof shall abridge his days. If he have a wife which as himself he loveth, although he see with his own eyes her chaste life given over to the lecher, and another enjoy that, only proper to himself, yet with heart's grief is he fain to smother so ugly and most odious abuse, doubting the revealing thereof should work his shame in the world, and his life thereby dangered.

Without the example of Arden, would Philip Gawdy have written in private correspondence of an "infamous" woman that her case was "worthy to be put in Holinshed's chronicle"? (She had "consorted herself with every companion," "misus[ed] her husband every way," plotted his death by bringing him to a charge of high treason, and with one lover assembled a group of accomplices, one of whom escaped justice.) Without Arden, would Thomas Gataker some seventy years after the murder have been able to declare that "evils are the more grievous, the nearer and the more inward they are," that "domestical evils vex a man most," that while "precepts show us what we should do, examples go further," and that "domestical examples are of all other the most powerful"?[124]

The long process of the recording, domesticating, and reconstructing of Thomas Ardern's story continued through the demand for two reprintings of the play and through many subsequent redactions; the process continued, too, in the literary successors and intellectual heirs that I take up in the following chapters. Cinthio aptly summarizes the import of such cultural process: "When we see that an entire nation,

124. *Most Horrible and Detestable Murder* (1595), sig. A2r; Philip Gawdy, *Letters*, pp. 99–100; Thomas Gataker, *A Good Wife, God's Gift* (1620), sigs. A3v–A4r and B1v. References to Holinshed's chronicle may have become conventional; see, besides that of Goodcole, cited above, the remark made of a murder that "England had never so much work for a chronicle," in the anonymous *True Relation of a Most Desperate Murder* (1617), sig. A3v.

over a space of several generations (except for some who are too fastidious), agrees as one in accepting a thing as valued and laudable, we must believe that this common consent does not merit being blamed."[125] Throughout this chapter, I have used the life and death of Thomas Ardern to illustrate the early modern place of the private. Here, in my fifth and final paradox, I discover that the story of Arden itself in many ways defined that place.

125. Cinthio, quoted in Weinberg, p. 962.

Alyce Ardern's Rapes

Sir Thomas Cheyney is my synecdoche for the extradomestic interests that may have conspired in Ardern's murder and my emblem for
the alternative constructions that the early modern period could have
placed upon that murder. While the multiple redactions of the Arden
story establish that the story was an object of cultural desire, Cheyney
defines the nature of that desire. The culture did not require Cheyney's collaboration, or municipal conflict, or tenant dissatisfaction. It
preferred an occasion for theorization of and reflection upon the private; it desired, in a contrary synecdoche, Alice.

But where, in the preceding investigation of an event transmitted to
history as "Alice Arden's crime," is Alyce Ardern? One subtext of the
endeavor to demonstrate how much of detail and substance has survived from the lives of Thomas Ardern and Thomas Cheyney is the
contrastive light it throws upon how little has remained of Alyce: the
color and value of some frocks, the golden chain for her "gentlewo-
man's" neck. Mine is a record-based report, and documentary records
are implicated in women's historical silence. The records that have
survived license me to speculate (insofar as records can) on the nature,
interests, and motivations of the two Thomases. But they yield no
Alyce Ardern; they merely reproduce the Alice of the Arden construct
and of the received tradition of Holinshed and *Arden of Feversham*.

Because it is also text-based, this afterword cannot recover Alyce
Ardern's voice. It does aim, however, briefly to restore her centrality
and to append to my earlier reflections on the place of the private in
early modern culture a chilling glimpse of the place of women in that

culture. My agenda reveals itself in my title, "Alyce Ardern's rapes," a phrase grammatically identical in structure to "Alice Arden's crime" but radically disjunct in significance with regard to the subject.

The roster of known early modern redactions of Thomas Ardern's murder is also completed here, with the addition of a previously unremarked reference to it. The unlikely source is a minor classic of resistance theory, *A Short Treatise of Politic Power*, published in Strasburg in 1556 by Marian exile John Ponet.[1] In a chapter titled "What confidence is to be given to princes," Ponet states that kings in their ambition to extend their sovereignty may employ either "open force" or—and this latter is Ponet's particular interest and implied indictment—"secret subtlety." He gives secret subtlety its alternative name of "policy." And he continues that one instrument of the policy of princes is the traitor, whom, Ponet warns, princes use for their imperialist purposes and then "cast them out on the dung hill."

To instance his discussion of traitors, Ponet recounts the story of a German king, Cacanus, who killed an Italian duke and then besieged the duke's city. The duke's widow, Romilda, observed Cacanus over the city walls, saw him to be "goodly and fair," and conceived a love for her husband's murderer. "She wisheth, that she might feel him enter in to her own hold" and went "half mad, for lack of her lust. To be short, contrary to all honesty and womanly shamefastness, she wooeth him to be her husband" by promising "to give him city, country, jewels, goods, and what so ever she could poll of her subjects, and make for him, so that he would marry her." This tale, in its demonstration of the way in which political and domestic betrayals are similarly, materially constructed, foreshadows the parallels of state and household governments that I consider in the next chapter. Romilda's treason is also echoed in the report of the Wardmote Book of Faversham that "Alyce the said Morsby did not only carnally keep in her own house here in this town, but also fed [him] with delicate meats and sumptuous apparel," all to the end "to have married with" him.

Ponet's Cacanus, knowing how dangerous an invasion of the Italian city would be, with secret subtlety accepted Romilda's treacherous invitation and conjugal terms. Ponet continues:

> according to his promise he married her, and one night took pains to shake up her lecherous rotten ribs. In the next morning he leaveth his chamber and her gates open free to every man: and (as some, God give them grace to repent in time, did to the wicked woman of Feversham in Kent, that not long since killed her husband) he gave every man liberty

1. John Ponet, *Short Treatise* (1556), sigs. H8ʳ–K1ᵛ, especially sigs. I2ʳ⁻ᵛ.

that would, to offer his devotion in to her torporess. So at length when he thought her tired, and her insatiable lust somewhat staunched (for belike it would never have been fully glutted), he caused her to be thrust on a stake naked, that all men might see those ugly parts, which to satisfy she was content to betray her natural country.

Ponet is a witness of some reliability. He had long ties to Kent, having been made canon of Canterbury in 1546, proctor for the diocese of Canterbury in 1547, and bishop of Rochester in 1550. He did not leave the county until after Ardern's murder and Alyce's sentence, when on 23 March 1551 he was made bishop of Winchester.[2] The very super-fluity of this report to his larger rhetorical purposes enhances its credi-bility, even though no other record survives to confirm that a punish-ment clearly considered appropriate to the sexual crime of Alyce's adulterous desire preceded her execution for the political crime of petty treason.

Can a cultural logic other than mob psychology be found for Alyce Ardern's repeated sexual brutalization? A first attempt to discover one might presume that some of those who had "liberty" of Alyce must, like Cacanus, have professed the moral efficacy of their actions. In 1629, Richard Cooke articulated such a philosophy of punishment for anoth-er domestic crime, writing, "let this day's punishment beat you home to God, and like a sovereign medicine work kindly with you, to purge your soul of your sins, for the health and recovery of your soul"; he con-cluded that "it must be no easy or ordinary repentance that will serve the turn: your offence hath been great, your humiliation must not be less."[3] But to apply Cooke to Alyce's case may be to attribute to Alyce's tormentors too modern an understanding of the psychological signifi-cances of rape for the victim. Ponet and Cacanus seem less preoccupied with a process of violent humiliation than with their conviction that women's presumed sexual voracity can be appropriately "served" only with the revenge of surfeit.

Alternatively—to advert to my earlier thesis of the communal prop-erty in private transgression—Alyce's rape, in all its immediacy of expe-rience, may have confirmed some in their sense of implication in one of the most notorious crimes of their time. Those who participated may have joined in a perverse celebration of her husband's death, exacting their own crime of violence against his memory, exercising the triumph of their survival of him, and exorcising the desires and dissatisfactions he had aroused—all on the enforced body of his "relict," who had

2. For Ponet, see the *DNB* and Winthrop S. Hudson, *John Ponet* (1942).
3. Richard Cooke, *White Sheet* (1629), sigs. F1^v–F2^r.

herself initiated a season of misrule by his carnal betrayal and murder. Worth noting with respect to the sexual nature of Alyce's punishment is the highly orgasmic language of Erich Neumann's description of "scapegoat psychology": "There is an urgent and redoubled need for the collective to liberate itself from aggressive drives which have accumulated within its bosom by some form of violent and explosive discharge; in this way, at least some transient relief can be obtained from the tension caused by these dammed-up energies. The resultant outbursts . . . wreak their fury on the scapegoat classes."[4] If Alyce played the scapegoat's role, then her subsequent execution was also critical to the ritual suppression of communal evil that had thus been exteriorized, so that her punishment promised collective as well as personal purgation.

The two respects in which Alyce may have acted the part of scapegoat are limited to the local action of civic justice: she was convicted for the murder of a widely despised man when others may have had a hand or an interest in the crime, and she was gang-raped, presumably with some official sanction. But I have resisted the larger notion that the historicized Alice, too, functioned solely as a scapegoat, that the cultural power of the murder's afterlife inhered in a displacement of the social, economic, political, and religious anxieties of the post-Reformation period onto the convenient figure of a "wicked" woman. Among other things, such a notion would restore the conventional hierarchies of historical consequence. By building a sense of the private out of the municipal, the juridical, and the ecclesiastical (rather than to their end), I have attempted to unsettle these hierarchies. To do otherwise is to make Alyce the victim not only of patriarchy and of history but also of a historiography that holds traditionally "public" matters to be of greater consequence than private ones. Of course this is not to rape her again, but it is certainly to deny her the meaning of her rapes.

As I began by suggesting, Alyce's rapes intimate something of women's place in post-Reformation England. They exhibit the early modern relational economy by which, as Keith Thomas has observed, the value of a man's "property" in his wife was maintained only by her chastity.[5] Because Alyce Ardern violated the exclusive rights of the man who had title to her, she made herself, by further analogy to property law, common ground. And as common ground she was correspondingly treated, of "liberty" to every man "that would."

The legal analogy was not unfamiliar. Within a few years of Ardern's

4. Erich Neumann, "Scapegoat Psychology" (1969), pp. 49–50. See also René Girard, *Scapegoat* (1982).
5. Keith Thomas, "Double Standard" (1959), p. 210.

death and Alyce's execution, Thomas Paynell translated into English a tract by Vives which argued that "the author of nature" held man, unlike animals, to the "more exact and straighter laws of matrimony. . . . And how many utilities and profits do spring and issue of matrimony? First, as all controversies and debates are removed and do cease among men, when lands be occupied and possessed and by the power of the law granted and stablished: even so when the woman is lawfully married, all such contentions do cease, which certainly would have grown among men, if women were common." Vives asserts that clear title to women is critical not only "for generation's sake" but also for what he terms "the society and fellowship of life," or peaceful coexistence. Because man "is a proud, a fierce, and a desirous beast to be revenged," any perception of his "injury" will result in "parttakings and factions" and then "war and cruel battle, both at home and abroad." (Vives demonstrates his thesis through reference to the reports of the consequences when women are ravished, and he adds—feelingly, one assumes—that "through Cava, Julian's daughter, we lost Spain." This reading of a rape narrative into the Moorish conquest of his native country resurfaces in my fourth-chapter discussion of another woman of disputed title, Desdemona.)[6]

Each trespass against the boundaries of Alyce Ardern's body ultimately served to reaffirm and to celebrate the notion of men's proprietary rights in women. And each was authorized by the conscious conviction not only that such punishment effected the moral amelioration of an individual woman but also that the terms of entitlement and exchange for all women were irreducible elements of the social order.

And yet the gender system had its discontents. Even persuaded that Alyce Ardern was a "wicked woman," Ponet wished for all those who raped her the grace to repent their actions. On the one hand his regret may have been inspired by the very hierarchization of public and private that Holinshed and other early moderns share with us. His chief anger is reserved not for Romilda but for Cacanus, whose "worm of ambition" Ponet calls the devil and whose practices Ponet insists must be suspect. He does not exonerate the traitor and, correspondingly, does not sentimentalize Alyce, but for Ponet the traitor is merely a pawn in the larger imperial policy that is his subject of choice and of despite. It may also be, in another privileging of the public sphere, that his dismay at Alyce's treatment and not at Romilda's stemmed from his conviction that Alyce's punishment was excessive for the lesser crime of

6. Joannes Ludovicus Vives, *Office and Duty of an Husband* (translated into English, ?1555), sigs. A4ᵛ–A6ʳ.

betrayal of an individual household rather than that of her "natural country." On the other hand Ponet's abhorrence may be located in a quite unrelated and apolitical ability to see Alyce as a suffering human being rather than a theoretically objectified property and a component of the social order. If so, and if the system and her crimes had conspired to dehumanize Alyce and to make of her merely a moral exemplum, then it was her rapes, ironically enough, that humanized her for at least one witness and for at least one gasp of recorded protest.

Chapter Two

PATRIARCHALISM AND

ITS DISCONTENTS

John Dod and Robert Cleaver opened their 1598 treatise on household government with a commonplace of early modern English thought: "A household is as it were a little commonwealth."[1] Earlier I argued for the cultural construction of private life in the period and, further, for the symbiosis of public and private in the post-Reformation cultural consciousness. Here I seek to characterize that construction more precisely and to taxonomize that symbiosis as political. The principal issue for investigation is this: what were the consequences for private life that it was informed by a political construct?

The notion that the household provided a structural model for the state originated with Aristotle, and his analogy retained its foundational authority throughout the early modern period.[2] The power of analogy as a process of thought or mode of argument derived from its transparently limitless utility: it served to explain phenomena that had no self-evident explanation or that could not be grasped in any other way. Analogy could also, as the instance of political argument makes clear, offer validation. The state needed to justify its concentration of wealth and power, and it did so in part by claiming a conceptual twinship with the primary, apparently natural, divinely mandated political

---

1. John Dod and Robert Cleaver, *Godly Form of Household Government* (1598), sig. B1r. In the 1560s, Thomas Smith wrote that "in the house and family is the first and most natural (but a private) appearance of one of the best kinds of a commonwealth" (*De republica anglorum* [1583], p. 59); see also George Whetstone, *Heptameron of Civil Discourses* (1582), sig. Y1r. The sentiment was traced to Socrates (via Xenophon): see John Aylmer, *Harbor for Faithful and True Subjects* (1559), sig. D1r.

2. See the discussion above, pages 72 and 73.

unit of the household. Post-Reformation English men and women understood the household to be a complex society with two basic communities, one the principal family and the other its subordinate servants, each of which had an internal hierarchy. The primary political function of the household society was the maintenance of order; because of its complexity, structure was necessary to domestic order. It followed that for a collection of households to sustain an analogous collective order, an analogous structure was required: a kind of super-family—that is, government in any one of its variant constitutions—that assumed its precedence over the subordinated units. By means of analogy, this government could be made to seem a natural extension of its own constituent elements.

If this fairly represents one process that motivated and shaped political ideology, then we must entertain the notion that, by extrapolation, conceptions of the family were remade in the interest of the state. In other words, the domestic analogy was manipulated to authorize the state in the specific form in which the state wished to imagine itself. The preferred political constitution in the period was monarchical, and this constitution found an analogy in the philosophy of domestic patriarchalism. For a monarchic government to reinforce the authority of the domestic patriarch was thus self-reinforcing; for that government to characterize patriarchy as natural was to naturalize itself. We have already witnessed one nonliterary means by which this ideological collusion was perpetuated: Thomas Ardern was a householder; his household was as a petty commonwealth; he was as a king in his commonwealth; the murder committed by his wife and servants was analogous to the assassination of a political overlord; and the state in its interest punished his wife and his two servants not for the crime of murder but for that of petty treason.

The form that domestic exhortation took in the Renaissance was fixed by the language and objectives of political discourse. Oeconomic sermons and manuals were grounded in the classical analogy of household and commonwealth; clergymen were apt to term the household "the state oeconomical" (as William Perkins did in the 1590s) or "this domestical kingdom" (as William Whately did in 1617).[3] But such texts also emphasized a biblical precedent for the prevailing patriarchal philosophy of obligation—and an effectual theory of obligation was a principal aim of political ideology. The commandment to "honor thy father and thy mother" was transferred from the natural parent to the head of household who received the children of the gentry in service,

3. William Perkins, *Christian Oeconomy* (composed, early 1590s; published, 1609), p. 436; William Whately, *Bride-Bush* (1617), sig. D1ᵛ.

to the craftsman who took the children of lower classes as apprentices, to the schoolmaster who shepherded children through their elementary education—in fact to anyone who, as Richard Bernard put it, "is any way to be preferred, either by his place, age, or gifts." Through its further extension to kings and magistrates, the fifth commandment was also put to political use, with Christopher Hegendorff, for example, contending (in an English translation of 1548) that "in this commandment both politic laws and household laws be ordained," and Bernard concurring that the commandment prohibited "all treason and rebellion," as well as "contempt of our betters, unreverent behavior towards them."[4]

What these texts suppressed, however, was the dualism of their purported moral authority: honor not only thy father (king, master) but also thy mother. Aristotle, who did not hold the early modern brief for monarchy, himself argued that the oversight shared by husband and wife rendered the political constitution of the household aristocratic rather than monarchic. And in fact, the administrative and economic requirements of the early modern household diverged often enough from those of the state that the monarchic model was not always applicable to domestic life. Given the self-authorizing agenda of monarchy, however, this was a practical matter that conventional political ideology in the sixteenth century was unable to accommodate. From this disaccommodation flowed others: problematics in the accepted nature and role of women, ambiguities in the inscription of domestic rule, the competing pulls of political and economic interest—in other words, ideological contention in the household—and the real hazards occasioned by the abstract analogies propounded in political thought.

Early modern apprehension of these philosophical insufficiencies reached a certain conceptual clarity in the 1590s. To the extent that the English Reformation is recognized as a crisis of authority, however, the issues trace themselves back to the 1530s and are among the intellectual consequences of the break with Rome. The unsettling of traditional understandings of the proper direction of political obedience, first addressed by such Tudor apologists as Stephen Gardiner, Richard Morison, and Thomas Starkey, was to persist for decades: in 1581, for example, Jesuits succeeded other missionary Catholic priests as immigrants to England and were described as seeking "to move the people

4. Richard Bernard, *Joshuah's Godly Resolution* (1612), sig. E4ᵛ; Christopher Hegendorff, *Domestical or Household Sermons* (translated into English, 1548), sig. D5ʳ. In his popular *Brief and Necessary Instruction* (1572), Edward Dering applied the fifth commandment to "princes, rulers, and magistrates, our pastors and teachers, our masters, and all others which are above us, in any calling, placed by God" (sig. A8ʳ). On broad applications of the commandment, see Gordon J. Schochet, *Patriarchalism in Political Thought* (1975), pp. 72–81.

by their secret persuasions . . . to acknowledge the Pope's authority, and to renounce the just authority of her Majesty. . . . to yield their obedience to the Pope as Christ's vicar."[5]

Meanwhile, the years following the Reformation were plagued by a series, first, of succession crises and, then, of threatened insurrections. These included the Lincolnshire rising in 1536, the Pilgrimage of Grace that same year, the Western rebellion in 1547–49, Kett's rebellion in 1549, Wyatt's rebellion in 1553–54, the Northern rebellion in 1569–70, Ridolfi's plot in 1571, Throckmorton's in 1583, Babington's in 1586, food riots in three counties (Gloucestershire, Somerset, and Hampshire) in 1586 and in two more (Oxfordshire and Kent) in 1596, and finally the Essex rebellion in 1600.[6]

The crown's reliance on hegemonic suasion in these years was all the keener because, in the absence of a state militia and an authoritarian priesthood, it had few enough arrows to its bow. This accounts for the urgency that informs the continued admonitory initiatives of such texts as the "Exhortation to Obedience," which appeared in the 1547 *Certain Sermons or Homilies, Appointed by the King's Majesty to be Declared and Read by All Persons, Vicars, or Curates Every Sunday in Their Churches*; Sir John Cheke's 1549 *The Hurt of Sedition How Grievous it is to a Commonwealth*; and the 1570 addition to the *Certain Sermons*, the six-part "Homily Against Disobedience and Willful Rebellion."

These second and then third generations of texts vested themselves in the analogy of public and private. Cheke, for example, observing that "dissension we see in small houses, and thereby may take example to great commonwealths. . . . and thereby learn to judge of great things unknown, by small things perceived," enlisted the private reader by acknowledging the applicability of his experience to public circumstance. The 1547 homily urged obedience to kings and magistrates as representatives of "God's order," without which "no man shall ride or go by the highway unrobbed, no man shall sleep in his own house or bed unkilled, no man shall keep his wife, children, and possessions in quietness." Richard Mulcaster declared in 1581 that "obedience towards the prince and laws is assuredly grounded, when private houses be so well ordered," and Thomas Floyd asserted in 1600 that "obedience formeth peace." (Peace was desired as much for relationships within the household as for the state of the nation.)[7] The hortatory

---

5. Anthony Munday, *Advertisement . . . for Truth* (1581), sigs. A2^{r-v}.

6. A helpful overview is provided by Anthony Fletcher in *Tudor Rebellions* (1983). See also Buchanan Sharp, *In Contempt of All Authority* (1980).

7. John Cheke, *Hurt of Sedition* (1549), sig. K3^r; "Exhortation Concerning Good Order and Obedience," in *Certain Sermons*, ed. Bond, p. 161; Richard Mulcaster, *Positions* (1581), sig. Oo2^v; Thomas Floyd, *Picture of a Perfect Commonwealth* (1600), sig. K2^r.

oeconomic literature invoked the homily's carrot of personal security less often than Mulcaster's stick of individual responsibility. But in both cases, political and domestic spheres were held to be thoroughly interdependent, the integrity of each reliant on order in the other, with obedience the universal cement.

I have argued in my first chapter that public and private did not sort themselves for early moderns in precisely the same way they do for us, but this is not to deny that a sorting process was engaged in the period. In the political ideology of the sixteenth century, we find the most extreme resistance to that process of differentiation. This might seem ironic were we not aware that ideology had its own uses for analogy. Outside the political discourse, however, the artificialities of analogy revealed themselves. Holinshed, for example, represented the common intuition that private matters were of a lower order of importance than affairs of crown and country.

As the century wore on, however, there appeared impulses even within the hegemonic discourse toward a mode of thought that was eventually to eclipse that of analogy and to displace the private. First, if government was conceptualized as a family writ large, then within the macrocosmic framework individual households were analogized to the servant, subordinated communities of the Platonic household. The household, in other words, succumbed to political hierarchy, as demonstrated by the fact that Alyce Ardern was executed for petty rather than high treason. At the same time, the accepted notion of the domestic monarchy, which was necessarily conceptualized in terms of the wife's political subjection to her husband, found itself disjunct from circumstance with the coming to the English throne of a female sovereign in 1553. Because political analogy had concentrated on the parental nature of the princely role (following the fifth commandment and as the term "patriarchalism" suggests), some theorists were able to make uneasy accommodation with the reigns of the two Tudor queens. But they did so by distinguishing royal from domestic rule—John Aylmer argued that a queen could "be the husband's inferior in matters of wedlock, and his head in the guiding of the commonwealth"[8]—and in this second way resorted to hierarchy in the service of monarchy. This process of progressive political hierarchization of public and private culminated in the theory of royal absolutism eventually propounded by James VI and I.

As I have suggested, the critical decade for the development of absolutist theory was the 1590s, when James published *The Trew Law of Free*

8. Aylmer, sig. C4^v.

Monarchies in Scotland and when the more traditional analogical ideology revealed its insufficiencies in England. Elizabeth I was aging and had been ill; the end of her reign was in sight; the succession was unsettled. Permeated as they were with intimations of Elizabeth's mortality and with the simultaneous awareness that the state must survive her, the 1590s found renewed import in the medieval theory of the king's two bodies.[9] When played out in anticipation rather than experience of a sovereign's death, though, the theory could not but engender a conflict of loyalties between present and future. Preeminent loyalty to the institution of monarchy entailed disloyalty to the person of the monarch.

Such anxieties climaxed a decade known as one of "crisis" for its failed harvests, population growth despite high death rates from plague and starvation, inflation and the collapse of real value in wages, and the acknowledgment of a substantial population of "laboring poor."[10] Common understanding linked the political crisis and the economic and demographic crises: because the latter disasters could be argued to be divinely ordained as punishment, and because accession to the throne by a tyrant was thought to be as ready a weapon of divine chastisement as was plague, the unsettled succession was acutely ominous. The coincidence of Elizabeth's aging and a decade of crisis with the end of a century only compounded popular foreboding. To the extent that a multivalent distress focused on the person of a female monarch, that distress lent further urgency to reflections on the nature of authority in every sphere and added evocative power to such literary figurations of women as those of Alice Arden and her textual sisters.

In 1592 *Arden of Feversham* conferred tragic stature on domestic example by exploiting the traditional analogy of the household to the state.[11] For all its generic impertinence—in fact, precisely in order to compensate for its generic impertinence—*Arden* in the first part of the decade relied on the orthodox analogies of public and private. In this chapter *Arden* thus serves as my control text: first, to establish a pattern for the theatrical deployment of those political analogies and, second, to introduce a more extended discussion of their problematics as they appear in both ideological writings and then in some successor play-

---

9. See Ernst H. Kantorowicz, *King's Two Bodies* (1957), and Marie Axton, *Queen's Two Bodies* (1977).

10. See chaps. 7 and 8 in Peter Clark, *English Provincial Society* (1977), as well as his Introduction to *European Crisis* (1985), especially pp. 4–7. On the laboring poor as a perceptual (as well as social and economic) problem in the late sixteenth century, see Paul Slack, *Poverty and Policy* (1988), pp. 27–32.

11. 1592 is the publication date of the first quarto of the play. It was undoubtedly written and first performed earlier, perhaps as early as 1587.

texts. The influence of *Arden* climaxed in 1599, when a second printing of the play coincided with the production of a Thomas Dekker–Ben Jonson collaboration on another domestic murder, *Page of Plymouth*, now lost, and also with the composition of *Arden*'s other immediate generic heirs. The surviving plays include the anonymous *A Warning for Fair Women*, Robert Yarington's *Two Lamentable Tragedies*, and Thomas Heywood's *1 and 2 Edward IV* (a two-part series that, for practical purposes, I consider as a conceptual unit).[12]

Produced in the last months of a critical decade, these playtexts are primary witnesses of the contradictions and fallibilities of contemporary theory. They permit us to uncover some sixteenth-century conceptualizations of "private matters" that offer alternatives to those more immediately available in moralizing and prescriptive literatures. They admit more fully of the doubts and vexations from which hortatory writing attempted to insulate itself. Most important, the texts anatomize some of the unhappy consequences of the imposition of political structures of thought on the private household. Through the display of conflicts among domestic, civic, and moral authorities (or between obedience and conscience), they also foreshadow the eventual disintegration of the system of correspondences into assertions of difference and hierarchy.

Arden of Feversham

As I argued in the first chapter, the trick of *Arden of Feversham* is that it succeeds both in raising its nonroyal protagonist to a tragic stature and in rendering his murder aesthetically acceptable. It accomplishes the former in the early scenes, by preempting any evidence of petty extortiousness, absolving him of the indignity of wittolry, and presenting him as a monarch in the little kingdom of his house. It then achieves the latter by abandoning him to willful credulity, depicting him as having ceded his domestic territory, and indicting him for household mismanagement. Arden's culpability is vital to the play's

12. Henslowe made payments to Jonson and Dekker for "pagge of plemoth" on 10 August and 2 September 1599. The two parts of *Edward IV*, published anonymously but attributed to Heywood, were entered in the Stationers' Register on 28 August 1599 and published the same year. (Felix E. Schelling [1902] called Jane Shore's domestic tragedy the "central story" of *Edward IV* [p. 151], and Henry Hitch Adams [1943] solidified the generic categorization.) The anonymous *A Warning for Fair Women* was entered on 17 November 1599 and also published before year's end. Yarington's *Two Lamentable Tragedies*, although not published until 1601, was associated with Henslowe payments in November and December 1599. See E. K. Chambers, *Elizabethan Stage* (1923), vol. 4, pp. 10 and 52, and vol. 3, p. 518; and Andrew Clark, "Annotated List of Lost Domestic Plays" (1975).

ideological project, because only those with some power over their own fate can be accountable for its eventuation. The text thus champions Arden's patriarchal authority, the right use of which would have averted murder and the abuse of which must end tragically. All depends on an exhaustive system of correspondences: Arden's house is a commonwealth; he is its sovereign; Franklin is his councillor; wife Alice and servant Michael are rebels against his authority; Mosby is an intended usurper; and the domestic language derives from the political discourse.[13] My aim here is to demonstrate the uses and consequences of the play's infusion with political constructs and vocabularies.

Alice Arden's infidelity, for example, is represented through the language of insurrection, her abuse of the terminologies of gender hierarchy and of religious and political authority and entitlement expanding the significances of adultery. When in the first scene Adam Fowle brings her the message that Mosby wishes to terminate their relationship and that she may no longer visit him where he lodges, at Fowle's Flower-de-Luce Inn, she vows an aggression monstrously transgressive of the contemporary notion of the female: "I'll see him. Ay, and were thy house of force, / These hands of mine should raze it to the ground" (1.117–18). She usurps the male role of wooer, too, sending Mosby her token of silver dice, vowing to make Mosby her own, refusing his reminder that he has sworn not to solicit her, pledging that instead she will "importune" him (1.432).[14]

When recruiting conspirators in Arden's murder, she twice promises Mosby's sister as a bribe to Michael, but she has no qualm about immediately thereafter making the same vow to Clarke, "As I am a gentlewoman" (1.286). For her, "Oaths are words, and words is wind, / And wind is mutable"; therefore, "'Tis childishness to stand upon an oath" (1.436–38). She dismisses even the sacrament of marriage as "but words," announces that her legitimate husband "usurps" the heart that she assigns instead to Mosby, states that "Mosby's title" to her is the best, and characterizes the husband to whom she should be fully submissive as instead a "block" preventing her meetings with her lover (1.98–102, 137). "Might I without control" enjoy Mosby, she declares, "then Arden should not die" (1.274–75).

Alice exhibits the "two repugnant desires" that William Thomas, writing around the time of Ardern's murder, warned against: "the one

13. See my "Man's House as His Castle in *Arden of Feversham*" (1985), pp. 57–89. In "Alice Arden's Crime" (1982), Catherine Belsey first offered a political reading of the play.
14. *Arden* critics tend to agree with Louis Gillet (1940) that Alice is "one of the most extraordinary figures in dramatic literature" (p. 153). Most have seen her as controlled by her passion, by Mosby, or by "a malignant destiny" (see John Addington Symonds [1884], p. 457, and A. H. Bullen [1887], p. xv); Belsey credits her with agency.

to rule, and the other not to be ruled."[15] During the course of the play, her refusal to be ruled escalates to an assertion of a right to self-rule, as she repeats her challenges to Arden's domestic sovereignty: "Why should he thrust his sickle in our corn"—what right has Arden to interfere with the lovers' ripe relationship?[16] "Or what hath he to do with thee, my love"—what authority does he have over Mosby? "Or govern me that am to rule myself?" (10.83–85).

Alice also initiates Mosby's aspiration to usurpation, beginning by promising him inheritance of Arden's wealth but then, when Mosby asks "leave to play your husband's part," dramatically raising the stakes of their liaison: "Mosby, you know who's master of my heart / He well may be the master of the house" (1.638–40). She will eventually proclaim him, willfully, "as gentle as a king" (8.140). Inspired by her ambition for him, Mosby imagines climbing to "the top bough of the tree" and seeking "to build my nest among the clouds" (8.15–16). To prevent a "downfall" and to consolidate his projected gains from the murder of Arden, he further plots independently to murder Greene, Michael, Clarke, and, finally, Alice: "You have supplanted Arden for my sake / And will extirpen me to plant another" (8.40–41). Making even more explicit his design of political arrogation, he characterizes the others as "Chief actors to Arden's overthrow" who may be a threat to him "when they shall see me sit in Arden's seat"; only with their dispatch "am I sole ruler of mine own" (8.30–36).

Mosby's usurpatory vision is briefly realized when Black Will choreographs Arden's murder: "Place Mosby, being a stranger, in a chair, / And let your husband sit upon a stool" (14.118–19). The typical Elizabethan dining chamber or parlor had only one chair, which was reserved for the master of the house and associated with his enthronement.[17] Thus, while Black Will's seating arrangement serves the

15. William Thomas, "Second Discourse" (written between 1550 and 1554, according to the *DNB*), p. 372. Thomas writes in reference not to individuals but to the "commonalty" (as opposed to the "nobility") of the kingdom.

16. See Robert Gray in *Alarum to England* (1609): "the husbandman thrusts the sickle into the corn when it is perfectly ripe." This image was often used metaphorically, as by Gray, who adds that "so destruction comes upon men, when the measure of sin is fulfilled" (sig. I5ᵛ). Alice's implication of violation is echoed proverbially—"Put not thy sickle in another man's corn" (Tilley, S420)—and in such uses as that of Henry Goodcole—"I was bold to put my sickle into another man's harvest" (*True Declaration* [1618], sig. B1ᵛ).

17. See M. Jourdain: "In domestic use the chair was the rightful seat of the master of the house, only given up by courtesy" (cited in M. L. Wine's edition of the play [1973], p. 117); and, similarly, Molly Harrison, *People and Furniture* (1971), p. 5. The association with state is made in *Two Lamentable Tragedies*: "virtue sat enthroned in a chair, / With awful grace and pleasing majesty" (sig. F3ʳ). A correlative association, suggested by Dod and Cleaver—"She must not think it enough to sit and command" (sig. G4ʳ)—is also represented in *Arden*, as Michael asks, "Susan, shall thou and I wait on them? / Or, and thou say'st the word, let us sit down too" (14.288–89). This is a further instance of his rebellion against service. The symbolic signifi-

practical function of easing his attack on Arden from behind, it also serves the symbolic function reconfirmed by Alice after the murder: "I pray you be content, I'll have my will.—/ Master Mosby, sit you in my husband's seat" (14.286–87).

If Mosby's expropriatory ambitions are recurrently expressed through a political language of place and displacement, so too is Arden's tenuous hold on his domestic sovereignty. His first mistake is in underestimating the nature of the threat to him: he thinks it is only sexual; he thinks the sexual is yet unconsummated; and he characterizes Mosby as one who "thinks to defile" (that is, expects to defile) merely Arden's marriage bed (1.40), not Arden's "seat." His second mistake is in heeding Franklin's advice to display patience, to profess no jealousy, to express no doubt, and to spend a term in London. Although the practice "abhors from reason," Arden accepts Franklin's principle that "women when they may will not, / But being kept back, straight grow outrageous" (1.44–54). Arden's third mistake is in exceeding even Franklin's counsel, urging Mosby to "frequent" his house during his sojourn in London so that "The world shall see that I distrust her not" (1.349–50). Here, as increasingly, Alice spells out the consequences of Arden's actions: she delights in his departure and, with "Be not afraid; my husband is now from home" (1.108), reassures Fowle that she more easily flouts Arden's authority in his absence.

In London, Arden briefly recognizes the reversal that he has encouraged: "My house is irksome; there I cannot rest." Franklin soothingly suggests that he not return to it, but Arden erupts, "Then that base Mosby doth usurp my room / And makes his triumph of my being thence" (4.27–30). "Room" here carries the sense of the "particular place assigned or appropriated to a person" or of "office, position, or authority"; James VI and I was to use the term in precisely this way when writing of political insurrection in *The Trew Law of Free Monarchies* (he complains of men who think to "rise up against" their sovereign, and, "when they think good, to slay him . . . and adopt to themselves any other they please in his room").[18] Arden thus represents himself as a household king, now in exile and supplanted by a base usurper; as long as he remains in London, the pretender will enjoy his place unchallenged.

But this is a lone instance of political acuity on Arden's part. En route

---

cance of Mosby's seating is suggested by its divergence from the playwright's source: Holinshed specifies that Mosby sat on a bench (*Chronicles* [1577], p. 155).

18. *OED*; James VI and I, *Trew Law* (1598; published in London, 1603), p. 65. Compare also Dod and Cleaver: "one father or one mother dieth, and another succeedeth and cometh in their stead and room" (sig. R2ʳ).

home from London, in a no-man's-land of travel, he entertains Frank-lin's tale of an unfaithful wife as if it has no grim significance for his own life, while Franklin suddenly chokes over the telling of it. Thus begins Arden's downward spiral to the final displacement.

Built on six failed attempts at murder, *Arden of Feversham* has been accused of artless, repetitive, and finally wearying construction.[19] I suggest, however, that the very key to the emotional power and moral balance of the text is its deceptively linear structure. As we experience the play, our allegiances are orchestrated to reverberate disturbingly among the poles of interest. Initially, caught up in Arden's anguish, observing him frustrate Alice's first stratagem of the poisoned broth, we may cherish hope that in this fictionalized version of the story Arden will escape. When introduced to Black Will and Shakebag, though, we may equally be engaged by slapstick comedy so appealing to Elizabethans that quarto copies of the play featured their names on the title page (a prominence anticipated in the Stationers' Register entry of "The tragedy of Arden of Feversham & Blackwill").[20] By the fourth scene we may lend our sympathy to the Michael who, in cowar-dice and conscience an Everyman, stole the 1982 Royal Shakespeare Company production of the play.[21] In the eighth scene Alice surprises our interest anew, entering on Mosby's determination to kill her with vows to reform herself "To honest Arden's wife" (8.73)—but then re-newed in purpose by Mosby's vile taunts. At scene 13 we may finally discover in Dick Reede a complainant against Arden who commands some credibility, both because he alone is not a collaborator in the murder and because Arden's "I assure you I ne'er did him wrong" rings so thin that even Franklin responds only, noncommittally, "I think so, Master Arden" (13.57–58).

One much-lauded invention of this text is Arden's escape from Black Will and Shakebag in the mist at the broom close (an enclosed field of bushes); as Black Will says in frustration at missing his target on that occasion, "I cannot see my way for smoke" (12.2–3). The sequential

19. Wine reviews those who, like F. W. Moorman, think the play "singularly devoid of constructive art." By contrast, Robert Speaight (1954) commends the play's "cumulative effect" (p. 122), and Wine also defends the pace that permits the characters to "persuasively evolve in all their ambivalence" (p. lxxv).
20. Reported in Wine, p. xix. In his unpublished dissertation for the University of Chicago, "Elizabethan Domestic Tragedies" (1925), Edward Ayers Taylor notes a Black Will in *When You See Me You Know Me* and an allusion to the character in *The True Tragedy of Richard III* (p. 47).
21. RSC staging had the assassins move threateningly around the *outside* of the corrugated tin walls of The Other Place in Stratford in scene 4, thus focusing attention on Michael's terrified response and creating a bond between the character and the audience "immured" with him. See reviews by Stephen Wall and James Fenton. In its London venue, too, reviewer Robert Cushman found Michael "the most fully drawn character in the piece."

challenges to our attention and dislocations of our sympathies are the ethical fog, I suggest, that permits the text to reverse itself on the subject of its protagonist's character. Although we are introduced to a protagonist who is enlarged by domestic sovereignty, who is ennobled by a sense of honor and calmed only by acknowledgment of the force of Franklin's advice, who is redeemed by Franklin's loyalty and (more surprisingly) by the testimony of conspirators against him, who is established in an ancient gentility rather than overweeningly ambitious for advancement, who avoids several attempts on his life either by native shrewdness or divine sanction, and who further benefits from contrast to a crew of villains and murderers, we eventually come to find a man who jests carelessly with the ferryman on playing the cuckold, who enthuses uxoriously over his wife's new kindnesses, who accepts her preposterous explanation of Mosby's provocation to swordfight at the fair, and whom Franklin (achieving his own complementary reversal of perception and position) describes as "bewitched" (13.153).

More to the point of the political theme, Arden also, for all his understanding while in London that absence disempowers him, on his return to Feversham leaves again at once. Summoned to dinner by Sir Thomas Cheyney, he for the first time acts out of what can be interpreted as career interest rather than misplaced domestic preoccupation. Arden's repeated forfeits of the castellated privilege of his house reach one culmination in a curious subtheme (and perhaps a main significance) of his interview with discontented former tenant Reede. Reede's preface to the encounter—"Here [en route from Cheyney's] I'll intercept him, for at his house / He never will vouchsafe to speak with me" (13.5–6)—may be glossed by George Meriton (writing in 1614): "When kings are in their courts and keep their Privy Chambers, none may speak unto them, nor yet approach near them, but nobles and personages of great account: but if they walk into the fields, take a journey, or ride a hunting, every shepherd and peasant of the country may have free access and speak his mind."[22]

The encounter with Reede underlines the fact that Arden has ceded his territory. Immediately thereafter he colludes in his own disempowerment by a headstrong derogation of his patriarchal role: he elects to ignore Franklin's warnings, saying, "I know my wife counsels me for the best." He further errs against domestic hierarchy by pledging, "Content thee, sweet Alice, thou shalt have thy will, / Whate'er it be" (13.149, 130–31). He invites Mosby into his house, and Alice's many feigned objections to her lover's presence keep our attention

22. George Meriton, *Christian Man's Assuring House* (1614), sig. E3ᵛ.

relentlessly focused on Arden's error in permitting the invasion. In the final challenge to his authority, his murder is enacted in the very place in which he should be most secure, his own home, as he cries, "Mosby! Michael! Alice! What will you do?" (14.233), numbering the hierarchy of the violations of his domestic order: the guest, the manservant, the wife of his house.

Dod and Cleaver's statement that "a household is as it were a little commonwealth" continues: "by the good government whereof, God's glory may be advanced, the commonwealth which standeth of several families, benefited, and all that live in that family may receive much comfort and commodity." In the oeconomic tracts of this period, the authority of the householder is never evoked without reference to his correspondent responsibilities and seldom without allusion to the manifold consequences of good or bad execution of those responsibilities. Indeed, for Whetstone, "every man's household, *well governed*, resembleth a commonwealth," as though the very cosmic analogy itself depended on the proper conduct of authority. The resultant consequences for the governor are outlined by Dod and Cleaver: "In matrimonial debate and discord, the man is more to be blamed, than is the woman." If the woman violates her role, "it is for the most part through the fault, and want of discretion, and lack of good government in the husband."[23]

The ideological tautology at the heart of *Arden of Feversham* is that Alice's rebellion itself validates her charge against Arden of "misgovernment" (13.113). Many readers of the play have sensed some justice in the death of its protagonist.[24] While I argue that their assignment of cause to Arden's "avarice" is misplaced, a holdover from Arden's life story and from its trace in Holinshed, I certainly concur with their sense of his limited culpability in his own murder. As signalled by the fact that the legitimacy of Dick Reede's claim is neither proved nor disproved, whether the theatrical Arden is covetous or corrupt is finally of small consequence to the ethic of the play. *Arden of Feversham* is focused strictly on its protagonist's sovereign domestic role and locates its claim to tragedy in his disastrous domestic misrule. The domestic

23. Dod and Cleaver, sig. B1ʳ; Whetstone, pp. 26–27 (emphasis added); Dod and Cleaver, sigs. N1ʳ and L6ᵛ.
24. Henry Hitch Adams and Sarah Youngblood (1963) most strenuously argue the case that Arden's murder is punishment for his avarice and land-grabbing. Others complain that Arden's murder is insufficiently motivated. For Symonds and Gillet, the plot would have been more logical had Arden remained a wittol. Those who apprehend that "the heavens abandon him" or that "providence forsakes" him witness a cultural phenomenon described by Mary Douglas in *Purity and Danger* (1966): "Consider the case of the man in a position of authority who abuses the secular powers of his office. If it is clear that he is acting wrongly, out of role, he is not entitled to the spiritual power which is vested in the role" (p. 106).

focus allows *Arden* both to fashion a "tragic" hero and simultaneously to motivate his death. Thomas Bilson provides an analogy from the political sphere: "A king you shall be, while you rule well, which except you do you shall be unworthy the name of a king and lose it."[25]

Domestic Patriarchalism

The patriarchal schema most familiar to us held the householder's relationship to his household in correspondence with that of the king to his people, Christ to his church, and the head to the body. Most common was the comparison of householder and sovereign, as in the frequently cited proverb, "every man is a king in his own house" and in such references as Whately's to "the household prince, the domestical king."[26] Because, as Henry Smith wrote, "a master in his family hath all the offices of Christ" (ruling, teaching, and praying), the analogy to Christ numbered among its variants those to a minister (as Bernard suggested, "the congregation is the minister's cure, so the family is the master's charge") and an ecclesiast (Hegendorff specified that the householder "is or ought to be a very bishop over his own household"). Smith, too, described the husband as "the head: to show that as the eye, and the tongue, and the ear, are in the head to direct the whole body, so the man should . . . direct his whole family."[27] What we understand to have been intellectually satisfying about patriarchalism in its fully developed form was this comprehensiveness, a philosophical nexus that incorporated the domestic, the political, the ecclesiastical, and the corporeal in an apparently inexorable logic of analogy and that served to authorize an inclusive system of obligation.

In fact, however, neither the comprehensiveness nor the rigor of patriarchal philosophy was fixed in the England of the 1590s. As implied both in the Aristotelian source of the political analogy ("The family is an older and more necessary thing than the state") and in the fifth commandment ("Honor thy father and thy mother"), domestic patriarchalism preceded political patriarchalism. While, as I have indicated, familial analogy was available to and exploited in political discourse throughout the sixteenth century, patriarchalism was not to be thoroughly appropriated to the political sphere as a systematic philosophy

---

25. Thomas Bilson, *True Difference* (1585), p. 250.
26. Tilley, M123; Whately, sig. F3v.
27. Henry Smith, *Preparative to Marriage* (1591), sigs. G2v and E5r–v; Bernard, sig. B3r; Hegendorff, sig. A3r. Meanwhile, Thomas Watts called the householder a bishop (*Entry to Christianity* [1589], sig. A5r); William Jones, "a captain of a company of soldiers in the church militant" (*Brief Exhortation* [1631], sig. B2r).

of *obligation* until the first decades of the seventeenth century.[28] When analogy between king and father appeared in early modern English thought, the supremacy of the father was understood to have the prior and unarguable claim, and monarchy both justified itself and inferred obligation by association with fatherhood. In the 1590s the authority of the father in his household was so sovereign that Henry Smith could write, "they which are called fathers are called by the name of God, to warn them that they are in stead of GOD to their children, which teacheth all his sons."[29]

Because, as Bilson argued, "there can be no king but in respect of his subjects," patriarchal authority was necessarily constructed in the relinquishing of power by women as well as by children and servants. Thus, the householder's godliness held with respect to his wife; in a 1541 translation, Heinrich Bullinger argued that "it followeth also that the disobedience which wives show unto their husbands displeaseth God no less than when he is resisted himself," and Thomas Gataker later observed that "when the husband admonisheth, God admonisheth in him, and hearkening to him, she hearkeneth to God in him." The matrimonial service in the Book of Common Prayer exhorted the wife to obedience, service, submission, subjection, reverence.[30] For John Dove, "a servant hath more liberty in the bondage of his service, than a woman in the freedom of her wedlock" (because "he may change masters, she may not change husbands, while her first husband liveth").[31]

<hr/>

28. Schochet reviews the political use of the familial symbol in Plato and Cicero as well as Aristotle, among others (pp. 18–28). I am grateful to John Guy for reminding me of Aristotle's influence on sixteenth-century analogical thought and also for referring me to Gardiner, who, as early as 1535, wrote of the "obedience which the subject is bounden to do unto the prince, the wife unto the husband, or the servant unto the master" (*De vera obedientia*, p. 99). Gardiner consistently figures absolutist doctrine as an immediate, two-person relationship between prince and subject, husband and wife, master and servant, avoiding the corporate images of the family and kingdom that were to enlarge later assertions of patriarchal obligation. Schochet argues the distinction between the political use of familial symbols and the post-1603 patriarchal theory of obligation (p. 16). See also J. P. Sommerville, *Politics and Ideology* (1986), especially pp. 27–34.

29. Henry Smith, sig. H1ᵛ. A character in John Ford's *'Tis Pity She's a Whore* says of the word *husband* that "in that name / Is hid divinity" (4.3.136–37).

30. Bilson, p. 194; Heinrich Bullinger, *Christian State of Matrimony* (1541), sig. H1ʳ; Thomas Gataker, *Marriage Duties* (1620), sig. C3ᵛ. For the "Form of Solemnization of Matrimony," see *Book of Common Prayer* (1559): "Wilt thou *obey* him and *serve* him. . . . Ye women *submit* yourselves unto your own husbands as unto the Lord, for the husband is the wife's head even as Christ is the head of the Church. . . . Therefore as the church or congregation is subject unto Christ, so likewise let the wives also be in *subjection* unto their own husbands in all things. And again he [St. Paul] saith, Let the wife *reverence* her husband" (pp. 292 and 298 [emphases added]).

31. John Dove, *Of Divorcement* (1601), sig. D7ᵛ. Dove is applicable only within the context of the marriage bond; elsewhere, writers concurred that "the husband is not to command his wife in manner, as the master his servant, but as the soul doth the body, as being conjoined in like affection and good will" (Dod and Cleaver, sig. O8ᵛ). The most frequently cited rationale for this stricture returned to woman's creation not from man's head nor feet but from his side; see Perkins, p. 428. For a discussion of Jean Bodin on this subject, see Schochet, p. 33.

The injunction to wifely obedience was authorized as a specific consequence of Eve's disobedience. Thus, Dod and Cleaver wrote that "because she sinned first, therefore she is humbled most"; Thomas Carter, that the wife is "committed" by God to the "subjection" of her husband "as a portion of her punishment for her disobedience unto him." We are more familiar with the notion that woman's suffering in childbearing was divinely decreed than with this understanding of marriage, too, as righteously punitive for her. But the 1547 "Homily of the State of Matrimony" confirms that "truth it is, that they [women] must specially feel the grief and pains of their matrimony, in that they relinquish the liberty of their own rule," as well as "in the pain of their travailing, in the bringing up of their children."[32] Given that the wife's subjection to her husband found this validation in primal Western myth, it is not surprising that it attained the status of "natural," or God-mandated, law. According to Torquato Tasso, whose oeconomic tract appeared in English in 1588, "by nature woman was made man's subject." In the early 1590s William Perkins wrote of the householder's political role that "he comes not unto it by election as it falleth out in other states, but by the ordinances of God, settled even in the order of nature. The husband indeed naturally bears rule over the wife." And Whately instructed the wife to tell herself that "mine husband is my superior, my better; he hath authority and rule over me. Nature hath given it him. . . . God hath given it him. . . . I will not strive against GOD and nature. Though my sin hath made my place tedious, yet I will confess the truth: Mine husband is my superior, my better."[33]

And yet, even within the idealizing confines of oeconomic prescriptive literature, the idea of the woman resisted full reconciliation to the rigor of the patriarchal schema. Aristotle had stated that "the association of husband and wife is clearly [that of] an aristocracy" rather than that of a monarchy; as early as 1530 Richard Whitford acknowledged that the fifth commandment enjoined authority to both father and mother, and in 1609 John Rainolds suggested that "whatsoever a man's mother should command him must be obeyed too, she being compre-

32. Dod and Cleaver, sig. Q7ʳ; Thomas Carter, *Carter's Christian Commonwealth* (1627), sig. E7ʳ⁻ᵛ; "Homily of the State of Matrimony" in *Certain Sermons*, ed. Rickey and Stroup, p. 243. Note that in the homily, as in the citation from Dove, above, emphasis is upon the woman's loss of liberty.

33. Torquato Tasso, *Householder's Philosophy*, trans. Thomas Kyd (1588), sig. C2ʳ; Perkins, pp. 436–37; Whately, sig. E4ᵛ. And see Richard Hooker: "To fathers, within their private families, nature hath given a supreme power" (*Laws of Ecclesiastical Polity* [1593], vol. 1, p. 99). Compare Dod and Cleaver, who argue that "no distinction or difference of birth and nobility can be so great but that the league, which both God's ordinance and nature hath ordained betwixt men and women, far exceedeth it: for by nature woman was made man's subject" (sig. L1ᵛ).

hended in the name of parents."[34] Thus was her subjection, despite the evident interest of ideology, "troublesome" (in the word of Matthew Griffith). The woman's dual role as wife who must obey and mother who must be obeyed resulted in such circuitous logic (and confused pronouns) as those in the "Homily of the State of Matrimony": "Ye wives, be ye in subjection to obey your own husbands. To obey is another thing than to control or command, which yet they may do, to their children, and to their family. But as for their husbands, them must they obey, and cease from commanding, and perform subjection." While Thomas Smith stated simply that man and woman "together rule the house," few others were able to conceptualize a rulership that was both partible and egalitarian.[35]

Henry Smith, for example, called husband and wife "partners like two oars in a boat; therefore, he must divide offices, and affairs, and goods with her . . . for she is an under officer in his commonweal." Dod and Cleaver identified both father and mother as the "governors" of a family, adding that there is "first the chief governor, which is the husband; secondly, a fellow helper, which is the wife." The oxymoronics of Smith's "partner" and "under officer" and of Dod and Cleaver's "fellow" and "helper" were symptomatic of a confusion that was to express itself for decades through such unhappy syntax as Whately's: "They must also be good rulers at home and join in guiding the household: the man as God's immediate officer and the King in his family; the woman as the deputy subordinate and associate to him, but not altogether equal; and both in their order must govern." In his "so cannot a house be ordered without an overseer, which must needs be man and wife," Thomas Gainsford witnessed a phenomenon that Sherry B. Ortner recognizes as the shared economic interest of husband and wife, because of which, she says, "the logic of hierarchical systems inherently tends towards . . . gender equality." But Gainsford continued that the two persons holding his notionally single political role must be "subordinate one to the other": the Renaissance ideology that apprehended joint economic interest strove all the more mightily, perhaps as a result, to preserve the internal hierarchy of gender inequality that was vital to its own political logic.[36]

34. Aristotle, *Ethics*, trans. Thomson, p. 276; Richard Whitford, *Work for Householders* (1530), sig. E1ᵛ; John Rainolds, *Defence of the Judgment* (1609), sig. E2ᵛ.
35. Matthew Griffith, *Bethel* (1633), sig. Y2ʳ; "Homily of the State of Matrimony" in *Certain Sermons*, ed. Rickey and Stroup, p. 242; Thomas Smith, p. 59.
36. Henry Smith, sig. E7ᵛ; Dod and Cleaver, sig. B5ʳ; Whately, sig. C2ᵛ; Thomas Gainsford, *Rich Cabinet* (1616), fol. 101ᵛ. See Sherry B. Ortner, "Gender and Sexuality" (1981), p. 397. Belsey has noted these contradictions in *Subject of Tragedy* (1985), p. 155. See also Susan D. Amussen, *Ordered Society* (1988), p. 41.

There were, of course, practical political consequences of patriarchalism's theoretical ambiguities. While Perkins stated that the "father and chief head of the family" had "the true right and power over all matters domestical," he also declared that the father "ought not in modesty to challenge the privilege of preserving and advertising his wife in all matters domestical, but in some to leave her to her own will and judgment." Thomas Smith insisted that in the aristocracy of the household commonwealth "not one always: but sometime and in some thing one, and sometime and in some thing another doth bear the rule." Dod and Cleaver were at some pains to establish those areas of household responsibility "in which the husband giveth over his right unto his wife: as to rule and govern her maidens; to see to those things that belong unto the kitchen, and to huswifery, and to their household stuff; other mean things, as to buy and sell certain necessary things, may be ordered after the wit, wisdom, and fidelity of the woman." Whately was eventually to insist that delegation of authority was necessary to maintenance of authority; because "he that will be drawing out his commandments for every light thing shall find it at length regarded in nothing," the husband should not "be charging, bidding, and intermeddling" in "brewing, baking, washing, and the particulars of these and the like businesses."[37] Regardless of the specificity attempted by the authors of domestic manuals in detailing the spheres in which the woman might assume authority, however, it was necessarily impossible for them to anticipate and categorize every quotidian instance of overlapping and conflicting responsibilities.

These ambiguities left the house, the very haven of the "domestical king," a contested space. On the one hand, as Edward Coke phrased the common understanding, "a man's house is his castle. . . . where shall a man be safe, if it be not in his house?" Coke's precedent can be traced back through William Lambard and William Stanford to a statute of 1478: "la maison de homme est a lui son castel et son defence"; but the phrase also enjoyed a life independent of legal thought in which it was asserted in support of the householder's authority, as in Mulcaster's declaration of the householder that "he is the appointer of his own circumstance, and his house is his castle."[38] On the other hand,

37. Perkins, pp. 437 and 428 (the latter was repeated nearly verbatim by Griffith, sig. X8ᵛ); Thomas Smith, p. 59; Dod and Cleaver, sig. M8ʳ; Whately, sigs. D2ʳ⁻ᵛ. The "Homily of the State of Matrimony" anticipated Whately: "Even as the King appeareth so much the more noble, the more excellent and noble he maketh his officers and lieutenants, whom if he should dishonor and despise the authority of their dignity, he should deprive himself of a great part of his own honor: even so, if thou dost despise her that is set in the next room beside thee, thou dost much derogate and decay the excellency and virtue of thine own authority" (*Certain Sermons*, ed. Rickey and Stroup, p. 246).

38. Edward Coke, *Third Part of the Institutes* (completed 1628, published 1644), sig. Y3ᵛ. William Lambard, *Eirenarcha* (1581): "A man's house is his castle, which he may defend with

the house was proverbially "the woman's place," a notion elaborated in one of the most frequently encountered set pieces of oeconomic prescription: "The good woman is called an housewife, because she commonly keeps the house—not a street-wife like Thamar, not a field-wife, like Dinah—but a housewife, because she is either at home or, if she go abroad, it is snail-like, with her house upon her head, and it is about household considerations."[39]

As Coke further articulated, "the house of every one is to him his castle and fortress, as well for defense against injury and violence, as for his repose."[40] While the external fortifications that characterized the castle form may have rendered it impregnable to assault from without (that is, from injury and violence), it remained vulnerable to challenge from within (that is, to repose). One challenge in "everyone's" castle was posed by an occupying female power that was anciently recognized in a proverb credited to Solomon, that resurfaced in *Piers Plowman* and *The Canterbury Tales*, and that also appeared in *Arden of Feversham* and Shakespeare's *1 Henry IV*: "Smoke [from hearth or chimney], rain [a leaking roof], and a very curst wife make a man weary of house and life."[41] Dod and Cleaver reminded the man contemplating marriage that his wife would "continually be conversant with thee, at thy table, in thy chamber, in bed, in thy secrets, and finally, in thy heart and breast." Griffith recognized the wife's power "to make her husband's house, his hell, by the strength of her will," which he called "as monstrous in nature, as to see one body having two heads."[42]

As is thus admitted, female power was *in practice* imperfectly contained by the deployment of an ideology relentlessly committed to the maintenance and articulation of male authority. Such power, Mary Douglas recognizes, reveals itself in the interstices of theory: "Where the social system explicitly recognises positions of authority, those holding such positions are endowed with explicit spiritual power, controlled, conscious, external and approved—powers to bless or curse.

---

force against any private army that shall invade him" (sig. L7ᵛ). William Stanford, *Pleas del Coron* (1557): "ma meason est a moy: come mon castel, hors de quel, le ley ne moy arta a fuer" (quoted from the second edition of 1560, sig. B6ᵛ). Stanford cites the statute from *Anni Regis Henrici Septimi* (1555), *Anno* 21 H 7, fol. 39ʳ. See also Mulcaster, sig. Ff1ʳ.

39. Griffith, sig. T5ᵛ; see also Henry Smith, sig. F6ʳ; Dod and Cleaver, sig. P8ᵛ; Carter, sig. G6ᵛ; and Griffith (again), sig. Dd7ᵛ.

40. Coke, Report on Semayne's Case (1605), translated into English in *Reports of Sir Edward Coke* (1658), sig. Pp3ʳ.

41. For medieval usages, see Whiting (1968), pp. 586–87, especially for Chaucer. For Renaissance examples, see Tilley, H781 and S574, especially *1 Henry IV*, 3.1.158–59. And see *Arden*, where the "smoke" of a mist is compared to "a curst wife in a little house, that never leaves her husband till she have driven him out at doors with a wet pair of eyes. Then looks he as if his house were afire, or some of his friends dead" (11.5–15). Many who employ the commonplace cite Solomon.

42. Dod and Cleaver, sig. L2ᵛ; Griffith, sig. Y4ʳ.

Where the social system requires people to hold dangerously ambiguous roles, these persons are credited with uncontrolled, unconscious, dangerous, disapproved powers."[43] Even without the evil animus of an Alyce Ardern, in other words, the woman posed a challenge to the very patriarchal philosophy with which society structured itself; the fact that that philosophy could not thoroughly integrate her conflicted status empowered her, even when virtuous and well intentioned, to unsettle her environment.

The woman's state of submission was at the same time *in theory* general; she was a subject in both domestic and political realms. She thus defined one extreme of the patriarchal scale; as Edmund Tilney wrote, "disobedience is a fault in all persons, but the greatest vice in a woman." For this reason, female characters were apt literary vehicles, in late sixteenth-century England, for the acting out of crises of authority and obedience. More specifically, as Natalie Zemon Davis has pointed out, "in early modern Europe, the relation of the wife—of the potentially disorderly woman—to her husband was especially useful for expressing the relation of all subordinates to their superiors."[44]

Alice Arden's Sisters

From this perspective it is particularly suggestive that the thoroughgoing political orthodoxy of *Arden of Feversham* is insufficient to one challenge to its intellectual integrity: it is fatally uncertain of how to treat, manage, and contain its disorderly woman. Franklin's conventional wisdom on the subject not only fails to avert Alice's rebellion, it nourishes it; and in so doing, it implicates the companion ideology of oeconomic prescription in tragic consequence. For Franklin displays an intimate familiarity with the tenets common to prescriptive literature, which, as he does, unanimously advised against the indulgence and expression of jealousy and suspicion. As early as 1530, a household manual suggested:

> If you suspect the woman of thy house, let other persons rather showeth than thou should be over busy to try out the matter. . . . it were better

43. Douglas, p. 99. I observe the distinctions proposed by Max Weber and summarized by M. G. Smith: authority is "the right to make a particular decision and to command obedience"; power, "the ability to act effectively on persons or things, to make or secure favourable decisions which are not of right allocated to the individuals or their roles" (quoted by Michelle Zimbalist Rosaldo in "Theoretical Overview" [1974], p. 21; Rosaldo applies these definitions to gender roles).
44. Edmund Tilney, *Flower of Friendship* (1568), sig. D3^r; Natalie Zemon Davis, "Women on Top" (1975), p. 127.

unknown. For once known, it is never cured; the wound is without reme-
dy. . . . The [b]est and most easy way therein is to dissimule the matter
(though it were privily known) and pretend ignorance, without any quarrel or countenance. . . . A noble heart and high gentle mind will never
search of women's matters. A shrew will sooner be corrected by smiling
or laughing than by a staff or strokes. The best way to keep a woman
good is gentle entreaty and never to let her know that she is suspected
and ever to be counselled and informed with loving manner.

Or, as was frequently quoted in the name of Socrates: "The best way
for a man to keep his wife chaste, is not to be jealous."[45] The plat-
itudinous Franklin is in fact precisely the sort of person of whom Cicero might have written: "Let the authority of friends (giving sound
counsel) bear great sway and force . . . and let such authority so given
be thoroughly obeyed."[46] We know the unfortunate consequences for
Arden of his "obedience" to Franklin.

Alice Arden represents both the theoretical threat posed by women
to patriarchal philosophy and the suspected inadequacy in practice of
an elaborate mechanism of domestic prescription. This understanding
of the uses of the female character also helps us to apprehend the
power of the four playtexts that succeeded *Arden of Feversham* and that
dramatized historical events and personages that might otherwise seem
insignificant to us: *A Warning for Fair Women* stages the collaboration of
a chaste wife in the murder of her merchant husband; *Two Lamentable
Tragedies* represents a murder committed out of petty avarice by a
tavernkeeper and concealed by the keeper's sister; *1 and 2 Edward IV*
recounts the well-known story of a goldsmith's wife who is taken from
her husband to become a king's mistress.

In fact, the cultural significance of these events was demonstrated
independently of the playtexts based on them, in notorieties not unlike
those accorded the murder of Thomas Ardern. *A Warning for Fair
Women*, for example, dramatizes the 1573 murder of London merchant
George Sanders by a circle of four conspirators: his wife, Anne; her
lover, George Browne; widowed neighbor Anne Drury; and the neighbor's manservant, Roger Clement. The historical cast was eventually
enlarged by a minister, George Mell, who grew enamored of the im-

45. Whitford, sig. H1ᵛ. William Baldwin cited Socrates in *Treatise of Moral Philosophy* (1547),
p. 316. Tilney similarly concluded that a woman cannot be "enforce[d] . . . to be true to her
husband, if she otherwise determine. Therefore to conclude to be jealous, either needeth not
or booteth not" (sig. C7ᵛ). And Leonard Wright added that "to be jealous without a cause, is the
next way to have a cause" (*Display of Duty* [1589], sig. D5ʳ).
46. Cicero, *De amicitia*, trans. Thomas Newton (1577), sig. C4ᵛ. Franklin's counsel seems to
be validated by experience: "it is not strange / That women will be false and wavering" (1.20–
21); "let your comfort be that others bear / Your woes twice doubled all with patience" (4.25–
26); of those who dream, only "Some one in twenty may incur belief" (6.39).

prisoned Anne Sanders and reportedly urged her to "conceal" her complicity. George Browne, meanwhile, himself refused to implicate Anne Sanders and was tortured on the rack until, as one Privy Council record chillingly notes, a physician was summoned "to look unto him." At the execution of the other three, "almost the whole field and all the way from Newgate was as full of folk as could well stand one by another. And besides that, great companies were placed both in the chambers near abouts (whose windows and walls were in many places beaten down to look out at) and also upon the gutters, sides, and tops of the houses and upon the battlements and steeple of St. Bartholomew's." Adding a further layer of implication and sensation was the presence at the execution of the earls of Bedford and Derby; Anne Drury apologized to Derby from the scaffold, denying that she had been responsible while in his service for his separation from his wife.[47]

These reports of the executions were included in a pamphlet authored by Arthur Golding and titled *A Brief Discourse of the Late Murder of Master G. Sanders,* issued promptly in 1573 and reprinted in 1577. Holinshed and Stow incorporated lengthy accounts of the murder; Anthony Munday included it in a collection of "sundry examples" of murders; it joined the Arden story in the anonymous *A World of Wonders, A Mass of Murders;* and Anne Sanders, like Alice Arden, inspired a ballad that pretended to voice her "woeful lamentation." The story also incited passing references of the sort that had been so strikingly associated with Ardern's. In 1596 Thomas Lodge described "unlawful Lucre" as a bawd who "will reckon you up the story of Mistress Sanders, and weep at it." In 1632 the author of *The Law's Resolutions of Women's Rights* (identified only as T. E.) explained that Anne Sanders was hung (rather than burned for petty treason) because she was only an "accessory" to murder, having "procur[ed] Browne to kill her husband."[48]

As Ardern's murder had entered Henry Machyn's diary, so the crime that informed the main plot of *Two Lamentable Tragedies,* the murder of chandler Thomas Beech by tavernkeeper Thomas Merry, surfaced in Philip Gawdy's private correspondence. "There was a very foul murder lately done in London," he wrote six days after the fact, on 29 August

47. Documentary sources include *APC,* vol. 8: p. 91 (26 March 1573); p. 92 (30 March 1573); p. 94 (1 April 1573); p. 96 (14 April 1573); p. 105 (12 May 1573); p. 121 (2 July 1573); and p. 142 (20 November 1573). See also Arthur Golding, *Brief Discourse* (1573), passim. And see Joseph H. Marshburn, "Cruell Murder" (1949), and E. St. John Brooks, "Pamphlet by Arthur Golding" (1938). On the use of the rack, see John Bellamy, *Tudor Law of Treason* (1979), p. 120.

48. John Stow, *Annals of England* (1592), sigs. Ffff8^{v}–Gggg1^{r}; Raphael Holinshed, *Chronicles* (1577), vol. 2, sigs. Yyyy5$^{r–v}$; Anthony Munday, *View of Sundry Examples* (1580), sigs. B1^{v}–B2^{v}; *World of Wonders* (1595), sig. F1^{v}. And see "Woeful Lamentation of Mistress Anne Sanders"; Thomas Lodge, *Wit's Misery* (1596), vol. 4, p. 38; and T.E., *Law's Resolutions* (1632), sigs. O8^{v}–P1^{r}.

1594, "by an alehouse keeper, the tapster, his sister, his maid, and a waterman consenting all unto it. There was a chandler and his boy murdered. They are all apprehended and have confessed." Gawdy drily added the gruesome cause that this murder had revealed itself: "The waterman should have had four shillings for carrying the dead body over the water," but he "left the one half behind." The crime inspired in addition a reference in *A World of Wonders, A Mass of Murders* and no less than five recorded ballads.[49] Even so, it was no rival in redaction for the story of Edward IV's mistress, Jane Shore, the multiple recastings of which—in the plays *1 and 2 Edward IV*, as well as in poem, ballad, chronicle, and moral exemplum—are widely familiar.[50]

By virtue of their comparable notoriety, these events would seem to lend themselves to theatricalization along the model of *Arden of Feversham*. But, some ten years on, they diverged from that model in the critical respect of the moral resolve of their female protagonists. Anne Sanders, Merry's sister Rachel, and Jane Shore transgress despite their demonstrated attempts to honor their obligations. Unlike Alice, these women do not resist the patriarchal system. Instead, they are trapped in ethical conflicts that that system does not equip them to resolve, and this is the source of their independent contributions to a cultural history of the private.

A Warning for Fair Women, Two Lamentable Tragedies, and *1 and 2 Edward IV* are products of their decade and of the fact that patriarchal philosophy was incompletely realized. That philosophy had yet to articulate fully the political component that would result in a comprehensive theory of obligation and had failed to reconcile the ambiguous role of the woman to the intended rigor of its domestic schema. Taken in turn below, these plays demonstrate the consequence of these irresolutions for a marriage, then a household, and finally the state. But this linear progression is merely a narrative convenience, ultimately irrelevant to my larger thesis, which is that ideological contradictions are here represented through the conflicts confronted by mere "private" characters and that the significance of these contradictions was understood to ramify far beyond them. Because each text thus exposes the

49. Philip Gawdy, *Letters*, p. 90. This is a previously unremarked reference to the murder and differs from the story as presented in *Two Lamentable Tragedies*; the bribing of the waterman to dispose of the body is unique to this account. In her unpublished 1978 dissertation for the University of Michigan, an edition of the play, Anne Weston Patenaude cites *World of Wonders* and reviews the Stationers' Register entries for ballads (pp. 22–23). The ballads included laments by Beech's ghost, Thomas Merry, and Rachel Merry. My focus on this plot of the play derives from its basis, like *Arden* and *Warning,* in a crime in near-contemporary England and from its categorization as a "domestic" tragedy.

50. For a review of the redactions, see Esther Yael Beith-Halahmi (1974) and Marilyn L. Johnson (1974).

problematics of the prevailing ideology, each plays a contributing role in the late Tudor discourse of order.

A Warning for Fair Women

In his insistence that Anne Sanders was only an "accessory" to her husband's murder, T. E. reads her crime in sympathy with the anonymous author of the dramatic text. Modern critics have typically failed to recognize this fact. So often has *A Warning for Fair Women* been taken for a pale replication of *Arden of Feversham,* so commonly has its action been described with reference to the wife-husband-lover triangle that defined *Arden,* so strong has been the presumption that the author intended another Alice, so further obfuscating (to modern readers) have been the dumb shows through which much of *A Warning's* action is communicated, that Anne Sanders has frequently been misread, her motivation obscured by the characterological displacement of her seduction.[51] The seducer in this play is not, as might be expected, George Browne, the cuckolder and murderer of her husband. Rather, in a first hint of the play's intellectual complexity, agency is located in the person of the Sanders's friend and neighbor, the widow Anne Drury.

Anne Sanders rebuffs Browne's one direct approach, an encounter at the door of her house, and, in amused soliloquy, reveals that she recognizes the motives of "arrand-making gallants" (2.394). Thus scorned by Anne Sanders, Browne determines to make Anne Drury his "mediator" with her (3.502). In Browne's presence Anne Drury confirms Anne Sanders's virtue and protests her own reluctance to accost it, but her remarks are affected largely to suggest the difficulty of her task and her consequent desert of reward. In Browne's absence she professes herself so certain that Anne Sanders "may be tempered easily like wax, / Especially by one that is familiar with her" (3.448–49) that she confidently and greedily anticipates "The money I will finger 'twixt them twain" (3.463).

Anne Drury finds her opportunity in an unhappy coincidence: Anne Sanders has commissioned the delivery of some household goods on the very day that her husband unexpectedly commandeers all available funds to repay a business debt. The manservant who is directed by Sanders to gather his ready cash objects on Anne Sanders's behalf three

51. On the dumb shows, see Otelia Cromwell (1928), p. 186; Adams, p. 125; Dieter Mehl (1964), pp. 90–96; Charles Dale Cannon (1975), p. 51; Alan C. Dessen, *Elizabethan Drama* (1977), pp. 136–37, and *Shakespeare and the Late Moral Plays* (1986), pp. 142–43.

times, informing his master of the household obligation and, most tellingly, protesting that he should not be made the messenger for Sanders's directive: the wife "will not so be answered at my hand" (4.586). But he is overruled, and all his apprehensions are fulfilled. Just as Sanders insists "take heed until my credit" and "I do not use (thou knowest) to break my word, / Much less my bond" (4.568–70), so Anne Sanders observes that "my breach of credit, in the while / Is not regarded" (4.629–30); she, too, considers herself to have undertaken a debt of honor, the forfeit of which jeopardizes her good name. To the manservant she bridles: "'Tis well that I must stand at your reversion, / Entreat my 'prentice, curtsy to my man" (4.618–19). And to her neighbor she frets,

> I am a woman, and in that respect,
> Am well content my husband shall control me,
> But that my man should over-awe me too,
> And in the sight of strangers, Mistress Drury,
> I tell you true, does grieve me to the heart.
>
> (4.655–59)

Anne Drury is quick to take advantage of Sanders's inattention to the delicate balance of order and command in his household. As the manservant delivers his message, she remarks in an aside, "Good fortune: thus incensed against her husband, / I shall the better break with her for Browne" (4.607–8). She makes her greatest capital out of the servant's part in the affair: "Your husband was to blame, to say the truth, / That gave his servant such authority." "What signifies it," she persists, "but he doth repose / More trust in a vild boy, than in his wife?" (4.660–63). Even though Sanders must presumably be forgiven for thinking his wife's concerns "trifling" in comparison with his own, the fact remains that authority is legitimately required of her in the management of her household, and he has undermined her. She "hath some things belonging to her," remind Dod and Cleaver; the husband ought "in some to leave her to her own will and judgment," advises Perkins.[52] That Sanders has carelessly encouraged a violation of the household hierarchy in his direction to his man compounds his error.

But while the violation of the Sanders's household hierarchy is the occasion for seduction, it is not the effectual persuasion to adultery. Anne Sanders's vexation with her husband is already fading when she observes some yellow spots on her fingers, associates them with foreor-

---

52. Dod and Cleaver, sig. E2ᵛ; Perkins, p. 428.

dained anger, and thus suggests that her husband is less responsible than is destiny. Wifely submission, however, does not suit Anne Drury's purposes, and she displays an improvisational genius in prolonging Anne Sanders's distress and advancing her own agenda. She seizes and studies the spotted fingers and, pretending an expertise in palmistry, purports to find a line that indicates "a dissolution" (4.681). This she interprets as incipient widowhood, and she further predicts remarriage to a better—that is, wealthier—man. Anne Sanders, who does not share Anne Drury's material ambition, resists the temptation of the projected "Ladder of Promotion" (4.699): "Yet had I rather be as now I am, / If God were pleased that it should be so." Anne Drury swiftly changes tactics, using Anne Sanders's own words and patent desire for spiritual rectitude as the defining elements of her next line of attack: "If God were pleased: O, but He hath decreed / It shall be otherwise." Anne Sanders's pause is chilling: "Your words do make me think I know not what, / And burden me with fear as well as doubt" (4.715–22).

Anne Drury then claims to find in her neighbor's hand the identity of the younger woman's next husband, a man with whom Mistress Sanders herself has talked recently, near her own door. Because Anne Sanders cannot suspect the collusion between her old friend and the newly met Browne, and thus cannot rationally account for Anne Drury's knowledge of that doorway meeting, she comes to subscribe it to the supernatural knowledge that Anne Drury has claimed for herself as a palmist.[53] Anne Sanders muses that only one man fits Anne Drury's specifications, Browne. Her "And he I must confess against my will, / Came to my door" (4.734–35), with its careful articulation of reluctant acquiescence, carries the force of moral as well as dialogic surrender.

By convincing Anne Sanders that Browne is to be her next husband, Anne Drury is correspondingly able to convince her that she must behave toward him as toward a husband: "use him courteously, as one for whom, / You were created in your birth a wife." Anne Sanders admits, "If it be so, I must submit my self / To that which God and destiny sets down" (4.753–56). In the scenes that follow, Anne Sanders mourns the "treachery," "complot," and "conspiracy" of the murder of George Sanders—even as she yields to the desires of Browne (10.1552–

---

53. Anne Drury's method was apparently a well-recognized means of cozenage in the period, judging by *Brideling, Saddling, and Riding . . . by one Judith Philips* (1595). Like Drury, Philips pretends to find by the "art of palmistry" knowledge that has in this case been given her by her criminal compatriots: "Thus is God's word made a cloak for all such devilish practices, only to blind the eyes of the simple and well-meaning people" (sig. B3^r).

53). While the actions of Anne Sanders may seem ambiguous, their rationale, seen from the perspective developed here, is clear: Anne Sanders is torn between the duty that she knows she owes her husband and the duty that she has been persuaded she owes Browne. She is uncertain of the proper direction of her obedience and obligation because Anne Drury has, in her supposed prophecy, conflated present and future and created an apparent conflict of authorities. To describe the confusion by analogy to the theory of the king's two bodies, Anne Drury has convinced Anne Sanders that the body politic—that is, her husband as head and domestic authority—resides simultaneously in two bodies natural—that is, Sanders and Browne.

In the dumb show that immediately follows, the allegorical character Tragedy emphasizes that "All we have done" to this point "hath only been in words" (D.S.1.776); the business of acting on those words is to follow. The seduction of Anne Sanders is, then, effected by rhetoric, not passion, and by Anne Drury, not George Browne.[54] The displacement of agency from Browne to Anne Drury is of critical ethical significance: to recognize it is to understand that what is at issue is not merely a woman's fickleness of affect but rather a crisis of obligation—even though that crisis is a false one.

The idea that Sanders must die is implicit in Anne Drury's argument: the first husband must be removed if Anne is to have a second. But Anne Drury is also the first to conceive of murder as the means to "compass Browne's desire." Even as she congratulates herself upon the success of the palm-reading device, she anticipates the need for "Some stratagem to close up Sanders' eyes" (4.765, 770). Again, the dumb show confirms Anne Drury's pivotal role: as the figure of Chastity pulls Anne Sanders away from Lust by one arm, Anne Drury pushes Chastity away. Only then does Anne Sanders accept Browne's toast to her, embrace Lust, and thrust a lamenting Chastity aside. Finally, with Chastity "quite abandoned," Murder uses a bowl of blood to stain the hands of Browne, Anne Drury, and Anne Drury's manservant Roger— and only one of Anne Sanders's fingers, so slight is her involvement in the deed. Tragedy glosses the masque for the audience, describing Anne Drury as "that instrument of hell / That wicked Drury, the accursed fiend" (D.S.1.824–25, 839).

Anne Sanders's recruitment to crime thus invokes the problematics of the Tudor notion of woman: possessed of an independent intellect, aspiring to goodness, and yet highly susceptible to the agency and

54. For a sympathetic reading, see Frances E. Dolan, "Gender, Moral Agency" (1989), especially pp. 206 and 209.

strategies of evil. "The woman," according to the "Homily of the State of Matrimony," "is a weak creature, not endued with like strength and constancy of mind, therefore they be the sooner disquieted and they be the more prone to all weak affections and dispositions of mind." Henry Smith warns the husband that he must not expect "that wisdom, nor that faith, nor that patience, nor that strength in the weaker vessel," which is expected in himself, the very wisdom, according to Thomas Carter, given him so that he may "bear with" her weakness.[55] A Warning for Fair Women suggests that the wife who is oeconomically tractable is also, ironically, more likely to be ethically manipulable and defraudable.

In this respect the play reauthorizes patriarchal control. Most readers of A Warning for Fair Women have viewed it as narrowly theological, "completely dedicated," according to its most influential critic, "to moral instruction."[56] Certainly the admonitory title seems to confirm such a reading. And the relatively brief essential action of the play is nearly overwhelmed by the long scenes devoted to its consequences—to the conspirators' trials, confessions, repentances, and executions. A Warning's affirmation of orthodoxy could not be more painstakingly detailed, nor more sentimental, as Anne Sanders at the hour of her execution advises her children to "learn by [their] mother's fall / To follow virtue and beware of sin" (21.2686–87).

But this resolution cannot, finally, obscure the more troubling aspects of her crime as they are depicted in this play: the occasion of Anne Sanders's seduction arises from the ambiguities and contradictions of the woman's coterminous roles in the household hierarchy. And the fundamental premise of her seduction is the fabrication of a crisis of patriarchal authority. The agent of disorder in this play thus invokes and manipulates the patriarchal principles that regulate domestic society so as to provoke the violation of those very principles. The play in fact exposes the hazards of such abstract thought as were expressed by Whately—who prescribes that the wife must regard her husband "as God's Deputy, not looking to his person but his place; nor thinking so much who and what an one he is, as whose officer."[57] The story of Anne Sanders demonstrates that the thorough abstraction of the person into the political role can result in the entertainment of unspeakable enormity.

55. *Certain Sermons*, ed. Rickey and Stroup, p. 241; Henry Smith, sig. E8ᵛ; Carter, sigs. D4ʳ⁻ᵛ.

56. Adams, p. 124. For a review of the criticism, see Cannon's Introduction, pp. 80–91.

57. Whately, sig. F1ʳ.

Two Lamentable Tragedies

A Warning for Fair Women resonates with the 1590s awareness of the mortality of Elizabeth's natural body and the conflict of loyalties thereby engendered. The coterminous Two Lamentable Tragedies engages another and equally timely set of anxieties and ideological problems. Like A Warning (and like Arden of Feversham), its main plot reenacts a notorious crime and ends with the execution of a woman. But Two Lamentable Tragedies diverges from its dramatic predecessors to find a new source of tragedy in the conflict faced by a woman subjected to the illegitimate commands of a profoundly disordered order figure rather than in a woman's rebellion against a flawed domestic authority. In so doing, the play implicates patriarchal philosophy in yet another radical failure.

The crime is committed by tavernkeeper Thomas Merry, who lures a chandler named Thomas Beech to a room above his tavern and there strikes him on the head with a hammer fifteen times. Of the many consequences of this murder that make up the Merry plot, one that does not materialize is the "gold expected hopes" for profit that motivate him. Instead he is occupied throughout with vain attempts at concealment: he fatally wounds Beech's boy, Thomas Winchester (who knew that Merry's tavern was Beech's last destination), dismembers Beech's corpse, and slowly purges the premises of body parts and blood. As a physical contaminant, Beech's body is the first and most obvious indication that Merry's house has been violated by the murder. A corollary sense of the ethical violation of the house pervades the reproach of Merry's man, Harry Williams: "Oh it was beastly so to butcher him . . . like a coward under your own roof. . . . I will not stay an hour within your house" (sig. B4^v). We are told not once but twice that Williams finds new lodgings in a hayloft at the Three Cranes Inn. His departure initiates the dissolution of Merry's household society; Williams's displacement and unmastering are aspects of the disorder that will require legal accountability from Merry and his sister Rachel.[58]

Rachel has no choice but to stay at home and incur her own share of

58. With reference to Williams, see Perkins: "A family is a natural and simple society of certain persons having mutual relations one to another under the private government of one. These persons must be at least three, because two cannot make a society" (p. 416). Given contemporary fear of masterless men and vagrants, Williams's displacement was more likely to have provoked anxiety than sympathy. Peter Clark estimates that the number of the homeless peaked during Elizabeth's reign. See Crisis and Order (1972), especially the Introduction; Clark's "The Migrant" and Paul Slack's "Vagrants and Vagrancy" (1974), especially p. 377. And see A. L. Beier, Masterless Men (1985).

the consequences of homicide. As an unmarried woman living in Merry's establishment, she characteristically owes her brother the obedience that a married woman would owe her husband—and in fact enjoys less independence than the mistress of a household.[59] We are frequently reminded of the hierarchical nature of their relationship by the directives that Merry issues regarding Rachel's role in the operation of the tavern, her conduct, indeed her every movement; even her first entrance is at his command. Her acceptance of her own subjection is suggested early, when she discovers the murder and cries, "Oh brother, brother, what have you done?" and then, at once, "We are undone, brother, we are undone. / What shall I say? For we are quite undone" (sigs. B4[r–v]). The immediate shift to the first-person plural, so automatic a reflex that she embraces complicity instinctively, shows the extent of her identification with her brother and her understanding that she is subsumed in him.[60] Later, when he admits the guilt of premeditation to her, she responds nonjudgmentally, "I am your sister, though a silly maid, / I'll be your true and faithful comforter" (sig. D2[v]).[61] And even after sighing that Merry's "deed would trouble any quiet soul," Rachel announces to the audience:

> Let others open what I do conceal,
> Lo, he is my brother, I will cover it
> And rather die then have it spoken rife,
> Lo, where she goes, betray'd her brother's life.
>
> (sig. F4[r])

The effect of Merry's homicidal act on Rachel's moral sense is the most moving of the violations that the killing engenders. She is plagued by regret that she had no opportunity to prevent the crime, by physical horror at the task of dismembering Beech and removing the bloody signs of his death, by ethical torment at her inability to stir Merry's conscience and effect his remorse, and by her own inability—unlike Merry himself—to sleep. Her moral dilemma is articulated most clearly when she says, with the emphases of soliloquy and of rhymed couplet,

59. Compare Anne in Thomas Middleton and William Rowley's *A Fair Quarrel*: "He's my brother, forsooth, I his creature; / He does command me any lawful office, / Either in act or counsel" (2.2.70–72). Rachel's subordinate role in Merry's household is, in terms of her obligations to him, a wifely one, and I use this frame of reference for my discussion.

60. Schochet writes that "so long as a person occupied an inferior status within a household . . . and was subordinated to the head, his social identity was altogether vicarious. . . . 'subsumed'" (pp. 65–66).

61. "Comforter" had a specifically religious resonance as a Protestant synonym for "confessor"; it could also refer to an "abettor" in criminal activity. Both meanings are relevant to Rachel's actions and fate.

"Ah, did not nature oversway my will, / The world should know this plot of damned ill" (sigs. E2ᵛ–E3ʳ). We tend to think loosely of sisterly affect as "natural," or instinctive, and could easily read her remark in this modern sense. But it is more likely that "nature" here refers us with some precision to the contemporary tradition of natural law, and the "natural," or God-mandated, direction of duty that is one of its fundamental tenets.[62]

This suggestion that the term is ideologically coded receives reinforcement in the alternate plot of *Two Lamentable Tragedies*, where the young Allenso functions as Rachel's foil and Allenso's father, Fallerio, commits a crime that is comparable to Merry's. Torn between, on the one hand, his sense of honor and his love for the young cousin whom Fallerio murders and, on the other, his recognition of his filial duty, Allenso, too, is an unwilling accomplice in a murderer's attempt to evade the consequences of homicide. At Fallerio's first misdeed, Allenso objects before capitulating, "to your will I do submit my self" (sig. B3ʳ). Fallerio denounces Allenso's later objections as those of a "rebellious tongue" (sig. C2ᵛ), he accuses Allenso of "attempt[ing] to contradict my will," and he calls Allenso "Forgetful of his duty" (sig. H1ʳ). Allenso recognizes, oxymoronically, that assisting his father constitutes "obedience to unlawfulness" (sig. C2ʳ), an insight that is repeated for emphasis when the finally remorseful Fallerio realizes that "Thou never yet were disobedient, / Unless I did command unlawfulness" (sig. K1ʳ). Allenso's conflict, in other words, is phrased in the political vocabulary that evokes hierarchy and submission to authority. While the Fallerio plot is more specific in this evocation than is the Merry plot, the language inevitably flavors our apprehension of the ethical framework of both. Thus, when Fallerio observes triumphantly of Allenso that "Nature in thee hath firm predominance" (sig. H2ᵛ), the rhetorical network reverberates until we understand that with both Rachel and Allenso the "natural" duty of moral law has prevailed over their individual wills, or moral election.[63]

Although the crime of which Rachel is accused, "concealment," is identical to that of Williams, he pleads benefit of clergy and is merely branded, while "wretched Rachel's sex denies that grace" (sig. I2ᵛ). She is condemned to hang with her brother.[64] She mounts the ladder pro-

---

62. On "the law of nature," see Sommerville, pp. 12–17.
63. Elsewhere, references such as Armenia's "Nature and love will have a double care" (sig. B1ᵛ) and Fallerio's "nature, love, and reason tells thee thus" (sig. C1ᵛ) clarify the uses of "nature" and "natural."
64. Rachel is actively complicit in the cover-up, while Williams is not. But the indictments do not distinguish between their actions.

claiming herself a mirror for all sisters, a warning against concealment of the crimes of brothers and friends. But she interrupts this profession of repentance to denounce Harry Williams for not having himself revealed Beech's death—a telling indication of her continuing inability to convince herself that she might have betrayed her brother and familial obligation. This moral hesitation colors both her appended declaration of her forgiveness of Williams and her concluding plea to others to "Conceal no murder" (sig. K2ᵛ).

The uneasy circling of her argument, from conventional exhortation to protests of innocence to renewed and decorous admonition, reflects the tortuous nature of a highly problematic tenet of patriarchy, which insists that the subject must not disobey her superior and yet stipulates that she must not obey him in actions that contradict God's moral laws: "Wives [a term that incorporates such other female subordinates as sisters] cannot be disobedient to their husbands [authority figures], but they must resist God also, who is that author of this subjection, and that she must regard her husband's will as the Lord's will. But yet withall, as the Lord commandeth one, that which is good and right, so she should obey her husband in good and right, or else she doth not obey him as the Lord but as the tempter."[65] Bullinger could argue the situation with deceptive clarity: because "they must esteem this obedience none otherwise than if it were showed unto God himself" and because "God delighteth only in goodness and forbiddeth evil everywhere," therefore "the said obedience extendeth not unto wickedness and evil but unto that which is good, honest, and comely." The difficulty of recognizing evil is, however, more apparent in Gataker: "as Peter saith of servants that they are to apply themselves even to their crooked masters: so here, though the husband's will shall be crooked, so it be not wicked, the wife's will is not straight in God's sight, if it be not pliable to his."[66] Thus rests to the individual conscience the onerous burden of distinguishing the crooked from the wicked, in Rachel's case a distinction further obscured from her by her brother's lies—his claim that he murdered Beech in self-defense and his denial that he murdered Beech's boy. But if the head of her household is called by the name of God, as Henry Smith declares, what role can her conscience play?

From this thesis of the godly derivation of patriarchal authority fol-

65. Dod and Cleaver, sigs. Q6ᵛ–Q7ʳ. They were anticipated by (and may have quoted from) Henry Smith, sig. F8ᵛ.

66. Bullinger, sig. H1ʳ; Gataker, sig. C3ʳ. See the "Homily on Obedience": "The holy apostle S. Peter commandeth servants to be obedient to their masters not only if they be good and gentle, but also if they be evil and froward." But it also advises: "we may not obey kings, magistrates, or any other, though they be our own fathers, if they would command us to do anything contrary to God's commandments" (*Certain Sermons*, ed. Bond, pp. 164 and 167).

lows, first, the common prescription that the subordinate has no right to any resistance other than the passive—which includes tears, prayer, and flight—and, second, the complementary doctrine of divinely ordained suffering—the notion of the tyrant imposed upon a people for their punishment. The "Exhortation to Obedience" reminded Elizabethans that "even the wicked rulers have their power and authority from God"; Hugh Latimer insisted: "If the king should require of thee an unjust request, yet art thou bound to pay it and not to resist and rebel. . . . And know this, that whensoever there is any unjust exaction laid upon thee it is a plague and punishment for thy sin."[67] Rachel's sense that she is implicated in Merry's crime through residence and kinship has its darker side in Renaissance theory, which is that any early modern subordinate would have been encouraged to accept this sort of violation as a providentially mandated chastisement.

Rachel's tragedy is the ambiguity that results when patriarchal and moral authorities collide. In *Two Lamentable Tragedies*, while the focus swerves from the actor of a murder to a reactor to it, a female character remains the locus of the most profound and moving explorations of the ethical issues addressed in the text. The notion that Rachel's dilemma dominates both her plot and the play is reinforced structurally, in that her execution for complicity closes the dramatic action.[68] The significance of this focus may lie in the fact that the woman's recourse is so much more limited than is that of any man: tears and prayers, yes, but where can a woman flee? Not to a hayloft in the Three Cranes Inn. The physical confines of "the woman's place" adumbrate and intensify the moral stringency of her dilemma. The patriarchal philosophy that denies her sanctuary is also that which finally refuses to any subject an application for conscience.

In the brief allegorical sequence that concludes *Two Lamentable Tragedies*, the simplest of admonitory warnings is issued and individual vigilance in the interest of civic order is exhorted.[69] The harsh ethic of the play—and of patriarchy—dictates that Rachel's life is forfeit because she has resisted Merry only verbally and morally; her execution is justified because she has collaborated in his cover-up. But while the

67. "Homily on Obedience" in *Certain Sermons*, ed. Bond, p. 164; Latimer quoted in Fletcher, p. 2. On prescriptions against anything other than passive resistance, see Sommerville, pp. 34–39; he notes that James I advised Parliament in 1610 that only prayers and tears could be used in connection with a sovereign.

68. I distinguish this action from the set speeches of the allegorical figures that frame the play.

69. The most influential reading of *Two Lamentable Tragedies* holds that it was "apparently intended to be a sermon cast in dramatic form" (Adams, p. 108; see also p. 186). For a review of the criticism, see Patenaude, cited in note 49.

officer at Rachel's execution hopes that the "spectacle" of her death will teach others to avoid "her misguided taciturnity" (sig. K2ᵛ), the play's allegorical framing figures judge her less severely as her brother's victim, even as Allenso is a martyr to his father.⁷⁰ As Homicide and Truth suggest, Rachel's dilemma was more likely to have occasioned some sympathy than was that of the adulteress Anne Sanders, and, finally, any sympathy for her dilemma subverts the play's conventional moral. Order in the macrocosm—civic order—is here shown, radically enough, to depend on the very betrayal of degree in the microcosm—household hierarchy. The text's eventual advocacy of resistance on the domestic level in the interest of obedience on the political level renders the traditional interdependence of the public and private spheres uneasy.

1 and 2 Edward IV

The scope of action in both *A Warning for Fair Women* and *Two Lamentable Tragedies* is pointedly enlarged beyond the immediate. In *Warning*, the roster of those who are affected by Anne Sanders's crime is carefully iterated as she begs pardon of God, of her children, of her husband, of his kindred, of her kindred, of her friends, and "of all men and women in the world, / Whom by my foul example I have griev'd" (21.2679–80). The allegorical figures of the induction and dumb shows, Tragedy, Comedy, History, Chastity, Lust, and Murder, suggest a further reach for general significance.⁷¹ In *Tragedies*, Merry is similarly held responsible for the deaths of Beech, Winchester, and Rachel, the disgrace of his family, and the dissolution of his household; Fallerio, for the death of his nephew, his wife, and his son, and for the "Blot and confusion of his family" (sig. I2ᵛ). Such allegorical figures as Truth, Homicide, and Avarice again embellish the action, and Truth voices the concern of "Eliza, Prince of piety" for peace and the prevention of murder in her kingdom (sig. K3ʳ).

In Thomas Heywood's two-part *Edward IV*, by contrast, such overt reminders of the symbiosis of private and public orders are unnecessary. While in the other plays the political world is present only by

70. Homicide anticipates how "father, son; and sister, brother may / Bring to their deaths with most assur'd decay," and Truth concludes that "The father, son; the sister, brother brings, / To open scandal, and contemptuous death" (sigs. F3ᵛ and K3ʳ).
71. Cannon emends the quarto character name of "Murder" in "*Murder sets down her blood, and rubs their hands*" to "Tragedy." I take Tragedy's statement "Here enters *Murder* into all their hearts" as an implied stage direction and prefer the original reading, thus adding to Cannon's cast list.

analogy to the domestic or by implication in the representations of civic justice, in *Edward IV* it coexists. The characters are choreographed in continuous movement between the two spheres, as indicated most simply, perhaps, by the king's visits to Hobs's cottage, to Crosby's house, and to Matthew Shore's shop, and by Shore's assistance in the suppression of rebellion, his trespass in the peace negotiated between England and France, and his presence in the Tower at the time of the English princes' murder. In this, *Edward IV* joins the two dramatic traditions of (political) chronicle and domestic tragedy under a single conceptual umbrella.

Issues and imagery that typically characterize each sphere are accordingly collapsed rather than differentiated. For example, the rebel Falconbridge's treasonous assault on London is repeatedly figured in terms of sexual conquest, and his followers think of the city's women as their plunder. Falconbridge himself promises to reward the first man to enter the gates of the city with London's "chiefest" wench—but reserves to his own use Jane Shore: "Shore, listen: thy wife is mine, that's flat. / This night, in thine own house, she sleeps with me" (p. 16). Had Falconbridge prevailed, Shore later muses (ironically, as it develops, and as members of Heywood's audience would have been aware), "where then had been our lives? / Dishonor'd our daughters, ravish'd our fair wives" (p. 23).

Meanwhile, Edward's seduction of Jane is reciprocally developed in terms of her besiegement. Jane describes how he "with a violent siege / Labors to break into my plighted faith"; how he visits, writes, gives her gifts, "all to win me to his princely will" (p. 73); and how:

> I must confess, I yielded up the fort,
> Wherein lay all the riches of my joy;
> But yet, sweet Shore, before I yielded it,
> I did endure the long'st and greatest siege
> That ever batter'd on poor chastity.
> And but to him that did assault the same,
> For ever it had been invincible.
>
> (p. 84)

Even Edward's queen acknowledges: "What fort is so strong, / But, with besieging, he will batter it?" (p. 129). The language that links the rebels' assault on London to the king's assault on Jane will eventually relate both to a third action, the king's invasion of France. Edward is presented as laying claim to Jane Shore as he does to London—an association underscored by her identification as "the flow'r of London"

(p. 16)—and to France—a parallel suggested by his desire for "A woman's aid, that hath more power than France / To crown us or to kill us with mischance" (p. 61). He is also to ask himself of her, "Lives there a king that would not give his crown / To purchase such a kingdom of content?" (p. 65).

These traditional topoi of the desired woman as a kingdom and of her seduction as an assault are extended by other correlative images. As Edward confronts internal rebellion in England, so he represents his infatuation for Jane as an insurgent attraction: "Down rebel," he says to himself; "back, base treacherous conceit" (p. 60). As the rebels are depicted in their attempt to invade London, so Edward is shown invading Shore's shop to press his suit with Shore's wife, "intrud[ing]" he says, "like an unbidden guest" (p. 75). As Falconbridge is executed for treason, so the enamored Edward chides himself, "What, and thou traitor heart, / Would'st thou shake hands in this conspiracy?" (p. 60). Finally, as members of Falconbridge's rabble cry, "the law is in our hands" (p. 9) and "we will be kings tonight" (p. 30), and as Falconbridge is described in his assault on the gates of London as "Commanding entrance as he were a king" (p. 15), so Edward inversely elects to dethrone himself: "it is the King / Comes muffled like a common serving-man" or like "a chapman, as it seems" (pp. 77, 65), to Shore's shop. When Jane discovers her suitor's true identity, she laments that he woos her "in most humble terms": "Oh, what am I, he should so much forget / His royal state and his high majesty?" (p. 73). Edward marvels to her: "How for thy sake is majesty disrobed! / Riches made poor and dignity brought low" (p. 75).

For Jane Shore, however, the distinction between private and public is acute. As a subject in both domestic and political spheres, she faces an apparently irreconcilable dilemma when domestic and political authorities conflict, and she articulates this dilemma more clearly than either Anne Sanders or Rachel Merry do their predicaments. When the king reveals himself to her in her shop, she kneels: "Whatever we possess is all your highness'; / Only mine honor, which I cannot grant"—because it is not hers to grant. Shore enters as she continues, "But here comes one to whom I only gave it; / And he, I doubt, will say you shall not have it" (p. 66). Torn between her duty to her husband and her duty to her king, Jane consults a friend and neighbor, Mistress Blague, who offers little reassurance and no simple solution.

> Believe me, Mistress Shore, a dangerous case;
> And every way replete with doubtful fear.
> If you should yield, your virtuous name were soil'd,
> And your beloved husband made a scorn;

> And if not yield, 'tis likely that his love,
> Which now admires ye, will convert to hate;
> And who knows not a prince's hate is death?
>
> (p. 73)

Mistress Blague, in her lust for status, wealth, power, and glory, high-lights Jane's lack of interest in such vanities, as did Anne Drury with Anne Sanders.[72] No disenchantment with her husband muddies Jane's motivation, however; her professions of love for him precede and succeed her enforcement by Edward.

Jane's demonstrated modesty of ambition and depth of affection only intensify her ethical dilemma, as, for example, she anguishes: "Oh, that I knew which were the best of twain, / Which for I do not, I am sick with pain" (p. 75).[73] When, in explaining his unseemly disguise, Edward addresses her as the lunar goddess, she invokes both the patriarchal and moral authorities that argue against her submission to him.

> King: The want of thee, fair Cynthia, is the cause.
> Spread thou thy silver brightness in the air,
> And straight the gladsome morning will appear.
> Jane: I may not wander. He that guides my car
> Is an immoved, constant, fixed Star.
> King: But I will give that Star a Comet's name,
> And shield both thee and him from further blame.
> Jane: How if the Host of Heaven at this abuse
> Repine? Who can the prodigy excuse?
>
> (pp. 75–76)

Edward dismisses the domestic authority, her husband, whom he can "shield" with preferment. But in response to her most potent argument, her appeal to the moral authority of "the Host of Heaven," Edward abandons their extended metaphor of the cosmos for the imagery of monarchy and drops the disguise of humility to affirm his sovereign identity:

> It lies within the compass of my power,
> To dim their envious eyes, dare seem to lour.

72. Earlier, when Shore had refused Edward's offer of a knighthood, Edward had remarked to Jane, "you had been a lady but for him"; then, too, Jane had protested her lack of ambition (pp. 59–60).

73. Compare Adams: Jane "is represented not as a creature of lust or pleasure, but as one caught by forces beyond her control" (p. 90). While Irving Ribner (*English History Play* [1957], p. 275) and Johnson (p. 64) agree, see Mowbray Velte (1922) for a contrary view (p. 30).

> But leaving this our enigmatic talk,
> Thou must, sweet Jane, repair unto the court.
> His tongue entreats, controls the greatest peer;
> His hand plights love, a royal sceptre holds;
> And in his heart he hath confirm'd thy good,
> Which may not, must not, shall not be withstood.
>
> (p. 76)

Edward, in other words, details his royal power and then announces that he expresses the royal will in this matter. Jane is thus made to understand that she has no right of resistance. She concedes: "If you enforce me, I have nought to say; / But wish I had not lived to see this day."

Throughout both parts of *Edward IV*, Jane perceives his conquest as her sin, and the intensity of her remorse is frequently emphasized. Her humility survives the temptations of perquisites and power to which her concubinage expose her, and her political incorruptibility compounds the sympathetic slant on her reluctant sexual corruption. When she exploits her influence over the king, it is only in order to do good works, even though "all the coals of my poor charity / Cannot consume the scandal of my name" (p. 121). Through her many acts of beneficence, Jane Shore assumes her public identity as a second queen and a dispenser of justice and mercy. Those who are jealous of her power and popularity include Richard, Duke of Gloucester; when Edward dies, she has no protection from Richard. At the new king's command her sustained private repentance is made public.

While Jane accepts every humiliation as just, she will not countenance the epithet of the "king's enemy," applied by Mistress Blague in consequence of Richard's opposition. Jane returns fiercely:

> When was it ever seen Jane Shore was false
> Either unto her country or her king?
> And therefore 'tis not well, good mistress Blague,
> That you upbraid me with a traitor's name.
>
> (pp. 159–60)

Jane's deference to royal authority has, after all, overridden her other duties and affections. There is fellow feeling in her forgiveness of those who enforce her penitence: "I know the King's edict / Set you a work—and not your own desires" (p. 165). In language reminiscent of Anne Sanders's "I must confess against my will" and Rachel's "Ah, did not nature oversway my will," Jane explains, "Against my will I wrong" Edward's queen (p. 123).

The edict of Edward often seems a harsh and arbitrary thing. This king is characterized by absences, omissions, trivial pursuits, and socially transgressive affections. The *First Part* opens with his widely condemned marriage to a widow. His determination to spend a night of crisis in "feast and jollity" allows Falconbridge to needle the Londoners who must fight without their "ling'ring" king (pp. 8, 27). He recuses himself from a politic feast at the house of Sir Humphrey Bowes in order instead to amuse himself with a visit to the cottage of Hobs the tanner. He effects a tear in the social fabric of his kingdom by intruding in Matthew Shore's proper (petty) commonwealth and by abducting Shore's wife. He occasions Frances Emersley's "wonder" that amid the serious preparations against France he can be "spared" to the pursuit of Jane Shore rather than of national honor (p. 78).[74]

That Edward is finally proved unnecessary to the defense of London and that he self-evidently *can* be spared in advance of the siege of France threatens not only to displace him but also to disable the kingship. These defaults are personalized and exaggerated through his interactions with Matthew Shore. The appropriation of Shore's wife is figured as a violation of the quasi-feudal obligation of a lord to a man who has offered his own life up to protect that of the lord and his possessions. When Shore refuses the offer of a knighthood for his defense of London, Edward promises some other "quittance," a promise Shore remembers later with grim irony: "And, Edward, for requiting me so well, / But dare I speak of him? Forbear, forbear" (pp. 33, 79).

This is an unusual lapse in Shore's otherwise unyieldingly loyalist posture. If Shore's mistreatment puts the hegemonic paradigm to its most extreme test, his response to it also embodies the fierce struggle of the text to recuperate its monarchic and patriarchal meanings. The moral paradigm of *1 and 2 Edward IV* differs from that of *A Warning for Fair Women* and *Two Lamentable Tragedies* in a critical respect. In *Warning* the household patriarch is inattentive, erring, and then, in consequence of his murder, absent. In *Tragedies* the head of household is the instigator of transgression. In neither is there a compensatory characterologic center of moral authority. The ethical lacunae seem to require the allegorical figures "who" establish ethical frameworks of arguable rigor. In *Edward IV*, by contrast, Shore serves as the moral arbiter of the play.[75]

---

74. Laura Caroline Stevenson emphasizes Edward's unprincely behavior (*Praise and Paradox* [1984], pp. 204–5).

75. On Shore's moral authority, see, for example, his refusal of a knighthood following the defense of London (he knows and is content with his place), his recognition of the king in disguise (whereas the watermen and Hobs are deceived), and his understanding that Edward

"What have subjects that is not their king's?" he observes most notably; "I'll not examine his prerogative" (p. 85).[76] He recognizes that the
king's "greatness may gild over ugly sin" (p. 77). He states that "Where
kings are meddlers, meaner men must rue. / I storm against it? No" (p.
78). And he refuses Jane's request to return to him: "No, Jane, there is
no place allowed for me, / Where once a king has ta'en possession";
"Thou go with me, Jane? Oh God forbid / That I should be a traitor to
my King!" (pp. 84–85). Finally, he moots the possibility of his own
chastisement: "Ah, Matthew Shore, how doth all-seeing Heaven / Punish some sin from thy blind conscience hid!" (p. 125). Shore defies only
Richard, and then only once, to offer Jane assistance in her
banishment.[77]

Edward IV argues for a loyalty that, while not easy, is necessary. The
text may fall short of its agenda, but that agenda is clear: the king's
political authority is enhanced by its ability to render personal failings
insignificant, the subject's obligation to defer made stricter by its un-
palatability. Distrust of individual conscience is again at issue: "What
shall subjects do then? Shall they obey valiant, stout, wise, and good
princes, and condemn, disobey, and rebel against children being their
princes or against indiscreet and evil governors? God forbid: For first
what a perilous thing were it to commit unto the subjects the judgment
which prince is wise and godly, and his government good, and which is
otherwise: as though the foot must judge of the head, an enterprise
very heinous."[78] Edward's transgressions are put into perspective by
the succession of Richard III, as Heywood's spokesman Matthew Shore
earlier anticipated: "God bless [this] King, a worse may wear the crown"
(p. 142).

As William Westerman wrote in his 1600 *Prohibition of Revenge*, "Private men have no further plea but complaints to their superiors or tears
and prayers to the Lord."[79] Shore, of course, cannot complain to his
superior of his superior, and so all recourse is denied him. His com-
pulsory deference initiates the ruin of his private life: he closes his

---

may be succeeded by a worse king (as is borne out when Richard III takes the throne). The
moral chorus includes Crosby, the Lord Mayor of London, who is grieved by his niece's "dispos-
sessment" but dares not voice objection (p. 81; see also p. 63). Even the Queen concludes: "Oh
God forbid that Edward's queen should hate / Her, whom she knows he doth so dearly love" (p.
129).

76. Compare Barnaby Rich, *Faults, Faults* (1606): "what subject (that knoweth his duty) dare
speak against a prince's prerogative?" (sig. Q4ʳ).

77. Shore's "And so persuaded, I myself will do / That which both love and nature binds me
to" (p. 174) establishes that this play, too, refers to the natural-law tradition.

78. From the "Homily against Disobedience and Willful Rebellion," *Certain Sermons*, ed.
Rickey and Stroup, p. 279.

79. William Westerman, *Prohibition of Revenge* (1600), sig. C8ᵛ.

goldsmith's shop and dissolves the society of his household, transfers his lands and goods to Jane's brother, changes his name, and expatriates. Besides being deprived of his wife, in other words, he is deposed from his domestic throne, disenfranchised, and displaced. He endures assault but has no privilege of defense. The interest of the king rudely enforces Shore's subordination.

The person of Matthew Shore thus embodies the limits of analogy. He may, as the *First Part* opens, be a king in the commonwealth of his own house, but he cannot exert authority in any larger setting. In *1 and 2 Edward IV*, the domestic and political spheres are, through shared imagery, actions, and issues, conflated as if into coincidence. But then they are exploded into two separate worlds again. The result of this dramatization of the breakdown of the system of analogy is an assertion of the necessary priority of royal absolutism, here expressed in the emblematic terms of royal power over a female body.

Political Patriarchalism

To return now to the primary analogies upon which early modern English society constructed itself is to recognize the extent to which those analogies were cast as similes rather than metaphors. Dod and Cleaver's well-known formula, "a household is *as it were* a little commonwealth," finds many echoes: Thomas Watts's "every well ordered and true Christian family ought to *represent the form and similitude*, as well of the commonweal as also in special of the Church"; Perkins's statement that the householder "exerciseth (*after a sort*) a power tyrannical over his servants. . . . he is, *as it were*, the prince and chief ruler"; Hooker's "all men have ever *been taken as* lords and lawful kings in their own houses"; and William Gouge's declaration that the husband "is *as* a king in his own house," one who "*resembleth* not only the head of a natural body, but also the glorious *image of* Christ" (emphases added). Analogy's blurrings of distinction were in fact incompletely accomplished, the differences between tenor and vehicle unable to disguise themselves. As Gouge spelled out, "there may be a resemblance where there is no parity, and a likeness where there is no equality."[80]

If at first English political theorists did not know how to conceptualize fully the distinction between public and private, if they were unwilling to articulate that distinction and jeopardize a synthetic world view,

---

80. Dod and Cleaver, sig. B1ʳ; Watts, sig. B1ʳ; Perkins, pp. 428 and 439; Hooker, vol. 1, p. 99; William Gouge, *Of Domestical Duties* (1622), sigs. S1ᵛ and Z4ᵛ.

increasingly they accepted the hierarchy of the two spheres. The household was relegated to its lesser position as one of many commonwealths comprehended by that of the state. Aristotle again anticipated this perspective: "We may now proceed to add that [though the individual and the family are prior in the order of time] the polis is prior in the order of nature to the family and the individual." A 1598 commentator on the *Politics* observed that Aristotle "findeth fault with such as confound the public and private governments together." And Thomas Smith much earlier argued from Aristotle that "in the house and family is the first and most natural (but a private) appearance of one of the best kinds of a commonwealth, that is called *Aristocratia*. . . . Marry, they cannot be called *Aristocratia*, but *Metaphorice*, for it is but an house, and a little spark as it were like to that government."[81]

One element of patriarchalism that survived undiminished by this hierarchization, notably, was the father's authority in his household. Dod and Cleaver insisted that "the husband without any exception is master over all the house, and hath as touching his family more authority than a king in his kingdom." The absolutist Jean Bodin identified the father as "the power private" or "domestical" and added that "natural liberty is such, as for a man next unto God not to be subject to any man living, neither to suffer the command of any other than of himself; that is to say, of reason, which is always conformable unto the will of God."[82]

As is first hinted in a work that he published in Edinburgh in 1598, *The Trew Law of Free Monarchies*, Elizabeth's successor was to champion his divine right, in part by claiming a patriarchal authority over all his people.[83] When the crown was inspired to absorb to itself not only the familial analogy for the commonwealth but also patriarchal obligation to the king, it succeeded in wedding the unchallenged authority of the father to the acknowledged preeminence of the kingdom and thus in generating a new justification for royal absolutism. Bilson had all but the most critical piece in place in 1585: "If private men be bound to train up their families in the fear of God and love of virtue, much more are princes (the public fathers of their countries and exalted to far

81. Aristotle, *Politics*, trans. Barker, p. 6; I.D., in *Aristotle's Politics* (1598), sig. C6ʳ; Thomas Smith, p. 59.
82. Dod and Cleaver, sig. M8ʳ; Jean Bodin, *Six Bookes of a Commonweale* (1576; English translation, 1606), sig. C1ᵛ.
83. In *Trew Law*, James argued, for example, that "if the children may upon any pretext that can be imagined lawfully rise up against their Father, cut him off, and choose any other whom they please in his room; and if the body for the weal of it may for any infirmity that can be in the head, strike it off, then I cannot deny that the people may rebel, control, and displace, or cut off their king at their own pleasure, and upon respects moving them" (pp. 65–66).

greater and higher authority by God's ordinance than fathers or masters)."[84] But where Bilson turned his argument to the responsibility of the king, James was to turn similar understandings to responsibility *to* the king. Almost without exception the comparison of the king to a father had been expressed in the request of a subject that the king undertake a fatherly charge or in an assurance by the crown that it would show a parental care; now, members of the populace were enjoined to honor the king as each should his own father.

Especially radical was a thesis that James developed by subverting the commonplace that "Love goeth downward: duty cometh upward." Gataker, the author in this instance, intended the prescription that the husband should be loving to his wife and the wife dutiful to her husband. James, however, argued that "although we see by the course of nature, that love useth to descend more than to ascend, in case it were true, that the father hated and wronged the children never so much, will any man, endued with the least spunk of reason, think it lawful for them to meet him with the line? Yea, suppose the father were furiously following his sons with a drawn sword, is it lawful for them to turn and strike again, or make any resistance but by flight?" By then applying this example to the public sphere, James argued that even if the king neglected his fatherly love, the people were nonetheless obliged to continue their filial duty to him. He also relentlessly promoted the dissemination of Richard Mocket's 1615 *God and the King*, which concluded that "there is a stronger and higher bond of duty between children and the father of their country, than the fathers of private families."[85] James perhaps intuited Clifford Geertz's understanding that "the function of ideology is to make an autonomous politics possible by providing the authoritative concepts that render it meaningful, the suasive images by means of which it can be sensibly grasped,"[86] and he found universally suasive images in the father and the household.

In his classic study of patriarchal philosophy, Gordon J. Schochet suggests that this "intentional assertion of political patriarchalism must finally be understood as the bringing to the level of consciousness of a series of related attitudes and assumptions that had previously been implicitly held and imperfectly understood. These notions had not really been challenged before and therefore had not been fully articulated." In other words, the theory of political patriarchalism *could* not have developed fully without the basis that was provided, in earlier

84. Bilson, sig. S5r.
85. Gataker, sig. B3r; James, p. 65. Mocket, quoted by Amussen, *Ordered Society*, pp. 55–56.
86. Clifford Geertz, "Ideology as a Cultural System" in *Interpretation of Cultures* (1973), p. 218.

years, in arguments about the familial model for the origin of government and about the role of the individual household in social order;
necessarily, the theories had antecedent, if incomplete, expression.[87]
But theories of political patriarchalism *would* not have developed—that
is, articulation would not have been required—without challenges to
the assumptions generated by the habit of analogical thought, challenges such as those expressed in the plays I have discussed.

Based on historic events and contemporary crimes, the plays offer
prima facie evidence that Renaissance ideas of political order were
vulnerable to experience as well as to their own philosophical irresolutions and contradictions. And political ideology was further sub-
verted in these texts by its translation from the rarified construct of
philosophical literature and prescriptive tracts to the multidimensional
context of lives and actions in dramatic representation. Rooted in the
daily operations of a merchant's household (*Warning*), a tavern (*Tragedies*), and a goldsmith's shop (*Edward*), these plays help us to apprehend, for example, the contradictions inherent in the woman's submissive and supervisory roles and how they originated in a clash of political
ideology and economic necessity.

The early modern household was a unit of production and con-
sumption as well as a locus of order and socialization; as Aristotle
recognized, "governance of household intendeth to have riches." The
wife was essential to this economic function—as is Anne Sanders, see-
ing to the feeding and provisioning of her household, protecting the
credit of her house; as is wife-surrogate Rachel, upon whom Merry, so
proud of the good governance of his tavern, depends; and as is especially Jane Shore, making "huswifery to shine" for her uncle, oversee-
ing her husband's workmen in his absence, and performing functions
so essential that with her removal Shore must dissolve both his shop
and house, incapable of maintaining them alone. So, an anonymous
pamphleteer wrote not only that "some matters of less weight are left to
the good discretion of those of the family" but also that "neither is it
otherwise possible to be."[88]

---

87. Schochet, pp. 56–57. For the use of the familial analogy, see also Gardiner, above. For a
significant anticipation of political patriarchalism, see Cheke: "If the servant be bound to obey
his master in the family, is not the subject bound to serve the king in his realm? The child is
bound to the private father, and be we not all bound to the common wealth's father? . . . If the
members of our natural body all follow the head, shall not the members of the political body all
obey the king?" (sigs. C1ᵛ–C2ʳ).

88. Aristotle, *Ethics*, trans. Wylkinson (1547), sig. A3ᵛ; *Remonstrance* (1590), sig. C1ʳ. The
oeconomic manuals did recognize the economic function of the house, although its incompatibility with political theory was not acknowledged and the issue of the competing domestic
governance of husband and wife was not recognized. See, for example, Tilney: "The office of
the husband is to bring in necessaries; of the wife, well to keep them. The office of the husband

In *A Warning for Fair Women, Two Lamentable Tragedies,* and *1 and 2 Edward IV,* we discover hints of the obsolescence to which patriarchalism would succumb, an obsolescence predicted by Geertz for cultural models "too comprehensive or too concrete to provide the sort of guidance such a political system demands." In its timid attempts at concreteness in the gendered division of household responsibilities, prescription revealed the inability of its theory of governance fully to admit the segmentation of authority as an economic necessity. And even as the theory integrated political obligation into its framework and thus realized comprehensiveness, it initiated the disintegration of the analogy between domestic and political that had been so striking a feature of its articulation and so compelling an element of its appeal. In other words, such philosophical synthesis as patriarchalism achieved (as in, for example, Robert Filmer's *Patriarcha*) was fleeting.

As Geertz argues, "whatever else ideologies may be—projections of unacknowledged fears, disguises for ulterior' motives, phatic expressions of group solidarity—they are, most distinctively, maps of problematic social reality and matrices for the creation of collective conscience."[89] *A Warning for Fair Women, Two Lamentable Tragedies,* and *1 and 2 Edward IV* diverged, as literature will, from the "actual" experiences of Anne Sanders, Rachel Merry, and Jane Shore. But they fairly reveal the experience of a culture grappling with a problematic social reality, and, through the experience of everyone who attended their performance or read their scripts, they played their part in the creation of the post-Reformation collective consciousness.

Admittedly, the plays balance subversion with orthodoxy: their conclusions, in the suffering, repentance, and just deaths of Anne Sanders, Rachel Merry, and Jane Shore, are far from heterodox. But their representations of the choices made by these women are complicated by the ethical double jeopardy each faces and the sympathy each may inspire. The text that has left the clearest trace of its conflict is Heywood's, and not only in the internal form of its overstrenuous apologist, Matthew Shore. In his defense of the theater, *An Apology for Actors,* Heywood later insisted that his purpose was that of the moral exemplum: "Women likewise that are chaste, are by us extolled and encouraged in their virtues, being instanced by Diana, Belphoebe,

---

is to go abroad in matters of profit; of the wife, to tarry at home and see all be well there. The office of the husband is to provide money; of the wife, not wastefully to spend it. . . . the office of the husband is to maintain well his livelihood, and the office of the woman is to govern well the household" (sig. C4ᵛ). Dod and Cleaver warned against "diversity, between the man and his wife" because it is "dangerous to thrift" (sig. G2ᵛ).

89. Geertz, pp. 219 and 220.

Matilda, Lucrece, and the Countess of Salisbury. The unchaste are by us showed their errors, in the persons of Phrine, Lais, Thais, Flora, and, amongst us, Rosamond and Mistress Shore."[90] But some members of the original audiences of *Edward IV* were less convinced of the "errors."

Instead they empathized with the reluctant adulteress Jane Shore. A fictional Richard III registers the fact in Christopher Brooke's stage play of 1614, *The Ghost of Richard III*:

> And what a piece of justice did I show
> On Mistress Shore? When (with a feigned hate
> To unchaste life) I forced her to go
> Barefoot, on penance, with dejected state?
> But now her fame by a vild play doth grow:
> Whose fate, the women so commiserate,
> That who (to see my justice on that sinner)
> Drinks not her tears, and makes her fast, their dinner?[91]

In *A Warning for Fair Women, Two Lamentable Tragedies*, and *1 and 2 Edward IV*, the troubled dialogue of rule and order has been internalized so that if there is a conventional moral, it is merely a last word, not an uncontested one.[92] In this the plays both participate in the evolution of early modern ideology and demonstrate that that ideology was not a fixed construct but a vexed process.

90. Thomas Heywood, *Apology for Actors* (1612), sig. G1ᵛ.
91. Excerpted by Arthur Melville Clark, *Thomas Heywood* (1931), p. 16.
92. Jonathan Dollimore has suggested that what Tudor audiences may have carried away from plays was not necessarily—or only—their endings, however tidy or moral (in discussion during an N.E.H. Summer Institute at the Folger Shakespeare Library, 1988).

Patriarchalism in Practice

On the face of it, prescriptive literatures and playtexts can seem an unpromising source of information about private life—if, that is, one imagines that one can recover private life as it was "really" conducted. To that other end, investigation can profitably be undertaken in diaries, personal correspondence, household accounts, parish registers, wills, inventories, and the records of ecclesiastical courts. But, to globalize the paradigm proposed in the first chapter, my overriding interest is how private life was constructed. I attempt an account that does not restrict private matters to the discipline of social history but that integrates them into and exploits the broader resources of cultural history.

Although it goes without saying that private life was not led according to the tenets of prescriptive literature or as dramatized in playtexts, it may nonetheless be to the purpose to inquire after any evidence that the precepts of ideological writing, in particular, were known outside their immediate genre—by those, say, who figure elsewhere in diaries, letters, and court cases. The question is whether some of those who violated prescriptive formulas knew that they were doing so, whether their lives were shaped or constrained by the ideology that has survived to us in printed literatures. The five instances rehearsed below demonstrate that this was not so esoteric a discourse that its doctrines did not circulate widely and impinge on private lives.[1]

---

1. *A Warning for Fair Women* offers some evidence that prescriptive literatures had cultural currency. In the last scene, Anne Sanders gives each of her children "a book / Of holy meditations" identified as "Bradford's works, / That virtuous chosen servant of the Lord" (21.2699–2710). *A Warning* expects its public-theater audience to recognize the name of a Protestant

Seventeenth-century lathe worker Nehemiah Wallington serves as exhibit number one. The personal papers of this literate and prolific artisan—be it noted, not a clergyman and not a gentleman—reveal that he knew the names of John Dod and William Perkins, for example. And, in the fifty-odd notebooks he compiled, incorporating auto-biographical reflection, contemporary observation, treatises, sermons, and letters, he not only produced original material but also transcribed from "above two hundred other books" he claims to have read in addition to the Bible. Of particular interest is the fact that, within a year of his marriage in 1621, Wallington had purchased William Gouge's massive and authoritative *Of Domestical Duties* in its first edition of 1622. Wallington's papers record that he did so because he felt "the charge of so many souls." As suggested in the previous chapter and as discussed in more detail in the next, marriage initiated a household, with the householder in charge of various subordinate communities, including the wife, the children, and the servants. In sober acceptance of convention, Wallington took Gouge as his guide "so everyone of us may learn and know our duties and honor God, every one in his place where God has set them."[2]

As Wallington's chronicler Paul S. Seaver has demonstrated, Wallington also copied into his notebooks letters from and to one James Cole, a tradesman and friend who is introduced here as exhibit number two. Cole fled London and his household responsibilities in the face of serious debt in 1634. In a letter to his wife, Cole asked her to take over his proper duties of religious instruction, to "catechize my children and nurture them in the fear of the Lord." He also requested the children and servants to accept his wife, in his absence, as their "governess." Wallington faithfully recorded the flood of reproaches that pursued Cole—from Cole's father, Cole's father-in-law, and Wallington's father. He himself subjected Cole to an epistolary roster of consequence reminiscent of those of *A Warning for Fair Women* and *Two Lamentable Tragedies*: "And how have you been a stumbling block to the weak! Oh, how have you grieved the hearts of your wife, your parents, and the rest of your loving friends. Oh how you have made the hearts of the righteous sad. . . . how have you given the Enemy cause to rejoice and triumph, and the name of God, your good God, to be dishonored by the wicked." Meanwhile, Wallington's father wrote in specific recall of the house-

---

martyr who was burned at the stake in 1555. John Bradford's *Godly Meditations upon the Lord's Prayer, the Belief, and Ten Commandments* were written while he was in prison, published posthumously in 1562, and reprinted several times through the early seventeenth century.

2. From Paul S. Seaver, *Wallington's World* (1985). On Wallington's papers, see pp. 1–13; on his reading, p. 5; on Gouge, p. 79.

holder's duty for the souls of his household, requiring Cole to return to London to "dwell with [his wife] as a man of knowledge and instruct her and your children in the ways of God, and appoint their work which are now all of them in a mournful maze and know not what to do till you come that should direct them all."[3] The head of the family, as Henry Smith wrote, "hath all the offices of Christ."

Cole's flight from responsibility acquires deeper resonance in my fourth chapter, which addresses a dawning suspicion that patriarchal authority was oppressive for the patriarch. For now, Cole may be viewed in the contexts provided by Ardern in his domestic mismanagement and by the hapless husband of the Montacute Skimmington Ride. With regard to derelictions of authority, Dod and Cleaver insist that if the wife errs, "it is for the most part through the fault, and want of discretion, and lack of good government in the husband." This sentiment carried legal weight, as appears from exhibit number three, the travel diary of a visitor to England in 1602. Philip Julius, Duke of Stettin-Pomerania, observed of judicial practice in Kent that "if the husband is an unfriendly or obstinate fellow, he is condemned to pay a fine in money; if, however, the mischief is on the wife's side, the husband is likewise punished for not having been able to keep up his authority." John R. Gillis has noted a court decision that follows this principle: a husband was fined for his wife's scandalous speech, "as a warning for husbands to keep their wives in check."[4]

Court practice also produces my fourth exhibit. In 1574 an Essex man was presented "for turning away his wife, saying that she [was] not his wife." This was a violation of his responsibility to cohabit with his spouse as well as to provide for her. His defense echoed the terms introduced in Arden of Feversham and repeated in William Thomas's characterization of the "two repugnant desires" to govern and to resist governance: the Essex husband declared that he had evicted his wife "for that she would not be ruled."[5] Not only did the accused expect his wife to understand her ideologically mandated subjection to him, he also expected her transgression to justify and excuse his own. Again, whether or not the woman actually transgressed is not at issue; what is, is that the doctrine and language of male rule was in circulation as a cultural convention. The habit of mind that conflates the role with the

3. Seaver, pp. 96–97.
4. Dod and Cleaver, sig. L6r. Philip Julius, "Diary" (1602), p. 65. John R. Gillis quotes Julius and the legal decision in For Better, For Worse (1985), pp. 76–77.
5. Frederick George Emmison, Elizabethan Life: Morals (1973), pp. 161–62. See also the 1589 case of William Markes, charged for "living asunder from his wife." He said that she was "a woman many times besides herself and will not be ruled, that he hath procured her to come to him, and after the same in her madness hath departed from him without cause" (p. 163).

proper execution of its responsibilities—if she will not be ruled, then she is no wife—accords with my reading of Whetstone's "every man's household, well governed, resembleth a commonwealth"—if it is not well governed, then the house is no commonwealth.

My final exhibit is the most self-aware, not only current in the language of prescriptive literature but also sensible of its internal contradictions and, moreover, able to exploit both to rhetorical effect. In 1702 Cassandra Willoughby compiled a history of her ancestors "taken out of the pedigree, old letters, and old books of accounts in my brother Sir Thomas Willoughby's study."[6] She included a report of dissension between Sir Francis Willoughby and Elizabeth Littleton; the two had married in 1564.

> After they had supper at Kingsbury Sir Francis Willoughby sent to his Lady (who had before refused to come to supper) to require her to speak with him; she sent word that she would speak with them in the gallery, where they all went. What Sir Francis said at first going into the gallery was not heard by the company, but his Lady answer'd in great choler, "I will blaze your arms and make you better known." Sir Francis pressed her to be reconciled to his sister, which she refused. He then asked her if in all other things she would be ruled by him. Upon which she answered she would not be ruled by him. Upon which Sir Fulke Greville said, "Why, madam, will you refuse to be ruled by your husband?"

So far, the account does little more than confirm, unremarkably, that the language of domestic rule was as proverbial as the presentment in Essex would suggest. But Elizabeth Littleton's subsequent retort to Greville specifically evokes the sort of conflict that I have argued was articulated for Jane Shore in *1 and 2 Edward IV*: "She answer'd she was the Queen's sworn servant and knew not but Sir Francis might command her something against Her Majesty's proceedings."

As I have hinted, it would probably be a mistake to burden Elizabeth's sharp return in this instance with any significance much greater than that of her evident rhetorical dexterity. But her challenge to her husband's rule was finally a matter of substance. Relations between the two deteriorated until Sir Francis, complaining of "her disorderly life, her watching late contrary to his liking, her keeping such company as he did mislike . . . her reviling him to his face. . . . her running out of the house and raising the town," ordered Elizabeth's house arrest. At that he gave her the freedom of only certain rooms within the house.

6. Cassandra Willoughby (1702), excerpted in Alice T. Friedman, *House and Household* (1989); see pp. 1–3 and 61–64.

He abrogated her authority over the household servants and, further, mandated the inversion of hierarchy that Anne Sanders had found so onerous, ordering her to submit to the commands of two of his men. He stripped her of all the duties that Dod and Cleaver (among others) would have argued were "belonging to her": he refused her any rights in caring for her children, prohibited her access to the household goods and linens, forbade her the funds to make household purchases, and allowed her "no authority to command anything in the house except necessary diet for herself."

Elizabeth was of sufficient status to seek financial and moral support outside her own home. In 1579 her father made her an allowance so that she could have some income independent of Sir Francis. In 1582 Elizabeth I commanded Sir Francis to provide his wife with separate maintenance in the amount of £200 per year. The estranged wife also solicited Burghley; this time she received in return merely advice. The response from Burghley's secretary, Sir Michael Hicks, demonstrates yet again the contemporary currency of prescriptive platitudes:

> according to the ordinance of God and the covenants of your marriage, you [must] endeavor to subdue and submit your will to the pleasure of your head, in all honest and lawful things seeking rather to win his good will with covering his faults and bearing with his infirmities, than to wrest him to your own, by revealing his shame and resisting his command- ments . . . the which although it may seem hard to flesh and blood, yet is it warranted by the word of God, which binds all women of what birth or calling soever they be, to yield due benevolence and obedience to their husbands.

In April 1588, after a separation of eight years, the couple recon- ciled. According to Alice T. Friedman, the cause may have had every- thing to do with the structure and maintenance of an ordered private life and nothing to do with affect.[7] In 1587 their daughter had mar- ried. Sir Francis had been forced to vacate his normal responsibility to host the wedding feast at his house, "because by reason of his wife's absence and the furniture of his house being much decayed, he had not designed to keep house this year." The incident replicates in this couple of great stature and wealth the mutual oeconomic dependence of hus- band and wife that was a decade later to be exampled in *Edward IV* by Jane and Matthew Shore. As a sidebar I refer to a letter of 19 Septem- ber 1601 by John Chamberlain, who describes a woman in a new home

---

7. Friedman suggests that the eventual reconciliation of the couple was due in part to Willoughby's need for help in the running of his households (p. 135).

who "will have much ado to bring that riotous and disordered house into any order, yet her virtue will shine the more if she can bring light out of darkness, or alter the frame of that confusion into any reasonable government."[8] For this level of domestic government, the wife of every status was responsible, and "neither [was] it otherwise possible to be."

In 1587 Sir Francis may have bowed to the same oeconomic necessity faced by Matthew Shore in his loss of a wife who had "made huswifery to shine," and in this Sir Francis may have lost a battle. But evidences are that he later won the war. As did that of the previous coda, this story concludes in a reminder of the place of women and in the defeat of female insurrection. Elizabeth sued (and repeatedly) for reconciliation, in the course of which she adopted the tenor of Hicks's advice. Elizabeth wrote Sir Francis that if he would receive her again as his wife, she would "study to conform all my words as I may best content and please you, as also to perform all good duties that do become a loving and obedient wife towards her husband." Sir Francis, economic exigency, and also the governing conventions of patriarchalism had evidently tamed a woman received to history as a shrew.

8. John Chamberlain, *Letters*, p. 47.

Chapter Three

VIRTUE AND DOMESTIC INTEREST

At the outset of this book, I cited recent work that has problematized our traditional relationship to historical documents and imperiled our comfortable reliance on them by identifying their narrativizing strategies: archives can be fictions. So to destabilize our research taxonomies should be to inspire a counterproposition: fictions can form an archive. At one level the present study is an extended investigation of this premise, an attempt to discover a contextualizing—or, rather, intertextualizing—method of sufficient rigor and subtlety to allow the use of literature in cultural history.

The method is tested most strictly here, where I approach Thomas Heywood's *A Woman Killed with Kindness* as a documentary record of broad cultural reformulation. Rather than presenting prescriptive literature as a "background" to the text, I begin (following this brief introduction) with the play, attempt to decode its moral philosophy, and then move outward in search of other evidences of its preoccupations. The aim of the experiment is to test the larger significances of the play's meanings. *Woman Killed* guides my correlation of classical ideals of friendship and magnanimity with post-Reformation notions of marriage and householding. The play leads me to locate the decay of friendship and hospitality in the Renaissance political and economic conditions of householding and, specifically, in concerns for the uncertain ownership of property and property's extension, accumulated domestic goods, as well as for their anxious symbolization in the trade in and title to women.

The play also provokes a revision of the traditional thesis that in the late sixteenth century the concept of "companionate" marriage developed as one residue of the depreciated ideology of friendship: at best, the term *companionate marriage* is misleading; at base, it refers to a concept of spousal relationships which is far less revolutionary than we have been encouraged to believe. *Woman Killed* marks instead the instantiation of a new ethic, what I call a domestic ethic, of keeping, protecting, and governing the persons and things of the household sphere—a material ethic that, like its political near-neighbor, patriarchalism, resists internecine competition and companionship. Because its synthetic sweep may be greater than that of any "nonfictional" text of the period, *Woman Killed*, when read to the purpose, allows us to recover the paradox that the Renaissance concept of domestic virtue which succeeds the moral philosophy of friendship and benefice is one lodged in the realization of its philosophical opposite, individual oeconomic interest.

To tease out this paradox, I read *Woman Killed* against Aristotle's *Nicomachean Ethics*, Cicero's *De amicitia*, Seneca's *De beneficiis*, and a number of Renaissance works of moral philosophy and domestic prescription—as well as Donne's first elegy, Shakespeare's *Timon of Athens*, and two other contemporary plays. *Woman Killed's* kinship with moral texts as well as literary ones can to some extent be inferred from Heywood's other works, which reveal the English playwright's classical training and contemporary reading. On the subject of marriage, for example, he knew and echoed the Dutch humanist Henricus Cornelius Agrippa von Nettesheim.

Marriage is, in fact, my first concern as well as the subject that opens the play. In 1602 William Segar declared that "men married are ever to precede men unmarried, *in pari dignitate*" (that is, if they are in other respects equal). Thomas Smith had earlier explained that "commonly we do not call any a yeoman till he be married, and have children, and as it were have some authority among his neighbors."[1] Marriage conferred social status because it inaugurated the household in which any man and every householder had the opportunity to realize the theoretically absolute political power of domestic patriarchalism.

But this rite of male initiation into the larger social community as a fully authorized member was not acknowledged as a function of marriage in works specifically devoted to the topic. These included the writings of Christian humanists such as Vives and Erasmus, the pro-

---

1. William Segar, *Honor Military and Civil* (1602), sig. X4^v; Thomas Smith, *De republica anglorum* (1583), p. 76.

testant office of holy matrimony that was recorded in the English Book of Common Prayer of 1559, the Elizabethan "Homily of the State of Matrimony" of 1563, the Counter-Reformation Roman catechism of 1566, and the late sixteenth- and early seventeenth-century sermons and treatises of the Puritan clergy. Emphasized instead were the notions that marriage, first, provided a man with a companion or helper; second, ensured the lawful propagation of his children; and, third, legitimized his sexuality (so that he might avoid fornication).[2] An early version of this traditional triad of marital objectives was presented by Cornelius Agrippa in his *De sacramento matrimonii* of 1526.[3] But Agrippa at the same time exceeded tradition by adding to each topic its biblical authorization, citing the book of Genesis for the first two and the preachings of Paul for the third.

Agrippa's search for learned precedent supplemental even to that of the Bible led him to diverge so far from traditional formulations as to anticipate some themes of this chapter: the developing social ethic for the early modern institution of householding, its derivation from newer ideas of marital relations and duties than those put forward in standard doctrine and prescription, and its divergence from inherited ideals of hospitality and benefice. "Socrates testified," Agrippa wrote to the point, "that he learned moral philosophy more of wives than natural philosophy, of Anaxagoras and Archelaus." As his *De sacramento* makes clear, moral philosophy in its three given branches—moral, political, and oeconomic, correspondent to the categories established by Aristotle's *Nicomachean Ethics* and *Politics* and by the pseudo-Aristotelian *Oeconomics*[4]—was experienced less in marriage itself than in householding. Thus the *De sacramento* continues: "For truly matrimony giveth a great exercise to moral philosophy. For it hath a certain household commonwealth annexed, in ruling the which a man may soon learn and have experience of wisdom, temperance, love to God and his kin, and all other virtues, by which in loving his wife, in bringing up his children, in governing his family, in saving his goods, in ruling his little house, in procreating and enlarging his stock, he may lead a life most

2. On the traditional functions and justifications of marriage, see especially Chilton Latham Powell, *English Domestic Relations* (1917); William and Malleville Haller, "Puritan Art of Love" (1942); John Yost, "Value of Married Life" (1976); Kathleen M. Davies, "Sacred Condition" (1977); Margo Todd, "Humanists, Puritans" (1980); and Edmund Leites, "Duty to Desire" (1982).

3. Henricus Cornelius Agrippa von Nettesheim's *De sacramento matrimonii* (1526) was first published among his *Opera* in Lyon with a 1531 imprint that may misrepresent an actual publication date of 1630. As *The Commendation of Matrimony*, however, it was available by 1540 in an English translation by David Clapham, from which I quote.

4. See Jill Kraye, "Moral Philosophy" (1988).

happy."[5] Even though the *De sacramento* was written for Marguerite, the future queen of Navarre, the text in this instance did not disguise its understanding that the woman's primary ethical standing was as an instrument of masculine fulfillment—through the exercise of householding which followed upon matrimony.

Thomas Heywood probably knew Agrippa's *De sacramento* from its inclusion in the Latin *Opera* rather than in its 1540 English translation (from which I have quoted). In his own oeconomic treatise of 1637, *A Curtain Lecture*, Heywood, too, first referred to the "excellent use" Socrates made of the moral philosophy he had learned from women and then repeated: "In marriage there is a domestic commonwealth in which the father of the family may express wisdom, temperance, justice, piety, and all other virtues: by loving his wife, instructing his children, governing his family, ordering his affairs, disposing his goods."[6] The most conspicuous difference between Heywood's version of Agrippa's statement and the original is Heywood's neglect even to hint that the expression of all virtues and the conscientious undertaking of household responsibilities will lead to "a life most happy." In 1603, in the play now generally thought to be the "finest example" of the domestic tragedy,[7] he had in fact already demonstrated the tragic consequences of conflict between, on the one hand, an aspiration toward classical virtue and, on the other, the contemporary exercise of household governance mandated by the interest coincident in householder and state.

As suggested above, *A Woman Killed with Kindness* recognizes the obsolescence, for the late sixteenth and early seventeenth centuries, of the received moral philosophy of the classical authors. It is not unique in doing so; many other works of the period record a disenchantment with inherited ideals. But, again, *Woman Killed* is a document of sufficient richness that it allows us to discover a principal cause of the falling

5. Agrippa, sigs. C7^v–C8^r. Socrates on moral philosophy was a commonplace; see, for example, William Baldwin's popular *Treatise of Moral Philosophy* (1547): "After that Socrates perceived that there was no fruit in the speculation of natural philosophy . . . he brought in the kind called ethic, that is, moral philosophy . . . and exhorted the people chiefly to learn those things which should instruct them in manners, which were needful to be used in their houses" (sigs. E7^{r-v}). On "matrimony giveth a great exercise to moral philosophy," compare Bacon: "Wife and children are a kind of discipline of humanity" ("Of Marriage and Single Life" [1612], *The Essayes*, p. 26).

6. Thomas Heywood, *Curtain Lecture* (1637), sigs. G10^{r-v}. To the best of my knowledge, Heywood's source is here identified for the first time. His version is undoubtedly translated from the Latin rather than paraphrased from Clapham; see Agrippa, *Opera* (?1630), sig. Mm4^r.

7. Quoted are both Peter Ure, "Marriage and the Domestic Drama" (1951), p. 148, and R. W. Van Fossen, Introduction to *A Woman Killed with Kindness* (1961), p. xv. Henry Hitch Adams numbers *Woman Killed* among the four "colossi" in domestic tragedy (*English Domestic or, Homiletic Tragedy* [1943], p. 187). Van Fossen also reviews other appraisals of the play.

off, which is the irreconcilability of the classical ethic to contemporary political theory and emerging economic reality—to, in other words, the motive agencies of householding purveyed in the philosophy of domestic patriarchalism, which has been discussed previously, and to its material foundation, my subject here.

My arguments on the discourse of gender in the period also have a place within this philosophical framework. Where the previous chapter considered the moral conflicts experienced by the subservient (female) population of three dramatized domestic commonwealths, this one addresses those of the (male) householder. *Woman Killed* has two plots, in each of which a gentleman proclaims his achievement of a "life most happy," in each of which happiness is located in domestic content, in each of which content is eroded and its ephemerality revealed, and in each of which the very incentive for happiness is devalued as the preeminent domestic goal is discovered instead to be the fulfillment of oeconomic duty. After considering the two plots in turn, I examine more specifically the notion of householding as an opportunity to "exercise" or "express" masculine virtue by reviewing the philosophical tradition available to the two protagonists. Anxieties about domestic authority and personal property are inextricably linked with the construction of gender, since they inflect notions of both homosocial and marital relationship, coalesce in the symbolization of the woman as the most valuable and potentially most fugitive of possessions, and thus nurture the persistent hierarchy of the sexes. This, to circle back to the theme with which the play begins, has its continuing consequences for conceptions of marriage.

Frankford's Household

Marriages both open and close *A Woman Killed with Kindness*. But the somber conclusion of the play, a deathbed affirmation of the marital union of John and Anne Frankford, is in no sense reminiscent of romantic comedy. And the first scene, which dramatizes the initial celebration of their nuptials, presents us with a compact confirmed, a courtship implicitly concluded antecedently, a ritual stripped of romantic illusion, and a ceremony revealed to be, as John R. Gillis has described it for the early modern period, a "strenuous, often conflicted social, psychological, and economic process."[8]

As Gillis further observes, the wedding celebration was primarily a

8. John R. Gillis, *For Better, For Worse* (1985), p. 11.

vehicle by which the community adjusted itself to the creation of a new social unit. William Bradshaw, writing of *A Marriage Feast* in 1620, censoriously described the form this adjustment could take: "what laughing and scoffing, what fleering, jeering, and nodding the head is there"; how "a marriage is accounted no marriage if it be not solemnized with beastly and profane songs, sonnets, jigs, indited by some hellish spirit and chanted by those that are the public incendiaries of all filthy lusts," so that the day of marriage is "as ignominious and reproachful as if it were the day of one's public penance or execution." Among the wedding guests were men who here lost the groom to a relationship preeminent to their former friendship as well as men for whom the bride had until then represented a potential mate. Bradshaw lacked the theory to understand that the marriage celebration offered a carnival outlet for expression and exorcism of their regret and envy.[9]

In the first scene of *Woman Killed*, the majority of the lines and the spirit of celebration—here manifested through the jests, music, and dance of which Bradshaw complained—are reserved largely to the ranking guests, Sir Francis Acton and Sir Charles Mountford. They enact the adjustments required, respectively, of kin and friend. The interests of a disappointed rival are represented by Mountford, who steps forward to dance "The Shaking of the Sheets" with Anne before reminding himself "But that's the dance her husband means to lead her"; who notes of her that "many a heart hath sought her"; who receives Frankford's subtle warning: "But that I know your virtues and chaste thoughts, / I should be jealous of your praise, Sir Charles"; and who consequently makes his accommodation to the marriage by shifting his focus from praise of Anne, in his first long speech, to praise of the union, in his second (1.2–3, 24–26). Meanwhile, Acton acknowledges the addition to his kinship network of "good brother Frankford" and cedes his responsibility for his sister Anne as, asking for a dance "By your leave, sister," he immediately corrects himself: "by your husband's leave / I should have said—the hand that but this day / Was given you in the church I'll borrow," that is, a hand given by Acton to Frankford and now borrowed only with Frankford's consent (1.73, 6–8).[10]

Through this exchange we see that Anne's essential political status is undisturbed by marriage, for she has merely transferred the direction of her duty from a brother to a husband. Early modern marriage was

9. William Bradshaw, *Marriage Feast* (1620), sigs. F2^{r-v}. Gillis also emphasizes the carnival uses of the wedding celebration, p. 67. And see on this subject Michael D. Bristol, "Wedding Feast and Charivari," in *Carnival and Theater* (1985), pp. 162–78.
10. On the wedding as transition for the guests, see also Frederick Kiefer, "Heywood as Moralist" (1986), p. 83.

thought far more profound a transition for men—friends, kin, and, especially, the groom—than for women. Frankford, to illustrate, has relinquished the "light and free" life of the bachelor. His initial attempt at wedding humor—"Marriage hath yok'd my heels"—has the unhappy ring of felt complaint and elicits the attempts of both Acton and Mountford to coax more gaiety from him (1.10–11).

While betrothal created a couple, marriage inaugurated a household, and thus the marriage celebration served to demonstrate the new husband's readiness for his communal oeconomic obligations.[11] To the point, Acton reminds Frankford of his duties to his guests. The radical shift in Frankford's position is emphasized by the fact that, with the sole exception of the wedding pair, the world of the first scene is a community of single males and that, after the departure of Frankford and Anne, the circle reconstitutes itself through the hawking challenge between Mountford and Acton which engages all those remaining in an affirmation of allegiances. Frankford is excluded from the circle, for he has exited "Into the hall" and "within," to the confines of a bigendered world of household responsibilities. His marriage thus defies the categories for the rites of passage delineated by Arnold van Gennep, for it is at once "preliminal," or before the doorway, a rite of his separation from the male community; "liminal," or on the threshold, a rite of his transition to a position of social responsibility; and also "postliminal," or in the house, a rite of his incorporation of a household.[12]

At this transitional moment of its first inauguration, the new household is at its most vulnerable. The daily responsibilities of Frankford's servants are relaxed, for example, as they salute the union in their own second-scene dance. More significantly, communal celebration renders the boundaries between household and world permeable; the nuptial festivities offer, after all, the first taste of Frankford's hospitality to Wendoll, who will be successively Frankford's guest, his cuckolder, and his challenger for control of the house. But in this first scene, the sense of risk is identified instead with Frankford's taking into his establishment of an other, Anne Acton. The sixteenth-century literary collections of William Baldwin and Francis Meres both include the warning that "like as no man can tell where a shoe wringeth, but he that weareth it: so no man knoweth a woman's disposition, but he that marrieth her."[13] All the anxieties intimated during the marital celebration form

---

11. On marriage as a male rather more than female rite of passage, see Gillis, pp. 75–76; on the wedding as an inauguration of a new household, p. 12.

12. Arnold van Gennep, *Rites of Passage* (1908).

13. Baldwin attributes this to Socrates, sig. V6ʳ; in *Palladis Tamia* (1598), Francis Meres cites Plutarch, sig. S4ʳ. The classical authorization is of more moment than the specific authority.

a subtext for and intensify the central—and in this scene unresolved—anxiety, concerning the nature of the new wife.

Although the second scene is often called a parody of the first,[14] the visual impact of the gendered pairing off of servants for a dance could scarcely be more unlike the first-scene clustering of six men about a solitary woman, assessing her, objectifying her. She is in that first scene the focus of attention even for guests Cranwell and Malby, but the burden of characterization is again carried by the two knightly characters, who initiate their unhappy rivalry in competing blazons of the new bride. To Mountford she is "beauty and perfection's eldest daughter" because of her noble birth and royal nurture; Acton finds her "A perfect wife already" because she is "meek and patient," "Pliant and duteous" (1.23, 37, 41). These descriptions seem less to reflect individual perspectives on Anne's perfections than they do conflicting notions of the ideal wife and, especially, ideal marriage, whether companionate or strictly patriarchal.

Undoubtedly Frankford is to be understood to apprehend the risk he takes in marrying Anne as well as the challenges he undertakes in establishing his household; the opening-scene indisposition to revelry in which other readers of *Woman Killed* have first located a coldness and "priggishness" in his character may be seen instead to present him as an exemplum of sober awareness of the consequences of matrimony. The character is not permitted to celebrate his domestic content until the fourth scene, when he can finally seem to confirm it by his experience of it.

> How happy am I amongst other men
> That in my mean estate embrace content.
> I am a gentleman, and by my birth
> Companion with a king; a king's no more.
> I am possess'd of many fair revenues,
> Sufficient to maintain a gentleman.
> Touching my mind, I am study'd in all arts,
> The riches of my thoughts, and of my time
> Have been a good proficient. But the chief
> Of all the sweet felicities on earth,
> I have a fair, a chaste, and loving wife,
> Perfection all, all truth, all ornament.
> If man on earth may truly happy be,
> Of these at once possess'd, sure I am he.
> (4.1–14)

14. Adams says the second scene "echo[es]" the first (p. 156); Van Fossen calls it a "comic counterpart" (p. xxxvii); for Lloyd E. Berry (1963), it is a "burlesque parallel" (p. 64).

In these early scenes the new husband enacts in full the Agrippan paradigm that Heywood had in *A Curtain Lecture* paraphrased only in part: "in loving his wife," "in saving his goods," and "in ruling his little house," Frankford finds that he leads "a life most happy." He has succeeded in founding a household that satisfies his needs and desires, reflects his status, and creates and sustains the mode of life appropriate to his gentility.

While it is not uncommon for scenes on the open stage of the English Renaissance to represent interiors in an unparticularized sense, *Woman Killed* immediately demonstrates by contrast how detailed its interest in the material surroundings of Frankford's "household" is and how demanding it will be of the perceptual imagination of its audience.[15] The play opens with what we are asked to picture as a kind of three-ring circus, a marriage celebration consuming three defined spaces: the great "hall," the floor of which will be "peck'd and dinted like a millstone" by dancing guests (1.74, 89); the "parlour," to which the main cast of characters has withdrawn for their private celebration and conversation (2.4); and the outer "yard," in which Frankford's servants enjoy their own dance (2.5). In later scenes we learn further that Frankford has a dining chamber for family and friends, while meals are "spread for the servingmen in the hall" (8.3, 15, 23). He uses the parlor, again, for after-dinner fellowship and games (8.13, 26); he also has a "study" (4.osd; 13.130). There are both a "withdrawing" (13.9) and then a "private" chamber for Frankford and Anne (8.204; 11.92; 12.2; 13.14),[16] as well as at least two other bedchambers for guests (8.195, 198; 11.95). To our mental map of the Frankford establishment, we eventually add the "cellar" (11.48), "fields" (6.71), and outer "gates" (12.21, 24; 13.8).

A range of theatrical languages articulates Frankford's domestic context.[17] One is the seemingly incidental verbal identification of spaces, including those cited above. A second is the narration of and call for stage business, as when Frankford and Anne command their servant Jenkin and when Jenkin himself requests of his fellows, "More lights in the hall there"; cries "Hark, within there, my master calls to lay more billets on the fire"; orders "One spread the carpet in the parlour and stand ready to snuff the lights"; summons "A pair of cards, Nich'las, and a carpet to cover the table. Where's Sisly with her counters and her

---

15. Otto Rauchbauer (1976) calculates that ten of the seventeen scenes in the play are set in Frankford's house (p. 203).

16. Although Wendoll and the servants refer to a bedchamber as Anne's when Frankford is away, elsewhere there are indications that Anne and Frankford share a room and a bed: see 8.204, 210–12; and 11.72.

17. On the theatrical realization of Frankford's house, see also Alan C. Dessen, *Elizabethan Stage Conventions* (1984), pp. 31 and 62–64.

box? Candles and candlesticks there"; or directs "the butler to give us out salt and trenchers" (8.10–15, 117–19; 11.13–19). A third stage language is direct address of the audience, as when, for example, Jenkin remarks, "You may see, my masters, though it be afternoon with you, 'tis but early days with us, for we have not din'd yet. Stay but a little, I'll but go in and help to bear up the first course and come to you again presently" (4.106–10). A fourth, extraverbal language is that of gesture, by the conventions of which Frankford enters *as it were brushing the crumbs from his clothes with a napkin* to indicate that he is *newly risen from supper* (8.21sd). A fifth, visual language is the stage property; contemporary stage directions variously call for a table, stools, carpet, tablecloth, napkins, salt, bread, trenchers, voider, wooden knife, cards, candles, candlesticks, "and other necessaries." The sixth theatrical language—and finally that of highest visibility on the Renaissance open stage—is that of the cast, here enlarged by the contextualizing inclusion of household servants, a full nine of whom are named characters; "altogether," as the author for an earlier generation wrote, such a group of servants "make[s] a world"—or a household commonwealth.[18]

In the domestic arena that is thus conjured up for us, the multiple functions of a household unfold. We see the implied structure as a place of shelter when the splashed and muddied Wendoll is first invited in and again when Frankford says that he will "make haste to bed" because "The night is raw and cold and rheumatic" (8.210, 205). We hear repeatedly of further occasions for rest, as Anne calls for a dressing gown for her husband and as Frankford invites his guest Cranwell to "see your chamber at your pleasure," bids his servant Jenkin "show him to his chamber," directs Wendoll to "go to bed," and asks Anne to come with him "into my bedchamber" (8.195–204). And we see the house nurture fellowship, social ritual, and leisure entertainment not only in the first, wedding, scene but also in the eighth, card game, scene. Perhaps most interesting theatrically, we are asked to picture the house as the site of spatial negotiation among its subordinate communities: even while supervising the clearing away of the family meal in the dining chamber, for example, Jenkin directs preparations for the ensuing meal of his fellow servants in the hall and simultaneously supervises the set-up of the principals' after-supper card game in the parlor.

The proliferation of domestic detail solidifies our perception of Frankford's status and, thus, of his investment in his household com-

18. *Civil and Uncivil Life* (1579), pp. 39–40.

monwealth. We learn, for example, that he holds "three or four" other manors (16.8–9) and, in addition, properties let out to tenants, among whom are three carters on whom he can call for service (13.167; 16.osd, 13). His fields and tenanted holdings support his assertion that he has "sufficient" income to "maintain" him, that he can, as William Harrison would have it, "live without manual labor," able to "bear the port, charge, and countenance of a gentleman."[19] Frankford's (court)yard and hall suggest an establishment of some size and antiquity, and the express dedication of the hall to public and servant use evokes community standing, long privilege, and household hierarchy of the sort for which Wendoll aptly denotes him one of the "best and chiefest / In Yorkshire" (6.39–40). The dining chamber, parlor, study, withdrawing room, and multiple bedchambers signal high levels of seclusion and comfort for guests and members of the principal family.[20] We discover, moreover, that Anne is expected to require her own maid and that Frankford numbers among his staff an unnamed coachman (16.osd). In a delegation of responsibilities that is yet another shorthand for privilege, authority has been vested in Jenkin to supervise the household servants in the many quotidian menial tasks that are dramatized. And Nicholas, in a further degree of specification that reinforces the elaborate subtext of household hierarchy, is at the outset an outdoor rather than domestic servant, as his fellow Jack explains: "we have been brought up to serve sheep, oxen, horses, and hogs, and such like" (2.10–13). For this reason, Nick is a witness to Wendoll's arrival.

Wendoll appears at Frankford's "house" immediately at the conclusion of Frankford's fourth-scene paean to his domestic content, in ominous punctuation of his self-proclamation as *beatus vir*. Wendoll's entrance initiates a chain of events that will in turn define a continuing evolution of Frankford's emotional response to his painstakingly created domestic environment. In his emotion, all the stage business regarding his household realizes an essential thematic significance. The eighth-scene supper that has been so carefully orchestrated in dialogue and through props ends with the audience Frankford grants Nicholas and with the airing of Nicholas's suspicions of Anne and Wendoll. At first Frankford rebukes this stablehand for transgressing against the household codes of place so far as to intercept him en route from dining chamber to parlor, but gradually Nicholas becomes his only sure

19. On Frankford's status, Rauchbauer and Nancy A. Gutierrez (1989) are more careful than most; elsewhere, the terms generally used are "bourgeois" and "middle-class" in contrast with the "aristocratic" Mountford. Both, however, are gentlemen: Mountford a knight and Frankford a "mere" gentleman. For clarification, see William Harrison, *Description of England* (1587), p. 114.
20. For more on the significance of these rooms, see my "Causes and Reasons" (1994).

ally in a household grown suddenly treacherous. During the ensuing card game, Wendoll's double entendres serve to confirm the secret game he plays with Frankford's wife, so that as the detailed domestic activity of the scene unfolds, Frankford's domestic content erodes. By the time the game ends and he retires for the night, Frankford says heavily to Nicholas that he goes "To bed then, not to rest" (8.221). That household function, too, is jeopardized in the newly uncertain world of his domestic commonwealth.

Our sense of Frankford's house is never keener than in the subsequent scenes of his investigation of Nicholas's accusations. The sequence opens with detailed preparations for yet another supper, is punctuated by Frankford's pretense that he has been summoned to York and by his leavetaking, continues with the removal of Wendoll and Anne to a private supper in her chamber, includes the closing down of the house for the night—"the gates shut in" (ironically against its owner's reentry), the keys sent up to Anne, and "the household all got to bed" (12.18–21)—and concludes with Frankford's surreptitious return to discover Anne and Wendoll together in his bed.

In counterpoint to the everyday props and the self-referential chatter of the servants that underline the routine household operations of supper and of evening shutdown, Frankford launches his extraordinary scheme to test Nicholas's report of treachery. The sober and taciturn bridegroom becomes a nervous host, chattering, questioning, urging "be merry, pleasant, / And frolic it to-night." Eager to set in train the ruse that will test his suspicions, he worries over domestic detail: "Where be those lazy knaves to serve in supper?" (11.38–43). He defaults on the obligation of a prominent gentleman householder by not intervening in the feud between Mountford and Acton, saying, when guest Cranwell chastises him for his omission, that "more weighty business of [his] own" occupies him (11.28). In a perversion of standard hospitality, he lends weight to his stratagem by bidding Nicholas "Have . . . into the cellar" for "A cup of our March beer" the "stripling" whom they pretend has borne a letter of urgent summons, a letter that Frankford himself has forged and Nicholas has delivered (11.46–49, 5). When Wendoll remarks that "The ways [outside] are dangerous," Frankford's reply that he and Nicholas will travel "Appointed well" (11.65–67), that is, well armed, both raises the level of suspense as to his response when soon thereafter he confronts the ocular proof of his betrayal and compounds the irony that for Frankford the dangerous ways will be the interior ones, those of the house that should be his castle, "as well for defense against injury and violence, as for his repose."

In moving, upon his return, through a space that is theatrically imagined as his darkened house, Frankford demonstrates that he knows his way blind: "This is the key that opes my outward gate, / This is the hall door, this my withdrawing chamber." Nicholas whispers that the door must be opened "with far less noise than Cripple-gate, or your plot's dash'd"; Frankford, too, warns that they must "Tread softly, softly," and Nicholas returns that "I will walk on eggs this pace" (13.8–9, 18–21). Creeping soundlessly into his offstage bedchamber (with a shuttered "dark-lantern" that we are to infer that he opens to cast light on the occupants of his bed), Frankford enacts the kind of convergence between self and place that occurs only in one's own home. And yet, in his preliminary scheme to provide himself with duplicate keys, involving the bribing of a smith (11.4); in the necessity for stealth that mandates that he tie his horse "Two flight-shoot off" rather than return to his own stables (13.2); in his enforced delay until "dead midnight" (13.6); and in his surreptitious progress to his bedside (all the more exaggerated for its miming on the daylit Elizabethan stage), Frankford at the same time assumes the role of intruder in his own house.[21] The house is true to spatial logic; it validates the corporeal memory he is able to summon; but it also defies his control of anything other than his own movement. During his iterations of the familiar, there grows the terrible sense that, rather than identifying, he is rediscovering his walls, his doors, his rooms. It is as if the house that no one knows better, his own house, has been transformed beyond his recognition:

> But this, that door that's bawd unto my shame,
> Fountain and spring of all my bleeding thoughts,
> Where the most hallowed order and true knot
> Of nuptial sanctity hath been profan'd.
> It leads to my polluted bedchamber,
> Once my terrestrial heaven, now my earth's hell,
> The place where sins in all their ripeness dwell. . . .
> (13.10–16)

The disjunction between Frankford and his house is confirmed by the contrast between its quiet—"A general silence hath surpris'd the house"—and his own unquiet: "And this is the last door. Astonishment, / Fear, and amazement play against my heart, / Even as a madman beats upon a drum" (13.22–25).

In the very moment of discovery, Anne is lost to him: "I am no more

21. Brian W. M. Scobie (1985) also notes that Frankford's return is "a subversion of domestic order" (p. xv).

your wife," she recognizes (13.83). Frankford exiles her to another of his manors, acting in sympathy with such arguments as Henry Smith's that "divorcement is not instituted for the carnal, but for the chaste, lest they should be tied to a plague while they live."[22] John Dove also recommended separation from an adulterous wife "because it is a public scandal." And William Whately offers us a striking seventeenth-century definition of "public"—"say she offend in public before the servants, children, strangers"—that is of particular moment here, when Anne offends in each respect. First, she laments, "See what guilt is: here stand I in this place, / Asham'd to look my servants in the face." Second, Frankford calls up her children to shame her. And third, Cranwell reminds us of his presence in the house when he briefly interrupts Frankford's "judgement" of her (13.150–51, 156–57).[23] To protect his children, already susceptible to the "stripe of bastardy," from further contamination by Anne's "infectious thoughts" (13.124–27) and to himself eschew a fornicator, Frankford sacrifices the third traditional motive for matrimony, companionship.

But he does not thereby despair of reclaiming his house, on which her adultery is the "blemish" (13.118). In his *De sacramento matrimonii*, Agrippa declares that "he that wanteth a wife hath no house, because he hath not settled a house. Yea, and if he have [that is, if he has a house but no wife], he tarrieth in it as a stranger in his inn."[24] In the action that follows Frankford's first-scene taking of a wife, his house, as if in correspondence to the Agrippan paradigm, materializes before us, "settled," with a cast of characters that embraces both gentles and servants and through scene-setting stage business that is unmatched in the English Renaissance theater for its detail. When Frankford entertains the suspicion that Anne has betrayed her matrimonial vows, we witness the complementary process of his estrangement from his house. But in exposing her and then deciding to exile her, he determines that he can no longer harbor the woman he has "lodged" in his bosom (13.113); that while she has served the Agrippan purpose of inaugurating Frankford's establishment and incubating his succession, the house he had settled with her is separable from her; and that in reclaiming the house,

22. Henry Smith, *Preparative to Marriage* (1591), sig. H5ʳ. In *Christian Oeconomy* (composed, 1590s; published, 1609), William Perkins argues that reconciliation is possible after adultery (p. 426). Anne's exile constitutes separation *a mensa et thoro* (from board and bed), the practical alternative to the legally and religiously difficult divorce *a vinculo matrimonii* (from the marriage bond). On relevant legal terms and issues, see Frederick George Emmison, *Elizabethan Life: Morals* (1973), pp. 164–65, and Martin Ingram, *Church Courts* (1987), pp. 145–47.

23. John Dove, *Of Divorcement* (1601), sig. C7ʳ; William Whately, *Bride-Bush* (1617), sig. D3ᵛ. Cranwell also makes public the scandal by reporting it to Anne's brother Acton (15.27–28; 17.10–11).

24. Agrippa, *Commendation*, sig. C8ʳ.

he can redeem for it and for himself domestic honor. In our last view of Frankford's theatrically imagined premises, he improvises a purification ritual, "search[ing] each room about," assuring himself that all are stripped of everything "That ever was my wife's" (15.1–4), reimprinting them with his own identity. Frankford is determined that *Anne* is to be "the stranger in the inn," the evidence of whose sojourn can be erased with the removal of every item "by whose sight being left here in the house / I may remember such a woman by" (13.161–62).

In discovering and dispatching Anne's lute after her, Frankford unconditionally restores a threatened integrity of space and governance. The marriage that was essential to the creation of his household is finally a threat to that household. And the household realizes its priority. In an apposite particularization of the value system put forward by Agrippa, John Dod and Robert Cleaver assert that "there is no honor within the house, longer than a man's wife is honorable";[25] and in the restoration of his house, Frankford confirms he is an honorable man.

Genius Domus

To suggest that there can be a priority of the house is to insist that it is more than a material structure, more than the aggregate of its hall, its dining chamber, its parlor, its bedchambers, and its outbuildings. This is to argue that it is a political association, an economic enterprise, a social institution, and, most particularly for John Frankford, a moral system.[26] The almost mystical association of Frankford with his house may become clearer with reference, first, to a poem by John Donne; second, to an allegorical moment in which the *Woman Killed* protagonist plays a part; and, finally, to the second plot of the play, to which I turn after this brief interval.

In my reading of the Frankford plot of *A Woman Killed with Kindness*,

25. John Dod and Robert Cleaver, *Godly Form of Household Government* (1598), sig. M5^r. On the honor of the house, compare Edmund Tilney: "At what time the married man determineth to keep a harlot, even the same hour doth he set fire to his honesty, destruction to his house, and loss of all that ever he hath" (*Flower of Friendship* [1568], sigs. B7^v–B8^r). On Frankford's honor, see Henry Percy's 1609 *Advice to his son*: even "if the act be public, there can no dishonour rise to a man by a woman's whoredom, being separated" (p. 95). Gutierrez also discusses the importance of the wife's chastity to her husband's honor (p. 272).

26. Others who note the importance of the "house" in the play include Yves Bescou (1931), p. 139; Michel Grivelet (1957), p. 212; Rauchbauer, p. 203; Scobie, pp. xv–xvi; and Diana E. Henderson (1986). Some contrast the house in the two plots; I would argue for complementarity. For example: Mountford's remark on the loss of his servants is significant out of proportion to its brevity because of the attention to servants and master/servant relationships in the Frankford plot; the brief appearance of the Frankford children is all the more meaningful for Mountford's articulation of his responsibilities to family honor.

the house assumes a dominant, even a characterologic, role. For a cynical twist on the adulterous affair of Anne and Wendoll which none-theless conveys a similar sense of the resistant force of the cuckold's house, compare John Donne's first elegy, "Jealousy":

> Fond woman, which would'st have thy husband die,
> And yet complain'st of his great jealousy;
> . . .
> O give him many thanks, he'is courteous,
> That in suspecting kindly warneth us.
> We must not, as we us'd, flout openly,
> In scoffing riddles, his deformity;
> Nor at his board together being sat,
> With words, nor touch, scarce looks adulterate.
> Nor when he, swoll'n, and pamper'd with great fare,
> Sits down, and snorts, cag'd in his basket chair,
> Must we usurp his own bed any more,
> Nor kiss and play in his house, as before,
> Now I see many dangers; for that is
> His realm, his castle, and his diocese.
> But if, as envious men, which would revile
> Their Prince, or coin his gold, themselves exile
> Into another country,'and do it there,
> We play'in another house, what should we fear?
> There we will scorn his household policies,
> His seely plots, and pensionary spies. . . .[27]

The cuckold's house, in other words, has its revenge on his betrayers. The violation of the marriage will continue, the aged and enfeebled husband will be cuckolded again, but the integrity of the house will reassert itself through its exaction of the exile of the lovers. "Jealousy" suggests the power of the domestic superstition that informs the fic-tional mentalities of both Donne's cuckolder and Heywood's cuckold.

The house of the ailing husband in Donne's elegy at first appears to operate independently, like a machine set in motion with no natural brake, exerting a field of force that seems all the stronger for its con-trast to its master's weakness and paralysis. In fact, however, it has anonymous human agents, its "pensionary spies." The personified house requires depersonalized subordinates who act in its institutional interest. The contemporaries of Heywood and Donne wanted to be-

---

27. John Donne, "Jealousy" (written, 1593–96; published, 1633) in *The Elegies* (1965), pp. 9–10.

lieve, even against clear evidence, in the communal ethic of the household servant. In a 1609 account of a murder, a witness "demand[ed] in the name of God, how such a wicked deed could be done, none being in the house, but they appertaining to the house?"—as if betrayal by the house's own subordinates defied common logic.[28]

A Woman Killed with Kindness cherishes the same conceit. Even the clown Jenkin, who has been assigned to serve Wendoll, articulates it: after Wendoll's disgrace, he asks smartly, "What, shall I serve you still or cleave to the old house?" (16.114–15).[29] Jenkin, for all his irreverence, imagines not a contest of loyalties between masters but an unequal opposition between transient person and transcendent place. Meanwhile, the perspicacious stablehand Nicholas is bent on an exaction more like that outlined by Donne. Nicholas is moved less by loyalty to Frankford—as he makes particularly clear in the discovery scene, when he seethes at Frankford's "patience" (13.66)—than by resentment of Wendoll for Wendoll's violations of the social and moral fabric represented by the household.

In addition to the supremely naturalistic Nicholas, there is one final household agent of whom we must take note: the quasi-allegorical "Maid in her smock," who arrests the sword Frankford has raised in vengeance against the discovered and fleeing Wendoll. To her Frankford says, "I thank thee, maid; thou like the angel's hand / Hast stay'd me from a bloody sacrifice" (13.67sd–69). Alan C. Dessen has remarked that her appearance defeats realistic expectation, that there is instead "clear symbolic value to this supernumerary figure."[30] Indeed, she is not Sisly Milk-pail, nor Joan Miniver, nor Jane Trubkin, nor Isbel Motley, all of whom have been painstakingly grounded by name and dialogue. At the same time, this unnamed maid wears a common smock rather than any more ethereal garment, and she fulfills the role of household servant when she does as Frankford directs and brings his children onstage. While I do not wish to rob her of her mystery, I relate it to that of the house. She is linked to the house in its material sense through her presence and agency, in its familial sense through her association with Frankford's progeny, and especially in its moral sense. She is the genius domus.

One commonplace of domestic prescription holds that "the very name of a wife is like the angel which stayed Abraham's hand when the

28. Bloody New Year's Gift (1609), sig. B4ʳ.
29. The assignment of Jenkin to Wendoll seems to result from a process of negotiation among the servants rather than a decision made by Frankford. Jenkin first assumes that "it will fall to [the] lot" of Nicholas, then fills in himself because Nicholas refuses the duty out of instinctive dislike for Wendoll (4.89–103).
30. Dessen, Elizabethan Drama (1977), pp. 75–76.

stroke was coming."[31] As she herself professes, Anne Frankford by her adultery has sacrificed the name of wife. But in the ethical system of *Woman Killed*, there remains to Frankford the spirit of the angel's hand, which is the spirit of the house and of its moral authority.

Mountford's House

At the center of the second plot of *A Woman Killed with Kindness* is Sir Charles Mountford, who, like Frankford, suffers a betrayal of his honor and becomes equally preoccupied with the integrity of his house.[32] His rival, Acton, refuses to accept Mountford's victory in the hawking match arranged at Frankford's wedding, draws a weapon in outraged pride, and, when Mountford also "hath the better" of the ensuing swordfight (3.41sd), pursues his revenge in court. Acton is so determined "to take [Mountford's] life" (5.5) that Mountford must expend his entire fortune to achieve acquittal of the charge of murder of Acton's men. Finally released from jail, Mountford finds his estate so depreciated that he is left with "only a house of pleasure, / [Worth] some five hundred pounds" (5.46–47).[33] Mountford is then betrayed twice more by false charity. First, the villain Shafton offers a loan of £300 only to sue for repayment, by this means attempting to force Mountford to sell him the "pleasure" house and its lands (which lie adjacent to property of his own). Second, in a scheme to ingratiate himself with Mountford's sister Susan, Acton purchases Mountford's freedom from debtor's prison. Like Frankford again, Mountford is determined to preserve the dignity of his house, in this case even at the expense of Susan's chastity.

He details the significances of his house in the interval between his two imprisonments. Echoing Frankford's declaration that he "em-

---

31. Henry Smith, sig. F1r.

32. Among the points of intersection: Anne and Acton are siblings; Acton and Mountford attend the Frankford wedding and plan their match there; Wendoll's entrée into Frankford's house is his news of the match; Frankford's houseguest Cranwell expects Frankford to take an interest in his brother-in-law Acton's case; Acton learns of Anne's shame from Cranwell; the wedding celebrants regather at Anne's deathbed. In 1946 Freda L. Townsend made the first attempt to redeem the play from earlier charges of disunity on thematic grounds.

33. The texts of *Woman Killed* read "a house of pleasure, / With some five hundred pounds." My emendation from "with" to "worth" recognizes that a house *with* sufficient attached properties to bring in an annual income of £500 would have been *worth* a great deal more in sale (including both the intrinsic value of the house and some multiple of the rental value, such as twenty-one times £500). Shafton thinks of the property as *worth* only £500. Had the property included an income of £500, some portion of it could have been sold to satisfy Mountford's debt without jeopardizing the whole, and there would have been no need for Mountford and Susan to work their own land.

brace[s] content" and that "a king's no more," Mountford proclaims of the modest life left to him that "Content's a kingdom, and I wear that crown" (7.8). His "poor house" no longer functions as has Frankford's household commonwealth, organized to serve his need for shelter and sustenance and provide his pleasures of fellowship and gentlemanly pursuits. Mountford has already "quite forgot / The names of all that ever waited on me." He and his sister Susan "labour hard" and "follow husbandry"; they "feed sparing" and "lie uneasy." He has also forgotten (in reference to a specifically gentlemanly pursuit) the names of hounds "Once from whose echoing mouths I heard all the music / That e'er my heart desired" (7.3, 44–55). As Mountford in this domestic interlude explains, the house nonetheless sustains the long tradition of privilege and honor to which he is heir and of which he is guardian:

> . . . this house successively
> Hath 'long'd to me and my progenitors
> Three hundred year. My great-great-grandfather,
> He in whom first our gentle style began,
> Dwelt here, and in this ground increas'd this molehill
> Unto that mountain which my father left me.
> Where he the first of all our house begun,
> I now the last will end and keep this house. . . .
>
> (7.15–22)

Unlike Frankford, Mountford cannot "live without manual labour," and he recognizes that "If this [house] were sold, [his and Susan's] names should then be quite / Raz'd from the bead-roll of gentility" (7.36–37). Because his hold on gentle status is so tenuous, he says, "we are driven to hard shift / To keep this poor house we have left unsold. . . . You see what hard shift we have made to keep it / Ally'd still to our own name. . . . To keep this place I have chang'd myself away" (7.1–2, 38–39, 56). He will accept even debtor's prison rather than alienate his property to Shafton, who interrupts Mountford's declaration of domestic felicity just as Wendoll entered on the conclusion of Frankford's.

In his 1604 "Advice to his son," Sir William Wentworth warned that friends should "not be such as are fallen into decay [such as Wendoll, "somewhat press'd by want"], nor unconscionable [such as Acton has been and will again prove himself to be], nor such as have lands lying within you or joining with you [such as Shafton]."[34] When Acton as-

34. William Wentworth, "Advice to his son" (1604), p. 15.

sumes Mountford's debt to Shafton, Mountford finds this fresh indebtedness so irredeemably unconscionable that he persuades Susan to "Grant [Acton] your bed, he's paid with interest so" (14.46). Of the many critics who feel that Heywood has mishandled this turn in the plot, Patricia Meyer Spacks is perhaps most censorious. She concludes that Mountford's sense of honor is "perverse": "Is the sacrifice of Susan really the only way this debt can be repaid? The pleasure-house still remains; we have found in a previous scene that Shafton considers it to be well worth five hundred pounds. Why cannot property rather than virginity be relinquished?"[35]

Such logic is, however, precisely contrary to the ugly ethic of the play. Dramatic coding establishes Shafton's villainy while dictating that aesthetic justice inheres in the defeat of his desire for Mountford's land. The story of Mountford's ill fortunes and Shafton's evil schemes demonstrates to us not that Mountford has something left to sell but that he has something left to protect. In his gentility and in the property that maintains that gentility, there survive values that he holds greater than either himself or his sister; the two are, after all, only temporary bearers of the family name. Because the patrimony is larger and longer-lived than any holder of it, Mountford perceives his overriding debt to be to his ancestors and his potential descendants.[36] As he understands it, that transcendent debt must be answered before any temporal debt occasioned by his own misspent individual "life."

At the moment that he refuses to "fly to save [his] life," yields to arrest, and faces the charge of murder rather than "sell / [His] country and [his] father's patrimony" (3.80, 90–91), Mountford begins a long decline in personal honor and self-determination in the interest of the preservation of his house. Of Mountford's second imprisonment for debt, Acton comments, "hast thou seen / A poor slave better tortur'd?" (7.75–76), and indeed, Mountford subsequently enters *"with irons; his feet bare, his garments all ragged and torn,"* calling himself "Thus like a slave ragg'd, like a felon gyv'd" (10.osd, 3). His sister Susan participates in this dishonor. She feels keenly the indignity of her petitions to Mountford's kin and friends for his relief: she protests, "I was not born a beggar," saying that only "his extremes" could "Enforce this language from [her]," and that "No [mis]fortune of [her] own could lead [her]

35. Patricia Meyer Spacks (1959) acknowledges that "the house represents . . . gentility, family honor, and tradition" without admitting the force of those values in early modern England (p. 328). See also on this subject Ure, p. 151; Irving Ribner, *Jacobean Tragedy* (1962), p. 58; and Leonora Leet Brodwin, *Elizabethan Love Tragedy* (1971), pp. 379–80, n. 7.

36. John Newnham, in his *Newnham's Nightcrow* (1590), argued that "the father should restore that to his posterity which he received from his ancestors" (sig. D4ʳ). Newnham was not disinterested, but the principle was widely accepted.

tongue / To this base key" (9.6–9). But these humiliations pale when Acton purchases Mountford's freedom from corporeal slavery and thus enslaves him spiritually to unrequitable benefit:

> Hale me back,
> Double my irons, and my sparing meals
> Put into halves, and lodge me in a dungeon
> More deep, more dark, more cold, more comfortless.
> By Acton freed! Not all thy manacles
> Could fetter so my heels as this one word
> Hath thrall'd my heart, and it must now lie bound
> In more strict prison than thy stony gaol.
> I am not free, I go but under bail.
>
> (10.88–96)

Susan, too, recognizes the nature of Mountford's obligation to Acton as "the slavery of your debts" (14.32).

For this plot with many romance elements, Northrop Frye's comment on the romance may be apposite: "In the social conditions assumed, virginity is to a woman what honor is to a man, the symbol of the fact that she is not a slave."[37] The symbiosis of slavery and virginity is certainly operative here; only Susan's virginity (to return to Spacks's largely anachronistic objection) is of sufficient substance to annul so otherwise unanswerable a debt as purchase from slavery. And yet, in a telling indication of the project of this text, the word *virgin* is never used in connection with Susan. Instead it is employed with reference to "this house, / This virgin title never yet deflower'd" (7.22–23) and "never yet . . . stain'd" (14.128). The word *virgin* occurs only one other time in the play, as Frankford enters his bedchamber expecting to confirm his wife's adultery: "Lend me such patience . . . / That I may keep this white and virgin hand / From any violent outrage or red murder" (13.30–32). In other words, in *Woman Killed* virginity is associated exclusively with male honor—that is, first, with the Mountfordian householding which is in Socrates and his philosophical heirs an exercise of male virtue and, second, with the Frankfordian right of judgment and rite of purification which household kingship authorizes.[38]

The ethical structure of the play eventually validates Mountford's

---

37. Northrop Frye, *Secular Scripture* (1976), p. 73. Heywood's source for the subplot is romance (see Van Fossen, pp. xvii–xx), as emphasized by Ribner ([1962] p. 53) and Herbert R. Coursen, Jr. ([1965] p. 184).

38. Townsend (1946) notes that in the Mountford plot "the honor of the man can be vindicated only through the sacrifice of the virtue of the woman" (p. 100). Margaret B. Bryan (1974) recognizes that the offering of a woman is also at issue in the Frankford plot (pp. 9–10).

tortuously reasoned decision to sacrifice Susan to his house, even as it celebrates Frankford's resistance of bloody revenge and his decision instead to exile the pollutant Anne from his house. In both cases the concluding perspective is fixed by the ranking character, Acton. Frankford is rewarded by Anne's profound and soul-saving repentance, as her own brother testifies: "had you with threats and usage bad / Punish'd her sin," then "the grief of her offence / Had not with such true sorrow touch'd her heart" (17.133–35). Similarly, Mountford's dubious gamble—with Susan at stake—succeeds when it inspires Acton's reform—"Stern heart, relent; / Thy former cruelty at length repent" (14.118–19)—and he marries rather than rapes her.[39]

But the extremity of Mountford's resolution does not pass without comment; even in succumbing to the force of it, Acton voices a reservation that frets at the edges of the text's purported moral consensus: "Was ever known in any former age / Such honourable wrested courtesy?" (14.120–21). In this association of Mountford's ethic with a former age and in the further evocation of a more current perspective by which that ethic appears strained or perverted, the text reveals its recognition of a contemporary sense of distance from an inherited moral philosophy. Whether the text regrets that distance is arguable; that the text remarks and finally reifies it is not.

Friendship and Benefice

From the two houses of Frankford and Mountford, I turn to the search for *Woman Killed*'s conceptual fellows. Again, the methodological ambition is to establish the playtext as an active contributor to a discourse from which we tend to think its fictional status excludes it. I look to works of moral philosophy not as "background" to the play but as texts in dialogue with it.

The play's title serves as the keystone of the countergeneric arch. In his edition of *A Woman Killed with Kindness*, R. W. Van Fossen writes that "no discussion of Heywood's sources would be complete without a reference to the title of the play," which he traces back to 1557 ("Then let us go hence, with kindness my her[t?] ye do kill"), to 1582 ("You will kill her [an old wealthy widow] with kindness"), and to its "most famous occurrence" in *The Taming of the Shrew*: "This is a way to kill a wife with kindness; / And thus I'll curb her mad and headstrong humour."[40] I

---

39. Richard Levin, *Multiple Plot* (1971), notes that Anne's repentance demonstrates the "superiority" of Frankford's "standard" (p. 95). I take issue with Spacks, p. 329; John Canuteson (1969), p. 141; and Ure, p. 150.

40. Van Fossen, pp. xxvi–xxvii. See also Arthur Melville Clark (1931), p. 37.

would like to raise as apposite two other contemporary occurrences of the proverb, in a sixteenth- and a seventeenth-century translation of Seneca's *De beneficiis*: "It becometh men to have an eye both to the beginning and to the ending of their benefits and good turns, and to give such things as may like a man not only at the receiving of them but also ever after. . . . Whether anger drive a man to do that he ought not, or whether the heat ambition withdraw him from his welfare: yet shall I not suffer him to mischief himself, neither shall I give him cause to say afterward, 'He hath killed me with his kindness.'" I quote from Arthur Golding's translation of 1578; Thomas Lodge in 1614 also rendered "Ille amando me occidit" as "He hath killed me with his kindness."[41]

My intention is not to suggest Seneca's *De beneficiis* as source for the title of Heywood's play but rather to introduce the work into this discussion of *A Woman Killed with Kindness* as one element in the contextual nexus of classical moral philosophy which also includes, most importantly, Aristotle's *Ethics* and Cicero's *De amicitia*.[42] By these lights Frankford can be viewed as an aspirant to classical magnanimity, as signalled by his name, "frank," which according to the *OED* means "liberal, bounteous, generous, lavish."[43] And, indeed, a review of the relevant precepts of the moral philosophy of friendship and benefice as the Renaissance received them strikes chord after chord with the play;[44] so, too, does the decay of ideals resonate with the play's tragic eventuation. To posit this context as relevant to *Woman Killed* is also to suggest that the dramatic and ethical energy in the main plot of the play is vested

41. Lucius Annaeus Seneca, trans. Golding, sigs. E1^{r-v}; trans. Lodge, p. 49. Below I employ Lodge's translation, which, although it postdates *Woman Killed*, is a nearer contemporary of the play and has the advantage of a more fluid and accessible syntax.

42. Laurens J. Mills, in *One Soul in Bodies Twain* (1937), argues that there was no one classical theory of friendship in the Renaissance; there were *theories* (p. 6). Among the Greeks he finds Aristotle more influential than Plato but asserts that Cicero eclipsed both. Caxton printed John Tiptoft's translation of the *De amicitia* as early as 1481; Rastell produced a second edition in 1530; John Harington's translation appeared in 1550 and 1562; Thomas Newton's translation (which I follow below), in 1577. As J. Wylkinson's 1547 translation of Aristotle's *Ethics* is incomplete, I use that of J. A. K. Thomson and Hugh Tredennick (1976). This approach took shape when Michael D. Bristol introduced me to gift-theory.

43. A more frequently encountered context for Frankford's character and actions is the theological one, reflecting the long-lived influence of Adams (p. 157). See Ribner, p. 53; Spacks, pp. 325–26; and Robert Ornstein (1976), pp. 128–29. Others call Frankford smug and priggish; see Brodwin, p. 108, and Robert Bechtold Heilman (1968), p. 214. If it is true, as I argue, that Frankford is fashioned on classical models of magnanimity, his "priggishness" may instead reflect prescribed deliberation and probity. His demeanor in the first scene is Aristotelian: the magnanimous man "will talk neither about himself nor about anyone else, because he does not care to be complimented himself or to hear others criticized" (p. 158); he "is not prone to express admiration, because nothing is great in his eyes" (p. 157).

44. In addition to benefice and gratitude, the points of correspondence between the *De beneficiis* and the play include the issues of revenge, pertinent to Frankford (pp. 306–11); the notion that benefits may proceed even from the bondman who "performeth more than that day's work to which he was hired," as does Nicholas (pp. 102–9); and the dilemma of ransom provided by an evil man, as Acton does for Mountford (pp. 60–62).

more in the relationship of Frankford and Wendoll than in that of Frankford and Anne.

That Frankford invites Wendoll to "be my companion" hard upon his hymn to domestic content is, as already suggested, ironic, because Wendoll will destroy that content. But the speech also establishes a Ciceronian context for Frankford's decision to adopt Wendoll as a friend and to share prosperity with him. The spirit in which Frankford describes his life—"How happy am I amongst other men," "I am possess'd of many fair revenues, / Sufficient to maintain a gentleman," "The riches of my thoughts, and of my time / Have been a good proficient," and "If man on earth may truly happy be, / Of these at once possess'd, sure I am he"—reverberates throughout such classical literature glorifying friendship as Cicero's: "so far off is it that friendship should be desired for neediness, that they which being endued with wealth and riches and specially with virtue (wherein is most aid) and not standing in need of any other, are men most liberal and bountiful." Cicero continues (in an English translation of 1577): "But what foolisher thing is there, than for a man (to th'end he may bear great port and sway through his wealth, riches, and revenues) to get other things that are sought for—as money, horses, servants, apparel, worship, and costly plate—and not to get friends, being the best and (as I may say) the goodliest furniture that can be in this life?"[45]

Friendship affords the opportunity to express generosity, according to Aristotle, for as "doing good to others is characteristic of virtue and the good man, and it is better to do a kindness to a friend than to a stranger, the good man will need friends to receive his benefits." Seneca advises the potential benefactor to make "choice of such (on whom we are to bestow our benefits) as are worthy to partake them." Cicero's ideal is modelled on his friendship with Scipio: "One house served us both, one fare and that even common." He warns that "as we be bountiful and liberal, not of purpose to get thanks therefore, . . . so likewise do we think that friendship is to be desired of men, not led thereto with hope of reward, but because all the fruit thereof resteth in very love it self"; and Seneca agrees that if a kindness is performed with hope of recompense, "then had it been no benefit, but a bargain." Aristotle asserts that "another mark of the magnanimous man is that he never, or only reluctantly, makes a request, whereas he is eager to help others."[46]

Thus, in a bow to Seneca, Frankford assures himself that Wendoll is

45. Cicero, sigs. C7^{r-v} and C8^v. Aristotle agrees that friends are "the greatest of external goods" (p. 303).
46. Aristotle, pp. 304 and 157; Seneca, p. 73; Cicero, sigs. F3^v and B6^v–B7^r.

worthy ("I have noted many good deserts in him"; he is "a gentleman / Of a good house" [4.29–33]). Aware that Wendoll is also "somewhat press'd by want" and in "possibilities but mean" (4.33, 64), he offers, like Scipio, to hold table and purse in common: "They are yours" (4.65–66). As Cicero and Seneca would wish, Frankford turns aside a lavish display of gratitude: "There needs no protestation, for I know you / Virtuous, and therefore grateful" (4.78–79). Wendoll later marvels that "This kindness grows of no alliance 'twixt us," that "I never bound him to me by desert," and that the benefit is all the greater because he himself is "A man by whom in no kind [Frankford] could gain!" (6.33–37). Frankford's only request of Wendoll, to "be my companion," may not be made with Aristotelian reluctance, but it is put as modestly as possible. Anne recognizes the nature of the relationship that Frankford has initiated: "It is my duty to receive your friend" (4.72, 82).

Wendoll four times refers to Frankford as his "friend" even as he seduces Frankford's wife. In accordance with its focus on friendship, the text subordinates Anne's character to its own ethical intent.[47] She never speaks of her own honor or affect in response to Wendoll's importunities; she alludes instead to Frankford's "kind friendship" and remarks that "you are much beholding to my husband; / You are a man most dear in his regard," "My husband loves you," "He esteems you," "It is my husband that maintains your state." She speaks of herself only as the "espous'd wife of so dear a friend." Wendoll, too, thinks of the injury to Frankford rather than to her chastity: "shall I wrong his bed," "shall I wrong this man," "I will not speak to wrong a gentleman / Of that good estimation." In the end he exploits the friendship itself as his most effective tactic in seduction, telling Anne that he will for desire of her risk even the loss of Frankford's hospitality and his own livelihood.[48] He begins by insinuating fellow feeling: "I love your husband, too, / And for his love I will engage my life." He baldly declares that the "sincere affection borne to you / Doth no whit lessen my regard of him." Finally, Wendoll's tributes to Frankford and to friendship undo her: "My soul is wand'ring, and hath lost her way" (6.21–151).

Betrayal of such magnitude is not entertained in the classical literature of friendship and benefice, which is, after all, premised on the notion that friendship is possible only between men of virtue and which

47. Van Fossen observes universal critical condemnation of Anne's easy submission (p. xlvi). In 1938, Hallett D. Smith undertook a defense that failed finally to persuade: witness Roger Stilling (1976), p. 179, and Leanore Lieblein (1983), p. 190. See also Gutierrez, pp. 276–77.

48. Louis B. Wright finds the play "almost a preachment against the violation of friendship" in "Male-Friendship Cult" (1927), p. 511. See also Van Fossen, pp. xlvii–xlviii; Stilling, p. 177; and Gutierrez, p. 276.

thus advises men of virtue how to find and be good friends. There are cautions: Cicero warns the would-be friend "to stay the vehement earnestness of his good will, even as he would stay his race in running: to the intent we may so use our friendships as men use to assay their horses, making somewhat a trial of the manners of our friends." He also laments that covetousness and ambition can occasion "great enmity . . . between right dear friends." But these caveats scarcely dim his praise of friendship as "the only thing in this world of whose profitableness all men with one mouth do agree"; "they seem to take the sun out of the world, which would take friendship from among us." And Plutarch's distinctions between flatterer and friend, reintroduced to the English Renaissance by Erasmus and thereafter a subject for unnumbered works of contemporary moral philosophy, are insufficient to predict Wendoll's perfidy. Seneca warns the benefactor to beware ingratitude as "the most grievous and greatest of crimes" but offers the consolation that "in effect all the injury that he did thee consisteth in this, that thou didst lose thy good deed: but comfort thyself with this, that thou didst not lose the better part thereof, which is, the honour to have given the same." This might seem cold comfort to Frankford, who loses a great deal more than his good deed. One last example from Seneca reveals how Wendoll challenges moral example:

> A certain man defendeth me, being accused and guilty of some capital crime, and afterwards useth infamous violence to my wife, and ravisheth her; he hath not taken away the good that he did me, but opposing an equal injury to the same, he dischargeth me of my debt; and if he hath hurt me more than he profited me before, the good turn is not only extinguished, but I have free liberty both to complain, and to revenge, where, in comparison of the benefit, the injury over-weigheth it: so, the benefit is not taken away, but overpressed and drowned.

Even here, mooting the rape of a wife as the most grievous example of injury, Seneca considers only violation committed by the giver of a benefit, not the recipient; nowhere in his treatise is put forward the example of a man who receives such benefits as Wendoll does and who returns such villainy.[49]

Wendoll himself explicates the monstrousness of his ingratitude: "When I but think of Master Frankford's love / And lay it to my treason"—the last a term he has already employed during his seduc-

49. Cicero emphasizes that "friendship cannot be but in good men" and "neither can friendship in any wise be without virtue" (sigs. A8^r and B1^v). Also cited: Cicero, sigs. D3^v, B8^v, E4^v, and C5^{r-v}; Seneca, pp. 20 and 225.

tion of Anne—"or compare / My murd'ring him for his relieving me, / It strikes a terror like a lightning's flash / To scorch my blood up" (16.37–41). Frankford also makes the terrible equation for his "many courtesies": when Wendoll "compare[s] them with [his] treacherous heart, / Lay[s] them together, weigh[s] them equally," then there will be revenge sufficient (13.72–75). Frankford concludes the latter passage by, for the second and third times, naming Wendoll a Judas. Wendoll seven times terms himself a "villain," as does Nicholas thrice and Frankford and Acton once each. Wendoll also twice calls himself a "traitor"; for both Nicholas and the repentant Anne, he is "the Devil," and for Nicholas, finally, "Satan." As Owen Feltham wrote: "If I shall receive any kindnesses from others, I will think that I am tied to acknowledge and also to return them, small ones out of courtesy, and great ones out of duty. To neglect them is inhumanity; to requite them with ill, satanical."

The title alone of Feltham's 1623 essay, "That Great Benefits Cause Ingratitude," is significant of a changing moral climate in early modern England. So is that of Daniel Tuvill's 1608 treatise "Cautions in Friendship."[50] In the disenchantment that Frankford experiences during the brief course of *Woman Killed*, he enacts a process that occupied moral literature throughout the sixteenth and seventeenth centuries, as cynicism corroded the ideals of friendship received from the great romances and from Aristotle, Cicero, and Seneca. Alberico Gentili explicitly challenged the classical authors: "We are speaking of the friendships of individuals which we see all about us, not drawing arguments from those ideal friendships which philosophy invents for our benefit, none of which we actually see, but at best we have merely read about some of them."[51] Thomas Elyot noted that "Cicero sayeth" that "men firm, and stable, and constant should be taken in to friendship," but he added that that sort of man is in "great scarcity and lack, and to judge which they be is a very hard thing."

Even when proposing that "there is nothing that so much delighteth the mind as faithful friendship," Elyot nonetheless warned that "thou shouldest a long time consider, whether thou shouldest take any in to thy friendship" and then should "commit nothing to him but that that thou wouldest commit to an enemy." Similarly, in 1589, Walter Dorke concluded a heavily Ciceronian "praise of friendship" on a discordant

50. Owen Feltham, *Resolves* (1623), sigs. X3^{r-v}. Daniel Tuvill, *Essays* (1608), pp. 47–55.
51. Benjamin Nelson, in his *Idea of Usury* (1969), quotes Gentili and others on the "exorbitant demands exacted by the classic and medieval canons of friendship"; he argues for "a turning-point in the history of moral sentiments" (pp. 155–57). Mills more mildly concludes that high ideals were often accompanied by "a sense of failure" (p. 112). Their theses qualify Wright's insistence on the continued "cult of male friendship" (p. 510).

note: "Yea, to make our full period (though friendship's praise be infinite) such is the force thereof, that mighty kings have desired it, it is so glorious; famous philosophers have honored it, it is so spacious; cruel tyrants have been amazed at it, it is so victorious; all men in general have praised it, it is so precious; and yet few have effectually at any time attained unto it, it is so miraculous."[52]

Meanwhile, warnings against friendship proliferated in moral works less specifically derived from the classical literature of praise. In 1579 Haly Heron stated that "the strength of one only virtue is not sufficient to knit the steadfast knot of true friendship. . . . In trust is treason and, to conclude, in fellowship ofttimes is found most wicked and deceitful falsehood." In 1606 Barnaby Rich called "the friendship of this time" one "more apt to enter into any exploit of vice than to relieve the necessity of his friend that wanteth." In 1622 Henry Peacham cautioned: "If among one hundred of your acquaintance, yea, five hundred, you meet with two or three faithful friends, think yourself happy. Such is the world in our cunning age"; and Feltham asserted, "it is prudence so to look upon men, as, though they be now friends, they may yet live to become our enemies. Stability is not permanent in the unstable heart of man; and therefore we are not oblig'd to trust them with that, which may deliver us into their power to ruin us, if after they shall once fall off. How often do we see dear friends decline into detested enemies?"[53]

Perhaps the best indication of a spreading recognition of the risks of friendship can be found in the frequency with which cautions are raised in private works of advice, which, as the twentieth-century critic Agnes M. C. Latham notes, are "strained . . . only in part through literary filters" and in other part through the authors' "own experience."[54] Around 1584 William Cecil, Lord Burghley, included among "Certain Precepts for the Well Ordering of a Man's Life" the advice that "it is a mere folly for a man to enthrall himself to his friend further than if just cause be offered he should not dare to become otherwise his enemy." In 1604 Sir William Wentworth warned his son in one marginal note, "your friend today, your enemy tomorrow," and, in his text,

52. Thomas Elyot, "Manner to Choose and Cherish a Friend," "sayings" collected from classical authors (1531), sigs. B5ᵛ and B7ᵛ; Walter Dorke, *Type or Figure of Friendship* (1589), sig. B2ᵛ.
53. Haly Heron, "Of Company and Fellowship," *New Discourse of Moral Philosophy* (1579), sigs. B8ᵛ–C1ʳ; Barnaby Rich, *Faults, Faults* (1606), sig. E3ʳ; Henry Peacham, *Complete Gentleman* (1622), p. 205; Feltham (in later editions of his *Resolves*; here, 1661), sig. Kk2ᵛ. John L. Lievsay (Tuvill's editor) notes: "Here is nothing of the generous or genial, nothing of idealism. Instead, the emphasis falls upon the niggling 'Cautions' of the title" (p. 181).
54. Agnes M. C. Latham, "Sir Walter Ralegh's *Instructions*" (1959), p. 199.

"your friend afterwards may become your enemy, a thing very common in these days." In 1609 Henry Percy, Earl of Northumberland, wrote of friends that "I have found so many and so weak hearted in cases of adversity, inclining so much to the overloving of their own particulars, that the very respects of common humanity and fortitude have been laid aside." Latham remarks the "sourness with regard to friendship" that Sir Walter Raleigh revealed in his *Instructions to his Son,* and Alan Macfarlane reports how, at some social remove, clergyman Ralph Josselin hesitated when confronted by a man who "desireth my friendship," because "friends are not hastily to be chosen."[55]

Traditional moral philosophy was being superseded not by a new ethic of friendship but by a psychology of distrust and resentment, built all too often out of immediate experience. In a speech to Parliament on 12 November 1586, Elizabeth I, interpolating the proverbial phrase cited by Haly Heron, above, institutionalized this psychology: "Good neighbors I have had, and I have met with bad, and in trust I have found treason. I have bestowed benefits upon ill-deservers, and where I have done well, I have been ill-requited and spoken of."[56] In her statement we see a revealing transition: where once classical allusion carried the force of moral prescription, it now served the lesser expediencies of rhetorical emphasis.

In *A Woman Killed with Kindness,* notions of friendship are similarly debased, especially in the subplot, where the term is used to refer to circles of allegiance, as those of Acton's, or of influence, as that of Shafton's over the prisonkeeper (7.61). The male relationships depicted in the play are, at the same time, relentlessly contestatory. We see this not only in Frankford's cuckolding by Wendoll but also and emphatically in Mountford's betrayals, first, by the "troop of friends" who came with him to the hawking match but who "all" flee, and, then, by Acton, Shafton, his uncle Old Mountford, his friend Master Sandy, his tenant Master Roder, and his cousin Tydy. We see it again and throughout in Mountford's and Acton's efforts to outdo each other in graceful speeches at Frankford's wedding; in the fact that all the men onstage are eager to take part in the hawking match; in the arguments among the servants Jenkins, Nicholas, Roger, and Jack over what to dance and with whom; in Acton's denial of the loss he first admitted in the hawking match and in the swordfight with which the contest is played out; in

55. William Cecil, "Certain Precepts" (1584), p. 13; Wentworth, pp. 18 and 23; Percy, p. 75; Latham, p. 212; Alan Macfarlane, *Family Life* (1970), p. 150.

56. Elizabeth I, *Public Speaking,* p. 89. The occasion was her reply to the petition for the execution of Mary, Queen of Scots.

Acton's legal suit and appeal; in Shafton's avidity for Mountford's land; in Wendoll's covetousness of Frankford's wife; and in the ruthless subtext of the card game in Frankford's parlor.[57]

Thomas Wright in 1601 wrote to this last example that "others in play . . . carry a secret pride and vehement desire to win because they would not be inferior to others, even so much as in play." Thomas Gataker, meanwhile, in 1620 observed that "there can be no ordinary intercourse and commerce or conversing between person and person, but there must be a precedency on the one part and a yielding of it on the other. Now where they be equals, there may be some question, some difficulty, whither shall have the priority"; as F. G. Bailey recognizes, "equality exacts its price."[58] So oppositional is homosocial relationship that Frankford's virtuous intention in benefit, to establish parity in friendship, is equally as oppressive as Acton's vengeful determination to humiliate, to establish precedence in rivalry. In this theme the two plots strike a harmonic chord of the end of virtue as Cicero and Seneca had construed it.

From Virtue to Interest

The advice that a Frankford might most usefully have heeded was in fact to be found not in works of classical moral philosophy but instead in the works of his contemporaries, and most particularly in their oeconomics and conduct books. These introduce the competing domestic ethic to which I have referred. In 1568 Edmund Tilney, for example, noted:

> many men blame their wives for ill life, when they themselves are the causers thereof for maintaining such companions, whereby he himself doth hardly escape infamy. And these good fellows do seek to creep into greatest friendship with the husband, to the intent they may have better opportunity with his wife. Yet may he use his tried friend or near kinsman familiarly, as well in his own house, as elsewhere, having always regard to the old saying that a man may show his wife and his sword to his friend, but not too far to trust them. For if thereby grow unto him any infamy, let him not blame his wife, but his own negligence.

57. Laura G. Bromley (1986) suggests that Wendoll's card game innuendoes reveal his "unrestrained pride and desire" (p. 272); Levin, that Mountford and Acton engage in "a contest of magnanimity" (p. 94).
58. Thomas Wright, *Passions of the Mind* (1601), p. 180; Thomas Gataker, *Marriage Duties* (1620), sig. B4ᵛ; F. G. Bailey, *Gifts and Poisons* (1971), p. 19.

The anonymous author of *Civil and Uncivil Life* warned in 1579 that "you see how easily you may be deceived in the love of your neighbors, and that haunting your house may be for other cause or occasion, as well as love [i.e., friendship]." Dod and Cleaver seconded in 1598 that "the wise husband shall never set himself so far in love that he forget that he is a man, the ruler and governor of the house and of his wife, and that he is set (as it were) in a station to watch and diligently to take heed what is done in his house, and to see who goeth out and in." And Thomas Gainsford observed in 1616 that "Oeconomic instructeth the husbands that they bring no suspicious person to their houses."[59]

In contemporary terms Frankford is implicated in and must accept responsibility for his own undoing. As the anonymous author of the *Court of Good Counsel* declared: "Let all men be assured that the greatest part of the faults committed by wives in this age take the beginning from the faults of their husbands. . . . if perchance the husband have some occasion given him to mistrust, let him examine his own life well, and he shall find how the occasion came from himself, and that he hath not used her, as he ought to have done."[60] This theme, first introduced with reference to *Arden of Feversham* and repeated in the second coda, is expressed most clearly in two other plays of the period, the anonymous *Second Maiden's Tragedy* and Heywood's own *Rape of Lucrece*. In both— grim parallels to Frankford's case—householders welcome into their very houses and themselves introduce to their wives the men who will cuckold them. They then absent themselves; as the maid Sisley quotes in *Woman Killed*, "When the cat's away the mouse may play" (12.5–6).[61]

In the subplot of *Second Maiden's Tragedy*, for example, a man who has no cause to distrust his (unnamed) wife nonetheless determines to test her virtue: "What labour is't for woman to keep constant / That's never tried or tempted?" (1.2.30–31). The husband, Anselmus, enlists in this objective his friend Votarius and, in that peculiarly Renaissance manner by which all social bonds are eventually perverted by any intentional violation of one, tests Votarius, too, demanding complicity in the very name of friendship: "Have I a friend?"—or can it be instead "That I must trust some stranger with my heart?" (1.2.62–65). His stratagem, one that throws into ominous relief Frankford's first absence from his

---

59. Tilney, sig. C6ʳ; *Civil and Uncivil Life*, p. 33; Dod and Cleaver, sig. M6ᵛ; Thomas Gainsford, *Rich Cabinet* (1616), fol. 103ᵛ.
60. *Court of Good Counsel* (1607), sigs. C2ʳ⁻ᵛ.
61. Of related relevance is the motif in both *A Warning for Fair Women* and *1 Edward IV* whereby the mere appearance of a woman outside her house seems to hint at her availability to a man other than her household lord and where public interchange engenders a desire for carnal exchange.

house, is to ensure that the reluctant Votarius has uninterrupted access:

> To give thee way,
> I'll have an absence made purposely for thee
> And presently take horse. I'll leave behind me
> An opportunity that shall fear no starting. . . .
>
> (1.2.147–50)

The deserted Wife reemphasizes that it is her lord Anselmus "That gives [Votarius] the house-freedom, all his boldness"; Votarius turns to the purpose her complaints that Anselmus's absence reveals him to have "lost his kindness, / Forgot the way of wedlock" (5.1.55–56; 1.2.107–8). Eventually seduced by the feigned act of seduction, Votarius follows the usurpatory progression recognizable in Mosby and Wendoll, from aberrant possessiveness of the Wife—"I do not like his overboldness with her; / He's too familiar with the face I love"—to ambition for exclusive control of the house—"Methinks 'tis not kindly / We two should live together in one house; / And 'tis impossible to remove me hence." He even exclaims, "I would he would keep from home like a wise man; / 'Tis no place for him now" (2.2.84–94, 39–40). And Votarius also details the irony of his access: while Anselmus "shall watch to keep all strange thieves out," he himself may "familiarly go in and rob him / Like one that knows the house" (2.2.140–42).[62] Discovery of the adulterous affair demands five deaths, including those of the cuckolder Votarius, the Wife (who, it is remarked, "ran upon two weapons and so died" [5.1.165]), and also the husband who set the intrigue in motion.

Heywood's *Rape of Lucrece*, too, is occupied with the erotic and tragic consequences of privileged access. Sextus Tarquin conceives his lust for Lucrece when Collatine enlists in the wager that brings the Roman soldiers to each of their houses at dead of night, to try the comparative excellences of their wives. He thus makes Sextus "an eyewitness of their beauties," and he pledges further to "commit my Lucrece wholly to the dispose of Sextus" for his selection of the fairest of them (1626–30). The "verdict" is, of course, for Lucrece (1643). Sextus finds opportunity to act on his lust when Collatine, returned to camp, sends him to

---

62. Not every member of the seventeenth-century audience would have seen so clearly Anselmus's responsibility for his own undoing—as even a modern reader can remind us. In "Double Plot" (1963), Richard Levin depicts the Wife as setting the plot in motion and considers her "failure" directly responsible for the sins, deaths, and damnation of Votarius and Anselmus (pp. 226–27).

Rome with the token of a ring "to purchase . . . kind welcome" at his house. As Sextus remarks ominously, "in this gift thou dost thy bed betray" (1718, 1725). Like Anne Frankford, Lucrece reads and honors her husband's signalled intent: "My love to my dear husband shall appear / In the kind welcome that I give his friend" (1794–95). Even before the "treason" of Sextus, she spells out that "Without that key you had not entered here"; "without this from his hand, Sextus this night could not have entered here"; "Without this ring" friends "can no entrance find in the night" (1793, 1862–63, 1867). And, after, she insists that the "cause of all my woe" and of her husband's "discontent" is "This ring, oh Collatine! this ring you sent" (2447–48). She has opened her household gates in deference to her husband's will, and, as in *The Second Maiden's Tragedy*, sexual violation (which here will require her suicide) follows from this spatial license.

The inexorable movement of these plays from favored entrance to seduction and rape (and from thence to tragedy) illuminates the way in which Frankford, too, sets in train his own cuckolding.[63] We see, if Frankford does not, that Wendoll is what Gainsford would call a "suspicious person." There is Wendoll's first-scene eagerness to affiliate himself with his betters through a wager that he can ill afford. By Sir William Wentworth's lights, ambition to useful connection is also what brings him to Frankford's house with news of the hawking match: "Whosoever comes to speak with you, comes premeditate for his advantage." His arrival, described by Nicholas, is ominous: his horse "Up to the flank in mire, himself all spotted / And stain'd with plashing"; because he has, with "Here goes my heart," joined the fatal fight after the match, we may assume that he is "stained" with the bloody marks of violence as well. Nicholas's further description—"horse and man both sweat; / I ne'er saw two in such a smoking heat"—is one of assault upon Frankford's house (4.22–25; 3.41).[64] Of such a situation Dod and Cleaver note: "There are certain things in the house that only do appertain to the authority of the husband, wherewith it were a reproach for the wife without the consent of her husband to meddle with all: as to receive strangers." And although Frankford has bidden Nicholas to "Entreat [Wendoll] in," Anne enters as his usher; she has already heard the visitor's report; and Frankford is in this way created the outsider in his own home, asking confusedly, "What news, sweet wife? What news,

63. For Spacks, too, Frankford's fate is "in a sense his own fault" (p. 326).
64. Cited: Wentworth, p. 14. In arguing that Wendoll brings a threat of the violence he has experienced to impinge upon Frankford's domestic content, I differ from Van Fossen, who emphasizes the contrast between the violence of scene 3 and the peacefulness of scene 4 (p. xxxviii); Rauchbauer, who sexualizes Wendoll's arrival (p. 204, n. 10); and Rick Bowers (1984), who sees "manly exertion and physical strength" (p. 297).

good Master Wendoll?" (4.26, 38). Thus early is suggested the violation of Alexander Niccholes's potent warning: "Make not thy friend too familiar with thy wife."[65]

Frankford nonetheless immediately thereafter solicits Wendoll's residence in his house. Frankford—in Wendoll's presence—asks Anne to "Use him with all thy loving'st courtesy" (4.80). And when away from home, he leaves behind a provocative invitation that he asks Anne herself to deliver:

> . . . he wills you as you prize his love,
> Or hold in estimation his kind friendship,
> To make bold in his absence and command
> Even as himself were present in the house;
> For you must keep his table, use his servants,
> And be a present Frankford in his absence.
>
> (6.74–79)

Like Mosby, Votarius, and Sextus, Wendoll is fully aware of the opportunity afforded by Frankford's absence; he insinuates to Anne that "Your husband is from home, your bed's no blab" (6.165). Later, when Frankford accompanies a second departure with the invitation "in my absence use / The very ripest pleasure of my house," Wendoll exults, "I'll be profuse in Frankford's richest treasure" (11.63–64, 116).[66]

Modern gift-theory helps us to comprehend Wendoll's perverse return of benefit. Lewis Hyde, for example, writes of how, until the recipient of benefice properly rises to the level of the benefice and achieves an equivalent act of giving, he must "suffer" gratitude, and so, presumably, Wendoll "suffers." We can read Wendoll in contemporary terms in the light of Feltham's "That Great Benefits Cause Ingratitude": "Extraordinary favors make the giver hated by the receiver, that should love him. . . . Benefits are so long grateful, as we think we can repay them: but when they challenge more, our thanks convert to hate. It is not good to make men owe more than they are able to pay."[67] Wendoll hints at the oppressiveness of hospitality in saying that Frankford "cannot eat without me, / Nor laugh without me" (6.40–41). We

---

65. Dod and Cleaver, sig. M8^r. Alexander Niccholes, *Discourse of Marriage* (1615), sig. G4^v.

66. The last invitation is also issued to Cranwell: the meaning is innocent to one not bent on interpreting it as Wendoll does. Frankford is, of course, by this point quite conscious of Wendoll's interpretation.

67. Lewis Hyde, *Gift* (1979), p. 47; Feltham, sig. X2^v. Seneca suggests that "what most of all maketh men ungrateful" is either "an overweening of our selves" or "covetousness or envy" (p. 66). See also Lieblein on Wendoll's indebtedness, pp. 190–91.

get another glimpse of his servitude to companionship when Anne describes how he is searched for when not found where expected (6.70–72). As in *Two Lamentable Tragedies*, here the alternate plot articulates with more clarity the phenomenon at work in the main plot; so, it is Mountford who explicitly despairs of his ability to repay Acton and who rebels against his enslavement to indebtedness: "His kindness like a burden hath surcharged me, / And under his good deeds I stooping go, / Not with an upright soul" (14.63–65).

The political language that characterized Alice Arden as a rebel against her husband is never used of Anne Frankford.[68] Instead it is Wendoll who is in revolt, here against surcharge. He is peculiarly the architect of Anne's fall, as Nicholas recognizes when he states that "It is that Satan hath corrupted her, / For she was fair and chaste" (6.179–80). Acton repeats: "O that same villain Wendoll! 'Twas his tongue / That did corrupt her" for "she was of herself / Chaste and devoted well" (17.12–14).[69] Frankford, too, accuses Wendoll of "robb[ing] me of my soul, of her chaste love" (8.183). And yet, although Wendoll is guiltily aware of the crime he has committed against Anne, "her whom I did kill" (16.99), Frankford has anticipated him and will with some insistence succeed him in self-accusation, speaking of "she whom her husband's kindness kill'd" (17.140). If Wendoll is the agent of evil, and if Frankford is responsible for welcoming Wendoll into his house, then according to the standards of contemporary prescription, he is finally responsible for her fall as well.

Cicero's famous definition of a friend as "th'other I"[70] undoubtedly informed Frankford's invitation to Wendoll to "be a present Frankford in his absence," but *Woman Killed* illustrates the politically expropriatory underside of Ciceronian correspondence. The abstract ground of philosophy permits of an idealization that Heywood's dramatic world, painstaking in its domestic contextualization, instead betrays. The household, more precisely, cannot accommodate another I, for the household hierarchy as ideally constituted is, again, bipolar—husband and wife, master and servant—and its dichotomous bias proves incapable of adapting itself to any such tripolar relationship as that threatened by, for example, Wendoll's introduction into its arena. His appropriation of Anne is effected in part through the authority he has been

68. Bromley, by contrast, argues for a political reading (p. 271).
69. Spacks calls Anne an "accidental sinner" (p. 325); Canuteson agrees that the decision is Wendoll's (p. 131).
70. Newton has "for he is a friend, which is (as it were) an other himself" (sig. E2ᵛ), but far more common in the period is "th'other I" (here, for example, from Baldwin, sig. L7ᵛ) or even the Latin "alter ego."

granted over Jenkin, whom he can command to "Vanish" to advance his venture in seduction (6.67).[71]

"The mixing of governors in an household, or subordinating or uniting of two masters," insisted Whately, "doth fall out most times to be a matter of much unquietness to all parties."[72] The consequences of Frankford's magnanimity radiate to the members of his extensive household in just the manner that domestic conduct books would insist, engendering incoherence of authority; Jenkin, most notably, launches a series of quibbles concerning his confusion about the direction of his duty (6.57–63; 8.5–10) that culminate in his eventual uncertainty as to whether his loyalty is owable to person or to household. Rather than establishing a coincidence of identity and interest, in other words, Frankford's expression of virtue has empowered a political rival.

But Frankford is distinguished from Anselmus and from Collatine by his motivation, and in that distinction lodges a particular interest of *A Woman Killed with Kindness* for the history of early modern thought. The proverb with which Heywood titled his play must find its full significance in the fact that Anne has been sacrificed to Frankford's aspiration not to test her virtue or to contest her excellence but rather to express toward Wendoll a "kindness" of Ciceronian or Senecan magnitude. In his return of betrayal rather than gratitude, Wendoll emblematizes the falling-off from classical ideals that early moderns experienced and that they chronicled, even in their idealizing literatures. The philosophical paradox is that Frankford's "expression" of classical virtue undoes his own domestic interest.

From Friendship to Companionate Marriage

The friendship of Cicero, I propose, could not survive the broad acquisition of private property in the early modern period, the proliferation of consumer goods, the attendant dispersal and intensification of felt distinctions between *meum* and *tuum*, and the correspondent imperatives regarding control of personal possessions.[73] Mountford

71. In our first view of the household following the seduction, Jenkin notes that "My master and the guests have supp'd already" (8.1–2), leaving unanswered for some twenty lines to which "master" he refers. On the subject of Wendoll's intrusion into what she terms the "dyad of husband and wife," see Gutierrez, pp. 275–76.

72. William Whately, *Care-Cloth* (1624), sig. A6ᵛ.

73. In related fashion Jean-Christophe Agnew suggests a "historical movement away from ritual, kin, and prescriptive bonds and toward contractual, commutable, and convertible forms of compensation" that were introduced by "market mechanisms" (*Worlds Apart* [1986], p. 8).

implies the causal relationship when he attributes to "covetous thoughts" the unwillingness of his friends to help him (10.16). So does Sir Walter Raleigh when advising the withholding of aid and surety, "for thereby millions of men have been beggared and destroyed, paying the reckoning of other men's riot." And Alberico Gentili makes the connection unambiguous: "Those ideal friendships [that philosophy invents for us] regard all the possessions of friends as common property, and there are many other differences between such friendship and those of real life."[74]

In insisting that benefits are "managed from will to will" (or, as a modern translater puts it, are "transaction[s]" that are "performed in our minds"), Seneca obscured the necessarily contaminating process through which generosity is translated into concrete form, as well as the determining effect of that form in focusing in material directions the emotions and escalating longings of the recipient. As hinted by a fact that Hyde points out, that etymologically "liberality is desire; libido is its modern cousin," Frankford through his hospitality is implicated in the actuation of the preeminently desiring subject of the play, Wendoll.[75] When Frankford offers Wendoll place, gelding, man, and table, asking in exchange companionship, he provokes a series of unhappy consequences: the occupation of the house confirms Wendoll in his material envy of property as well as his social envy of connectedness to community; the maintenance of his horse prolongs his self-identification as a gentleman even as it preserves his antisocial will to detachment, his power to flee accountability; the offer of an attendant from among Frankford's men releases a political ambition that will expand from authority over one to usurpation of all; the provision of sustenance arouses in Wendoll, as in so many other banqueters on the Renaissance stage (including among them Browne of *A Warning for Fair Women* and Edward IV of *1 Edward IV*), sexual appetite; the offer of homosocial bonding carries expectations not only of friendship but also of entitlement, homosexual relationship, and rivalry.[76] All these desires are entangled in the specific desire that the character Wendoll enacts, which on the face of things is (hetero)sexually appropriatory.

In this displacement of multiple desires onto Anne, *A Woman Killed with Kindness* offers us one further insight about notions of property and anxieties of possession in the early modern period: these notions and anxieties could be and often were transferred to and cathected in women. Such a symbolization of women requires in its turn the denial

74. Raleigh, quoted in Leites, "Duty to Desire," p. 393; Gentili, quoted in Nelson, p. 157.
75. Seneca, p. 76; see also John W. Basore's translation, p. 119. Hyde, p. 35.
76. See Eve Kosofsky Sedgwick, *Between Men* (1985), p. 1.

of their subject status, the withholding of even such characterologic substance as a playtext can confer. *Woman Killed* is extreme in this regard: Anne is introduced to us as a blank canvas on which male characters may limn, as do Mountford and Acton, in their dissimilar portraits of her; as does Frankford, who subsumes her personality in her dependent roles by speaking of her exclusively in terms of what she has not inherited from her father, how she is unlike her brother, and how she "Hath to her dower her mother's modesty" (1.49–54); and as does Wendoll. His imagery conflates possession of Anne's body with entrance, occupation, and appropriation of Frankford's house as well as Frankford's exile from it. Thus, he accompanies his first physical contact with Anne by speaking of "The path of pleasure and the gate to bliss, / Which on your lips I knock at with a kiss" (6.162–63). Thus, during the card game, he insists on partnering Anne because when Frankford does "I sit out." And thus, he seconds Cranwell's call for the game of "post and pair" because he and Anne "shall be soonest pairs, and my good host, / When he comes late home, he must kiss the post" (8.126, 161–62; Van Fossen glosses "kiss the post" as "be shut out").[77] Three scenes later, with Frankford locked out, Wendoll finally accepts the full, only quasi-sexual meaning and consequences of his deepest desires, declaring, "I am husband now in Master Frankford's place / And must command the house" (11.89–90). It appears that Anne is rather more the vehicle for Wendoll's economic ambitions and political aggressions than the tenor of them.[78]

If Anne is allowed a voice of "her" own, it is only when, discovered, she awaits Frankford's pronouncement of her fate. In this brief interval she declares a philosophy of suicide. She would willingly commit the sin of self-murder and jeopardize her eternal salvation, she suggests, to effect temporal moral recuperation:

> O to redeem my honour
> I would have this hand cut off, these my breasts sear'd,
> Be racked, strappado'd, put to any torment;
> Nay, to whip but this scandal out, I would hazard
> The rich and dear redemption of my soul.
>
> (13.134–38)

77. Heywood engaged an architectural symbolization of women most directly in his *Rape of Lucrece*. There the complex integration of the wife's identity with her unhusbanded house is represented by a ring, traditional symbol of female sexuality, that serves as a "key" to her household door and, in turn, to her own "conceal'd" door. Heywood alone makes Lucrece's oeconomic skill the grounds of her triumph in the contest of wives and, in a song in praise of Lucrece, figures her beauty in architectural terms.

78. Lieblein also finds that Wendoll enjoys adultery as "mastery" over Frankford (p. 191).

Strikingly, the terms of this philosophy are echoed in the succeeding scene, but by Susan rather than Anne and almost as prophecy instead of project. Susan foresees for herself a similar end when, solicited by Mountford to sacrifice herself to Acton in requital of Mountford's debt, she asks if she must "cut off [her] hands and send them [to] Acton" or "Rip up [her] breast"; she, too, finally determines to kill herself "To save [her] honour" (14.57–58, 85). The ethical problematics of self-murder are scarcely at issue here, because female suicide is substantially a convenience for the male characters, freeing Frankford from his ambiguous state as a "widower ere my wife be dead" (15.30) and releasing Mountford to offer Susan to Acton without serious qualm.

While most readers of *Woman Killed* have remarked the "contrast between Mistress Frankford's easy yielding of her honour and Susan's Roman staunchness," and while it is true that elsewhere, in his 1624 prose *Gunaikeion*, Heywood enjoyed the play of distinction between women "Chaste and Wanton,"[79] I argue here for a conceptual pattern that contrasts the two women only superficially (characterologically) and that conflates them functionally (ethically) by submerging any prospect of their agency.[80] The polarity of Susan's chastity and Anne's wantonness is diminished by Susan's forecast of her identical fate and by the fact that that fate is circumvented not by her own "Roman staunchness" but by Mountford's "honorable" gamble on it. Only male honor, in other words, has the moral purchase to inspire such reform as Acton voices: "You overcome me in your love, Sir Charles" (14.133). At the same time, the axiological focus is exclusively male: Wendoll never doubts that Anne will succumb to him or that the decision to betray Frankford is his to make (and Anne justifies the assumption).

79. I quote Ure, who acknowledges Townsend (p. 149). Others who contrast the two women include Felix Sper (1929), p. 550; Coursen, pp. 183–84; Ornstein, p. 139; and Bonnie L. Alexander (1978), p. 7. See also Heywood, *Gunaikeion* (1624), sig. A5^r.

80. The linguistic parallels are marked. Frankford says that Anne "takes not after you, Sir Francis. / All his wild blood your father spent on you" (1.49–50); Acton says Susan is "ne'er descended from old Mountford's line" (7.101). Frankford remembers how before her exile Anne sang with a "ravishing voice" and made her lute "Speak sweetly many a note" (15.18–22); Susan's cousin remembers how before her poverty she "sung well" and "play'd sweetly"—on what the first quarto calls a "flute" but the second quarto has (more plausibly) as a "lute" (9.24). Wendoll says, "when I meditate—O God, forgive me— / It is on [Anne's] divine perfections" (6.10–11); Acton describes himself as "rapt in admiration / Of [Susan's] divine and chaste perfections" (9.60–61). Wooed by Wendoll, Anne says, "My soul is wand'ring and hath lost her way," and speaks of "This maze I am in" (6.151, 160); discovering Mountford's release (intended by Acton to woo her), Susan says, "I am rapt into a maze of wonder," and "My wits have lost themselves" (10.59, 78). At her presentation to Acton, Susan asks, "Brother, why have you trick'd me like a bride?"—in other words, in striking theatrical replication, like Anne in the first scene (14.1). The penultimate scenes find each in her only moment of self-determination, each resolved to die, each for sexual shame. Frankford is moved by Anne's penitence to "wed [her] once again"; Acton is reformed by love of Susan to "seal" her his wife (17.117; 14.146).

Mountford confidently uses the language of a lover himself in persuading Susan to accept his stratagem for repaying Acton (and she as readily transfers her loyalty from him to the reformed Acton).[81]

As these last instances suggest, the worldview that identifies women as the ultimate signifier for male property requires their own complicity in their depersonalization. Anne in her first speech empties herself of content: she declares that the "perfections" described by Mountford have value, "Such as they be, if they [her] husband please." Their only end is his approval: "They suffice me now I am married." She is incapable of self-evaluation: "His sweet content is like a flattering glass, / To make my face seem fairer to mine eye." His mood determines hers: "the least wrinkle from his stormy brow / Will blast the roses in my cheeks that grow" (1.31–36).[82] Both Anne and Susan, moreover, give voice to the preeminence of masculine honor and the right of patriarchal authority. Awaiting Frankford's judgment, Anne predicts: "He cannot be so base as to forgive me" (13.139). Deferring to Mountford, Susan reasons, "But that I know / These arguments come from an honour'd mind . . . I should condemn you." Instead, she accedes: "So Charles will have me, and I am content" (14.76–83). Even the resolutions of suicide function less importantly at the characterologic level (by lending Anne and Susan their textually unique approximations of agency) than they do at the plot level (by releasing Frankford and Mountford to the less complicated pursuit of their own ethical, political, and economic interests).

Neither Anne nor Susan, moreover, participates in the system of benefice operative in the text—as giver or as recipient. As Vives wrote, "A woman that giveth a gift, giveth her self: a woman that taketh a gift, selleth her self. Therefore an honest woman shall neither give, nor take." Instead she is herself the gift; Thomas Gataker found in Proverbs the title of his treatise, *A Good Wife, God's Gift*. Hyde concludes that "where men alone may give and receive, and where women alone are the gifts, men will be active and women passive, men self-possessed and women dependent, men worldly and women domestic, and so on, through all the clichés of gender in a patriarchy." According to Claude Lévi-Strauss, marriage is the most basic form of gift exchange—as

81. In Heywood's *Curtain Lecture*, Galdrata Bertha parallels Susan in certain respects: without her consent or knowledge, her father offers her to an emperor; when she objects, the emperor instead makes her a "gift" to one of his noblemen; and in this case of legal marriage she makes no complaint (sigs. D1ʳ–D11ʳ). Bertha's father is guilty of "base Pandarism"; Mountford, by contrast, exacts Susan's consent.

82. This is reminiscent of Tilney: the husband's "face must be her daily looking glass, wherein she ought to be always prying to see when he is merry, when sad, when content, and when discontent, whereto she must always frame her own countenance" (sig. E4ᵛ).

Hyde observes, the woman "moves when she marries"—and the text gestures toward this fundamental significance with Acton's reference to Anne's hand as "given" to Frankford in marriage (1.8).[83] But the implications of the theme are more pronounced in Mountford's resolution to offer Susan to Acton in order "In one rich gift to pay back all [his] debt" (10.124) and in Acton's affirmation, "Your metamorphos'd foe receives your gift / In satisfaction of all former wrongs" (14.141–42). Heywood would have found this theme of female exchange in the source for his subplot, *The Palace of Pleasure*, where the Mountford character declares: "And I which am her brother, and have received that great good will of her, as in my power to have her will, do present the same, and leave her in your hands, to use as you would your own, praying you to accept the same, and to consider whose is the gift, and from whence it cometh, and how it ought to be regarded."[84]

Notable is not only the assertion that his is the power to "have" her will but also the insistence as to "whose is the gift, and from whence it cometh, and how it ought to be regarded": this passage demonstrates Julia Kristeva's and Gayle Rubin's contention that the desired woman is a "pseudo-center, a prize the winning of which, instead of forging a male/female relation, serves rather to secure male bonds." Or, in an inversion of terms but not of sense, the desired woman serves to focus the grounds of male contestation. Gift-giving, as Marcel Mauss recognized, has among its "underlying motives . . . competition [and] rivalry"; as F. G. Bailey noted, it "may be interpreted as a challenge"; as even Seneca was aware, it could initiate a "contest of benefits"; as Heywood's contemporary William Westerman pungently observed, "gifts be as birdlime, they entangle the wings, and make that the receiver is not his own man, but standeth in awe of the giver."[85]

My argument has circled back to the moral philosophy of friendship and benefice. Historians Lawrence Stone and Louis B. Wright along with philosopher Edmund Leites would appreciate the way in which a discussion of the place of women in Renaissance society has returned

83. Joannes Ludovicus Vives, *Instruction of a Christian Woman* (1529), sig. O1ᵛ. Thomas Gataker, *Two Marriage Sermons* (1620); Hyde, pp. 102 and 96; Claude Lévi-Strauss, *Elementary Structures of Kinship* (1949), p. 65. He calls the woman "the supreme gift among those that can only be obtained in the form of reciprocal gifts." And see on this subject Gayle Rubin, "Traffic in Women" (1975), especially pp. 170–83.

84. William Painter, *Palace of Pleasure* (1580), quoted in Van Fossen, p. 114. See also Gifford Hooper (1974). Perhaps the reason so many critics have found Heywood "sympathetic" to women is that he depicts them as gifts rather than commodities (see Hyde on the distinction, p. 60). Arthur Melville Clark, for example, has written of Heywood's "championship of women and his praise of marriage" (p. 172), especially in *Gunaikeion* and *Curtain Lecture*.

85. I quote Karen Newman (1987) on Kristeva, p. 21; see also Rubin. Marcel Mauss, *The Gift* (1925), p. 26; Bailey, p. 24; William Westerman, *Sword of Maintenance* (1600), sigs. C3ʳ⁻ᵛ. Gutierrez makes a similar point, pp. 280–81.

me to notions of friendship. For they have argued that in this period the ancient ideals of friendship were recycled to ground theoretically the paradigmatic relationship of husband and wife.[86] They depict the early modern ascendance of a concept of companionate marriage as the final triumph of the classical philosophy of friendship. Prescriptive literature can seem to bear them out; to the examples given by Leites, I might add that of Feltham: "Questionless, a woman with a wise soul is the fittest companion for man: otherwise God would have given him a friend rather than a wife. . . . It is the crown of blessings, when in one woman a man findeth both a wife and a friend." Of particular significance is the "Homily of the State of Matrimony," which introduced marriage as "instituted of God, to the intent that man and woman should live lawfully in a perpetual friendship" (as well as "to bring forth fruit, and to avoid fornication").[87]

The sophisticated discourse of friendship is without doubt adapted to what has been called the "exaltation" of matrimony in the sixteenth and seventeenth centuries,[88] and so the term "companionate marriage" is rhetorically apt. But at the same time, it is functionally misleading, as Tilney's *Brief and Pleasant Discourse of Duties in Marriage, Called the Flower of Friendship* hints: "Because no friendship or amity is, or ought to be, more dear, and surer, than the love of man and wife, let this treatise be thereof, wherein I would the duty of the married man to be described. For the knowledge of duty is the maintenance of friendship." Into the formula of friendship and benefice has been inserted the ingredient peculiar to matrimony, "duty." Indeed, for Richard Greenham, even desire is in this manner to be domesticated: "One may know whether his wife be brought unto him of the Lord. . . . when they desire mutually to do the duties which they owe one unto another."[89]

Early in this chapter I (disingenuously) suggested that in the first scene of the play, Acton touts wifely submission to old hierarchies while Mountford advances the new virtues of equality in marriage. Wright, Stone, and Leites would similarly dichotomize domestic patriarchalism, the construct for male/female relations that the sixteenth century inherited, and companionate marriage, the construct that the century inaugurated. Kathleen M. Davies, too, notes the coexistence of these

86. Lawrence Stone, *Family, Sex, and Marriage* (1977); Louis B. Wright, *Middle-Class Culture* (1935). I cite Leites's "Duty to Desire" (pp. 393–94), but see also his *Puritan Conscience* (1986). And see Theodore Zeldin, "Personal History" (1982).

87. Feltham, sigs. Z3^{r-v}; "Homily of the State of Matrimony" in *Certain Sermons*, ed. Rickey and Stroup, p. 239.

88. Todd, p. 18; see also pp. 21–22.

89. Tilney, sig. A6^v; Richard Greenham, *Works* (1599), sig. D2^r.

theoretically opposed views of marriage in the period, remarking that contemporaries "took the paradox in their stride."[90] But I suggest that this, like other paradoxes I have mooted above, reads as a contradiction only to us, not to Renaissance Englishmen. In celebrating the play-closing nuptials of one woman "too poor" to be her social better's bride (Susan) and of another who "prostrates" her soul in shame before her moral superior (Anne), *Woman Killed* finally helps bring us to the recognition of how essentially similar these two perspectives on marital relations were in the view of most early moderns. In the unsettled times that followed the Reformation, the companionate relationship of male and female could be valorized as companionate precisely *because* it was fundamentally hierarchical. William Perkins defined a couple as "that whereby two persons standing in mutual relation to each other are combined together, as it were, into one. And of these two the one is always higher and beareth rule: the other is lower and yieldeth subjection."[91] The "one" into which the two combine is by definition he who bears rule; the woman can never be anything other than a lower "other," cannot really threaten (as can a male friend) to be another "one" (or other I).

A Woman Killed with Kindness takes issue with Cicero's argument that "if you take out of the world the knot of friendship, certes, neither shall any house be able to stand," for only *without* "friendship" is Frankford's house in fact able to stand. The text adopts instead Henry Smith's contention that "masters should receive none into their houses, but whom they can govern"—and because there was available an unrelenting ideology for the governance of women, that of domestic patriarchalism, this was more likely to be a female other than a male "other I."[92]

The Ethic of Interest

The resolution that *Woman Killed* achieves does not escape the specter of the generic impertinence of *Arden of Feversham*: the epilogue apologizes that "some will judge [our play] too trivial, some too grave." The text's "triviality" is that characteristic of the domestic tragedy: its cast of gentles, its focus on marital dispute, its address of private matters. Its "gravity" is that of the topics it engages: the issue of private

90. See Stone (1977), p. 325; Wright (1927), p. 227; and Davies (1981), p. 60.
91. Perkins, pp. 418–19.
92. Cicero, sig. B3^r; Henry Smith, sig. G3^v.

revenge, the punishment of female adultery, the legitimacy of divorce, the sin of suicide—heated topics all, as the many contemporary publications on these subjects reveal.[93]

Even independent of these grave and current issues, however, *A Woman Killed with Kindness* is a moral document of some significance. This claim for it may be put into final perspective with reference to *Timon of Athens*, of which John M. Wallace writes: "Shakespeare, in the first decade of the century, saw and felt more vividly than anyone before him that gratitude and good turns were not a glue that could be trusted to keep society stuck together"; the play exposes "Seneca's culpable naiveté in thinking that benefits could be made into a workable system of social behavior." But Shakespeare, according to Wallace, offered no alternative to the Senecan tenets; *Timon* "concludes, for want of anything better, by leaving them still in place."[94] *A Woman Killed with Kindness* displays in the same decade the same disillusionment with received moral philosophy, but we can extrapolate from it an alternative, one that—in yet another apparent paradox—springs from the very political and economic motives that rendered that philosophy obsolescent. Virtue inheres in domestic duty, in the right ordering of the individual's household commonwealth and the careful supervision of its associated possessions, in a new domestic ethic.

As Wallace also notes in his discussion of *Timon*, "Neo-stoicism is less concerned with finding a 'basis for a healthy society' . . . than it is with describing personal development."[95] But *Woman Killed* admits no such bias. It sees the virtue of the (male) self and the order of society as seamlessly integrated, through the identification of the householder's honor with his household and through the recognition of the household as the building block of social stability. The notions found their most typical expression among the third of the traditional functions of marriage, as during the early modern period reference to the lawful propagation of children was "expanded" to incorporate Puritan notions of socially responsible child rearing (a phenomenon Margo Todd has charted). As the author of *The Christian Man's Closet* put it, this "end

93. On the punishment of female adultery, which for William Heale still "lawfully" included wife murder (though he admitted there had begun to attach to it "the guilt of heinous offence"), see his *Apology for Women* (1609), sig. H1ʳ. On private revenge, which occupied so many tragedies that it has defined a theatrical subgenre, see Fredson Bowers (1940), especially p. 225. On suicide, see John Donne, *Biathanatos* (?1608). On divorce, see George Joye (?1549), Erasmus (?1550), *Work of the Holy Bishop S. Augustine* (1550), John Dove (1601), John Howson (1602), Edmund Bunny (1610), and John Rainolds (1609); among domestic oeconomies, see especially William Whately, *Care-Cloth* (1624), reversing *Bride-Bush* (1617). Interest in divorce motivated Clapham to translate Agrippa (see Yost, p. 32).
94. John M. Wallace, "*Timon of Athens*" (1986), pp. 362 and 360.
95. Wallace, p. 362.

of lawful matrimony" was "the procreation of children, to be brought up in the fear and nurture of the Lord, and praise of God, that they may be meet for his Church and the commonwealth."[96]

In the "person" of the maid in her smock, who interrupted Frankford's revenge on Wendoll in a clear echo of the angel who stayed Abraham's sacrifice of Isaac, *A Woman Killed with Kindness* was capable of conflating into sympathetic impulses the domestic and the divine. Elsewhere, in a defense of stage players against antitheatrical prejudice, Heywood further celebrated the hegemonic synthesis of self, house, and society. The rhetorical emphasis of that text reveals his confidence in the universal power and suasive capacity of the domestic ethic: "Many amongst us, I know to be of substance, of government, of sober lives, and temperate carriages, *housekeepers, and contributary to all duties enjoined them.*"[97]

96. Todd, p. 22; Bartholomaeus Battus, *Christian Man's Closet* (1581), sig. A4ᵛ.
97. Thomas Heywood, *Apology for Actors* (1612), sig. E3ʳ (emphasis added).

The Key and the Cogito

Both as a historical personage and as a literary character, George Sanders, the murdered householder of *A Warning for Fair Women*, is in all respects but one a cipher when compared with his generic progenitor, Thomas Ardern.[1] That one distinction is a literary report to the effect that the historical figure left behind a quasi-autobiographical fragment. A coda to Arthur Golding's *Brief Discourse of the Late Murder of Master G. Sanders* transcribes "A note of a certain saying which Master Sanders had left, written with his own hand, in his study":

> Christ shall be magnified in my body whether it be through life or else death. [The text is Philippians 1:20.] For Christ is to me life, death is to me advantage. These words were Master Nowell's theme which he preached at the burial of my brother Haddon upon Thursday, being the twenty-fifth day of January Anno Domini 1570, Anno Regina Elizabeth 13. Among other things which he preached this saying of his is to be had always in remembrance, that is, that we must all (when we come to pray) first accuse and condemn ourselves for our sins committed against God before the seat of his justice, and then after cleave unto him by faith in the mercy and merits of our Savior and Redeemer Jesus Christ, whereby we are assured of eternal salvation.[2]

Philippe Ariès, who associates the English incubation of privacy with its fad for the keeping of diaries, would locate our sense of encounter with

---

1. Sanders's single appearance in the *State Papers* is his commission for the sale of Spanish goods; see *CSPD*, 1547–80, p. 437: vol. 85, no. 59 (February 1572).
2. Arthur Golding, *Brief Discourse* (1573), p. 230. The note may be apocryphal, but the issue here is the material framework that serves to certify it.

the "private" thoughts and emotions of George Sanders in his apparent literacy and in this attribution to him of a scrap of memoir. With this I have no quarrel. To advance my speculation on the relationships of privacy and property, however, I also focus on the telling detail of the discovery of this document in Sanders's study.

To convey my sense of the significance of the material medium that produced this fragment, I must, first, remark on the study as a domestic space; second, address the early modern uses of locks and keys with regard to the security of the study; and, third and finally, return to John Frankford's study and to the scene in *A Woman Killed with Kindness* which prompts this excursion. The scene represents in emblematic form a pivotal moment in the process of the construction of modern (male) subjectivity.

In *Some Rules and Orders for the Government of the House of an Earl*, Richard Brathwait interrupts a catalogue of the earl's officers and their duties to describe a place. In his view the room at issue is essentially a strongbox writ large, a space for the storage of account books, correspondence, and documents of property, venture, and inheritance:

> I digress to a matter, which albeit the same belongeth not to the secretary his place, yet I think here fittest to insert the same, being necessary for the Earl to know; which is, that I wish the Earl to have in his house a chamber very strong and close. The walls should be of stone or brick; the door should be overplated with iron, the better to defend it from danger of fire: The keys thereof the Earl himself is to keep. In this chamber should be cupboards of drawing boxes, shelves, and standards, with a convenient table to write upon; and upon every drawing box is to be written the name of the manor or lordship, the evidence whereof that box doth contain. And look what letters patents, charters, deeds, feoffments, or other writings or fines are in every box; a paper roll is to be made in the said box, wherein is to be set down every several deed or writing, that when the Earl, or any for him, hath occasion to make search for any evidence or writing, he may see by that roll whether the same be in that box or not. In the standards and upon the shelves are to be placed court rolls, auditor's accompts, books of survey, etc. Also empty boxes both for letters patents and other evidences, when there is cause to carry them out of that chamber. If there be occasion of search to be made for any evidences in this house (the Earl himself not being present), under two persons at the least should not enter therein; and if they take out any evidence or writings, in the same box out of which they be taken they are to leave, under their hands, in writing, the name of every such deed or writing as by them is taken forth, and the cause for which they did it, and the day and year of their so doing, and also by what warrant. For the Earl ought to have more care of the safe keeping of his evidences, than either

of his plate or jewels. But I will end this digression and return to other household officers and offices.[3]

Brathwait's overdetermined procedures for the exigency of the house-holder's absence emphasize the normative exclusivity of his relation-ship to his strong and close chamber. The association obtains in *Arden of Feversham*, when, in one of his first plots against Arden, Mosby pro-poses to commission Clarke to create a poisoned portrait of Alice so that in gazing on it Arden may die. Alice objects feelingly that anyone else "Coming into the chamber where [the portrait] hangs may die" as well. But Mosby replies: "Ay, but we'll have it covered with a cloth / And hung up in the study for himself." In Alice's continued protestation of the danger of this strategy, she cannot conceive of being brought her-self into the study to see the portrait; instead she imagines it brought out of Arden's exclusive space for her viewing: "Arden, I know, will come and show it me" (1.227–41).

Arden also, notoriously, has a countinghouse, the room in which Black Will and Shakebag hide on the evening of his assassination. This room, too, as they emphasize, is lockable. While Brathwait elsewhere distinguishes the countinghouse from the study as a more public room in which, among other things, servants are held to account, the two were, in fact, companion spaces.[4] In the house of a man of less proper-ty, the separate functions of the countinghouse and the study might be pursued at different times in a single chamber, but always at the discre-tion of the householder. The parallel history of the two is reflected in *A Woman Killed with Kindness*, as, in his study, Frankford does his stocktak-ing of advantages concrete as well as abstract—status, birth, estate, income, education, wife—with the final metaphorical *summum*: "If man on earth may truly happy be, / Of these at once possess'd, sure I am he." And as the activities of the study ingrained themselves in cultural practice, abstract accountings, encouraged in their own way by a "con-venient table" and its writing implements, came to characterize men whom we would otherwise associate with the countinghouse, like the merchant George Sanders.

Brathwait's rigorous concern with the control and preservation of the "evidences" of a man of wealth involved, by extension, control of access to them. In this respect the study was a domestic space without

---

3. Richard Brathwait, *Some Rules and Orders* (n.d.), pp. 17–18. Although Brathwait does not give his "strong and close" chamber a name, it is described in an account of "The Secretary his Place."

4. Brathwait, p. 5. Volpone, Barrabas, and Arden have countinghouses. Arden's is re-vealed to be relatively easy of access when his murderers hide there.

precedent in the Elizabethan and Jacobean household, the chambers of which were otherwise communal and multipurpose.[5] No surer indication of the difference between early modern notions of physical "privacy" and our own can be found than in the practices of the bedroom.

Household inventories of the sixteenth and seventeenth centuries list beds in nearly every conceivable space—halls, parlors, stair landings, outbuildings, and kitchens, as well as bedchambers proper—in houses of all size, status, and regions. At the same time, even the bedchambers of householders had trundles or pallets added for their attendants. The basic distinction available to early moderns, in other words, was not that of the public and the individual space but that of the public and the shared. Admittedly, householders had some experience of environmental control, for, in the case of shared space, discretion could be exercised in the selection of authorized sharers.[6] Although the paradigm for the staging of retreat and the election of co-occupants was the royal suite,[7] even a gentleman like the fictional John Frankford could have a withdrawing room as well as a bedchamber. This means that access to Frankford in notionally private moments was sequenced in terms of floor plan as well as floor level. But *private* is a relative term when the presence of a servant's pallet meant that the highest degree of somnolent and sexual seclusion in the early modern household expressed itself solely and by our lights inefficiently through the drawing of bedcurtains. Thomas Heywood emblematizes spousal intimacy in titling his oeconomic treatise *A Curtain Lecture*, for this token of privacy.

All indications are that privacy was not an object of the architecture of the period. How could it be, when early moderns had so little domestic experience of it? In the one critical instance of the householder's study, however, privacy was a by-product of architectural ambitions to protect and preserve records and objects of value. Further, the association of the study with the strongbox imported with it the notion that the room, like its lesser antecedent, required a lock and key. This accessory to the function of the study, its capacity to be locked and its concern with the keeping of the key, in yet another way distinguished it from other household spaces and practices.

A Woman Killed with Kindness illustrates for us the most common function of household keys, which existed in single copies for outer doors, which locked household residents in, in safety, during the vulnerable night, and which passed through many household hands. Thus

5. See my "Causes and Reasons" (1994).
6. The fictional Frankford makes it clear that the passageway between his dining chamber and his parlor is off limits to a stablehand (see page 147, above).
7. See David Starkey, Introduction to *The English Court* (1987).

Jenkin is required to lock the gates and "send up the keys" to Anne in her "private" bedchamber when she and Wendoll retire there; thus Frankford is required to make copies of his own keys to effect his later entry. William Wentworth generalizes the practice in his 1604 advice to his son: "Let there be good orders and peace in all your house and let the doors at night be surely shut up by some trusty ancient servant." And one Thomas Ellwood records how this shutting up was accomplished in the early seventeenth century: "There were four outer doors, and the keys of all of them were kept on one chain and taken up to the father's chamber at night."[8]

As with other conventions, this one, too, revealed itself in violations. There is the case of John Scacie, who was jailed for "having been in the habit, whilst apprenticed, of conveying himself through his master's doors at midnight . . . notwithstanding that he endangered thereby his master's goods, and the safety of his person, through leaving the doors open at night." And there is the further example of a notorious alcoholic named Mistress Killingworth, whose neighbors would carry her home at night and who, "at their going from her, used to shut the door and throw in the key, thinking (as indeed it was) the best security for her self, and the goods she possessed."[9] Note in both instances the twinning of persons and possessions, an adumbration of my proposition that identity is constituted in ownership.

The study, meanwhile, invented and required a new use for lock and key, a daylight use. Like a chest, the study contained its objects securely. But, unlike a chest, it also admitted its owner within its boundaries. Closeting himself inside, the householder discovered a space that was unique to him, that accepted his exclusive imprint upon it, that rejected the incursions of others, that welcomed him into the comforting embrace of his proofs of possession, that celebrated an identity independent of relational responsibility, and that put ready to hand the impedimenta of authorship. More, the association of the space with valuables and with prohibited access invested his own isolation with a derivative prestige. That Brathwait's fictive earl is to keep the key to the study

8. William Wentworth, "Advice to his son" (1604), p. 14. Ellwood quoted in Maurice W. Barley, *English Farmhouse* (1961), p. 148.

9. For Scacie, see Ann Jennalie Cook, *Privileged Playgoers* (1981), p. 79. This anecdote throws some light on Michael's betrayal in unlocking the doors of Franklin's town house to assassins in *Arden of Feversham*. See also Michael Dalton, *Country Justice* (1618): "A servant conspireth with a stranger to rob his master, and at a time appointed in the night, he letteth in the stranger into the house and led him to his master's chamber, and the stranger killeth his master, the servant standing by; this is petty treason in the servant and murder in the stranger" (sig. S6v). For Killingworth, see *Apprehension . . . of Elizabeth Abbot* (1608), sig. A2v.

"himself" indicates the link between the householder and a precursive privacy unattainable by any other member of his household. The housewife, in particular contrast, was to have no room of her own for some generations.[10]

In a discussion that furthers our postmodern understanding of the construction of subjectivity, Jean-Christophe Agnew quotes John Hall: "Man in business is but a theatrical person, and in a manner but personates himself. . . . in his retired and hid actions, he pulls off his disguise, and acts openly." Agnew comments that "Hall's observation suggests a number of things, not least of which is a new concept of privacy, one centered within the self rather than within the household, as had earlier been the convention."[11] In fact, no intuition of this process of centering within the self, in distinction from the household, can be more striking than that realized and dramatized in the discovery scene of *A Woman Killed with Kindness*, when Frankford's entitlement to "retired and hid actions" is pointed by his withdrawal to his study.

The discovery opens with Frankford's exit to what we are to understand is his bedchamber. There, offstage, he finds his wife in bed with his cuckolder. He returns to the stage to deliver a moving lament: "O God, O God, that it were possible / To undo things done, to call back yesterday" (13.52–53). He exits for a second time to startle the lovers awake. Wendoll, in a nightgown, crosses the stage in flight. Frankford pursues him and is prevented from making a third exit only by the interruption of his good genius, whose angelic gesture persuades him to patience and dissuades him from vengeance. Anne then enters, herself in "night attire," for their highly charged scene of confrontation and remorse. Frankford raises the emotional pitch by summoning their children, tormenting Anne with a last view before he banishes them from her "infectious" presence. She grovels at his feet: "In this one life I die ten thousand deaths."

At this moment of highest sensation, Frankford interrupts:

> Stand up, stand up: I will do nothing rashly.
> I will retire awhile into my study,
> And thou shalt hear thy sentence presently.
>   (13.128–31)

10. In "Mercantile Writing and the Construct of Privacy," Stephanie H. Jed relates secret rooms, secret books, and secret writing to the protection of female chastity. She quotes Leon Battista Alberti: "I always kept my writings not in the sleeves of my clothes, but shut off and organized in my study almost as a sacred and religious thing. I never gave my wife permission to enter this place, either with me or alone" (*Chaste Thinking* [1989], p. 80).

11. Jean-Christophe Agnew, *Worlds Apart* (1986), p. 97.

A stage direction indicates his exit. When he returns, he prefaces his decision with the evidence of how he has occupied himself: "My words are regist'red in Heaven already" (13.152). In the privilege of his study, Frankford has reached his "judgement" unadvised, taking counsel only of himself and his conscience in a space that precludes any influence or intervention. The point is underlined by Cranwell's aborted interruption of the announcement, which seems to suggest that he would have argued with it, given opportunity. But the study exerts its preemptive authority.

During the interval of Frankford's retreat, Anne is left onstage in her smock and dressing gown. At first she is alone in the bright gaze of the voyeuristic audience; then she is displayed to a second audience of "all the Servingmen," who cry accusingly, "O mistress, mistress, what have you done, mistress?" (13.145). Her exposure, "public" by William Whately's definition of the term and starkly contrasted to Frankford's remove, indicates again that Agnew's divorce of self from household pertained only to the householder.

Above I referred to George Sanders's study as "producing" his autobiographical fragment. It did so in two respects. First and most obviously, it presumably preserved the physical document until Arthur Golding transcribed it (as, similarly, the Willoughby study preserved the marital history reviewed in the previous coda). In this respect the study served the protective function of the strongbox and of the countinghouse. But second and more significantly, it also generated the discursive practice recorded in the document. Unlike a strongbox or a countinghouse, it allowed of private meditation and linguistic formulation; it permitted this creation of the perceived individualism of George Sanders. If the study similarly produced Frankford's judgment, and if (as I propose) his judgment valorized his agency, then the study authored him as an apparently determinate male self.

The study not only inaugurated the experience of a private behavior but also nourished the apprehension of individual selfhood. This is to take one step further Alice T. Friedman's remark that "spaces and boundaries exert their own influences on the patterns of behavior enacted within them."[12] One suprabehavioral end of the study's influence is the philosophy of Descartes, who dichotomized the physical and the mental, then privileged the mental. If this, too, is so, consider the irony: the very idea of the mental was delivered by the midwifery of the material, by the accidental sensory experience of isolation afforded by four walls, a door, a lock, and a key, all consecrated to the accumula-

12. Alice T. Friedman, *House and Household* (1989), p. 7.

tion, inventory, and administration of goods and properties. In short, the key in the hand eventually enabled the *cogito*.

At the same time, the inanimacy of the study rendered its role invisible to its occupant. In this way yet again the discovery scene of *A Woman Killed with Kindness* offers a parable of cultural process. Frankford is confident in a self independent of its inscription by society. His conviction of his invention of his judgment is revealed in his declaration of responsibility for its result: "Here lies she whom her husband's kindness kill'd." The study is in this sense the symbol of society and its scripting work. It has left its unacknowledged imprint upon Frankford, upon Descartes, and upon all heirs to the Enlightenment.

Chapter Four

DOMESTIC ABDICATIONS

Remembering the dissolution of Roche Abbey in June 1539, Michael Sherbrook wrote (sometime between 1567 and 1591) that sight of both the "sorrowful departing" of monks, friars, and nuns and also "the sudden spoil that fell the same day of their departure" "would have made an heart of flint to have melted and weeped." Both displacement and despoil figure in his vivid recollection of an encounter between his uncle and a monk of the abbey: "Which monk willed my uncle to buy something of him; who said, I see nothing that is worth money to my use. No, said he; give me two pence for my cell door, which was never made with five shillings. No, said my uncle, I know not what to do with it (for he was a young man unmarried, and then neither stood need of houses nor doors)."[1]

Without doubt, at the time of his solicitation by the monk, Sherbrook's uncle had a place of residence. But Sherbrook will not give that residence the name "house" unless it is his uncle's own house (and his uncle the householder). In this distinction some of the original power is restored to a word so common that for us, centuries later, it is easily emptied of any significance other than the grossly generic architectural one. If we take this word as if it is a metaphor, if we grant that to the Renaissance, too, it had already in many uses become a dead metaphor, if we nonetheless begin the search for its associations, we will discover one clue in Sherbrook's casual assumption that the "house" is initiated by marriage. And if we recall *A Woman Killed with Kindness*, we will

1. Michael Sherbrook, "Fall of Religious Houses," p. 123.

connect marriage and householding to the assumption of social role and oeconomic responsibility. A second clue can be located in Sherbrook's synecdoche for house and correlative of wife, that is, the door, signifying ownership, exclusion, and the enclosure and protection of possessions, principally including the wife. Written decades later, in 1663, Balthazar Gerbier's architectural treatise similarly focuses householding, the possession of a wife, and jealous proprietorship on the totemic image of the door: "A good surveyor shuns also the ordering of doors with stumbling-block-thresholds, though our forefathers affected them, perchance to perpetuate the ancient custom of bridegrooms, when formerly at their return from church, did use to lift up their bride and to knock their head against that of the door, for a remembrance that they were not to pass the threshold of their house without their leave."[2]

Clifford Geertz declares that "semiotics must move beyond the consideration of signs as a means of communication, code to be deciphered, to a consideration of them as modes of thought, idiom to be interpreted. It is not a new cryptography that we need . . . but a new diagnostics, a science that can determine the meaning of things for the life that surrounds them."[3] Cryptography assumes a one-to-one relationship of term and meaning and implies stasis; Geertz's "diagnostics" permits of the variable, the multiple, and the dynamic in "modes of thought." In my own attempt at a diagnostics of the sign "house" in the early modern period, I have seen it as the locus of the private, in the first chapter; as a center of political definition, economic function, and ideological contention, in the second chapter; as a unit of social realization, a force of moral restraint, and the embodiment of both temporal and transcendent values, in the third chapter; and finally as a material agent in the construction of personal identity, in the third coda. In this chapter I turn to some further moral significances of place, which, especially through contemporary domestic prescription, are relatively accessible to us. I turn also to what Ernst Cassirer has called the "mythical" meanings of place. These are more remote; my window on them is Shakespeare's *Othello, the Moor of Venice* (1604).

In mythical thinking, Heinrich Nissen has demonstrated, the heavens are "an enclosed, consecrated zone" likened to "a temple inhabited by one divine being and governed by one divine will." That is, first, all space is contained; as Cassirer confirms, "there is no detached, no merely abstract, form of space; instead, all intuition of form is melted

2. Balthazar Gerbier, *Counsel and Advice* (1663), sig. C3ʳ.
3. Clifford Geertz, *Local Knowledge* (1983), p. 120. His recommendation for semiotics is to render it "of effective use in the study of art."

down into the intuition of content." Second, each container has an occupying and sensible power. Nissen continues that this twofold conceptualization of space is ineluctably transferred "to every sector of juridical, social, and political life," so that the Renaissance habit of analogous thought constructs, first, boundaries and, second, spatial sovereigns in every sphere. The principle of analogy requires that there be spatial containers within spatial containers, or worlds within worlds, so that the cosmos operates rather like the successively encapsulated volumes of a Russian doll. The notion that cosmic space is necessarily inhabited by an occupying power replicates itself in terms of a subordinate power for each subsidiary container. Cassirer emphasizes that this understanding of the cosmos forms "the basis for the development of the concept of property"; in other words, in the instance of the primary domestic space, it authorizes the door.[4] It also, by extension and with reference to Henri Lefebvre, forms a basis for a concept of authority and, in consequence, for a theory of obligation or exaction of obedience.[5] In other words, again in domestic terms, it legitimates the householder. It is in large part by such an intuition of space that in the late sixteenth century Jean Bodin could without hesitation declare it "the law of nature, which willeth, that every man should be master of his own house."[6]

In Bodin's cosmology, this last statement requires no proof. Instead it is the unargued and unarguable validation for his contradiction of a "Roman" law "that the married daughter, except she be before by her father set at liberty, although she have forsaken his house and dwell with her husband, shall not yet for all that be in the power of her husband, but of her father." For Bodin, by contrast, the critical transfer of political responsibility is realized not de jure, by patriarchal permission, but de facto, by physical relocation, when the woman "forsakes" her father's house to dwell with her husband. Bodin's forceful objection that contemporary "custom generally exempteth the married woman out of the power of her father" can be read with some relevance into the first act of *Othello* and the transfer of power signified therein by Desdemona's removal from her father's house; the early modern understanding of the mythical significance of place is implicated in her elopement. But Bodin's customary moral exchange is also aborted there, incomplete, because while Desdemona moves away from a space governed by her father, she does not move to one governed by her

---

4. Ernst Cassirer, *Mythical Thought* (1955), pp. 99–101 and 89. Cassirer cites Nissen.
5. Henri Lefebvre, *Production of Space* (1974). See especially pp. 11 and 21–24.
6. Here and below: Jean Bodin, *Six Bookes of a Commonweale* (1576; English translation, 1606), sigs. C2^{r-v}.

husband. The full consequence of Othello's violation of Bodin's locational law of nature ("Every man should be master of his own house") is communicated and compounded in the play by the operative subtext of a mythical system of spatial meanings, a system keynoted for us by the name of her interim residence in Venice, the "Sagittar/y."

Cassirer attributed mythical thinking primarily to ancient societies, but the force of mythical thinking maintained currency in the Renaissance through occult philosophies. Like domestic and political patriarchalism, occult philosophy aspired to a comprehensive world view, but one incorporating the material and the conceptual rather than the governmental and familial. Brian Vickers explains that this is a symbolic construct in which nature achieves its significance as "a system of signs."[7] In *Othello* the decipherer and manipulator of the occult system of signs is the ensign, or sign-bearer, Iago. Iago's intuitions enable him to establish an early and predictive dominance of mythical space that adumbrates his moral influence over Othello; Iago's plot advances, in one deep structure of the play, through a nonlinear apprehension of cause. Although investigation of the occult constructions of the text will at first necessarily be cryptographic, my interest remains diagnostic: I am concerned with mythical significances of place to the extent that they inform and empower the moral conceptions that finally determine the construction of private tragedy.

Othello's tragedy is in part located in his unwitting violations of the moral code of domestic place and of those obligations for governance entailed by spatial sovereignty. He initially abdicates his domestic responsibilities but then, in wild overcompensation, asserts his patriarchal rights in the Roman form of domestic murder.[8] This pattern holds for the protagonist of another roughly contemporaneous play, the anonymous *Yorkshire Tragedy* (1605). In these two tragedies we can discover some early seventeenth-century apprehensions about marriage. These include anxieties that male ownership of the female could inspire a proprietary disequilibrium, that the experience of material possession and of political authority coincident in householding could itself engender possessiveness and tyranny, that some men perceived the onerousness of their theoretically comprehensive responsibilities, that they revolted against the burdens contingent on authority, and that prevailing domestic formulas were in these instances ineffectual.

7. Brian Vickers, *Occult and Scientific Mentalities* (1984), p. 9.
8. J. P. Sommerville discusses the extension of patriarchal theory that would give the father power to punish his children with death in *Politics and Ideology* (1986), pp. 29–30. Its typical characterization as a Roman practice is exemplified in Bodin's chapter title: "Of the power of a Father, and whether it be meet for the Father to have power of life and death over his children, as had the ancient Romans" (sig. C4ᵛ).

Male collapse under the burdens of oeconomic responsibility is the theme of this chapter. The long theatrical interrogation of conventional wisdoms, one for which I have argued in the previous two chapters and through an analysis of five Elizabethan plays, advances with *Othello* and *A Yorkshire Tragedy*. These latter texts challenge not only the operative prescriptions of ideology but also its underlying myths or formative conceptualizations. Finally, the playtexts hold certain thematic affinities with an anonymous prose pamphlet, *The Bloody Book* (1605), that details the criminal career of another misgoverning householder. *The Bloody Book* lodges its own indictment of conventional ideology and, in its coincident date of publication and semiotic redundancy, compounds an intuition of the textual definition of a distinct historical moment. This brings me full circle to a topic engaged in my first chapter: the shape (or shaping) of domestic evil in the early modern period. In the Jacobean years, one prototype is revised from rebellious wives to renouncing husbands. With the defaults of the patriarch, the domestic arena, finally, is feminized, undoing old integrative ideologies and mythologies of the house.

Mythical Thinking in *Othello*

Through the odd insistence of designatory repetition (1.1.158; 1.3.115), the text of *Othello* emphasizes for us an act of naming that might otherwise pass unnoticed as a rhetorical flourish. Othello and Desdemona elope to a building called the Sagittar in the first quarto and the Sagitary in the Folio; I compromise on the spelling Sagittar/y. Although the Sagittar/y's primary identification is with the newly married couple, we are also told that Iago "best know[s] the place" (1.3.121), and his introduction of the name is resonant with implication:

> Though I do hate [Othello], as I do hell's pains
> Yet, for necessity of present life,
> I must show out a flag, and sign of love,
> Which is indeed but sign. That you shall surely find him,
> Lead to the [Sagittar/y] the raised search.
> And there will I be with him.
>
> (1.1.154–59)[9]

9. Although I have frequently consulted Lawrence Ross's (1974) edition of *Othello*, references are to M. R. Ridley's (1958) edition for The Arden Shakespeare as the more generally accessible text. References to other Shakespeare texts are to the Riverside edition. For reviews

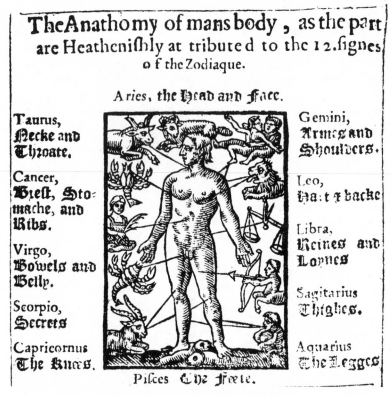

The Anathomy of mans body , as the part
are Heathenifhly at tributed to the 12.fignes
o f the Zodiaque.

Aries, the Head and Face.

Taurus,
Necke and
Throate.

Cancer,
Breſt, Sto=
mache, and
Ribs.

Virgo,
Bowels and
Belly.

Scorpio,
Secrets

Capricornus
The Knees.

Pifces the Feete.

Gemini,
Armes and
Shoulders.

Leo,
Hart & backe

Libra,
Reines and
Loynes

Sagitarius
Thighes.

Aquarius
The Legges

FIGURE 8. The zodiacal man, from Thomas Bretnor's *New Almanac and Prognostication for the Year of our Lord God 1615.* Reproduced by permission of the Folger Shakespeare Library.

Having already identified himself as "his worship's ancient," or ensign, Iago reconstructs his very profession as the hallmark of his avowed duplicity.

Besides marrying himself and his malignity to the place, however, his iteration of "flag," "sign," and "sign," a noun sequence culminating in "Sagittar/y" and punctuated by "there will I be with him,"[10] serves in addition the subliminal function of summoning up for the listener or reader a mental image of the sign with which an inn or public house

---

of *Othello* criticism, consult the following bibliographic entries: New Variorum *Othello* (1886), Helen Gardner (1968), James Ruoff (1973), Peter Davison (1988), and John Hazel Smith (1988). Also helpful is Susan Snyder, *Critical Essays* (1988).

10. I except "love" from this noun sequence because it participates in a different sequence, the hate-love dichotomy.

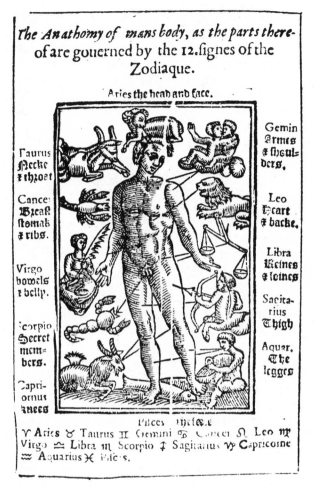

The Anathomy of mans body, as the parts thereof are gouerned by the 12.fignes of the Zodiaque.

Aries the head and face.

Gemin
armes
& shoul=
ders,

Taurus
necke
& throat

Cancer
Breast
stomak
& ribs.

Leo
Heart
& backe,

Virgo
bowels
& belly.

Libra
Reines
& loines

Scorpio
Secret
mem=
bers.

Sagita-
rius
Thigh

Capri-
ornus
knees

Aquar.
The
legges

Pisces feete.

♈ Aries ♉ Taurus ♊ Gemini ♋ Cancer ♌ Leo ♍
Virgo ♎ Libra ♏ Scorpio ♐ Sagitarius ♑ Capricorne
♒ Aquarius ♓ Pices.

FIGURE 9. The zodiacal man, from Richard Allestree's *Prognostication for this Present Year of Grace 1623.* Reproduced by permission of the Folger Shakespeare Library.

would have been identified. In this case, the image is of a celestial sign, the technical term in astrology for any of the twelve elements of the zodiac. The "zodiacal man" of the English almanac—according to Ruth Samson Luborsky the most familiar printed secular image in Tudor England—fixed in universal currency the figurative nature of the Sagittarius as a centaur with drawn bow (see figures 8 and 9).[11] And, in

11. Ruth Samson Luborsky, "What Tudor Book Illustrations Illustrate," a paper delivered at the Folger Shakespeare Library on 20 March 1987.

fact, editors seeking an explanation for the name of the Sagittar/y and a clue to its nature make frequent analogy to the "Centaur" of *The Comedy of Errors*.[12] A more common related name for a public house in early modern England was perhaps the "Archer." This much is hinted in John Taylor's comic tour of the taverns of London in 1636, purportedly a search to record in their signs the twelve signs of the zodiac and so to "imitate" the sun in its monthly journey. He notes that, "For Sagittarius, I was forced to make use of the sign of the Archer, near Finsbury-fields, or Grub-street end."[13]

In the first of two lengthy detours that further identify Iago with the Sagittar/y and that advance on the mythical level his influence over Othello, I take Taylor's cue and begin with the sign of the archer.

And he [the tongue] is an archer also. The tongue is bent like a bow for lies, and lo, the wicked bend their bow: they make ready their bow upon the string, that they may privily shoot at the upright in heart. And there be four principal arrows which it doth shoot forth.

The first arrow is envy, an arrow made in hell by that envious one the Devil. The feathers of this arrow are two: 1. Sadness at others' prosperity. 2. Gladness at the adversity of other men. It is headed with the rusty iron of self-consuming emulation, and this is *Sagitta venenata*, an arrow full of deadly poison. . . .

The second arrow of an evil tongue is the arrow of hatred, an arrow made in hell by that old Serpent who is a murderer from the beginning. The feathers of it are ill will and spight; it is headed with a desire to do hurt. And this is *Sagitta occulta*, the secret or hidden arrow, like the javelin which Saul darted against David, thinking therewith to have nailed him to the wall: he that shooteth it, is a manslayer and a murderer. And where this arrow is in request, there is confusion and every evil work.

The third arrow of an evil tongue is mocking, an arrow framed in the shop of the scornful; the feathers of it are morology and eutrapely,

12. For attempts to identify the Sagittar/y, see the New Variorum *Othello* and Ross, Introduction, p. 12. Most scholars conclude that it is an inn, as is the Centaur in *Errors*. It is implicitly distinguished from both private house and military lodging: from Brabantio's house (1.1.74, 80, 106, 138); from Bianca's house (3.4.169; 5.1.118); and from quarters for Iago (1.3.374), Roderigo (2.3.370), and Cassio (3.3.326; 3.4.6–10, 170). The fact that Brabantio and others do not know its location adds to its mystery. Ross first discussed the thematic significance of the name in his 1956 dissertation for Princeton University, "The Shakespearean Othello," pp. 566–71; I am grateful to Leeds Barroll for directing me to it. For more on the centaur image in *Othello*, see Abby Jane Dubman Hansen, "Shakespeare's *Othello*" (1977), and Martin Elliott, *Shakespeare's Invention of Othello* (1988), pp. 252–53, n. 23.

13. John Taylor, *Taylor's Travels* (1636), sig. A4ʳ; see also sig. B1ʳ. And see Jacob Larwood and John Camden Hotten, *English Inn Signs* (1951), for seventeenth-century public houses named "Arrow," "Archers," and "Sheaf of Arrows" (p. 197).

scoffs and jests. It is headed with a desire to disgrace. And this is *Sagitta volans*, the flying arrow, drawn out of the quiver of the proud and vainglorious. . . .

The fourth arrow of an evil tongue is the arrow of backbiting, made by Satan and shot by Satanists; the feathers of it are lies and slanders, and it is headed with a desire to defame. And this is *Sagitta parthica*, the Parthian arrow shot behind one's back, a most pernicious arrow to the prejudice of others' credit and reputation, an arrow that woundeth afar off, and which killeth three men: the slanderer, the party slandered, and the receiver of the slander, with one stroke. And as this unruly tongue doth go with one of these four arrows always ready upon his string; so, it carrieth with a vial full of deadly poison. . . .

The arrow which is shot out of the strongest bow and sent forth with the greatest force can hurt no farther than it can reach. But let a man be never so far off, let him be beyond the seas, let him be in never so far remote regions and distant countries, the arrow of an evil tongue will reach him and wound his good name. Other weapons only hurt the present, this hurteth those also who are absent; there is none that can be privileged from its stroke. . . . A tongue enraged is harder to be tamed than a strong city is to be conquered.[14]

The ways in which I think this passage from George Webbe's 1619 *Arraignment of an Unruly Tongue* connects Iago with the Sagittar/y should be apparent: he is full of envy, he hates the Moor, he desires to disgrace, he lies and slanders, he calls his practice poisonous, his tongue and not the defense of Cyprus defeats Othello; he is an archer shooting forth the terrible verbal arrows, *sagitta venenata*, *sagitta occulta*, *sagitta volans*, *sagitta parthica*.

The primary source for *Othello*, the seventh story in the third decade of Cinthio's *Hecatommithi*, contains a hint of this association of ensign and archer. After the nameless prototype for Iago succeeds in inspiring the Moor's jealousy, "the unhappy Moor went home," according to the *Hecatommithi*, "feeling as if he had been pierced by a sharp arrow."[15] In *Othello* the imagery resurfaces in Lodovico's lament for the "much chang'd" Moor:

14. George Webbe, *Arraignment of an Unruly Tongue* (1619), sigs. D2ᵛ–D5ʳ and E6ᵛ–E8ʳ.
15. Per Ridley's translation of Cinthio (p. 242); Ross has "dart" (p. 267), as does Geoffrey Bullough (p. 246). For John Payne Collier: "The poor Moor went home with a barbed arrow in his side" (p. 11). Compare the original: "Il misero Moro, come tocco da pungentissimo strale, se n'andò à casa" (sig. Oo5ᵛ). Also of relevance is: "Ben che lasciarono tali parole, cosi pungente spina nell'animo del Moro . . . et se ne stava tutto maninconoso" (sig. Oo4ʳ). Ridley translates this as "these words had left such a thorn in the soul of the Moor that he . . . became quite melancholy" (p. 240).

> Is this the noble Moor, whom our full senate
> Call all in all sufficient? This the noble nature,
> Whom passion could not shake? whose solid virtue
> The shot of accident, nor *dart* of chance,
> Could neither graze, nor pierce?
>
> (4.1.260–64 [emphasis added])

Later, apprehending the innocence of the wife he has murdered, Othello cries, "Here is my journey's end, here is my butt" (5.2.268). Lawrence Ross notes that "the butt is the structure on which the targets are placed in archery, and thus the utter limit of the aimed arrow's flight."[16] But Iago has aimed this arrow; "your reports," says Emilia, "have set the murder on" (5.2.188).[17]

In the 1576 Geneva Bible, a marginal gloss for "arrows" is "false reports and slanders." In other words, even though Webbe's treatise postdates *Othello*, it was grounded in scriptural precedents that had been commonplace years before. *The Arraignment* serves my purposes by reminding us, as John Taylor does, how readily the translations from *sagitta* to arrow and *sagittary* to archer were effected in the period and for providing a richly suggestive amplification of their association with the tongue.[18] Webbe's sermon is scarcely idiosyncratic. His text was James 3:8, which says, "the tongue can no man tame. It is an unruly evil, full of deadly poison"; Proverbs 25:18 states, "A man that beareth false witness against his neighbor is like an hammer and a sword, and a sharp arrow." The gloss with which I opened this paragraph accompanies the verses cited below from the Geneva Psalms:

> Hide me from the conspiracy of the wicked and from the
>   rage of the workers of iniquity,
> Which have whet their tongue like a sword and shot for
>   their arrows bitter words
> To shoot at the upright in secret: they shoot at him
>   suddenly, and fear not.
> . . . But God will shoot an arrow at them suddenly: their
>   strokes shall be at once.
> They shall cause their own tongue to fall upon them. . . .
>
> (Psalms 64:2–4, 7, 8)

16. Ross edition, p. 240.

17. Meanwhile, from Othello's reference to Cupid, Elliott develops a nexus of arrow images (pp. 10–11). Arrow imagery runs through Kenneth Burke's rhetoric in "*Othello*" (1951).

18. See also the *OED* entries for *archer* (4: "Sagittarius, that is to say, the Archer" [1594]) and for *arrow* (sb. 6: "Sinus versus . . . is also called in Latin *Sagitta*; in English a Shaft or Arrow" [1594]).

Undoubtedly because of these biblical associations—and in evidence of their wide familiarity—the comparison of the tongue to an arrow was proverbial in the sixteenth and seventeenth centuries.[19] In the 1588 *Marvelous Combat of Contrarities*, for example, William Averell's personified Tongue announces: "I counterfeit laws, I tell lies, I sow seditions, I stir up traitors, I slander princes; under color of truth I beguile and deceive, I swear and forswear, I break promise, I allure to whoredom, to theft, to murder, and to all mischief." The Tongue's corporeal opponent in Averell's fantastic contest, the Belly, accuses: "Her words are but light, because they lightly fly, and although they fly swiftly, yet they wound deeply, sting grievously, and pierce inwardly. . . . she is more slippery than an eel, more piercing than an arrow." In the 1598 *Palladis Tamia*, similarly, Francis Meres anticipates many of Webbe's analogies, speaking of an "unruly and a malicious tongue" in a passage immediately preceding reference to an arrow; comparing "an ill tongue" to "bow and arrows, which are sent from far, and wound the absent"; and advising that "a cunning archer is not known by his arrow, but by his aim: so a friendly affection is not known by the tongue, but by the faith."[20]

Iago's announced aims are "to abuse Othello's ear" with false suspicions of Cassio and Desdemona (1.3.393) and to "pour this pestilence into his ear" (2.3.347): T. McAlindon has characterized *Othello* as "the tragedy of the tongue and its terrible potency."[21] In nominating Iago the Archer, I do not intend merely to suggest a variant metaphor for the part he plays in Othello's tragedy, a part that scarcely needs rehearsing. Rather, the metaphor of the arrow advances my argument in that it effects an identification of Iago with the Sagittar/y, in an association fundamental to the mythical constructions of place which inform the text and put in play the factor of Othello's race.

Race is a subtext of my second detour, which continues the association of Iago with the Sagittar/y and which turns to centaurs, the history of the Moors in Spain, Christianized astrology, and Iago as the Astrolo-

19. Tilley cites "A Word spoken is an arrow let fly" and quotes Thomas Lodge from 1596: "Words are like to arrows, which are easily shot out, but hardly got in again" (W780). The relationship between the tongue and poison is also of interest; see Walter Dorke: "tongues so tipped [i.e., like arrows] with taunts and bitterness" (*Type or Figure of Friendship* [1589], sig. B1ᵛ), and Wendoll's plea in *Woman Killed with Kindness*: "Give me a name, you whose infectious tongues / Are tipp'd with gall and poison" (6.81–82).

20. Shakespeare certainly knew William Averell's *Marvelous Combat* ([1588] sigs. A1ᵛ and C2ʳ⁻ᵛ), at least by the time he wrote *Coriolanus* (for which it has been cited as a source). He is also likely to have known Francis Meres's 1598 *Palladis Tamia* (sigs. Z5ʳ and Z5ᵛ–Z6ʳ), because Meres mentions him therein. See also Thomas Wright's *Passions of the Mind* (1601ʳ): "Rash men in speech have an arrow in their tongues" (p. 169). And compare Owen Feltham's *Resolves* (edition of 1661): "Anger is the fever of the soul, which makes the tongue talk idly: nor come words clothed as at other times, but now as headed Arrows, fly abroad" (sig. Ii3ᵛ).

21. T. McAlindon, *Shakespeare and Decorum* (1973), p. 18.

ger. If to call Iago the Archer is to recall the terrible potency of his tongue, then to call him the Astrologer is to provoke a reconsideration of the nature of the pestilence that he pours into Othello's ear.

In the early modern period, centaurs were most often associated with the violent sexuality they displayed in the individual insult to Deianira, the wife of Hercules, by Nessus (to which Shakespeare alludes in *All's Well That Ends Well* and *Antony and Cleopatra*) and in the group assault on the Lapith women at the wedding of Pirithous and Hippodamia (to which he refers in *Titus Andronicus* and *A Midsummer Night's Dream*).[22] Of related interest is the political use to which human rape narratives have been put. In her study of this phenomenon, Stephanie H. Jed remarks "how many incidents of sexual offense registered in ancient historiography are necessary markers of change in a legal and political system. From the earliest historiographic records, some "erotic" offense . . . is always required in order to justify the overthrow of tyrants. Aristotle abstracts from this narrative pattern a political formula: one of the primary reasons that tyrants are ruined is that they offend the honor of their male subjects by raping and violating their wives and breaking up their marriages."[23] Jed is concerned with the significance for Republican Rome of the rape of Lucrece. For me her observation registers with respect to medieval Spain and to the mythology of rape that gave the Spanish, even down to the Renaissance, a way of redeeming national pride despite their conquest by the Islamic peoples known in England as Moors or Saracens.[24] Aristotle's formula is of particular relevance to my case and to this national narrative, for, as Jed clarifies, he emphasizes the offense to male honor rather than female, the challenge to male possession rather than to female integrity.[25]

The legend of the Islamic conquest of Spain was widely known in England; the version that I follow dates from the 1575 *Notable History of*

22. For Shakespeare's association of centaurs with lechery, see also Lear's complaint of his daughters that "Down from the waist they are Centaurs" (4.6.124). Compare Edward Topsell: "Centaurs . . . are described by the poets to have their forepart like men, and their hinder part like horses, the occasion whereof is thus related by Pindarus: that Centaurus the son of Ixion committed buggery with the mares of Magnetia, under the mountain Pelius, from whence came that monstrous birth in the upper part resembling the father and in the nether the mother" (*History of Four-Footed Beasts* [1607], sig. Gg1ʳ). The part of the body governed by the sign of Sagittarius is the thigh, which was historically coded as the male seat of sexuality.
23. Stephanie H. Jed, *Chaste Thinking* (1989), p. 3.
24. See Richard Eden's "Preface . . . to the Reader" in Petrus Martyr Anglerius, *Decades of the New World* (English translation, 1555): "[Ferdinand of Aragon] hath quite driven out of Spain the Moors or Saracens" (sig. A4ʳ).
25. In the *Politics*, Aristotle argues that because men, "feeling themselves insulted," may attempt to assassinate sovereigns, a tyrant should "abstain" from sexual violation except when "genuinely in love" (trans. Barker, pp. 238 and 248–49).

the Saracens.[26] According to report, Saracen invasions of Spain were of
limited success until 712. At that time, Spain was ruled by a Visigoth
king named Roderick, who entrusted the defense of his country to one
Julian, Earl of Cepta.

> This Julian had a daughter named Caba, a beautiful young lady, inso-
> much that for her personage she was no less pernicious to Spain than fair
> Helena was to the Trojans. For Roderick falling in love with her, whether
> it were by force or by fraud (for it is reported both ways) made a breach
> into her virginity. Which unprincely trick she (as soon as she conveniently
> could) uttered and discovered unto her father. Who, dissimuling as
> though he had known nothing of this injury done to him in his daughter
> and keeping to himself the desire of just revenge till a time for his
> purpose convenient, desired leave of the king to depart the court and to
> go to Cepta, because being there (as he said) he could much better defeat
> the Saracens' intended enterprises. Which request obtained, he trussed
> up all his furniture of household and with his wife went to Cepta. When
> he was come thither, feigning an excuse that his wife was sore sick, he
> desired the king to give Caba his daughter leave to come home and see
> her languishing mother, who was never like to see her any more. For
> Caba with other princes' and lords' daughters (as the manner was) at that
> time waited in the court. Having by this means received home his daugh-
> ter, he went to Mucas, who was (as before we showed) the head ruler of all
> Libya under Vlite, and unto him he opened from point to point the
> whole cause of his coming away from the court, and promising to make
> him lord of all Spain if he would give the adventure and take the enter-
> prise in hand. (sigs. K1^{r-v})

Among his own friends, kin, and countrymen, Julian "forgot not to tell
them the king's ungratitude and the spightful dishonor done unto his
house by the ravishing and deflowering of his daughter" (sig. K2^r),
adding to the story an accusation of usurpation against Roderick. Julian's kin, "feigning that they went to repulse this Saracenical invasion"
of 12,000 troops sent by Mucas, instead joined the Moors (sig. K2^v).
Roderick gathered a great army; Mucas answered with more troops
and a renewed assault. There resulted for a while "an equal match,"
despite the Spanish disadvantages of years of dearth, plague, and military unpreparedness (sig. K3^v). The Saracens were finally triumphant
(according to myth) only with the aid of Julian's own (Spanish) men and
with further betrayal by two sons of Roderick's royal predecessor, Witi-

26. Caelius Augustinus Curio, *Notable History of the Saracens* (English translation, 1575). The
story of Julian's revenge for rape is apocryphal. For some of its chronological inconsistencies,
see Derek W. Lomax, *Reconquest of Spain* (1978), pp. 12–15.

za. Eventually, Roderick fled the "merciless slaughter of his men on every side, moved with repentance because *he knew himself to be the cause and occasioner of all this mishap*" (sig. K4ʳ [emphasis added]). And indeed, Western history attributes the conquest of Spain not to Saracen might nor even to Julian's treason but instead to Roderick's rape. His purported epitaph reads that his "sensual reign brought dull and deadly sting / To Spanish soil" (sig. K4ᵛ). The narrative of conquest adds that Valencia was thereafter "pestered and peopled with Moors" (sig. L2ʳ). In a passage of some relevance to the interracial anxieties of *Othello*, another commentator notes that during the ensuing eight-hundred-year occupation, "we must not think that the Negroes sent for women out of Aphrick."[27]

According to legend, one of the first of the Spaniards to "take heart" against the invaders was Pelagius, whose life and motivations were reportedly intersected by yet other rape narratives. Because his father had been killed by Witiza "to th'intent he might carnally abuse his [the father's] wife" (sig. M1ʳ), Pelagius and his sister had taken sanctuary with a Saracen ally, Mugnuza, Duke of Gigion. Mugnuza sent Pelagius on a diplomatic mission to the Saracens so that in Pelagius's absence he might, while insinuating marriage to the sister, have the "spoil" of her "maidenhead" (sig. M1ᵛ). Pelagius in revenge inspired the resistance of other Spaniards with an oration reminding them of how the Saracens "do perforce ravish and like devils pollute infinite Christian women and virgins," how they "despoil" men "of their temporal goods, wives, and children" (sig. M2ʳ), how resistance was required so "that your wives and children shall not be constuprated, harmed, nor uncourteously handled" (sig. M3ᵛ).

The theme of sexual appropriation resurfaced once more in Spanish national myth. In the next major recorded confrontation of the occupation, a Spanish king, Ramiro I, reportedly took up arms rather than render an annual tribute of one hundred virgins exacted by the Moors. In a battle launched inauspiciously near Clavijo, Ramiro in desperation "sought his only refuge at God's hands." In apparent response, "Saint James the Apostle seemed personally to appear unto him, promising him his help and furtherance":

> Ramire the next day [came] into the field in good array of battle against his enemies, with an assured confidence of divine help and assistance. The said holy Apostle Saint James was seen in the battle, sitting upon a white horse and bearing in his hand a red cross, and that in the

27. Edward Daunce, *Brief Discourse of the Spanish State* (1590), sig. E3ʳ.

same battle were slain of Saracens seventy thousand. Then were Albaida, Clavigium, Calagurra, and many other towns thereabout regained by the Christians. In token and remembrance of which victory by the divine assistance of celestial presence achieved, the noble Order of the Knights of Saint James was by the king instituted. (sigs. T2ᵛ–T3ʳ)

In 834 Ramiro reportedly inaugurated a national tax in substitution for the tribute of virgins; he called it the Voto de Santiago.[28]

With my naming of this tax in Spanish, one of the most obvious links between *Othello* and these narratives of rape and invasion in Moorish Spain becomes evident. As G. N. Murphy first pointed out and Barbara Everett has more recently reminded us, "Iago" would have been recognized by Shakespeare's contemporaries as the Spanish name for "James." The name was specifically associated in medieval and Renaissance Spain with the third apostle taken by Jesus in the Gospels. He was first called "James the Greater" to distinguish him from another apostle also named James (the Less); he came to be known in Spain as Santiago, its patron saint, with a shrine at Santiago de Compostela second only to Rome as a destination for pilgrimage; and, dating from the battle of Clavijo, he was also known to Spaniards as "Santiago Matamoros," that is, Saint James the Moor-killer.[29]

The fact that the Ensign in Cinthio was nameless throws into bolder relief Shakespeare's choice of a name that seems tantalizingly to forecast Iago's fatal effect on *Othello*'s protagonist. This suggestion of symbolic naming seems one further step removed from the purely conjectural when we remember that the character of Roderigo, whom Iago calls "my dear countryman" (5.1.88), does not even exist in Cinthio but is sheer invention on Shakespeare's part. The eighth-century king Roderick is in other accounts given his proper Spanish name, Roderigo, and it is difficult not to make the association between the Roderigo of legend, who was known to have betrayed his homeland to the Moors for the sake of illicit desire, and the Roderigo of *Othello*, who vows to "sell all my Land" (1.3.377–80) to pursue by proxy his adulterous courtship of Desdemona.[30]

28. See T. D. Kendrick, *St. James in Spain* (1960), pp. 34–38, as well as James S. Stone, *Cult of Santiago* (1927).

29. G. N. Murphy, "Note on Iago's Name" (1964), pp. 38–43; Barbara Everett, *Young Hamlet* (1989), pp. 189–91. I am grateful to Alan Sinfield for directing me to Everett and Santiago Matamoros. Murphy records a poetic version of the Othello story, ostensibly recorded not long after the play, that identified Iago as "a false Spaniard." But this poem was discovered by Collier.

30. As Roderigo's vow is from the Folio and second-quarto texts only, it is not included in Ridley's copytext. Roderigo was also the Christian name of the Cid (who fought in the name of Santiago and with the slogan that as one Roderigo had lost Spain, a second would redeem it). In

In his introduction to the Riverside *Othello*, Frank Kermode suggests that "the richness of the tragedy derives from uncancelled suggestions, from latent subplots operating in terms of imagery as well as character."[31] The associative subplot I am tracing seems not to confine itself to *Othello*, for the Sagittar/y is a focal element in a nexus of images for unquiet relationships, violent sexuality, and murderous jealousy which works itself out through a number of Shakespearean texts. In *The Comedy of Errors* a woman boasts of her "reprehension" of her husband that "In bed he slept not for my urging it; / At board he fed not for my urging it" (5.1.63–64), much like Desdemona, advancing Cassio's case by making Othello's "bed . . . a school, his board a shrift" (3.3.24). The woman is held responsible for her husband's "hind'red" sleep, "Unquiet meals," "jealous fits," and mad behavior (5.1.71–74), although the real cause lies in the confusion of his identity and reciprocal dislocation with a twin who lodges at an inn named the Centaur. In *Titus Andronicus*, the cast of which includes Aaron the Moor, a father revenges the rape of his daughter by preparing a banquet "More stern and bloody than the Centaurs' feast" (5.2.203). He makes two "pasties" of her assailants, Chiron and Demetrius, called by him "Rape" and "Murder" (5.2.189, 156). Chiron bears the name of the centaur that, wounded by a poisoned arrow (in some versions at the Lapith wedding, by Hercules), was transformed by Zeus into the constellation Sagittarius. In *A Midsummer Night's Dream*, Theseus, friend of the Lapith who battled centaurs attempting the kidnap of his bride, Hippodamia, has himself "woo'd" Hippolyta "with his sword" (1.1.16). In memory of the "glory of [his] kinsman Hercules," he tells his bride of the "battle of the Centaurs" (5.1.44–47). In *Antony and Cleopatra*, the most valiant of soldiers, undone by love, cries that "The shirt of Nessus is upon me" and vows that the "witch" shall die for it (4.12.43–47). Perhaps most striking, particularly in view of the play's rough contemporaneity with *Othello*, in *All's Well That Ends Well* a woman heals a fistula, an ailment generally governed (according to occult medical tracts) by Sagittarius.[32] Deserted by her husband, she travels as a pilgrim to the shrine of Saint Jaques le Grand (that is, Santiago de Compostela). And her husband is

the thirteenth century an Archbishop Roderigo of Toledo referred in a chronicle to the apparition of Saint James at Clavijo; see Kendrick, p. 36. Add to this the Visigothic count Cassius (with obvious resonance of Cassio) who joined Musa and became a Muslim; see Lomax, pp. 13–14. I am grateful to J. G. A. Pocock for turning my attention to Roderigo and thus to these circles of association.

31. Frank Kermode, Introduction (1974), p. 1200.

32. William Lilly, for one, notes that Sagittarius "ruleth the thighs and buttocks in the parts of man's body, and all fistulas or hurts falling in those members" (*Christian Astrology* [1647], sig. N1ʳ).

slyly affiliated with the centaur Nessus by Parolles, whose name identifies him as the Archer of this play.

This tracing of coincident names and patterns of association is, to cite Geertz again, largely cryptographic. Its diagnostic significance inheres in one as-yet-unrecognized twist on this identification of *Othello*'s Iago with Saint James the Greater, the recovery of which requires some glancing familiarity with the history of astrology. The science began in the correlation of celestial and terrestrial maps, in the association of constellations with specific portions of the planet or with, as Ptolemy put it, "the inhabited world." His classic *Tetrabiblos* established that Spain was among the countries "in familiarity" with Sagittarius.[33] When astrology later came to be Christianized, practitioners of numerology and the occult sciences recognized that among the significances of the number "twelve" are its enumeration both of the signs of the zodiac and of the Christian apostles. They devised a scheme in which each apostle "ruled" one of the twelve signs. It was probably because Sagittarius was already associated by Ptolemy with Spain and because James the Greater was known as the patron saint of Spain that James the Greater came to be identified as the ruler of Sagittarius. Cornelius Agrippa's chart of the "cabalistical" correspondences of the number "twelve" (see figures 10 and 11), offers just one instance of the identification of "Jacobus major" or "James the elder" with "Sagittarius" (and, in another notable association, with the "tempters or ensnarers" among the "degrees of the damned, and of devils").[34]

If, in other words, James the Greater/Santiago rules the sign of Sagittarius, then, by eloping to the Sagittar/y, Othello and Desdemona place themselves in some sense under the influence of the ensnarer Iago, an influence that exerts itself throughout the course of the play as

33. Ptolemy, *Tetrabiblos*, II.3, pp. 133–37 and 159. For help with this section, I am grateful to Betty Jo Teeter Dobbs.

34. Agrippa was far better known for his three-volume *De occulta philosophia* (1531; translated into English, 1651) than for his *Commendation of Matrimony* (1526; translated into English, 1540). On the text's wide influence, see Charles Garfield Nauert, Jr., *Agrippa* (1965). Book 2 presents the "Cabalistical scale" of the number twelve shown in figures 10 and 11 (sigs. P5ᵛ–P6ʳ); Book 3 notes "the twelve Apostles of Christ, who (as the evangelical truth saith) sit upon twelve thrones, judging the twelve tribes of Israel, who in the Revelations are distributed upon twelve foundations, at the twelve gates of the heavenly City, *who rule the twelve Signs*, and are sealed in the twelve precious Stones, and the whole world is distributed to them. . . . The third . . . is James the greater" (sigs. Gg3ᵛ–Gg4ʳ [emphasis added]).

The identification of James the Greater with Sagittarius can also be found in Francesco Giorgio, *De harmonia mundi totius* (1525), sig. cccxiv. (I am grateful to Georgianna Ziegler for confirming this in the University of Pennsylvania collections.) On Giorgio, see also D. P. Walker, *Spiritual and Demonic Magic* (1958), p. 116. The tradition continues in, e.g., Dal Lee, *Dictionary of Astrology* (1968): "The twelve apostles of Jesus Christ sometimes are compared with the twelve signs of the zodiac." Although his correspondences differ significantly from Agrippa's, he too associates James the Greater with Sagittarius.

SCALA DVODENARII

In Archetypo — In mundo intelligibili

Nomina dei: אהיה · הוא (ipse) · ברוך (Benedictus) · קדוש (Sanctus) · אב בן רוח הקדש — Pater filius, & Spiritus sanftus

	1	2	3	4	5	6	7	8	9	10	11	12
Nomina dei duodecim literarum	יהוה	יהוה	יהוה	יהוה	יהוה	יהוה	יהוה	יהוה	יהוה	יהוה	יהוה	יהוה
Nomen magnum in duodecim vexilla renolutum	יהוה	יהוה	יהוה	יהוה	יהוה	יהוה	יהוה	יהוה	יהוה	יהוה	יהוה	יהוה
Duodecim ordines beatorū spirituum	Seraphim	Cherubim	Throni	Dominationes	Potestates	Virtutes	Principatus	Archangeli	Angeli	Innocentes	Martyres	Confessores
Duodecim angeli praesidentes signis	Malchidiel	Asmodel	Ambriel	Muriel	Verchiel	Hamaliel	Zuriel	Barbiel	Adnachiel	Hanael	Gabriel	Barchiel
Duodecim tribus	Dan	Ruben	Iehuda	Manasse	Asser	Symeon	Isachar	Beniamin	Nephthalim	Gad	Zabulon	Ephraim
Duodecim prophetae	Malachias	Aggeus	Zacharias	Amos	Oseas	Micheas	Ionas	Abdias	Sophonias	Naum	Abacuc	Iobel
Duodecim apostoli	Mathias	Thadeus	Symon	Iohannes	Petrus	Andreas	Bartolomeus	Philippus	Iacobus maior	Thomas	Matheus	Iacobus minor

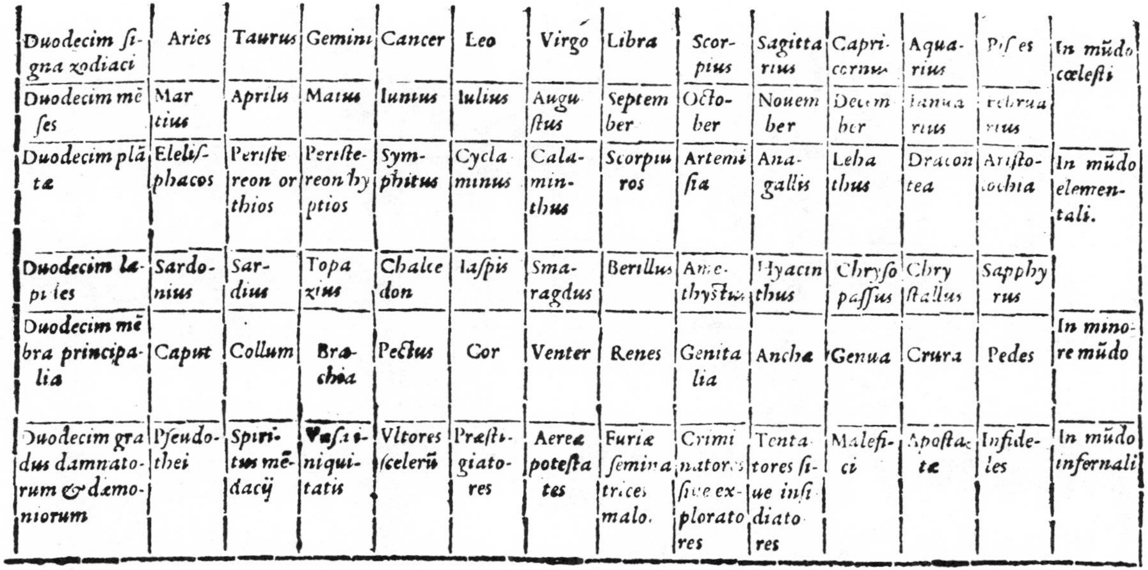

Duodecim signa zodiaci	Aries	Taurus	Gemini	Cancer	Leo	Virgo	Libra	Scorpius	Sagittarius	Capricornus	Aquarius	Pisces	
Duodecim menses	Martius	Aprilis	Maius	Iunius	Iulius	Augustus	September	October	Nouember	December	Ianuarius	Februarius	In mūdo cœlestis
Duodecim plātæ	Elelisphacos	Peristereon orthios	Peristereon hybptios	Symphitum	Cyclaminus	Calamintus	Scorpiuros	Artemisia	Anagallis	Lebaltus	Dracontea	Aristolochia	In mūdo elementali.
Duodecim lapides	Sardonius	Sardius	Topazius	Chalcedon	Iaspis	Smaragdus	Berillus	Amethystus	Hyacinthus	Chrysopassus	Chrysoprassus	Sapphyrus	
Duodecim mē bra principalia	Caput	Collum	Brachia	Pectus	Cor	Venter	Renes	Genitalia	Anche	Genua	Crura	Pedes	In minore mūdo
Duodecim gradus damnatorum & demoniorum	Pseudothei	Spiritus mendacij	Vasa iniquitatis	Vltores scelerū	Praestigiatores	Aereæ potestates	Furiæ seminatrices malo.	Criminatores siue exploratores malo res	Tentatores siue insidiatores	Malefici	Apostatæ	Infideles	In mūdo infernali

FIGURE 10. Chart of the number twelve, from Book 2 of Cornelius Agrippa's 1531 *De occulta philosophia.* Note column 9: *Jacobus major, Sagittarius,* and *Tentatores sive insidiatores.* Reproduced by permission of the Folger Shakespeare Library.

The Scale of the Number twelve.

The names of God with twelve letters.				הוא Holy	ברוך Blessed	הקדש He
The great name returned back into twelve banners.	יהוה	יההו	יוהה	הוהי	הויה	ההיו
Twelve orders of the blessed Spirits.	Seraphim.	Cherubim.	Thrones.	Dominations.	Powers.	Vertues.
Twelve Angels ruling over the signs.	Malchidiel.	Asmodel.	Ambriel	Muriel.	Verchiel.	Hamaliel.
Twelve Tribes:	Dan.	Ruben.	Judah.	Manasseh.	Asher.	Simeon.
Twelve Prophets.	Malachi.	Haggai.	Zachary.	Amos.	Hosea.	Micha.
Twelve Apostles.	Mathias	Thadeus.	Simon.	John.	Peter.	Andrew.
Twelve signs of the Zodiack.	Aries.	Taurus.	Gemini.	Cancer.	Leo.	Virgo.
Twelve Moneths.	March.	April.	May.	June.	July.	August.
Twelve Plants.	Sang.	Upright Vervain.	Bending Vervain.	Comfrey.	Lady's Seal.	Calamint.
Twelve stones.	Sardonius.	A Carneol	Topaze	Calcedony.	Jasper.	Emrald.
Twelve principall members.	The head.	The neck.	The arms.	The breft.	The heart.	The belly.
Twelve degrees of the Falfe gods damned, and of Divels.	Lying spirits.	Vessels of iniquity.		Revengers of wickedness.	Juglers.	Aery powers.

FIGURE 11. Chart of the number twelve, from Book 2 of Cornelius Agrippa's *Three Books of Occult Philosophy*, translated by J.F. in 1651. Note column 9: James the elder, Sagittarius, and "Tempters or ensnarers." Reproduced by permission of the Folger Shakespeare Library.

the Moor "changes with [Iago's] poison" (3.3.330). The occult thread reasserts itself in Othello's throwaway line to the Senate that he has "some nine moons wasted" in Venice (1.3.84); because Sagittarius is the ninth sign, the detail places him in yet another way under the influence of the Sagittar/y. Of course, the passage of nine months also resonates

FIGURE 11. *(continued)*

		אב בן ורוח הקדש Father, Son, Holy Ghoſt.				In the originall world.
וההי	יוהה	והיה	היהי	היוה	ההוי	
Principalities.	Archangels.	Angels.	Innocents.	Martyrs.	Confeſſors.	In the Intelligible world.
Zuriel.	Barbiel.	Adnachiel	Hanael.	Gabiel.	Barchiel.	
Iſſachar.	Benjamin.	Napthalin	Gad.	Zabulon.	Ephraim.	
Jonah.	Obadiah.	Zephaniah	Nahum.	Habakuk	Joel.	
Bartholomew.	Philip.	James the elder.	Thomas.	Matthew.	James the yonger.	
Libra.	Scorpius.	Sagittarius	Capricorn	Aquarius.	Piſces.	In the Celeſtiall world.
September	Oƈtober.	Novemb.	December	January.	February.	In the Elementall world.
Scorpiongraſs.	Mugwort.	Pimpernel.	Dock.	Dragonwort.	Ariſtolochy.	
Berill.	Amethyſt.	Hyacinth.	Chryſopraſus.	Cryſtall.	Saphir.	
The kidnies.	Genitals.	The hams	Knees.	Legs.	Feet.	In the Elementary world.
Furies the fowers of evils.	Sifters or Tryers.	Tempters or eninarers.	Witches.	Apoſtates.	Infidels.	In the infernall world.

with implications of gestation, but the progeny of *this* incubatory period is Iago's practice: "I ha't, it is engender'd; Hell and night / Must bring this monstrous birth to the world's light" (1.3.401–2). Among Iago's monstrous progeny is the Cypriot "night-brawl" of Cassius, Roderigo, and Montano, but his alternative account of its genesis—that it erupted "As if some planet had unwitted men" (2.3.173)—both intimates his own identification of self with celestial signifier and integrates Othello into his astrological belief system. As Iago's practice achieves its end, Othello falls into an epileptic fit that (even without Iago's self-congratulatory "Work on, / My medicine, work" [4.1.44–45]) is its own confirmation of the ensign's occult efficacy, for according to Ptolemy, Sagittarius is one of two signs "responsible for those [diseases] that come about with falling fits or epileptic seizures."[35]

Of some relevance is the fact that the source story for *Othello* concludes as a cautionary tale about the determinative capacity of names. In the *Hecatommithi* the story is purportedly told to a group of travellers, whose responses point the moral: "It appeared marvellous to everybody that such malignity could have been discovered in a human heart; and the fate of the unhappy Lady was lamented, with some blame for her father, who had given her a name of unlucky augury. And the party decided that since a name is the first gift of a father to his child, he ought to bestow one that is grand and fortunate, as if he wished to foretell success and greatness. No less was the Moor blamed, who had believed too foolishly."[36] Disdemona, in Greek "the unfortunate one," is the sole named character in Cinthio.

The 1590 *Brief Discourse of the Spanish State* alleges that the name *Spain* is also Greek in origin and means "neediness, penury, and rarity." But in its report that "after the division of tongues" Spain was inhabited by Tubal, meaning "confusion," the *Discourse* is able to advance an English nationalistic agenda grounded in an apparently disinterested linguistic significance. The common manifestation of Spanish confusion, it declares, is a violation of natural law: "For the father to kill his innocent son, or the husband his chaste wife . . . I know no authentic proof, unless Spain can yield some precedent for both. . . . so small a thing it is in Spain, for a father to murder his son, and a husband his wife." The *Discourse* continues that "in what place the Spaniards display their ensigns, nothing is to be looked for but cruelty and slaughter, and all misery."[37] The Spanish name subsequently given the ensign in *Othello*, coupled with the name for his general's place of elopement, provides a suprapsychological explanation of influence, of why (to return to Cinthio) the Moor believes the ensign, otherwise "too foolishly,"

---

35. Ptolemy, III.12, pp. 329–30.
36. Cinthio, *Hecatommithi*, trans. Bullough, p. 252.
37. Daunce, sigs. B1ʳ, C3ʳ⁻ᵛ, C4ʳ, and D2ᵛ. See also the story of the prince of Spain, imprisoned by his father at the behest of the duke of Alba in 1568. His mother "the Queen of Spain (presuming much on her place, and pitying his innocency and tender years) solicited the king to receive him again into favor: but the malice of the prince's adversaries prevailed" (sig. C3ᵛ). She was punished with death for her intervention (the prince also died), in analogue to Desdemona's fate after intervening for Cassio.

and murders his own chaste wife. The Sagittar/y casts a long shadow, and it is the shadow of Iago.

Othello's credulity, in other words, begins in his inscription in a rape narrative. His inscriber is Iago. But, in a distinction that marks the ultimate divergence of Othello's narrative from those of Moorish Spain, Republican Rome, and Aristotle's axiom, Iago's first subscriber is not Othello. Instead, it is Brabantio, who bears the name of a territory (the Netherlandish Brabant) already under the rule of Spain. Iago begins by testing his case there and succeeds in convincing the incredulous Brabantio that "an old black ram / Is tupping your white ewe," that "you'll have your daughter cover'd with a Barbary horse," that "your daughter, and the Moor, are now making the beast with two backs" (1.1.88–89, 110–11, 115–17). Typically depicted in profile, with the spines of both man and horse outlined (as shown in such illustrations of the zodiacal man as those reproduced in figures 8 and 9), Sagittarius literalizes the beast with two backs.

Thus infected with the myth of the centaur—of Othello he might say, as does Parolles of Bertram, "For rapes and ravishments he parallels Nessus" (4.3.251)—Brabantio makes the conceptual leap from rape narrative to political consequence. His early resistance—"What, tell'st thou me of robbing? this is Venice, / My house is not a grange"—reveals the civic conviction that will underlie his ensuing determination to recover his daughter: "at every house I'll call, / I may command at most: get weapons, ho!" (1.1.105–6, 181–82). In his worldview,

> . . . any of my brothers of the state,
> Cannot but feel this wrong, as 'twere their own.
> For if such actions may have passage free,
> Bond-slaves, and pagans, shall our statesmen be.
> (1.2.96–99)

He bursts in upon the Senate's emergency session to complain that Desdemona "is abus'd, stol'n from me and corrupted, / By spells and medicines" (1.3.60–61). When Brabantio's confidence in his domestic rule, in his political influence, and in the fellowship of Venetian patriarchs is nonetheless betrayed, the Duke of Venice attempts slight and aphoristic consolation: "The robb'd that smiles, steals something from the thief, / He robs himself, that spends a bootless grief." Brabantio's retort—"So let the Turk of Cyprus us beguile, / We lose it not so long as we can smile"—maintains the analogy between the daughter who has been "stolen" from him and the threat to the Venetian title to the island of Cyprus (1.3.208–11, 60). He follows the Aristotelian formula that enmeshes the fate of a community's women, the surety of its posses- sions, and its political stability.[38]

But again, Iago's method is not limited to portraying Othello to the increasingly receptive Brabantio as the Centaur. Rather, the evil genius of this "ensnarer" is to infect Othello himself with the dual associations of the Sagittar/y, the monstrous beast armed for conflict.[39] First, with his reference to the "old black ram," Iago the Archer initiates a net- work of allusions to the transformation of men into beasts (1.1.116; 2.3.256, 284, 297), horses (1.1.111–13), baboons (1.3.316), asses (1.3.400; 2.1.304), goats (3.3.184, 409; 4.1.259), toads (3.3.274), dogs (3.3.368; 5.1.62; 5.2.362), monkeys (3.3.409; 4.1.259), and wolves (3.3.410).[40] These intersect with the half-man, half-beast, and mon- strous nature of the centaur and culminate in Othello's misconceived self-identification that "a horned man's a monster, and a beast" (4.1.62) as well as in his dying self-association with a bestial antagonist: "I took by the throat the circumcised dog, / And smote him thus" (5.2.356– 57).[41] Second, with "it was a violent commencement," Iago the Astrolo- ger reconstructs the elopement of Othello and Desdemona as the "an- swerable sequestration" (1.3.345) that he predicts and then negotiates, Othello's violent murder of Desdemona.

As "sequestration" implies, however, this remains a domestic mur- der. Here is the end of the divergence to which I referred: in *Othello* the formula of Aristotle exhausts itself with Brabantio's role, in the first act of the play. The text's characteristic shift of focus from the political to the domestic, a central concern of the next section of this chapter, is forecast here, where Brabantio's projection of the rape narrative onto Venetian jurisdiction is voided and where only Iago's projection of Othello into a rape narrative persists and reverberates. Brabantio's final warning is of marital rather than political consequence: "Look to her, Moor, have a quick eye to see: / She has deceiv'd her father, may do thee" (1.3.292–93).[42] This construction of the event is put to the

38. Michael Neill suggests that Venice "offers to supply each individual with a clearly de- fined and secure position within an established social order" ("Changing Places" [1984], p. 118).

39. On Othello's sexual initiation, see Edward A. Snow, "Sexual Anxiety" (1980), and Stan- ley Cavell, "Stake of the Other" (1987).

40. Caroline F. E. Spurgeon concludes that over half the animal images are Iago's and all are pejorative (*Shakespeare's Imagery* [1935], p. 335).

41. Referring to Othello's "mumbling of goats and monkeys," Susan Snyder concludes that "he has internalized Iago's reductive view of man as animal" ("Conventions of Romantic Come- dy" [1972], p. 133).

42. Neill has also remarked that Iago "presents the abduction of a daughter as though it were an act of adultery" (p. 122).

specific purpose of Othello's torment in Cyprus—Iago reminds him meaningfully: "She did deceive her father, marrying you" (3.3.210)— but it is a limited purpose. The subject of the remaining acts—and the object of Iago's mythical practice—is catastrophe not for a state but for a marriage.

Othello and Oeconomic Thought

In their *Godly Form of Household Government,* John Dod and Robert Cleaver offer one moral perspective by which is suggested immediate tragic potential in the marriage of Othello and Desdemona: "For the first year after marriage, God would not have the husband go to war with his enemies, to the end that he and his wife might learn to know one another's conditions and qualities, and so afterwards live in godly peace, and not to war one with another. And therefore God gave and appointed that the new married husband that year is to stay at home and settle his love, that he might not war and jar after: for that God of peace dwelleth not in the house of war." Behind this statement lie two commonplaces of early modern domestic prescription: first, that the foundation and objective of a marital relationship is peace and, second, that a newly married couple must establish a home of their own (according to what Bodin called a law of nature).[43] The characterologic precursors of Othello and Desdemona, in Cinthio's *Hecatommithi*, followed the prescriptive formulas. Setting forth their love and marriage, Cinthio concludes: "And they lived together in such harmony and peace, while they were in Venice, that no word passed between them that was not loving."[44] But Othello and Desdemona ominously

43. John Dod and Robert Cleaver, *Godly Form of Household Government* (1598), sig. P4ʳ. See also Henry Smith, *Preparative to Marriage* (1591), sig F1ᵛ. William Perkins cites Deuteronomy 24:5: "When a man hath taken a new wife, he shall not go out to war, neither shall he be charged with any business: but he shall be free at home one year, and shall cheer up his wife which he hath taken." Perkins says that marital duties are "principally two: cohabitation and communion" (*Christian Oeconomy* [composed, early 1590s; published, 1609], p. 423). Dod and Cleaver emphasize another familiar prescription, that the new couple must "depart from their parents, to keep house by themselves" (sig. O1ʳ). And see William Gouge: "Dwell together they must: but without peace there is no dwelling together" (*Of Domestical Duties* [1622], sig. Q2ᵛ). The social requirement for independent housing for a married couple helps account for the relatively late age at marriage in the early modern period, according to Peter Laslett: "Marriage could not come about unless a slot fell vacant and the aspiring couple was able to fill it up. It might be a cottage . . . which became available" (*World We Have Lost* [1983], p. 101).

44. I cite Ross's translation (p. 263). Those in Ridley (p. 238) and in the New Variorum (p. 377), both reading that they lived in "harmony and peace" in Venice, by omitting the "living *together*" obscure a point explicit in both the Italian and the French translation to which Shakespeare may have had access. Cinthio reads: "e *vissero insieme* di si concorde volere, & in tanta

enjoy neither the "living together" nor the "harmony and peace" in Venice.[45]

Throughout much of this book, I have juxtaposed dramatic literature with works of moral prescription in order to clarify disjunctive, alternative, and informing views of private life in the Renaissance. As the passage from Dod and Cleaver suggests, it would seem that *Othello*, too, can profitably be read in the light of contemporary oeconomic theory. In the following pages I accordingly pursue three first-act violations of prescription which appear to feed its tragic denouement: the marriage of this couple does not initiate a household; the new husband goes immediately to war; and the wife is indulged in an agency that results in her accompanying him on his military expedition. Nonetheless prescription once more proves itself to be inadequate to Othello and Desdemona's case, inapposite to their tragedy.

The prescriptive companion text, like the occult one, in some senses begins with the Sagittar/y. Or so it seems to me as I read a passage so often isolated for critical discussion that its central importance cannot be doubted. Describing to the Venetian Senate his "courtship" of Desdemona, Othello says:

> Her father lov'd me, oft invited me,
> Still question'd me the story of my life,
> From year to year; the battles, sieges, fortunes,
> That I have pass'd:
>
> . . .
>
> And of the Cannibals, that each other eat;
> The Anthropophagi, and men whose heads
> Do grow beneath their shoulders: this to hear
> Would Desdemona seriously incline;

---

tranquillità, mentre furono in Venetia, che mai tra loro non fu non diro cosa, ma parola men, che amorevole" (sig. Oo2ᵛ); Gabriel Chappuys (1575): "& *vesquirent ensemble,* en si grande union & tranquillité, tandis qu'ils furent à Venise que jamais ne se dirent un mot de travers" (sigs. Ss4ʳ⁻ᵛ [emphases added]).

45. There are a range of differences between Cinthio and *Othello.* Othello and Desdemona do not live together in Venice for a period of concord and tranquillity: the play opens on the night of their elopement. The two do not establish a household: they elope to the liminal Sagittar/y. Othello is not called to a routine assignment in Cyprus: he is summoned in a state of emergency. Othello and Desdemona do not discuss the assignment privately: they must speak to it publicly, before the Venetian Senate. The notion that she remain behind in Venice does not imply only their separation: there is no place for her in Venice. Desdemona does not choose one of her husband's two options for her disposition: she makes her own proposal to accompany him to Cyprus. She does not prefer her request to her husband in private: she petitions the duke. The two do not travel to Cyprus together: Othello assigns Desdemona to a different vessel, in the company of Iago. There is no tranquil passage to Cyprus: a storm delays Othello's trip.

But still the house-affairs would draw her thence,
And ever as she could with haste dispatch,
She'ld come again, and with a greedy ear
Devour up my discourse; which I observing,
Took once a pliant hour, and found good means
To draw from her a prayer of earnest heart,
That I would all my pilgrimage dilate,
Whereof by parcel she had something heard,
But not intentively: I did consent,

. . .

She lov'd me for the dangers I had pass'd,
And I lov'd her that she did pity them.

(1.3.128–68)

The passage establishes a telling dichotomy: on the one hand, Othello's stories of sieges and monsters and, on the other, Desdemona's duties in managing Brabantio's wifeless household. The house exerts a socializing force that "ever" and "again" she attempts to frustrate, but her responsibilities repeatedly "draw her" away from Othello and, it is re-emphasized, prevent her from hearing anything other than interrupted "parcels." Finally, an intentive dilation initiates a movement from Brabantio's sphere to Othello's that culminates in elopement. As she has hastened "house-affairs" for tales of monstrous men and battles, so Desdemona flees her father's house for a building named after a creature that is monstrously half-man, half-horse, and poised for attack.[46]

I deliberately suggest an agency in her elopement. In the Senate, Brabantio accuses Othello: "O thou foul thief, where has thou *stow'd* my daughter?" (1.2.62), and he is not alone in figuring the movements of Desdemona as those of a kind of inanimate cargo. Roderigo, too, describes her as having been *"transported"* to the Moor (1.1.124); Othello admits that he has *"ta'en* [her] *away"* (1.3.78); the Duke commands, *"Fetch* Desdemona hither" (1.3.120). Later, Othello "crave[s] fit *disposition"* for her (1.3.236) and, for the journey to Cyprus, turns her over to Iago: "To his *conveyance* I *assign* my wife" (1.3.285); "My Desdemona must I *leave* to thee" (1.3.295).[47] In Cyprus, Cassio repeats that she

46. See also on this subject McAlindon, p. 115; Peter Erickson, *Patriarchal Structures* (1985), p. 91; Peter Stallybrass, "Patriarchal Territories" (1986), p. 136; and, for a different set of referents, Stephen Greenblatt, *Renaissance Self-Fashioning* (1980), p. 238. My sense of the passage differs markedly from that of G. Wilson Knight, *Wheel of Fire* (1930), pp. 107–8.

47. On "conveyance" Ross notes: "other Shakespearean meanings of this word support the audience's anticipatory qualms about the meaning of this plan—particularly: (1) removal; (2) document by which transference of property is effected; (3) underhand dealing" (p. 42).

has been *"Left* in the *conduct* of the bold Iago" (2.1.75). This verbal pattern is congruent with another (widely recognized) set of images that characterize Desdemona as a valuable possession.[48]

Because it misrepresents Desdemona's actual enterprise, however, the pattern exposes little more than the nature of gynephobic fantasies of female location. Desdemona in fact enacts her own preference for placement, unconfined by the passivity wished on her by male language. As Roderigo indistinctly reveals, Othello has "ta'en her away" only metaphorically, through marriage. Physically, she has taken herself away to Othello: "Transported with no worse nor better guard, / But with a knave of common hire, a gondolier, / To the gross clasps of a lascivious Moor" (1.1.124–26). Although Roderigo resorts to a passive voice that threatens to obscure the facts, on careful rereading they disclose themselves. Desdemona has travelled unprotected, without the "better" escort of, say, Brabantio or one of his men, without even the "worse" escort of Othello or one of his. She has travelled with only a gondolier. To follow the pattern of Roderigo's evasive verbs is also to suspect that Desdemona herself has employed the "knave of common hire."[49] Brabantio, taking the point and echoing the diction, will later describe her as having "Run from her guardage to the sooty bosom" of Othello (1.2.70). The contrast between prevailing masculine constructions and Desdemona's action fuels Roderigo's and Brabantio's respective characterizations of her elopement as a "gross revolt" and an "escape" (1.1.134; 1.3.197).[50]

As Iago and Roderigo rouse Brabantio with their cry of thievery in the night—"is all your family within? / Are all doors lock'd?" (1.1.84–85)—they play to the conventional notion that Brabantio's familial integrity requires the enclosure of his house around its members and (especially for female members) their confinement within. So confident is the first-scene Brabantio of his household security that Roderigo must challenge him to seek Desdemona "in her chamber, or your house" by vowing that the Venetian senator may "Let loose on me the justice of the state" (1.1.138–39) if the alarm is false. Even then only the correspondence of an obscure dream convinces Brabantio to test this challenge to his governance. When he finds that Roderigo has told "too true an evil," he demands, "Where didst thou see her?"; "how got she out?"; and "How didst thou know 'twas she?" (1.1.160–69).

48. See, for example, Burke and Snow.
49. The common notion is that Cassio escorts Desdemona to Othello, an idea that undoubtedly originated in the later description of him as intermediary between them during their courtship. But in scene 2 he is ignorant of the marriage and of the Sagittar/y.
50. See also Greenblatt, p. 240.

Only enchantment, magic, foul charms, drugs, minerals, "arts inhibited" (1.2.63–79), spells, medicines, witchcraft (1.3.61–64), "practices of cunning hell," "mixtures powerful," or "some dram conjur'd" (1.3.102–5) could have transformed beyond all recognition "A maiden never bold of spirit." Otherwise it is impossible that "perfection so would err / Against all rules of nature" (1.3.94, 100–101). In other words, by fleeing his house for the Sagittar/y, Desdemona has become as alien to her father as are Othello's cannibals and anthropophagi.

At his first opportunity to confront his daughter directly, Brabantio does not ask her, "Is this true?" Instead, because now, as before, "Belief of it oppresses me already," he speaks directly to the meaning of her "escape": "Do you perceive in all this noble company, / Where most you owe obedience?" (1.3.179–80). Desdemona's "place" in a patriarchal familial and social structure is defined by the direction in which she tenders obedience; as the earlier description of her "hasty dispatch" of household duties implied a dereliction of them, so, too, her spatial displacement implicates her in a violation of the patriarchal hierarchy. The issue of her obedience has been skillfully mooted by Roderigo, who twice interrupts his story of her elopement to ask Brabantio's permission to proceed, "If't be your pleasure, and most wise consent" and "If this be known to you, and your allowance" (1.1.121, 127). But, as Roderigo also says, "if you have not given her leave," then is it a "gross revolt" (1.1.134–35), then is it "treason of the blood" (1.1.169), then can Brabantio accuse himself of insufficient "tyranny" (1.3.197) as the monarch in the little world of his house.

Desdemona's displacement, her elopement not to a "settled" house but to the temporary and public one named the Sagittar/y, can also be read through the prescriptive filter of Cornelius Agrippa's derogation of the life of "a stranger in his inn."[51] The liminality of the Sagittar/y is suggested anew when, with the marriage reconfirmed and with Othello's order for Cyprus issued, the new husband "crave[s] fit disposition" for Desdemona in Venice. He entertains no thought of her continued sojourn at the site of their elopement; indeed, he rather implies its inadequacy to her needs with his overelaborated request for "Due reference of place, and exhibition" and "such accommodation and besort / As levels with her breeding" (1.3.236–39).[52]

Othello's abdication of his householder's responsibilities is com-

51. See above, p. 150.
52. Ross glosses: "assignment to some appropriate residence and allowance of money for maintenance" and "such befitting arrangements (for her) . . . as corresponds with her upbringing" (p. 37). Ridley notes that "the passage seems overloaded with words expressing 'suitability'" (p. 34); Elliott also finds "anxiety" in the language (p. 6).

pounded by his appeal to the Duke on the matter, in a preposterous extension of the interruption of state affairs by mere domestic concerns. The Duke properly refuses any civic accountability for Desdemona's housing, for, as he gently admonishes, it is an issue to be "privately determine[d]" (1.3.275). He does, however, venture the suggestion that Desdemona return to her father during the siege of Cyprus. As Brabantio and Othello bluster out their monosyllabic protests, the locational insufficiency of the Sagittar/y empowers Desdemona to advance her own agenda, rejecting not only a return to Brabantio's house, rejecting even the idea that she should remain in Venice. She insists instead: "I did love the Moor, to live with him . . . let me go with him." Her statement that "my heart's subdued / Even to the utmost pleasure of my lord" (1.3.248–59) scarcely obscures the fact that Othello has given no sign that it would be his pleasure for her to accompany him. And she directs her plea to the Duke because, again, Othello has ceded his own authority over her placement.[53]

On the inappropriateness of such behavior, the prescriptive text could not be more clear. "I deny not," says William Whately, "that the service of the country and needful private affairs may cause a just departure for (even) a long time," but he allows of nothing other than the husband's departure alone in these pursuits. The domestic conduct books repeat countless times the rule that "God hath made the man to travail abroad, and the woman to keep home."[54] It goes unsaid—because it needed no saying—that these dicta presuppose a house already "settled" for the woman's occupation. But because he has established no material context for her as his wife, it is all the easier for Othello to yield to Desdemona's desire to accompany him. Still abdicating his domestic prerogative to the Senate, he "beseech[es]" and "beg[s]," "let her will / Have a free way" (1.3.260–61)—in default of such advice as Edmund Tilney's that the new husband must, in the interest of domestic peace, make it an immediate objective to "steal away [his bride's] private will."[55]

53. Ridley also notes that Othello does not hint that Desdemona might accompany him (p. 35). In Cinthio, the Moor initiates discussion of whether to take Disdemona or leave her behind; only then does she declare her will. Elliott emphasizes that, unlike Cinthio's Moor, Othello expresses no concern about exposing Desdemona to the dangers of either sea voyage or military siege (p. 5).

54. William Whately, Bride-Bush (1617), sig. A4ʳ; see also Smith, sig. E2ʳ; Dod and Cleaver, sigs. M4ᵛ–M5ʳ; Francis Dillingham, Golden Key (1609), sig. I6ᵛ; and Thomas Gainsford, Rich Cabinet (1616), fol. 101ᵛ. In The Comedy of Errors, Adriana asks, "Why should their liberty than ours be more?" and Luciana answers, "Because their business still lies out a' door" (2.1.10–11).

55. "Let her will / Have a free way" (in Ridley) is from the 1622 quarto; editors more commonly give the 1623 Folio reading, "Let her have your voice." The quarto version is the

Desdemona's sojourn at the Sagittar/y is thus pivotal, on the one hand representing her determination both to deny the patriarchal text that has in Brabantio's house defined and confined her and to rescript her own story along the lines laid out by Othello's tales of monsters and battles; on the other, prefiguring her commitment to move outside the Venetian social order entirely by following Othello to a "warlike isle" and the "fortitude" of a Cypriot citadel (2.3.53; 1.3.222). That is, the theme of domestic incorporation in the shadow of war, rather than in consecration of peace, has already been intimated with the couple's residence under the sign of the Sagittar/y, the legendary military prowess of which (especially in the Trojan War) is documented in *Troilus and Cressida,* where "The dreadful Sagittary / Appalls our numbers" (5.5.14–15). Desdemona disavows the universal goal of marital relations in her desperate resistance to being left behind in Venice, "a moth of peace," and Othello declares his indisposition for that goal when he protests himself "little blest with the set phrase of peace" (1.3.256, 82).

The incompatibility of Othello's occupation with marriage is emphasized from the first. His commission for Cyprus, notably, sabotages even his wedding night. Asking the bridegroom to "slubber the gloss of your new fortunes" by accepting the assignment, the Duke admits that Othello's command is not absolutely required: "we have there a substitute of most allowed sufficiency"; mere "opinion, a sovereign mistress of effects"—nothing more tangible—"throws a more safer voice on" the Moor. Yet Othello defers to this "sovereign mistress" rather than to the claims of a new wife, and to the "tyrant custom" of his occupation rather than to that of marital ritual. The ruling metaphor of his acceptance—that occupational practice "Hath made the flinty and steel couch of war / My thrice-driven bed of down"—indicates at least a dim recognition that his "new fortunes" properly involve the marriage bed, the "right and lawful use" of which William Perkins defines as "an essential duty of marriage" (1.3.223–31).[56] His muddled attempt to assure the Senate that his "appetite" will not interfere with his employment further suggests his apprehension of the tension between marital consummation and martial profession. Repeated figurative commin-

more interesting, given the link between sexual possession and conquest of the will in the early modern period. According to Edmund Tilney, "in this long and troublesome journey of matrimony, the wise man may not be contented only with his spouse's virginity, but by little and little must gently procure that he may also steal away her private will and appetite, so that of two bodies there may be made one only heart" (*Flower of Friendship* [1568], sig. B6r). See also Dod and Cleaver, sig. M4r. For both, this advice is essential to marital "peace."
56. Perkins, p. 424.

gling of the military and the marital ("'tis the soldiers' life, / To have their balmy slumbers wak'd with strife," he will tell Desdemona in Cyprus [2.3.249–50]) highlights their disjunction.[57]

Henry Smith described marriage as "the hardest vocation of all other: and therefore they which have but nine years prenticeship to make them good mercers or drapers have nineteen years before marriage to learn to be good husbands and wives, as though it were a trade of nothing but mysteries, and had need of double time over all the rest."[58] The "warlike Moor Othello" has by no means apprenticed himself to marriage, and the institution seems to hold for him nothing but mysteries. So innocent is he of his proper patriarchal role that he appears to invite his own overmastering both by giving his wife a handkerchief that did "subdue [his] father / Entirely" to the love of his mother (3.4.57–58) and in musing of Desdemona that she "might lie by an emperor's side, and command him tasks" (4.1.180–81).[59]

Although marriage was understood to initiate a household, Othello has defined himself in opposition to "chamberers" (3.3.269), as one who has made his residence instead in the "tented field" (1.3.85). Roderigo terms him "an extravagant and wheeling stranger, / Of here, and every where" (1.1.136–37); Iago calls him "an erring"—that is, wandering, vagabond—"barbarian" (1.3.356–57). The newly wed Othello does anticipate the transformation that marriage will entail, but his anticipation is not happy:

> But that I love the gentle Desdemona,
> I would not my unhoused free condition
> Put into circumscription and confine
> For the sea's worth.
>
> (1.2.25–28)

Despite his declaration of willing translation, Othello, in this, our first view of him, resists domestic "confine." Warning that Brabantio and his allies—as well as three senatorial search parties—are in pursuit of Othello, Iago urges the Moor, "You were best go in." But Othello says largely, "Not I, I must be found," that is, found outside, unhoused, and

57. The figurative encroachment of the military upon the marital recurs when Iago suggestively describes the "opposition bloody" of Cassio and Roderigo as having begun with them "In quarter, and in terms, like bride and groom, / Devesting them to bed" (2.3.171–75). See also McAlindon, p. 103.

58. Henry Smith, sigs. H7^{r-v}.

59. This is predicted by Iago. That marriage may subjugate Othello is hinted in the reference to Desdemona as "our great captain's captain" (2.1.74); Iago, too, says that "Our general's wife is now the general" (2.3.305–6) and that "His soul is so infetter'd to her love . . . her appetite shall play the god / With his weak function" (2.3.336–39).

free (1.2.30). Only a scene later, he will promise the Venetian Senate that marriage will not reduce the scope of his activity; if it does, then, worst of all fates, let him be wholly domesticated, "Let housewives make a skillet of my helm" (1.3.272), in his abhorrence revealing his stubbornly unaccommodated inclination.

Othello's unhousedness, the Sagittar/y's insufficiency, Desdemona's agency, Cyprus's disaccord: these are the multiple terms by which the first act of the play challenges prescription and seems to call down its tragic predictions. Like the name of Iago, these terms (with the exception of the last) have no source in the *Hecatommithi*. But despite this and every other evidence that it directly engages oeconomic thought as a companion text, *Othello* nonetheless denies prescription its consequence.

Again, the polysemous image of the Sagittar/y introduces the theme. Although insistent references to both Othello's and Desdemona's displacements in Venice seem engineered to impress on us that they live as "strangers in an inn" rather than by "settling" a house,[60] the Sagittar/y sustains some element of its mystery. While it houses homeless strangers and is, through the story of Desdemona's escape, made to seem antidomestic, it is never called an inn (as the Centaur repeatedly is in *Errors*).

This first-act ambiguity of place is anticipatory; it escalates significantly in Cyprus. There, on arrival, Othello bids, "Come, let us to the castle . . . come, Desdemona." He asks Iago to "disembark my coffers; / Bring thou the master to the citadel," and Iago advises Roderigo to "meet me by and by at the citadel: I must fetch his necessaries ashore" (2.1.201, 208–11, 278–79); as late as the fifth act, Iago bids Emilia "run you to the citadel, / And tell my lord and lady what has happ'd" (5.1.125–26). Because of Desdemona's association with the citadel and the repeated mention of personal possessions in terms of their apparent conveyance there, we may assume that Othello and Desdemona will establish residence within it, a space the "fortitude" of which is "best known" to Othello.

But as the tragedy unfolds, our fix on Othello and Desdemona's residence slips. In the briefest of scenes—only six lines long—Othello informs Iago that he "will be walking on the works" and invites others to accompany him: "This fortification, gentlemen, shall we see't?" (3.2). Iago has said that he will "devise a mean to draw the Moor / Out of the way" (3.1.37–38) for Cassio's free access to Desdemona, and Othello's exit creates the opportunity. But as a plot device, the scene is hardly

60. Cf. Agrippa's *Commendation of Matrimony.*

necessary; it is almost always cut in production. In establishing a new sense of domestic environment, on the other hand, it marks a significant point of departure. That the fortifications are "out of the way" suggests the spatial distance of the stronghold from the residential area. And only a scene later, Othello tells Desdemona, "I shall not dine at home, / I meet the captains, at the citadel" (3.3.59–60)—speaking again as if their home is elsewhere, at some remove from rather than within the citadel.

Meanwhile, intimations of a settled domesticity proliferate. The much-discussed uncertainty about the consummation of the marriage is resolved (in my view) when the whole island joins in "celebration of [Othello's] nuptials" (2.2.7).[61] A motif of hospitality surfaces as Othello remarks that his wife "feeds well, loves company, / Is free of speech, sings, plays, and dances well";[62] as he invites "generous islanders" to dinner (3.3.188–89, 284–85); and as the couple welcomes Lodovico and Gratiano. Dod and Cleaver's inclusion of household linens among a woman's proper matronly concerns reverberates with Desdemona's sentimental identification with her wedding sheets (4.2.107; 4.3.22–25). And where she had embarked for Cyprus without an assigned female attendant, on the island she develops a domestic allegiance with Emilia. They share intensely private preparations for bed, idle chatter about Lodovico, intimate memories of her childhood maid, the willow song, and a philosophy of marital fidelity.

At the same time, Othello, who has opposed himself to "chamberers," now finds himself imagining betrayal by his wife in "*my* chamber." His statement that the memory of Iago's insinuations comes over him "As doth the raven o'er the infected house" reveals a startling identification with domestic space (4.1.139, 21).[63] The problem is that Othello's domiciliary transformation expresses itself solely in his developing jealousy. There is his growing fixation on the door of Desdemona's chamber, for example, a totem Iago insinuates into his consciousness. By painting word pictures of Desdemona and Cassio "bolstering," by asking whether for proof Othello must himself "Behold her topp'd," by suggesting instead that "imputation and strong

61. For a contrasting view, see especially the heavily characterologic reading of T. G. A. Nelson and Charles Haines, "Othello's Unconsummated Marriage" (1983). For me, one point of the interruption is that it reminds us that the newlyweds have been sharing a bed.

62. Like the reference to Desdemona's speculation on Lodovico, below, this passage can seem to confirm Desdemona's "liberality," as other critics have made clear (see for example Ross, p. 119). The purposes to which I cite it do not exclude those meanings.

63. For an analysis of Desdemona as a cornered "chamber" entrapping Othello, see Elliott, p. 68.

circumstances, / Which lead directly to the door of truth," may give him "satisfaction" (3.3.400–414), Iago undoubtedly accomplishes what M. R. Ridley describes: "Othello is led in imagination to stand outside the closed bedroom door," picturing the activities of the chamberers within.[64]

In a succeeding interrogation of Emilia, Othello asks her to take him in imagination beyond the door to which Iago has introduced him, enquiring if she has seen Desdemona and Cassio together, overheard their conversations, ever left them (in defiance of custom) alone. When Emilia's protestations of Desdemona's chastity fail to "satisfy" the conviction that Iago has bred in him, when the door has not been opened on the scene he wishes to see in his mind, he dismisses her as "A closet, lock and key, of villainous secrets" and opens the door himself. He chambers himself with Desdemona, requiring Emilia's withdrawal: "Some of your function, mistress, / Leave procreants alone, and shut the door" (4.2.1–28). In an earlier scene, just after hearing Iago's original word pictures, Othello has encountered Desdemona and declared that her hot, moist hand "requires / A sequester from liberty" (3.4.35–36), succumbing to the common compulsion of the period to confine the woman behind doors in the need to be sure of her. But the chambering of Othello's imagination ironically results in his own physical imprisonment, as Montano says of the discovered wife killer, "Come, guard the door without, let him not pass" (5.2.242).

Domestic props—the bed, its curtains, its sheets, the candle—crowd the final scenes. These so confirm the sense of an established household that Lodovico's judgment that Gratiano shall "keep the house, / And seize upon the fortunes of the Moor" does not jar at all (5.2.366–67). Further, it can be argued that the growing signals of domestic instantiation themselves participate in Othello's fatal jealousy: his acquisition of the trappings of a household and his acceptance of the door accompany his discovery of the anxiety of secure possession of the wife:

> O curse of marriage,
> That we can call these delicate creatures ours,
> And not their appetites! I had rather be a toad,
> And live upon the vapour in a dungeon,
> Than keep a corner in the thing I love,
> For others' uses. . . .
>
> (3.3.272–77)

64. Ridley, p. 118.

Here Othello elucidates the problematics of the patriarchal system as a marital text; it both asserts possession and finds possession always uncertain. Brabantio's warning—"Look to her, Moor, have a quick eye to see: / She has deceiv'd her father, may do thee"—has been counterpointed many times over by apprehensions of the insufficiency of the eye. Brabantio has also cried that fathers cannot know their daughter's minds "By what [they] see them act" (1.1.171), and Iago has insinuated that the women of Venice "do let God see the pranks / They dare not show their husbands" (3.3.206–7). Thus Othello's demand for "ocular proof" of Desdemona's infidelity is doomed; Iago will argue that "Her honour is an essence that's not seen" (3.3.366; 4.1.16). He has no ocular proof of guilt; more significantly, there can be no ocular proof of innocence.

The prescriptive text we might have used to read Desdemona, to resolve her radical inconsistencies, in fact offers no useful supplement. She defies the text: for all the inclination and determination she displayed in the first scene, she is chaste and obedient to the end. And this, as I have suggested, is not the only first-act promise that goes unfulfilled. Where Othello and Desdemona earlier had no "place" other than the ominously liminal Sagittar/y, they now, in all theatrical, moral, and symbolic respects, inhabit a "house." Where they violated the marital ideal of "peace" by travel to a Cypriot citadel, they soon learn that the threatened invasion has not materialized, that the "wars are done, the Turks are drown'd" (2.1.202). The project of applying domestic prescription dissolves into mere irrelevance.

The ill omens of the first act are not essential to the narrative. The source story depends for its effect more on a reversal of fortune than on the tragic foreboding that informs Othello from the start. But to suggest that Othello's transgressions of oeconomic convention do little more than establish an ominous opening that is appropriate to tragedy is to depreciate, it seems to me, their conceptual interest. Rather, these transgressions seem directly to dispute custom. In defiance of all contemporary oeconomic doctrine, disaster occurs when the couple is most rooted in domesticity, when Othello is at his least martial, when Desdemona is at her most obedient. The calculative capability of domestic prescription is disproved (and all the more clearly in the face of the predictive capacity of the occult).

Most striking of all, the final scenes of Othello challenge the ethicality as well as the efficacy of conventional oeconomic ideology. The text most directly ventures this challenge in Emilia's scene of appalled discovery, when it valorizes her refusal to be silent and obedient. These female attributes, too, were constructed locationally in the oeconomic literature, as Henry Smith makes clear. He begins with the first virtue in the triad of which silence and obedience are traditionally constituent members: "Paul biddeth Titus to exhort women that they be chaste, and keeping at home: presently after chaste, he sayeth, keeping at home, as though home were chastity's keeper." Using language that presumes female obedience, he continues: "a wife should teach her feet, go not beyond the door; she must count the walls of her house like the banks of the river which Shimei might not pass, if he would please the King." And finally, Smith observes of the looked-for silence of the wife that "as it becometh her to keep home, so it becometh her to keep silence."[65]

This last pairing of place and peace is precisely keyed to Cassio's displeasure with Bianca, by means of which Emilia's theme is previewed. Cassio complains of Bianca's not keeping home and her not keeping silent.[66] Afraid of being found "woman'd," he greets her at her first appearance onstage with "What make you from home?" and "I'faith, sweet love, I was coming to your house" (3.4.193, 167–69); later he complains that "she haunts me in every place" (4.1.131) instead of confining herself to her "proper" place, at home, where he can fix the time and control the nature of their interaction. At one point, Cassio even follows Bianca, saying he "must" because "she'll rail i'the street else" (4.1.159). She offends not only as an unsilent woman but, even worse by Cassio's conventional standards, by railing publicly rather than privately, in the street rather than behind the closed doors of her house. Because Bianca is neither physically contained nor vocally controlled, she becomes liable to accusations of unchastity, as was predicted by Henry Smith (and as will be true for Emilia as well). Iago terms Bianca a prostitute, Cassio treats her like one, and the "Names of the Actors" appended to the 1623 Folio text lists her as a "courtesan." But, as Susan Snyder has pointed out, Bianca herself presents her relationship with Cassio as one of romantic (and jealous) love.[67] She resists the label of whore which the misogyny of this play imposes on each of its unsilent, disobedient, and displaced women.

The association of female dislocation and loquacity achieves its most radical significance when Iago chastises Emilia for speaking out of

65. Henry Smith, sigs F6ʳ–F7ʳ. Gouge declares that "too much speech implieth an usurpation of authority" (sig. T5ᵛ).
66. Bianca's loquacity has often been discussed in the criticism; her dislocation has been noted by Stallybrass, pp. 126–27. Carol Thomas Neely relates Emilia's rejection of the three wifely virtues to "unhousing" herself ("Women and Men" [1977], p. 131); Stallybrass remarks that silence and chastity are "homologous to woman's enclosure within the house" and that "Emilia must open the closed mouth, the locked house" (pp. 127 and 142).
67. Susan Snyder, "A Modern Perspective" (1993), p. 296.

place and remands her to her "proper" place. He has inaugurated the issue with his command to her to "Speak within doors" (4.2.146), and in the last scene, during her denial of Desdemona's infidelity, he orders Emilia first to "charm [her] tongue" (a phrase that reasserts his occult identity),[68] then to "get [herself] home." Her challenge to the decree of silence is explicit: "I will not charm my tongue," "I am bound to speak," "let me have leave to speak," "I hold my peace sir, no," "I'll be in speaking, liberal as the air," and "yet I'll speak." This rebellion implicates her in another: "'Tis proper I obey him, but not now: / Perchance, Iago, I will ne'er go home." And in response to his repeated "Be wise, and get you home," she declares, "I will not" (5.2.184–224). Her refusal to be silent and obedient provokes Iago's impeachment of her chastity, too; in an accusation that invalidates itself more readily to modern readers than does that of Bianca, he brands her a "Villanous whore!" As Emilia's articulation of insurrection escalates, so does Iago's determination to control her, until he finally silences her tongue and sends her to her last home in the play's second uxoricide.

Othello's self-recognition, the revelation of Desdemona's chastity and Iago's duplicity, and the resolution of the tragedy all depend on Emilia's resistance of her husband, her disclosures of fact, her refusal to obey the locational imperatives of patriarchy, and her willingness to attract to herself the label of a whore. To achieve its closing gesture toward justice, in other words, the text relies on Emilia for truth. Truth can be advanced only through her violation of the most familiar tenets of domestic prescription. In *Othello,* prescription is proved incompatible with moral principle. The fact that principle is gendered female has resonance for my continuing argument.

Walter Calverley's Crime

In the *Hecatommithi,* the Ensign is a single malign individual practicing on a Moor. If in *Othello* he is the "ruler" of the zodiacal Sagittarius, then the whole constellation of anxieties he embodies generalizes him from a particular personality to an influence notionally operative upon every man, and especially every married man. The long history of readers who have blamed Desdemona for her own victimization demonstrates that, while not every man is Othello, Iago can act on any man.[69] The protagonist of *A Yorkshire Tragedy,* named only the "Husband" as if to underline the paradigmatic aspects of this domestic

68. Ross observes that Iago wishes Emilia to silence her tongue "as though it were constrained by a magical spell" (p. 233).
69. Othello witnesses Desdemona's initial violations of domestic prescription: she half-woos him, flees her father's house, elects to accompany Othello to Cyprus. But the play also plants

tragedy, seems also to have come under the influence of the Sagittar/y and to share Iago's violent misogyny. The character's historical prototype, Walter Calverley, of Calverley Old Hall in the town of Calverley, was, as eponymy implies, secure in his wealth and status, centered in regional English geography, and thoroughly "housed" and "chambered." He was the furthest thing from a "new" man, the term that characterized Thomas Ardern and that has some applicability to Othello—to the extent that he can be translated into an English social setting—as well.[70] And yet Walter Calverley committed crimes for which only Spain, according to an English contemporary, could "yield some precedent," violating the natural law forbidding "the father to kill his innocent son, or the husband his chaste wife." As Yorkshire antiquary Roger Dodsworth remembered the case:

> On the other hand standeth Calverley, the seat of the knightly family of the Calverleys, who lived in the best rank till . . . Calverley stained his progeny by his barbarous cruelty in murdering his own children and etc., out of a desperate humor, after he had greatly entangled and consumed his estate by his riotous courses. He killed two children and stabbed his wife, who by reason of their bodies was saved, and, riding to the nurse's with intent to murder his [third] son, his horse stumbled and threw him down, so that, being apprehended before he recovered his horse, his son was spared by God's gracious providence, who doth limit man's courses, and etc. I saw him executed in primo Jacobi. He was pressed.[71]

Walter Calverley was buried near his place of trial, where a church register records that he was "executed for murdering unnaturally two of his own children."[72]

Like Thomas Ardern, Walter Calverley had a considerable life in the documentary archives as well as an afterlife in sensational literature. To review some parts of the archival record is to complete the bracket of

---

suspicions that are unknown to Othello, are incapable of fueling his jealousy, and thus can resonate only in the mind of the audience: she banters with Iago at the dockside, advises Emilia not to learn from her husband, vows to make Othello's "bed . . . a school, his board a shrift," speculates about Lodovico. There is a long history of critics who, even knowing Desdemona's chastity with a certainty unavailable to first viewers or readers of the play, have nonetheless succumbed to the temptation offered them and placed upon Desdemona the burden of responsibility for her victimization. It may be that some, entrapped by the misogyny of this text, are brought to a terrible self-recognition at its denouement; Davison notes the intense reactions that the play provokes, including the "*personal* acrimony, betrayed by some critics" (p. 10). The tendency to blame Desdemona has been challenged by Neely; W. D. Adamson, "Unpinned or Undone?" (1980); and Ann Jennalie Cook, "Design of Desdemona" (1980).
70. Stallybrass discusses Othello as a "class aspirant" (p. 134).
71. Roger Dodsworth, *Yorkshire Church Notes*, pp. 42–43.
72. Cited by A. C. Cawley and Barry Gaines, Introduction to *A Yorkshire Tragedy*, p. 11.

case histories that have opened and now nearly closed this book. Calverley's record as I report it is material rather than political or economic. Material history is essential to understanding the notoriety of his crime, for this was not a murder that was motivated by ambition and competition. The gentleman from Yorkshire rewrote domestic history by derogating not only the natural law but also ancient privilege.

Family myth has it that the Calverley line was founded in 1100 when John Le Scot, a member of the royal family of Scotland and steward of the household to Maud (daughter of Malcolm III of Scotland and wife to Henry I of England), wed Larderina, heiress to Alphonsus Gospatrick, lord of Calverley and Pudsey.[73] (In all likelihood there was a remote Scottish ancestor, though probably not a royal one, who acquired the property in Calverley through marriage.) The descendants of the union were for six centuries the preeminent family in this Yorkshire locality, as the eventual adoption of the Calverley surname formally recognized. Between 1154 and 1181, a William Scot donated the parish church of Calverley to the archbishop of York. Later, a John Scot endowed Kirkstall Abbey with one manor and Esholt Priory with another. (This Scot's daughter was installed as Prioress of Esholt, and subsequent gifts as well as the unmarried daughters of subsequent generations found their way there.) Here is a telling distinction between Thomas Ardern and Walter Calverley: at the time of the Dissolution, the unpropertied Ardern seized the opportunity to create an estate out of the monastic lands claimed by the crown, while Walter Calverley's ancestors were among those who had anciently invested the monasteries with properties from their own vast holdings.[74] A strong sense of family tradition undoubtedly accounts for their post-Reformation recusancy, another difference between Calverley and the reformist Ardern.

By 1358 the Calverley seat, in continuous occupation since the twelfth century, included a hall house with "diverse" chambers, a kitchen, a barn, a stable, an oxhouse, a sheepfold, a kiln, and a cattleshed. Over the years, the house was entirely rebuilt (see figure 12).[75] The

73. The account that follows is based on a family history compiled for the Landmark Preservation Trust by Charlotte Haslam (1985) from the Calverley papers deposited at the British Library. I am grateful to Haslam for sending me a manuscript copy of her work.
74. A hint of the Calverley's proprietary ambitions survives from 1391, when a Calverley seized some Kirkstall Abbey lands (which may or may not have been among the endowments provided by John Scot). The abbot sued him, and Calverley and his collaborators were fined and imprisoned.
75. Information on the house was compiled by D. J. H. Michelmore (updating the work of Jack Sugden) for the West Yorkshire Metropolitan County Council Archaeology Unit and deposited at the Historic Monuments Trust in London. See also Henry Stapleton, *Memorials*, in the private collection of Hilda Bartel. Ms. Bartel kindly showed me the family chapel at Calverley Old Hall and a room in the seventeenth-century dining extension.

Figure 12. Calverley Old Hall. The projecting wing to the left is the family chapel. Next to the chapel is the ancient solar wing, originally of timber construction. Photograph © RCHME Crown Copyright, reproduced by permission.

oldest surviving portion, the central solar wing of the main living quarters, is of early to mid-fifteenth-century timber-framed construction. Like Thomas Ardern's solar, it is two stories high, with the upper level open to the rafters of its great roof. According to his will of 1488, a William Calverley appended to the solar section another wing for a family chapel, a remarkable architectural luxury for a private establishment. This was of stone, two-storied, with a hammerbeam roof and ornamental beams and boards. The altar area at the front was open to the roof, but the rear of the structure was partitioned into an upper gallery reserved for family members and a lower level, with access by outer door, for household attendants and associates. At about the same date, the great hall was rebuilt. With a width of thirty feet, large as the nave of a cathedral; a hammerbeam roof, again more common in churches than in private houses; and its stone construction, the hall made a second claim of considerable status. (Its chimney stack alone is so large that today it houses a bathroom and a larder.) In 1550 Sir William Calverley, High Sheriff of Yorkshire, added a chamber wing behind the chapel, creating extensive new family accommodations.

The Walter Calverley of *A Yorkshire Tragedy* did not make his mark on the house before his execution on 5 August 1605—not, at least, through building or remodelling—but his surviving son, Henry, did. At her death during his minority, Henry's mother left documents itemizing income from rents (for some of which Henry had to sue his stepfather in the Court of Wards on reaching majority), assessing the state of repair of his properties, and inventorying his furniture and goods. He subsequently encased the solar wing in stone; warmed the ground-floor room of that wing with wainscoting; inserted great mullioned windows in the solar; enlarged windows in the hall, too; extended the low balustrade of the gallery in the chapel by adding elaborate ornamental panels to form a screen; and built a wing behind the chamber block to incorporate a new dining chamber and kitchen. An inventory taken shortly after his death in 1651 lists the hall, kitchen, great chamber, four other chambers (including one for servants), two parlors, and a lodge.

Henry's son Walter, given the name used in alternate generations despite his homicidal grandfather, married Frances Thompson, heiress to the manor of Esholt and, ironically enough, owner of the manor house that had been created on the site of Esholt Priory when her ancestors purchased it at the Dissolution. Walter Calverley and his bride made Esholt their primary residence. When Walter died, his body was returned to Calverley Old Hall, where it rested in the household chapel for three days before burial in the family vault in the church

that his ancestor had given to the archbishop. This was a last revisit by
the Calverleys. Since the late seventeenth century, the medieval hall has
remained comparatively untouched by structural modification. With
the exceptions of the loss of its service rooms and outbuildings and of
the addition of Henry's amenities and extensions, the house survives
very much as Henry's father knew it.[76]

Walter Calverley's stature helps to explain the notoriety of his crime,
which was memorialized in numerous texts: a 1605 pamphlet titled *Two
Most Unnatural and Bloody Murders: The one by Master Calverley, a Yorkshire
Gentleman, Practiced upon his Wife and Committed upon his two Children*; a
1605 "Ballad of Lamentable Murder Done in Yorkshire by a Gent[le-
man] upon two of his own Children, sore wounding his Wife and
Nurse"; a second pamphlet of 1605 titled *The Arraignment, Condemnation, and Execution of Master Calverley at York in August 1605*; descriptions
in Stow's 1607 abridged *Chronicles* and his 1615 *Annals*; Dodsworth's
report; a 1633 pamphlet recording another murder to which Calverley's was compared, *A True Relation of a Barbarous and most Cruel Murder,
committed by one Enoch ap Evan*; a reference in Thomas Heywood's 1635
Philocothonista; and, based on *Two Most Unnatural and Bloody Murders*,
the 1605 stageplay *A Yorkshire Tragedy*.[77]

The domestic tragedy that dramatizes Calverley's crimes is thoroughly preoccupied with his long pedigree and with his privilege. His
honor is so "ancient" that its origin seems obscure beside, for example,
Sir Charles Mountford's precise location of his "gentle style" in a great-
great-grandfather. Like Mountford, the Husband defiles his inherited
estate. But, unlike Mountford, he has no remorse for his derogation, so
that his place and prestige live for us through the distress of others: his
Wife, a visiting Gentleman, even a maidservant. The Husband himself
eventually joins this chorus as he comes to recognize the consequences
of his addiction to gambling and his defiance of family responsibility:
"How well was I left? Very well, very well. My lands showed like a full
moon about me. But now the moon's i' th' last quarter, waning, waning,
and I am mad to think that moon was mine. Mine and my father's and
my forefathers', generations, generations. Down goes the house of us;
down, down it sinks. Now is the name a beggar, begs in me. That name,

76. That similarity is more pronounced following the restoration efforts of the Landmark
Preservation Trust.
77. In their edition of *A Yorkshire Tragedy*, Cawley and Gaines cite all references save that
from *True Relation of a Barbarous . . . Murder*, which reads: "We may read of a Gentleman, one
Master Calverlee of Yorkshire, who laid violent and wicked hands upon his own children, and
intended the like unto his wife, but melancholy and jealousy were things that before had much
wrought upon him, and therefore might in some small degree extenuate the cruelty of the act"
(sig. A3ʳ).

which hundreds of years has made this shire famous, in me and my posterity runs out" (4.69–77).

For early moderns, the mystery of the Calverley murders was motive. The problematic first scene of *A Yorkshire Tragedy* hints that the Husband's dissipation may have begun with his violation of a previous betrothal;[78] the last scene imputes demonic possession. But when the Wife asks "the cause of this . . . discontent," he replies viciously, "A vengeance strip thee naked, thou art cause, / Effect, quality, property; thou, thou, thou!" (2.32–35). His specific complaints of her, like his frequent and casual accusations of his children's bastardy, seem spoken maliciously according to familiar formulas rather than out of any personal disaffection or conviction, invented, like Iago's motivating myth of his own sexual displacement.[79] What rings more true is the Husband's lament, "I hate the very hour I chose a wife, a trouble, a trouble" (2.101–2). He is tormented not by the nature of this wife, who is a type of the patient Griselda, but by being wived.

In close recall of Othello's apprehension, the *Yorkshire* Husband articulates the profound discontent occasioned by the patriarchal role. He recognizes that marriage engenders a possessiveness that can never be wholly satisfied: "If marriage be honourable, then cuckolds are honourable, for they cannot be made without marriage." He apprehends that the only end of marriage is responsibility: "Fool, what meant I to marry? To get beggars?" (2.42–45). He finds marital responsibilities oppressive: "Midnight, still I love you / And revel in your company. Curbed in?" (2.78–79).[80]

Those who remonstrate with the Husband repeatedly plead the cause of his noble wife, begging him to remember her birth, her alliances, her virtue, her kindness, her obedience, her chastity. Given the marital root of his discontent, however, these protests feed his mania rather than diverting it. The turning point of the play comes with the complaints of a college Master, who reminds the Husband of the youn-

---

78. The Husband's earlier betrothal is mentioned only in the first scene of the play; in the source pamphlet, *Two Most Unnatural and Bloody Murders* (1605), it calls down God's revenge.

79. Baldwin Maxwell similarly suggests that the Husband's accusations display not conviction but "a desire to torture" (*Studies in the Shakespeare Apocrypha* [1956], p. 166).

80. The Husband's imagery reveals his misdirected preoccupation with the carnal and progenital concerns to which marriage has introduced him. His addiction to gambling is expressed as a sexual compulsion: "I was never made to be . . . A bawd to dice; I'll shake the drabs myself / And make 'em yield" (2.97–99). He fancies that his beggared "second son must be a promoter and my third a thief, or an underputter, a slave pander" (2.48–50). And he vows to the Wife that he will "never touch the sheets that cover [her]," will "be divorced in bed," until she authorizes the sale of her dowry "to give new life / Unto those pleasures which I most affect" (2.86–89). That is, he deflects into gaming the sexual passion proper to marital sheets and bed as well as the procreative energy that would produce "new life" in heirs rather than in continued addictions.

ger brother imprisoned for the Husband's debts, who in declaring that "you have killed the towardest hope of all our university" may initiate the older man's self-conceptualization as a murderer, and who enlarges even further the scope of the Husband's accountability by numbering the "ten thousand souls" who might have been made "fit for heaven" had the brother been allowed to continue his studies (4.14–20).[81]

In *A Yorkshire Tragedy*'s source, *Two Most Unnatural and Bloody Murders*, the university Master is the first to introduce us to the brother's plight, and this seems to account for his unique efficacy with the Husband. The pamphlet affords a telling contrast to the play, where the issue is instead previewed both in the first scene (1.48–50) and by the Wife (2.70–71). What is peculiar to the *Yorkshire Tragedy* Master's chastisement is his failure to mention the Wife, the subject that has so preoccupied all other bearers of "instructions" and "admonitions" and the very object of the Husband's loathing: "My strumpet wife, / It is *thy* quarrel that rips thus my flesh" (2.181–82 [emphasis added]). In their insistent probing at the festering source of his discontent, the other complainants have undone themselves. Through his silence on this subject, the Master releases the Husband to apprehend in horror what he has effected: "In my seed five are made miserable besides myself. My riot is now my brother's jailor, my wife's sighing, my three boys' penury, and my own confusion!" (4.77–79). In this scene of self-recognition, the Husband is for the first time able to separate his wife, personalized by her sighing, from the institution of marriage. Of this, he says with sudden clarity: "That heaven should say we must not sin and yet made women; gives our senses way to find pleasure, which being found confounds us. Why should we know those things so much misuse us?" (4.56–60). ("Why," as Othello put it more simply, "did I marry?" [3.3.246].)

Because oeconomic prescription has proved itself unable to induce his amendment, however, the suddenness of the Husband's conversion finally conveys a sense of moral randomness. Prescription is tested in the person of the Wife, who seems to have modelled herself on Robert Snawsel's oeconomic ideal. Snawsel argues that a woman should avoid criticizing her husband to others, but he also admits that "if the matter be of such a nature, that it cannot well be helpen by the wife's counsel, it is a seemlier course that the wife make complaint to her husband's parents, or some of his kindred, rather than to her own; and also that she moderate her complaint and temper her speech, so that she may

81. In an N.E.H. Summer Institute at the Folger Shakespeare Library in 1992, J. M. Massi suggested that the Husband determines to enact the role into which the college Master has already cast him, that of a murderer.

seem not to hate her husband's person, but only his ill conditions."[82] The *Yorkshire* Wife, accordingly, will not admit her husband's "abuse," "usage and unkindness"—"Why should our faults at home be spread abroad?"—especially when it is her own uncle who quizzes her on the subject (3.3–12).

Further, she returns submission for insults and spurns; she attempts "counsel" at every opportunity.[83] She says, "I never yet / Spoke less than words of duty and of love" (2.40–41), with the two words "duty" and "love" conveying her awareness and observance of the directives issued by Edmund Tilney and his fellows. Tilney writes that wives must "seek gently to redress them, endeavor to please them, and labor to love them, to whom we have wholly given our bodies, our goods, our lives, and liberty. . . . how much more the husband be evil, and out of order, so much more is it the woman's praise, if she love him."[84] The Wife's behavior follows the formulas and when measured against Tilney's recommendations merits praise, but it is nonetheless inadequate to reform the Husband.

Through no consequence of the Wife's punctiliousness, only through the accidental nature of the college Master's intervention, Calverley finally comes to recognize his defaults. But even then, the action that he proposes to take in response to this discovery is perverse. His acknowledgment of the results of his dissipations engenders only despair and the grim determination to hasten the conclusion toward which his actions have tended, to "knock my house o'th'head" (9.18). His "remorse" expresses itself in a resolve to commit mass murder. Having abjured domestic duty so obsessively, he now seizes domestic entitlement at its most radical extreme. By the strictest construction of patriarchal sovereignty, a Roman construction, the lives of his children are at his disposal. But, as Jean Bodin had already observed, Roman patriarchalism no longer obtained for early moderns, either in theory or in fact. There is nothing but condemnation for the Husband's acts of infanticide (except perhaps from the Wife, who remains to the end as the text had created her, so thoroughly subsumed in her husband that

82. Robert Snawsel, *Looking Glass* (1610), sigs. D6^v–D7^r. For Henry Smith, "it is an evil bird that defileth his own nest" (sig. F7^v); Whately concurs that "the wife is worthy all hard measure that spreads abroad every thing which she sees amiss in her husband" (sig. C1^r).

83. While husbands were universally enjoined from striking their wives, the wives are nonetheless advised, as by Henry Smith, that if "he doth strike thee, thou must bear him" (sigs. F2^r–F3^r). For the Wife's repeated attempts at verbal communication, see 2.23, 32, and 55; 3.39–40 and 43. The Wife adheres to the most difficult tenet of patriarchy, the injunction to honor a higher conscience when it diverges from direction by her husband: "what the law shall give me leave to do / You shall command" (2.91–92).

84. Tilney, sigs. D4^v–D5^r.

grief over his fall from grace outweighs even her anguish over her children's deaths).

In *Mythologies*, Roland Barthes has analyzed the process by which ideology naturalizes itself, so that its most basic assumptions seem reasonable, incontrovertible, and sufficient to themselves. In early modern England, the tenets of oeconomic prescription were accepted as matters of common apprehension; they seemed true to prevailing wisdom; they were consistent with what was regarded as the most basic common sense. What could seem more logical than that a father would protect his son(s); that privilege such as the Husband's would fight to sustain privilege; that, as Bodin asserts without remark, every man should be (and should welcome being) master of his own house? From the church register recording Calverley's execution to the pamphlet describing his murders, the emphasis was on the "unnaturalness" of the murders. As *Othello* required racial distinction to particularize its protagonist and obfuscate its heterodoxy, so *A Yorkshire Tragedy* invented its ethical distraction of the Husband's demonic possession. Given the shape of the early modern moral order, what else but an invasion of the devil could be understood to have inspired such "unnatural tragedies" (10.22–26)?

A New Domestic Mythology

If a nineteenth-century transcription of his now-lost confession to infanticide is accurate, the historical Walter Calverley had learned the lesson of Alice Arden's crime.

> And being likewise examined whether at any time he had any intention to kill his said children, to that he said, that he hath had an intention to kill them for the whole space of two years past, and the reasons that moved him thereunto was for that his said wife had many times theretofore uttered speeches and given signs and tokens unto him, whereby he might easily perceive and conjecture, that the said children were not by him begotten, and that he hath found himself to be in danger of his life sundry times by his wife.[85]

In my discussion of Thomas Ardern's murder, I suggested that one of its cultural uses was that it put a face to disorder, that in its construction of Alice Arden it created an archetype for the agent of domestic evil. I

---

85. Excerpted by Cawley and Gaines, app. B, pp. 111–12.

quoted the anonymous pamphleteer of 1595 who universalized the Arden paradigm: "If he have a wife which as himself he loveth, although he see with his own eyes her chaste life given over to the lecher, and another enjoy that, only proper to himself, yet with heart's grief is he fain to smother so ugly and most odious abuse, doubting the revealing thereof should work his shame in the world, and his life thereby dangered." If the transcription of the Calverley confession is true—and even if not—the period had readily available to it a means of constructing this crime, too, along those familiar lines.

Instead, however, the Calverley murders present us with a new paradigm for domestic transgression and a new malefactor in the husband. As I argue of Ardern's murder, what is at issue is not the specific legal disposition of an "actual," historical crime but which particular crimes the culture chose to totemize and in what forms it did so. *Othello* provides some further evidence of a Jacobean preoccupation with the crimes of householders rather than housewives. From this viewpoint we can chart a certain historical progression of the manifestations of domestic distress, beginning in the 1570s with a coalescence of anxiety on the person of the adulterous and murderous wife in the prose criminal literature and in the chronicles, continuing during the 1590s in that same vein on the public stage, but shifting in the first decade of the seventeenth century to a focus on transgressive and murderous husbands in the drama and also in some examples of the prose literature. Joy Wiltenburg, taking a longer view in her survey of the popular literature of domestic crime, has proposed an alternative symptomatic structure: a preoccupation with murderous wives up to 1650 and a focus on tyrannous husbands thereafter.[86] But in the narrow cultural trace that I have been following, one that can be read in a linear and transhistorical fashion only because subsequent literary criticism has imposed the linkage of genre identification on a small collection of playtexts, the interpretive schism occurs between 1603 and 1605. At that point we see either a shift to male violations of oeconomic order or, at the least, an enlargement of the repertoire of criminal misconduct to include male as well as female.

If we are facing merely an expansion of the field, then we have come upon a variation no more historically profound than that theorized by Cinthio, who knew that the dramatic form would seek new sources of

---

86. There is no complete bibliography of ballads and prose tracts devoted to contemporary crime; my gross generalization is based on an unsystematic survey of about 180 examples dating from around 1550 to 1640 and treating of murder, treason, counterfeiting, robbery, perjury, adultery, piracy, arson, and swearing. Cf. Joy Wiltenburg, *Disorderly Women* (1992), especially chap. 9. It should be noted that *Yorkshire Tragedy* was published in 1608; I follow Cawley and Gaines that it was written shortly after its source pamphlet, in 1605.

conflict as soon as it had exhausted others. In this case, the theatrical appetite brought into the foreground the recurrent subtext of the husband's responsibility for disarray in his household, figuring him as the new locus of disorder. Thus *Othello* and *A Yorkshire Tragedy* represent one climax in an extended dialogue between the public stage and popular prescription. Their focus on the male transgressor served to release the most direct engagement yet of hegemonic ideals of household function, and it underlined the dysfunction of those ideals.

But say, more largely, that there was a paradigm shift: especially because the evidence for it is so delicate, so subject to qualification and counterevidence, it may be an act of overinterpretation to freight it with causal significances of historical moment. To do so would presumably be to suggest that the shift may have been occasioned by the succession to the English throne for the first time in five decades of a king, a phenomenon that would have inspired its own anxieties about rule and order, now gendered male rather than female. It would be to suggest that the accession of James may have released a misogyny that was denied certain of its outlets during the reign of a queen, as hinted in Sir John Harington's happy anticipation in 1602 of a king rather than "a lady shut up in a chamber from her subjects and most of her servants."[87] It would also be to observe that anxieties other than gender, such as those aroused by the succession of a foreigner or those of transition of any sort, could have been displaced onto gender. One alien element in James, for example, was that he was himself disburdened of the long tradition of English hostility toward Spain, so that his professed wish for peaceful coexistence with the old enemy may have distantly informed the anti-Spanish countertext of *Othello* and may additionally have intersected obscurely with the naming of Iago.[88]

To the evidentiary mix I now add a nondramatic text, a pamphlet account of murders almost immediately coincident with those of Walter Calverley. *The Bloody Book, or the Tragical End of Sir John Fites (alias) Fitz* was, like the source pamphlet for *A Yorkshire Tragedy*, published in 1605, and it also relates male transgression to ideological challenge. The tragedies of Fites and Calverley correspond in so many points that they seem to confirm the suggestion that we are witnessing the construction of a new formula for domestic disorder with its own conventions and stereotypes.

87. Quoted by Simon Adams in "Eliza Enthroned?" (1987), p. 77.
88. I do not imply any political significance in the use of Iago's name, even though it is the cognate of James. James may have threatened reconciliation with the enemy, but he was also neither Catholic king nor apologist for the occult sciences; in his 1597 *Daemonologie*, he specifically engaged Agrippa (pp. 13–14).

The Fites story is located in an "ancient" place, South Tavistock in Devonshire. There, a gentleman who has given up any hope of children belatedly fathers an heir. John Fites's father, like Walter Calverley's, dies while his son is still in his minority, leaving him "large possessions" (sig. A3^r). Like Calverley, Fites promises to be "the complete mirror of an accomplished gentleman" (sigs. A3^v–A4^r). Like Calverley, he marries well, in this instance to the daughter of Sir William Courtney, a man of "ancient stock" and "honorable mind." Like Mistress Calverley, Fites's wife gives "evident proofs of a virtuous wife" (sig. A3^v). Again like Calverley, despite the moral agency of his wife, Fites falls "into the careless race of a dissolute life" (sig. A4^r), his crimes including murder, drunkenness, rioting, disturbing the peace, breaking windows, quarrelling, blaspheming, and whoredom. At a critical point, he, too, numbers the accounts of his "inordinate disorders" and despairs: he has "impaired his estate, sever'd himself from his wife, wedded himself to willful obstinacy, abused his neighbors, murdered his friends, consorted himself with villains, and caused himself to be so odious" that he begins "to fall into a desperate kind of lunacy" (sigs. C3^v–C4^r). As was the case for Calverley, the devil is described as being "strong in him" (sig. E1^v), motivating his catastrophe. In the variation that finally most distinguishes his career from Calverley's, Fites's lunacy manifests itself in a second murder (here, of a stranger rather than a friend) and then in self-murder.

Pride in his position—or, more precisely, in his possessions—inspires the crime that first sets Fites on the path to disgrace. Fites was widely known to be fast friends with another area gentleman named Slanning. But at a neighbor's house, Fites displays the same intolerance of rivalry which I have suggested was responsible for the early modern decay of friendship:

> Amongst other their table talk, Sir John was vaunting his free tenure in holding his land, boasting that he held not a foot of any but the Queen in England. To whom master Slanning replied that, although of courtesy it were neglected, yet of due and common right, he was to pay him so much by the year for some small land held of him, the rent being by reason of friendship long time intermitted. Upon which words, Sir John (grounding his occasion upon choler, and heating that choler with disdain and pride) told him with a great oath, he lied, and withal, gave fuel to his rage and reins of spite to the unjustness of his anger, offering to stab him. (sigs. A4^v–A5^r)

A "feigned reconciliation" briefly averts disaster. En route home, however, Slanning orders his men to walk his horses separately, so that he is alone when Fites overtakes him, determined to "revenge himself" for what he thinks of as a personal "disgrace" (sigs. B1^{r-v}). One of Fites's men (seeming kin to the fractious followers of Thomas Cheyney) strikes Slanning on the head from behind, enabling Fites to run Slanning through with his sword.

As intimated by the rarified ground of this dispute, an ongoing theme of the pamphlet is Fites's privilege. In a strategy briefly entertained by Sir Charles Mountford and subsequently adopted by Wendoll, Fites flees England and escapes punishment for the murder. After a year in France he is able to return with a conditional pardon negotiated by his wife. The pamphlet coaxes from us our most extreme unease with its revelations of the impregnabilities of contemporary social status when it reports that Fites, despite his criminal history and his dissolution, is among those knighted by the newly crowned James. The text acknowledges that this honor emboldens Fites in his offences: "Now began he to think that the world should wink at his impieties, his credit and knighthood was a sufficient privilege" (sig. B3^v). *The Bloody Book* thus links its antihero's course to the accession of the Scottish king.[89]

Privilege further displays its perquisites when, on a journey to London, Fites seeks overnight lodging. At a gentleman's house his claim to fellow gentility is unavailing, but at a "victualling" house his cry of "Here is a Gentleman, and I want lodging" (sig. D1^v) causes the owner to turn his wife out of their own bed to make room for their better.[90] After a restless night, Fites rises "in his shirt, with his naked rapier in his hand" (sig. D4^r) and leaves the house, passing through its back gate. His host, trying to close the gate protectively behind the "frantic" guest, instead draws Fites's angry attention, and Fites stabs him. The victualler's cry "I am killed" rouses the wife, who runs out in her smock and is herself assaulted by Fites. (Her wound is not mortal.) According to the pamphlet, the inspiration of the devil is such that Fites "will not be satisfied unless he shed his own blood likewise" (sig. E1^v). Fites fixes the hilt of his sword in a mud wall and twice runs on it, subsequently refuses medical attention, refuses also to confess, and finally dies after being bled. Although he is found guilty of the victualler's death and of his own, he is buried in the chancel at Twickenham, in a last remark on privilege, "because he was a Gentleman born" (sig. E4^v).

As was the case with the Calverleys, the textbook virtue of Mistress

89. It also works one variation on *Woman Killed*'s anticourt sentiment regarding Wendoll's parting resolve for his future (16.124–36).

90. This reported incident is more immediately revealing of the status of the gentry than any number of abstract descriptions of the class.

Fites has no ameliorative effect. Like the earl of Essex, Fites makes their house the "safest sanctuary" for his riotous companions (sig. B4^v), bringing home whores ("not esteeming the precious modesty of his wife's bed" [sig. C1^r]) and, despite her patient willingness to "wink at" his abuses, exiling her from the house. He "would neither vouchsafe her maintenance or houseroom, but with words of disgrace turned her out of his doors," unlike Frankford, "not leaving her attended by any to conduct her" (sig. C1^v). Fites attributes his fatal mental torment to fear of retribution from his father-in-law Sir William Courtney. As was true of the textualized Calverley, thus, he assigns to his wife a power to unsettle and threaten him, although here in the more displaced and indirect form of power lodged in the kinship network of a woman of status.

The Bloody Book defies convention so far as to applaud Mistress Fites's enforced exile, "for by these means she avoided further peril of death. . . . so that herein she was most fortunate, that she was safe" (sig. C1^v). Mistress Fites is thereafter abandoned to "great cause of sorrow" and the uncertain future of widowhood; the pamphlet follows the subsequent career only of Fites's daughter, in a brief note of her wardship to "an honorable earl" which is more a report on the disposition of the Fites property than acceptance of any responsibility to complete a human—read "female"—history. Significantly, however, *The Bloody Book*'s brief attention to Mistress Fites also provokes a radical rereading of the domestic oeconomy. The pamphlet attributes to her a power that her social status does not account for and that the tenets of conventional ideology cannot admit of: "This lady being by him in this wise turn'd away, he now knew himself to be the only master of himself, and might as he thought now be emboldened to follow his own looseness. Now was his own house, without contradiction or controllment, open to his associates, where now (if they please) they may erect a little commonwealth of many iniquities and much imputation" (sig. C1^v–C2^r).

With terms like "master" and "a little commonwealth," the text proclaims its intersections with analogical thought even while subverting them. In my earlier discussion of domestic patriarchalism, I reviewed the vigorous attempts of theory to suppress the contradictory roles of the mistress/mother who must be obeyed and the wife who must obey; the pressure to subordinate shared oeconomic interest to discriminated political hierarchy; the rage to contain and dismember any threat of female power. Only with the overdetermination that betrays unease was ideology capable of acknowledging a role for the wife in the economic terms of her contribution to the maintenance and supervision of household operations. *The Bloody Book* not only recognizes the essential administrative conflict of the prescribed household structure, it also celebrates that tension as a creative and ethically corrective one. At least in this instance of a husband in rebellion against his socially mandated role, the moral pressure exerted by the wife has assumed a legitimate and desirable social purpose.

The Place of the Private, Revisited

Maintaining distinctions between public and private spheres has been essential to my argument. In my first chapter I sought to problematize their parameters, to shift their borders and adjust their range in order to differentiate them from the constructions with which we are most familiar. But the binary structure itself held for my analysis of the public and private lives of Thomas Ardern and informed my discussion of domestic and political patriarchalism. Whatever the implications of one realm for the other, public matters essentially remained those concerned with the state, private matters those concerned with the household.

With *Othello*, however, this binary reveals its artifice and insufficiency. The first-act career of Othello introduces instead a tripartite structure organized around "worldly matters," "direction," and "love" (1.3.299). First, there is the role he plays in the public or, let us say for clarity, political sphere, as an agent of the Venetian Senate and its instrument against the Turkish threat to its Cypriot territory. Second, in his report to the Senate of his wooing of Desdemona and in his reassurance that marriage will not derail his militancy, Othello reveals his awareness of a private or, more properly, professional history, of his personal record of exploit and accomplishment, and of the individually managed commodity of his reputation. Then, third, through his marriage, Othello commences a second private or, more specifically, domestic life. His initiation into this third sphere as a novice highlights its separability from the professional private.

It is only with difficulty that the precapitalist society of early modern England accepted the contrast between professional and domestic. A similar social scale could have been played out for Thomas Ardern or for Matthew Shore, for example, had their textualizations been more amenable to it. Ardern's public career—that is, his dealings with and on behalf of central and town governments, his economic advancements, and his material instantiation—could as easily have been read in terms of his private ambition as of a public persona, but this story of a private life was suppressed. Instead, we are given the domestic life with which

his culture was so much obsessed, and we infer the larger public significance that, in early modern terms, is afforded through analogical
thought or that, in our own time, is derived from anecdotal thought.[91]
A more explicit hint of the tripartite does flare in *1 and 2 Edward IV*,
when the consequences of Matthew Shore's cuckolding by the public
figure of the king include his abandonment of the private, his shop and
his profession, as well as the dissolution of the domestic, his marriage
and his house. But this glimpse of multiple distinctions is brief, for the
spheres of domestic life and private occupation almost immediately
fold in on each other without further articulation, and Shore's pro-
longed preoccupation is with his wife rather than his trade. The public
theater required the city comedy and its alternative generic paradigm
in the career of Simon Eyre to fully admit private ambitions and
achievements in men of nonnoble status.[92]

In the early modern fragmentation of the binary structure, however,
the long contest between the house as man's castle and the house as
woman's place finally moved toward a resolution that we today would
recognize. A contemporary formula for marital roles held that "the
duty of the husband is to get goods; and of the wife, to gather them
together and save them. The duty of the husband is to travel abroad to
seek living, and the wife's duty is to keep the house."[93] This model
unwittingly predicts a distinction that should also have been apparent
from my introductory discussion of mythical thought: where Cornelius
Agrippa and Jean Bodin spoke of the rulers and masters of spaces and
places, Ernst Cassirer and Heinrich Nissen referred not only to governing but also to occupying powers, and the latter two were not always
one. The woman who kept the house in her governor's absence was also
a woman in occupation of it. As the house became less the central
institution of production and was succeeded by the various offices and
stewardships of an Ardern, the merchant travels of a Sanders, and the
nomadic professionalism of an Othello, it was feminized.

And as literature totemized the closed door beyond which Gerbier's
bride and Brabantio's daughter were not to pass and before which
Frankford and Othello paused in dread, it emblematized the space

91. By "anecdotal" thought I do not mean to refer only or even primarily to the New
Historicism, although its penchant for the telling anecdote has been noted (see, for example,
Jean E. Howard, "The New Historicism" [1986], pp. 38–39) as well as much imitated. I regard
much traditional history as anecdotal, in that the career of a Thomas Ardern, for example, is
held to be of historical significance to the extent that it is representative of or was multiplied
many times over in the careers of other new men, reformers, government officials, and proto-
capitalists.

92. Thomas Dekker, *The Shoemaker's Holiday* (1600).

93. Dod and Cleaver, sigs. M4^v–M5^r. See also on this subject my "Performance of Things in
The Taming of the Shrew."

behind the door as the woman's place. This was a transformation to which the texts of the early seventeenth century pay prophetic tribute. In *Othello*, the resistant Moor is imported into a domestic sphere that is represented, through stage synecdoche, by a bed and bed linens. In this play and in all contemporary oeconomics, these are goods inextricably associated with the wife. For the *Yorkshire* Husband, house, wife, instructions, and admonitions are synonyms, collusive in exerting social regulation. He can attempt to regain control in his house only by destroying it and her part in it, the children. In *The Bloody Book*, John Fites's house takes on the character of his virtuous wife. He must exile her to redefine it in his own image, as a site for his iniquities.

From this perspective, Dod and Cleaver's warning to the new husband takes on a more ominous cast: the wife will "continually be conversant with thee, at thy table, in thy chamber, in bed, in thy secrets, and finally, in thy heart and breast."[94] The sense of a mythical domestic paradise lost may account for the backlash of extreme misogyny and gynephobia in these texts of male abdication. All their chaste women, including Bianca, are branded with a relentless string of accusatory, sexualized epithets; Desdemona and Emilia are murdered onstage; the *Yorkshire* Wife is kicked and stabbed before us; Mistress Fites is exiled and abandoned.

The intuitions of these texts were proleptic. The culture that produced them had not yet processed or acknowledged the feminization of the domestic sphere, and the domestic tragedies of fifteen and twenty years later were to resist the notion strenuously, struggling to recover the integrated house of sixteenth-century patriarchal theory. Even in *Othello*, *A Yorkshire Tragedy*, and *The Bloody Book*, the phenomenon is only dimly perceived. It is not related to social or economic change on a large scale. Instead, it can be figured only in the local terms of male abdication and of the statistically insignificant incidence of interracial marriage, lunacy, satanic possession, uxoricide, infanticide, and suicide. The feminization of the house gave the biggest lie to a question that Edward Coke had meant to be rhetorical: "Where shall a man be safe, if it be not in his house?" As these early modern texts reveal, his was a question that domestic ideologies and mythologies could not claim to have answered.

94. See above, p. 103.

CODA FOUR

Impertinent Tragedies

The framework upon which I have built this partial and eccentric investigation of private matters in the English Renaissance is a literary kind. The generic architectonics are primarily a tool for delimiting an unwieldy subject; secondarily, they suit my methodological ambition to liberate the private from the purview of social history alone and to explore the uses of literature in constructing cultural history. To this point the generic argument has advanced implicitly and unexamined, a deliberate silence this coda finally redresses.

Neither the canon of the domestic tragedy nor its character has been conclusively established in the critical literature. I have adapted the canon proposed by the most disinterested and synthetic of writers on the topic, Keith Sturgess, diverging from it to add *1 and 2 Edward IV* and, perhaps more problematically, *Othello*.[1] Meanwhile, I have engaged the generic definition formulated by the recognized authority on the subject, Henry Hitch Adams. Adams characterizes the domestic tragedy as a genre of "obvious lessons" and "egregious moralizing." In his view its characters experience no "inner conflict as to which of two courses is morally right," nor are they "asked to select one of two alternatives neither of which seems to be entirely good or entirely bad." He concludes that the genre "failed . . . to deal significantly with moral problems which were subtler than the obvious equating of providential

---

1. Keith Sturgess (Introduction [1969]) lists *Arden, Warning for Fair Women, Two Lamentable Tragedies, Woman Killed, Yorkshire Tragedy, Witch of Edmonton*, and *English Traveller*. He also mentions *Miseries of Enforced Marriage* (1607) as "an interesting near relation of *A Yorkshire Tragedy*" (p. 8).

operations and the popular conception of right and wrong" and thus fell short of the "larger reach" of orthodox tragedies.[2]

These citations from Adams should serve to indicate well enough the grounds of my dispute with him.[3] In the first chapter, I borrowed from Holinshed the term "impertinent," which the chronicler used with reference to his inclusion of the Arden story in a national narrative and which I used with reference to *Arden of Feversham*'s violation of the dramatic conventions that reserved tragedy to matters of state and the doings of kings. My notion is that the domestic tragedy was authorized or, more precisely, enabled by analogical thought, by the persuasion that the microcosm enjoyed the same principles of order as the macrocosm and suffered corresponding challenges of disorder. By this logic, the individual household was as susceptible to violations of order as was the state, and, moreover, those violations had an equal theoretical resonance for the state and its constituents. While the generic impertinence of *Arden* served to dramatize the cultural phenomenon of the fractious claim of private matters on public consciousness, I have also sought to uncover an impertinence of another sort, the ideological impertinence of *Arden*'s successors. These plays seem to have performed, in the space made available to them by *Arden*, the social work of a public laboratory for the testing of conventional thought on private matters and for the diagnoses of systemic failures of that thought (but not, admittedly, for the development of radical alternatives).

While I have pressed the case for *Othello*'s impertinence with respect to oeconomic issues (and have included it for that reason), the case for its generic impertinence remains untried. In fact, I do not intend to argue that *Othello* is or is not a domestic tragedy; the issues surrounding the play's genre are more interesting than is any actual conclusion as to its label. For although G. Wilson Knight termed the play "eminently a domestic tragedy," both those writing on the

2. Henry Hitch Adams, *English Domestic or, Homiletic Tragedy* (1943), pp. 189–90 and 184. Adams's subtitle reads, "Being an Account of the Development of the Tragedy of the Common Man Showing its Great Dependence on Religious Morality, Illustrated with Striking Examples of the Interposition of Providence for the Amendment of Men's Manners."

3. I must also acknowledge my debt to Adams, who raised the level of the discourse with respect to plays that had earlier surfaced primarily in arguments of authorship and among the Shakespeare apocrypha. Also important to the genre's critical tradition was the pioneering 1925 dissertation of Edward Ayers Taylor for the University of Chicago, "Elizabethan Domestic Tragedy"; he enlarged the canon by identifying a number of lost domestic tragedies. Through their emphasis on the family in the plays, Peter Ure ("Marriage and the Domestic Drama" [1951]), Michel Grivelet (*Thomas Heywood* [1957]), and Andrew Clark (*Domestic Drama* [1975]) rendered the domestic tragedies more susceptible to appropriation for a cultural history of the private. More recently, with "Alice Arden's Crime" (1982), Catherine Belsey has demonstrated that the time is ripe for a rethinking of the genre and its cultural import. See also my "Man's House as His Castle" (1985), Frances E. Dolan's "Gender, Moral Agency" (1989), and Dolan's *Dangerous Familiars* (1994).

kind and those specializing in Shakespeare display a lingering discomfort with the categorization.[4] My reading of this discomfort has nothing to with bardolatrous superstitions—that the preeminent English playwright would not have lowered himself to what many regard as a minor genre—nor with any concern of authorship or aesthetic quality. It bears instead on the assumptions that underlie our generic definitions.

Two obvious causes for uneasiness about calling *Othello* a domestic tragedy are its non-English setting and the superstructure of matters of public concern which Shakespeare imposes on this story of domestic murder. This is not to say that the play can be taken at once for an orthodox tragedy, however. The first scenes, in which concerns of state are most prominent, have been persuasively described as an abbreviated romantic comedy: Brabantio is the blocking character whose machinations are defeated in the triumphant match of Othello and Desdemona.[5] But, as I have suggested, it is also possible to see the Venetian scenes in terms of cultural myth rather than dramatic genre, as an abortive rape narrative, with "rape" signifying abduction if not violation, with Brabantio and Othello engaged in a contest for control and possession of a disputed woman, but with the conventional political upheaval finally averted.

The rape-narrative structure is another means by which public valences enter the drama. Its examples (such as the stories of the Moorish conquest of Spain and of Spanish resistance) are quintessentially public histories dealing with empire and war. At the same time, the rape narrative evades what I have termed the professional private, for while its prototypical events are constructed as the acts of single individuals, its protagonists are motivated only in what might be called domestic terms: not in terms of self-interested aggression and the desire for private gain or glory but instead in terms of response to the sexual dispossession of women. In the cases of Helen of Troy, Lucrece, the Sabine women, and Caba of Spain, revenge for rape is a universally acceptable motivation—is in fact the preeminent motivation—for aggressive actions with global consequences. England well knew the rationale of sexual provocation, for the secular myth of its Reformation was

4. G. Wilson Knight, *Wheel of Fire* (1930), p. 108. In his edition of *Othello* for The New Cambridge Shakespeare (1984), Norman Sanders calls it "the greatest domestic tragedy in the English language" (p. 9); see also S. L. Bethell, "Shakespeare's Imagery" (1952), and G. R. Hibbard, "*Othello*" (1968). In the Arden *Othello* (1958), M. R. Ridley more cautiously terms the play "the nearest approach which Shakespeare made to a 'domestic' tragedy" (p. xlv).

5. See especially Barbara Heliodora C. de Mendonça, "*Othello*" (1968), and Susan Snyder, "Conventions of Romantic Comedy" (1972).

one of the king's desire for Anne Boleyn (and her son), not for monastic wealth and a centralized political and ecclesiastical authority.

But from rape narrative *Othello* switches to what seems more credibly to be domestic tragedy, the domestic focus of the former providing a bridge to the latter. I have proposed that *Othello* and *A Yorkshire Tragedy* together established a new paradigm for the first decade of the seventeenth century. I don't mean to overlook, however, that *Othello* has far closer affinities with the playtexts of the preceding decade than does *A Yorkshire Tragedy*, even if only because it works some inversions on them. Like *Arden of Feversham*, *A Warning for Fair Women*, *1 and 2 Edward IV*, and *A Woman Killed with Kindness*, it involves the sexual displacement of a woman. But in *Othello* the cuckolding is at first figurative (inasmuch as it is a father rather than a husband who is cheated) and then fallacious (inasmuch as Desdemona is innocent of adultery). Othello is an outsider because of his race, as is Mosby because of his artisan status, Browne because of his Irish nationality, and Wendoll because of his depreciated wealth. In *Othello*, however, the Other is the protagonist-husband, the man who achieves title to the contested woman rather than the adulterous challenger for her. Iago, the evil agent who disrupts the balance of domestic relationships, does not, like Mosby, find his political and economic ambitions released by an adulterous affair and does not, like Wendoll, discover a focus for his diffuse longings in the person of another man's wife. Instead, Iago's presence interrupts the classic triangular paradigms of Brabantio-Desdemona-Othello in the first act and of Othello-Desdemona-Cassio in the remaining four. In each case, Iago creates a triangle and sets the plot in motion. But in each case, and here is the critical point, he himself exhibits no desire for the woman whom he places in exchange. He deploys the domestic or (as Stephanie H. Jed would term it) the erotic—without partaking of either.

This, I submit, is why Iago's malignity has seemed motiveless to us: it is not directed in the familiar ways by desire for a woman or even by desire displaced onto a woman. By comparison, readings of *A Woman Killed with Kindness* have long been concerned with the mysterious motivation of Anne; none questions the motivation of Wendoll, no matter the anguish with which he regrets his betrayal of Frankford and recounts the personal jeopardy of that betrayal, because masculine sexual desire implicitly requires no motivation other than occasion. In the world of these Renaissance textual conventions, betrayal without a sexual component, revenge for professional complaint rather than sexual slight, seems either obscure or overdetermined and finally mysterious.

Othello in its impertinence toys with our suppositions about desire by inventing Iago's voiced suspicion that Othello has cuckolded him, but the text also marks that suspicion with its own incredulity and in this way mocks both the motive and our anticipation of it.

Othello is generically ambiguous because it doesn't employ its disputed woman in the expected ways. Acknowledging the mystery of motives that are professionally private, it refuses to dramatize the obvious motives that are domestic and in this can seem to disengage from a flirtation with the domestic tragedy. To put the case this way is to rediscover how often *domestic* translates for modern readers as *woman-centered*. But the mistake is to believe that in the early modern period domestic concerns were either centered on women's issues or proto-feminist. Julia Kristeva again informs my argument that the domestic tragedy of the Renaissance was centered not on the woman as agent but on the woman as putative object of desire, the woman as pretext for dispute, the woman in whom anxieties and aspirations coalesce, and the woman as device of the dramatic plot. By and large the domestic tragedy seems to me to share the biases of the rape narrative, insisting on the signifying woman as essential to its mechanism and to its evasion of the process of absorbing and acknowledging the private man of self-generated ambition.

The semantic emptiness of Anne Frankford and of the *Yorkshire Tragedy*'s Wife is one symptom of this signifying system; the characterologic discontinuities of Desdemona are another.[6] To look to the later plays generally associated with the genre, moreover, is to find the system achieving its end, with the woman finally and thoroughly displaced even from the symbolic and motivational center. The collaboratively authored *Witch of Edmonton* (1621) proposes a series of traditional triangles of two men in sexual competition for a single woman, but it then dramatizes its own explosion of those triangles.[7] It introduces us to a young gentleman, Frank Thorney, in service to the principal local knight, Sir Arthur Clarington. Thorney engages in an affair with a serving girl, Winnifride, who is already carrying Clarington's child. The knight happily anticipates that his relationship with Win-

6. My argument for Desdemona's characterological discontinuities was made in a seminar paper for the Shakespeare Association of America in 1987, "Desdemona's Disposition." At about the same time, Alan Sinfield wrote "*Othello* and the Politics of Character" for presentation at the University of Santiago de Compostela. I am grateful to him both for sharing that paper with me and for offering helpful advice for my continued work on *Othello*. See also his "When Is a Character Not a Character? Desdemona, Olivia, Lady Macbeth, and Subjectivity," chap. 3 of *Faultlines* (1992).

7. The text is Thomas Dekker, John Ford, and William Rowley, *The Witch of Edmonton*, ed. Fredson Bowers (1958). My discussion engages only one plot of the play, that usually termed a domestic tragedy, not the plot regarding Elizabeth Sawyer, the witch of Edmonton.

nifride will continue after her marriage to Frank Thorney, and, with Thorney summoned to his father and Winnifride left behind with her uncle, he believes the way is clear for their continued "interchange" of "pleasures." But Winnifride surprises him—and perhaps us as well— by refusing Clarington, resolving to change "From a loose whore, to a repentant wife," and removing herself from the usual competition between men (1.1.171, 192).

Meanwhile, Thorney's father has summoned him to an arranged (and bigamous) marriage with a wealthy yeoman's daughter, Susan Carter. Susan makes her first entrance accompanied by a young gentleman named Warbeck, an apparent rival for Thorney. But there is no rivalry in fact; Susan refuses to encourage Warbeck, while she tells Thorney directly that he has the "possession" of her heart, in a second abortion of sexual contestation (1.2.209–10). The theme reaches its climax when Thorney informs Susan that he is leaving, and she, wanting to believe in romantic triangles and casting herself at the center of one, poignantly misconstrues the occasion as a "pre-appointed meeting / Of single combat with young Warbeck" (2.2.154–55). Instead, Thorney intends to elope with Winnifride, who has disguised herself for travel as Thorney's male attendant. The irony is compounded as Susan gives parting instructions to Winnifride, in a scene of gender confusions, double entendres, and the image of two women repointing the conventional triangle by exercising their competing claims upon a single man.[8]

Thomas Heywood's *English Traveller* (1625) redesigns its triangles, too, scrambling the relationships of a young gentleman traveller, Geraldine; his doting older friend, Wincott; Wincott's Wife, a childhood friend of Geraldine's whom he plans to marry after Wincott's death; the Wife's sister, Prudentilla, who flirts with Geraldine; and Geraldine's friend Delavil, who cuckolds Wincott and in this betrays Geraldine, too. When a maidservant warns Geraldine of the adultery of Delavil and Wincott's Wife, Geraldine prefers to fantasize that the maid has her own amatory ambitions for him and seeks to eliminate a rival— thus inventing an alternate triangle with himself at the center. Wincott, however, sees himself in the pivotal position, as he muses to Geraldine that he knows not "Which of you two"—Geraldine or Wife—"doth most impart my love" and as he figures a secret midnight conference

---

8. The play includes also a parody of the theme: Young Cuddy Banks confides his infatuation with Susan's sister Kate, while we know that Kate already has a suitor, Somerton. But the clown Cuddy never shares the stage with Kate or actualizes a romantic triangle; the witch of Edmonton arranges for him to meet instead an evil spirit in the "shape" of Kate, who misleads him into a near drowning.

with Geraldine as his own act of infidelity ("I have parted beds . . . to give you meeting; / Nor can be ought suspected by my Wife, / I have kept all so private") (p. 68). Wincott employs the prior relationship of his own wife and Geraldine ("you, in youth were play-fellows") and encourages their continued intimacy ("nor now be strangers") in order himself to purchase Geraldine's presence (p. 10).

The Wife, in other words, is not a contested object of desire but the pretext for and intersection of homosocial, homoerotic, and testamentary longings. The play closes with a triangle of moral misdirection, for Wincott is so removed from associations of either affect or interest with respect to his Wife that when her affair with Delavil is revealed, *The English Traveller* attempts to summon our disapproval and sympathy on behalf of Geraldine only. And because she is displaced from the center of transgressive sexuality and acquisitive ambition in the play, Wincott's Wife cannot by means of her death serve the generically restorative and ideologically conservative role pioneered by Alice Arden. The world that survives her celebrates its masculine exclusivity: the aim of this text is its arduous reclamation of the domestic sphere from the intrusive female.

The Witch of Edmonton and *The English Traveller* render transparent that which is more opaque in but which is nonetheless true of their generic predecessors: the early modern domestic tragedy is man-centered, that is, concerned with men's issues. Principal among these issues is the management of troublesome women, from which interest proceeds much of the thematic confusion on this matter. But recognition of the masculinist focus is one end of my argument for the constitutive role of the private household in these plays, an argument that also requires some sense of the ideological burdens carried by the early modern house and its complex political, economic, social, and ethical—read not "merely" woman-centered—meanings. Because our own borders for the territories of the private have shifted, because we have incorporated the professional private into our worldview and have reduced the house to the woman's domain, the formative mythologies of the Renaissance domestic tragedy have been obscure to us.

CONCLUSION

No one has ever been able to make much sense of the first scene of *A Yorkshire Tragedy*. Its most recent editors for the Revels Plays, A. C. Cawley and Barry Gaines, argue that the text was "worth re-editing" in the Revels format both for "its intrinsic merit as a domestic tragedy" and for the opportunity to address in some detail the "problems" of the play. Principal among these are its unknown authorship and, the topic I address here, the relationship of the first scene to all that succeeds it.[1] Having followed the critical convention of ignoring this scene in the preceding chapter, I return to it, first, to recover some strands of a material argument implicit throughout this book; second, to tease these strands out as a means of remarking the impact of an expanding market economy on constructions of the private (male) self; third, to relate this theme to my continuing preoccupation with the meanings of the house; and, fourth, to make one last case for the way in which early modern English playtexts register the concerns of their cultural environment.

One difficulty with *A Yorkshire Tragedy*'s first scene is that it seems by modern aesthetic judgments to be both topically and tonally unlike those that succeed it. Admittedly, it refers to a man who "beats his wife, and has two or three children by her," who "has consumed all, pawned his lands, and made his university brother stand in wax for him," and who "calls his wife whore" and "his children bastards as naturally as can be" (1.40, 48–50, 53–55). The referent for all these phenomena seems

1. A. C. Cawley and Barry Gaines, Preface (1986), p. ix. Other "problems" include date and sources.

to be the Husband of the following scenes, and, framed in language heavily indebted to the source pamphlet, these issues dominate the plot concerns of the rest of the play. But the opening scene also introduces the story of a woman formerly betrothed to this man who beats his wife. She remains in "a pitiful, passionate humour for the long absence of her love" (1.1–2), apparently unaware that he has married another so many years ago that he has fathered "two or three" children (1.40). Although the source pamphlet devotes considerable attention to this story of vow-breaking, the play never returns to it, and its far briefer report does not contain the sort of verbal parallels with the pamphlet that mark the text in later scenes.

The first scene also names its servingmen—Oliver, Ralph, and Sam—in contrast to the socially descriptive designations that serve in the next nine scenes: "Wife," "Husband," "Gentleman," "Master of the College," "Son," "Servant," and "Knight." The servingmen's jocular exchanges are radically disjunct in tone from the later action, which has been memorably characterized by John Addington Symonds: "Like the asp, [the play] is short, ash-coloured, poison-fanged, blunt-headed, abrupt in movement, hissing and wriggling through the sands of human misery."[2] Without question, this initial scene poses a challenge to readers in search of a unified authorial voice, and critics have used its anomalous features to construct elaborate hypotheses concerning collaborative (and Shakespearean) authorships, successive rewritings, generic redirections, and theatrical marketing strategies.[3]

To take this document on its own, admittedly puzzling terms, we must dismiss these textual anxieties and fantasies and forget, at least for the moment, the thematically unifying report of the vow-breaker's dilapidation of his estate and abuse of his wife. Looked at afresh, the scene offers an opening reference to the grieving former betrothed and turns it into a jest about a woman gone overripe on the marriage market and consequently made available "for every man to take [her] up" (1.7). Next, Sam enters, *"furnished with things from London"* (1.15sd). He describes them: "three hats and two glasses bobbing upon 'em, two rebato-wires upon my breast, a cap-case by my side, a brush at my back, an almanac in my pocket, and three ballads in my codpiece" (1.22–25). Sam also brings news of the man who beats his wife, but he interrupts his report to ask rhetorically, "what have we here? I thought 'twas somewhat pulled down my breeches. I quite forgot my two poting-

2. John Addington Symonds, *Shakespere's Predecessors* (1884), p. 434.
3. See Cawley and Gaines, Introduction, pp. 13–15. They conclude that the first scene was added "later" and "ineptly" by "a different playwright."

sticks. These came from London; now anything is good here that comes from London" (1.55–59).

The exploding availability of consumer goods in the early modern period was a cultural preoccupation. William Harrison, for example, observed that his contemporaries "do yet find the means to obtain and achieve such furniture as heretofore hath been unpossible." His loving catalogue of arrases, tapestries, silk hangings, fine linens, "Turkey work," carpets, napery, vessels, plate, pewter, and brass is its own tribute to an expanding consumer culture. He remarks in particular that possessions of this variety and excellence have "descended" along the social scale from nobles and gentlemen to yeomen and merchants and "even unto the inferior artificers and many farmers . . . whereby the wealth of our country . . . doth infinitely appear."[4]

Household inventories support even the most radical of Harrison's observations concerning the "descent" of provision. In Oxfordshire, for example, we can compare the movable goods of two generations of husbandmen who had farms of about equal size. According to an inventory dated 16 May 1553, John Sims lived in a one-room house furnished with only the barest cooking equipment and tableware, his goods valued at 18s. out of a total estate of £36 19s. Thirty-four years later, as recorded on 11 May 1587, Richard Collins lived in a ten-room house (hall, kitchen, parlor, five chambers, buttery, dairy) with four chairs and a joined table in his hall, painted cloths on the walls of hall and parlor, and several beds and sets of bed linens in his parlor and chambers, all assessed at a value of £42 14s. out of a total estate of £119 15s. That is, over a third of his estate was invested in his household goods. Near Banbury, a similar comparison is possible for two farmers with comparable amounts of land, livestock, and farm equipment. Edward Kempsale in January 1560 lived in a two-room house with goods worth £19 8s. 2d.; Thomas Gyll in December 1587 in a four-room house with goods worth £67 16s. 8d. Kempsale's farm stock made up three-quarters of the value of his personal estate, Gyll's little more than half. Kempsale had six trenchers; Gyll, twenty-eight pieces of pewter and five silver spoons. Kempsale had three pairs of sheets, one blanket, one coverlet, one bolster, two tablecloths, and two towels; Gyll, thirteen and a half pairs of sheets, two blankets, six coverlets, three

4. William Harrison, *Description of England* (1587), p. 200. Harrison's "furniture" are the most commonly described consumer goods in the period. But their stage display was impractical; this helps account for *A Yorkshire Tragedy*'s alternative strategy of showing fashionable items of clothing and personal grooming. These items may seem to represent different orders of objects, but they *function* in identical ways: I see Sam's objects as stage synecdoches for the world of goods available to early moderns.

bolsters, four tablecloths, and three towels, as well as four pillows and pillowcases and twelve table napkins.[5]

These case studies do not suggest that the gap between the privileged and laboring classes had narrowed dramatically. Geoffrey Tyack disabuses us of such a notion with his reminder that even a wealthy yeoman farmer like John Fetherstone left at his death in 1634 a parlor with bed, tables, cupboards, chairs, stools, and a chest together valued at only £16, whereas eight years earlier the contents of the parlor of a nearby great house, Stoneleigh Abbey, had been worth £129.[6] What does seem true, however, is that *relative* improvement was essentially nondiscriminating among the housed population. Victor Skipp's history of the Arden region indicates that during the sixteenth and seventeenth centuries the household goods of the wealthy increased by over 289 percent, those of the "substantial" by 275 percent, those of the middling sort by 310 percent, and those of lesser peasants by 247 percent.[7]

Twentieth-century economic anthropologists know that the accumulation of goods promotes nothing so much as an ambition for the accumulation of more goods and that such ambition enlarges exponentially. The seventeenth century supplied its own evidence of this geometric principle in the form of Randle Holme's *Academy of Armory*.[8] Holme aimed to identify, depict, and classify all objects that appear in heraldic badges; in fact, he compiled an exhaustive illustrated repository of early modern names, objects, trades, and customs. The bulk of the *Academy* seems to have been prepared by 1649; one volume appeared in 1688 with a comprehensive table of contents that also introduced a second volume, but this second volume was to remain unpublished until the twentieth century. The massive project defeated its executors. The first of the unprinted chapters, as if the chapter that in its excess occasioned defeat, deals with "household goods."

Holme illustrates his household goods on a grid of what he calls "quarters" (see figure 13). His folio page accommodates ninety-five quarters, each presumably intended to feature a single household item, numbered for cross-reference with an explanatory text. But the goods strenuously resist the meticulous efforts to predict and contain their number. A first glance shows that the structure is inadequate to its subject: two beds, for example, demand double and quadruple space, respectively. Moreover, a count demonstrates that one hundred twenty items are crowded into the ninety-five quarters, straining the clearly

5. *Household and Farm Inventories*, pp. 30–34.
6. Geoffrey Tyack, *Making of the Warwickshire Country House* (1982), p. 52.
7. Victor Skipp, *Crisis and Development* (1978), p. 70.
8. Randle Holme, *Academy of Armory* (1649), bk. 3, chap. 14; see BM Harl. MSS 2026–35.

FIGURE 13. A chart of household goods, from the second (unpublished) volume of Randle Holme's *Academy of Armory, or a Storehouse of Armory and Blazon*, completed 1649, BM Harl. MSS 2026-35. Illustration from the Roxburghe Club facsimile edited by I. H. Jeayes (1905), reproduced by permission of the British Library.

articulated borders and belying the numbering system. There are two items in fourteen of the quarters and three items in four of them.

These sorts of visual copia are not unique to the chart of household goods, but a survey of Holme's other illustrations reveals one variation that is. The full measure of overplus in this one instance is communicated by three ghostly items that have been superimposed on the very borders themselves, as prodigal addenda: a stand for dishes strays from quarter 32 into quarter 22; a drinking jug claims territory of both quarters 28 and 29; a looking glass violates the border between quarters 58 and 59. None of Holme's other illustrations tolerates the transgression of such excessive afterthoughts.

This superabundance is compounded by repetition to display variation: the accompanying text identifies two kinds of saltcellars (quarters 1 and 2), ewers (quarters 7 and 8), candlesticks (quarters 20 and 21), tongs (quarters 27 and 28), forks (quarters 36 and 37), pot hooks (quarters 39 and 40), cushions (quarters 60 and 61), tables (quarters 78 and 79), and beds (quarters 80 and 81). There are three kinds of pot racks (quarters 18, 25, and 34) and stands for dishes (quarters 9, 19, and 32); four kinds of pots (quarters 4, 5, 38, and 44), trivets (quarters 30–33), chairs (quarters 67–70), and lamps (quarters 49–52); six kinds of stools (quarters 71–76) and baskets (quarters 59 and 83–87); seven kinds of pans (quarters 11, 34, 35, 45, 46, 54a, and 54b). At another level of hypertrophy, most of the visual images are exploded verbally into multiple significations, so that the chamber pot (quarter 4) is also called a bed pot, a rogue with one ear, and a piss pot; the three-square trivet (quarter 30) has the additional names brandreths, brandirons, and iron crows; the vial (quarter 6) is identified also as a vinegar bottle and cruet and is distinguished from a urinal (quarter 48). The knives of quarters 11 through 13 remind Holme that there are chopping knives, cook's choppers, spreading knives, and also Turk's knives, Dutch cleavers, hacking knives, Scotch bibby knives, and "an other kind of desperate Knife called an Irish skene." The brush of quarter 43 calls forth the names of besom, broom, birch, rush, heath besom, long brush, handle brush, brush with a handle, hand brush, bristle brush, and beaver brush. Of chairs (quarters 67–70) there are thrones, chairs royal, cathedres; turkey-work chairs; stool chairs, back stools; joined chairs, buffet chairs; arm chairs, chairs of ease; turned chairs; settle chairs; twiggen chairs, groaning chairs, and child-bed chairs.

Holme frequently admits amplificatory digressions. He sometimes distinguishes subspecies of goods by their compositions in clay, glass, wood, or metal. He also pauses to observe some items in such detail that he catalogues their parts, as for a knife, dish, flagon, candlestick, lantern, cup, bellows, flesh pot (a pot for cooking meat), and grate. These, for example, are the parts of a candlestick enumerated in the text referring to quarter 21:

> The socket is the place where the candle is set.
> The nose is the length from the socket to the broad rim round the middle of it.
> The buttons or knobs are those outswelling or works made on the nose or shank or neck of the stick to adorn it.
> The flower is the round rim or broad brim set in the middle of the stick on which the tallow drops.
> The bottom is all the remaining part of the stick from the flower to the edge it stands upon.
> The edge or cord or flourish round the bottom, if there be any.
> The hollow is in the in part or under side of the bottom.

When he catalogues combs (quarter 63), Holme lists "the parts of a comb" (end teeth, middle teeth, small teeth, wide teeth, round teeth, flat teeth, teeth slender and thin, bastard teeth, open teeth, teeth wide asunder, sides and back), "sorts of combs" (horse or mane comb, wisk comb, back-tooth comb, beard comb, double comb, merkin comb, periwig comb, and small-tooth comb, each described), "comb makers' terms" (cutting, pressing, marking out of patterns, chopping, shaving, bordering, "dantaching," grailing, "priting," "plantum," rounding, redishing, polishing, sorting, and binding, each described), and "of what combs are generally made" (wood, boxwood, horn, ivory, bone, tortoise shell, cocus wood, and lead, with some sources and uses). Mention of the types of table (quarter 79) leads him to itemize "things necessary for and belonging to a dining room." From the illustration of the bed royal (quarter 80) comes two lists of "useful" things, one for the bed itself and one for the bed chamber.

If Holme's dizzily comprehensive lists have a totem, it is the dish stand of quarter 19: "This is to set on a table full of dishes, to set another dish upon, which kind of stands, being so set, *make the feast look full and noble*, as if there were two tables, or one dish over another" (emphasis added). Holme is semantic twin to *A Yorkshire Tragedy*'s Sam, who has not just one hat or one ballad but three hats and three ballads, not just one looking glass or one rebato-wire but two of each; who has, moreover, a cap-case, a brush, and an almanac; and who has his own prodigal possessions to add belatedly to the initial catalogue, as he rediscovers his two temporarily overlooked poting-sticks.

Given such evidences of material fixation, it is no wonder that goods so frequently surface as motivating devices in the plays I have examined:

In *Arden of Feversham* Arden sees the ring he has given Alice on Mosby's finger; Alice sends Mosby silver dice as a love token; Franklin's story of an erring wife turns on a glove that incriminates her; the Mayor of Feversham indicts the murderers on the evidence of a bloodied hand towel and knife dropped in the household well and the purse and girdle found at Mosby's bedside. Unique to the play, perhaps reflecting an independent local knowledge, and serving no immediate plot function is *Arden's* extended discussion of plate, for the theft of which Bradshaw is unjustly accused and the mysterious Jack Fitten is nominated.

In *A Warning for Fair Women* Anne Sanders's vulnerability to the agency of evil stems from her frustrated attempt to purchase goods: linens worth £30 and delivered by a draper, gloves and an Italian purse displayed by a milliner. The forfeited linen resonates when George Browne dips a handkerchief in the wounds of the murdered George Sanders and then sends the bloody cloth to Anne as token of her widowhood. Her legacy to her children are books of meditations.

In *Two Lamentable Tragedies* the allegorical figures of Homicide and Truth are joined, notably, by Avarice, also labelled in speech prefixes as Covetousness. In the main plot Thomas Merry murders Thomas Beech because he has a shop well stocked and a score of pounds, while Merry complains that he lacks the coin to purchase food and coals. In the companion plot Fallerio murders his nephew for the sake of possessions that he several times catalogues: plate, jewels, hangings, and household stuff, as well as castles, houses, meadows, lands, and also the turkeys, capons, pigeons, pigs, and geese offered by the orphaned boy's tenants.

In *1 Edward IV* rebels attack London with dreams of Cheapside, talking of new-minted gold coins, horses shod in silver, tankards of ipocras, chains of gold, and pearls, velvet, silks, satins, plate. The loyal citizens, as the Mayor declares, fight to "preserve our goods" as well as wives and children. In *2 Edward IV* betrayal is figured personally rather than nationally but again in terms of possessions: Mistress Blague's treason to friendship is emblematized in her appropriation of the trunks of jewels, coin, and plate (worth £20,000) with which Jane Shore had intended to maintain herself after the death of her royal protector.

In *A Woman Killed with Kindness* stage business heightens our awareness of the prescribed household clutter of tables, stool, tablecloth, napkins, carpet, voider, wooden knife, trenchers, bread, salt, lights, candles, candlesticks, cards, counters, box, and other impedimenta of dining and gaming. Frankford completes his separation from his unfaithful and exiled wife by purging his house of her possessions, saying that he will not live with so much as a bodkin, a cuff, a bracelet, a necklace, or a rebato-wire that carries the imprint of her use, banishing also, and more significantly, the larger symbol of her lute. Meanwhile, he expresses his Janus-faced "kindness" by installing her in another of his houses and providing her with a bed and its hangings.

In *Othello* a cultural novice is initiated into the "mystery" of marriage as he accumulates the trappings of a household: bed, curtains, linens, candle. For his history to achieve closure, the machine of society must complete its economic work even in the immediate face of his death; Lodovico, the representative of social order, must fix Othello's house and "fortunes" on a new caretaker. Finally, at one reductive but essential level, this play is the tragedy of a misplaced handkerchief.

The material theme has also run through the nondramatic discourses engaged by this book, beginning with Faversham's role as a distributor of London goods through Kent, its need for a customer, the controversy over two boats of grain exported to Flushing, the dispute over a piece of church silver, Thomas Ardern's passage of "An Act for Orphan's Goods," and the town's seizure of the clothing and jewelry of its malefactors. In Faversham's inventory of these reversions survives our only archival contact with the person of Alyce Ardern, just as a commission for the sale of Spanish goods permits George Sanders's sole entry into the *State Papers*. The dramatic invention of Anne Sanders's thwarted housewifery can be paired with the unhappy history of Elizabeth Littleton, Lady Willoughby, whose husband forbids her access to her household goods and linens and prohibits her purchase of domestic supplies. Fallerio luxuriates in the listing of his nephew's possessions in just the manner of William Harrison, itemizing the wealth of furnishings available to Englishmen. The rebels against Edward IV's London define the city as Ponet's Romilda does her own, as a storehouse of jewels and goods. Edward's loyal citizens fight to protect their women and their possessions even as Pelagius motivates his fellows to resist the Moors in Spain. And Mistress Blague helps make Alberico Gentili's case that no modern friendship can suffer possessions to be held in common.

As documentary archives report that Alyce Ardern's daughter and Walter Calverley's son sued for the return of their parents' goods and incomes, so fictionalized narratives track material histories: we are told of the descent of Fites's property; Lodovico assigns Othello an heir; and the English story of Moorish Spain reassures us that before Julian defected to Cepta, he "trussed up all his furniture of household" and took it with him. The reader's imagination is not permitted to distract itself with fantasies of property unaccounted for and in open circulation. As Donald R. Kelley has suggested, the acquisition, retention, use, and inheritance of things were English cultural fetishes.

The historical Ardern's acquisitiveness may have made him no friends, but his urge to own was nonetheless more comprehensible than the textual *Yorkshire* Husband's disdain for his possessions. I should note that the historical Walter Calverley behaved more seemingly and more to the English spirit at his trial and execution. He refused to plead and was pressed to death, thus preventing the forfeit of his properties to the state. His widow, unable to influence her husband's course, undoubtedly regained some sense of equilibrium when itemizing those properties for her one surviving, underage son.

Or, rather, she regained some illusion of control. As the stories of Ardern and Fites particularly remind us, possessions stimulate the desire for their domination as well as for their multiplication. Ernst Cassirer traces their power to the erosion of the primitive integration of inner and outer, subjective and objective, self and world; in its place, he suggests, man defines himself through his ownerships.[9] But property is a dangerous vessel in which to lodge identity, for it is inherently unstable. As Maurice Godelier has argued, "by property is meant a set of abstract rules governing access to and control, use, transfer and transmission of any and every social reality *which can be the object of a dispute.*"[10] Even as objects inspire the desire for control, they resist it; in their resistance, the desire is intensified, so that the cycle escalates.

This desire can metastasize in culturally significant ways. For example, it is socially conservative and reinforces the structures of status. As William Segar observed in 1602, "rich men are to be preferred, because the more a man possesseth in the state, the more careful he will be to conserve it: but poor men desiring to better their fortune are apt to innovation."[11] Sam's goods from London are of a kind with the *Yorkshire* Husband's admonitory neighbors, equal agents in the hegemonic conspiracy to promote the Husband's protection of his estate. Through its jesting linkage of a "common" woman and Sam's city commodities, the first scene of *A Yorkshire Tragedy* also reminds us of the commodity

9. Ernst Cassirer, *Mythical Thought* (1955).
10. Maurice Godelier, *The Mental and the Material* (1984), pp. 75–76 (emphasis added). My perspective on early modern material goods has also been informed by Joan Thirsk, *Economic Policy and Projects* (1978), and Chandra Mukerji, *From Graven Images* (1983).
11. William Segar, *Honor Military and Civil* (1602), sig. X5ᵛ. This is from the chapter titled "Of Precedency among persons of mean and private condition."

status of women, in which the possessive desire sustains the traditional gender hierarchy.

The social work of things with regard to status and gender is long-standing. New to the developing market economy of the sixteenth and seventeenth centuries was what Jean-Christophe Agnew traces textually to Hobbes, namely, the notion of "a commodity self: a mercurial exchange value or 'bubble' floating on the tides of what attention others were disposed to invest."[12] Such analyses of the effect of commercialization and capitalism on identity formation largely neglect to emphasize that this effect was gendered: the most primitive economies had long before marked women for exchange, but the incorporation of men—free men, skilled men, propertied men, even gentlemen—into such economic equations was a phenomenon of the early modern period.

Again, it was a phenomenon marked in the drama. The last two domestic tragedies produced before the closing of the theaters, *The Witch of Edmonton* and *The English Traveller*, work one significant variation on the paradigm of their generic precedents. In their main plots, they present their male protagonists, not contested women, as what Godelier terms "objects of dispute."

In *The Witch of Edmonton*, it will be remembered, the inheritance of a young gentleman, Frank Thorney, is economically threatened. He is placed in service to the principal local knight, Sir Arthur Clarington. There, Thorney engages in an affair with a serving girl, Winnifride, who has already conceived a child with Sir Arthur. The knight determines to solve the problems of his paternity by having the two servants marry. Convinced that he is himself responsible for the pregnancy, Thorney obeys Sir Arthur and honors moral obligation by marrying Winnifride. In a desperate attempt to keep the marriage a secret from his disapproving father, he lodges Winnifride with her uncle. Old Thorney, meanwhile, plans to preserve the family estate by marrying his son to Susan Carter, the daughter of a wealthy yeoman. Thorney soon bows to paternal authority and weds Susan, too. Ricocheting from demand to demand, Thorney epitomizes what Agnew has termed "a serial self, not a cumulative self."[13] His duplicate masters and bigamous marriage emblematize this refiguration of the male as the object of evaluation, liquefication, and contestation.

A reactive vector sends Thorney back to the reformed Winnifride,

12. Jean-Christophe Agnew, *Worlds Apart* (1986), p. 13 and passim, especially pp. 98–99.
13. Agnew, p. 83.

and the couple determines to flee. Sir Arthur has defaulted on his promise of a £200 portion for Winnifride, but Thorney has acquired control of Susan's dowry. A discussion of his economic resources fosters Thorney's recognition that he has prostituted himself and that his father was the pander.

> Frank.   . . . Are we not now set forward in the flight,
>   Provided with the dowry of my sin,
>   To keep us in some other nation?
>   While we together are, we are at home
>   In any place.
> Winnifride.   'Tis foul, ill-gotten coin
>   Far worse than usury or extortion.
> Frank.   Let my father then make the restitution,
>   Who forc'd me take the bribe: it is his gift
>   And patrimony to me; so I receive it.
>   He would not bless, nor look a father on me,
>   Until I satisfied his angry will.
>   When I was sold, I sold my self again
>   (Some knaves have done't in lands, and I in body)
>   For money, and I have the hire.
>   (3.2.16–29)

When Susan appears and presses her competing emotional claim on him, Thorney rebels against the irreconcilable demands of his multiple commodifications: he murders her. In the end the law lays yet another claim on the body of the besieged Thorney, as he is taken offstage to his execution. Old Thorney laments "the sad Object" of his son and sighs, as that object defeats his plans for it, "Would I had sunk in mine own wants" (5.3.53–59).

In *The English Traveller* competition similarly focuses on the young male protagonist, Geraldine. The main contest is engaged by the childless Wincott and Geraldine's own father, competing for an heir; another is suggested between Wincott's wife and her sister, Prudentilla, vying for his attention; a dishonest friend, Delavil, plays a variation on the theme in his envy of Geraldine's knowledge and popularity. So accustomed is Geraldine to his status as the universal beloved that when a maidservant impugns the honesty of Wincott's wife (for whom Geraldine in turn harbors his chaste and deferred affection), he muses, "the young wench may fix a thought on me; / And to divert me from her Mistress' love, / May raise this false aspersion" (p. 58).

Describing Wincott's love for him, Geraldine himself uses terms

of commercialization—"He studies to engross me to himself"—
feminization—he "is so wedded to my company"—and alienation—
"He makes me stranger to my father's house" (p. 9). The economic
vocabulary, freighted with the argot of use and here pointed by the
metacommentary of Delavil, is of immediate interest:

Old Geraldine.	You have took him from me quite, and have I think
	Adopted him into your family,
	He stays with me so seldom.
Wincott.	. . . By trusting him to me, of whom your self
	May have both use and pleasure, y'are as kind
	As money'd men, that might make benefit
	Of what they are possessed, yet to their friends
	In need will lend it gratis.
Wincott's Wife.	And like such,
	As are indebted more than they can pay;
	We more and more confess our selves engaged
	To you, for your forbearance.
Prudentilla.	Yet you see,
	Like debtors, such as would not break their day;
	The treasure late received, we tender back,
	The which, the longer you can spare, you still
	The more shall bind us to you.
Old Geraldine.	Most kind ladies,
	Worthy you are to borrow, that return
	The principal, with such large use of thanks.

"What strange felicity these rich men take," remarks Delavil, "To talk of
borrowing, lending, and of use; / The usurer's language right" (pp.
41–42).

Objects in the commodity stage of their existence are things in motion, and the commodification of Frank Thorney and Young Geraldine
is expressed, too, through their motility, a migrant status reflected in
their movement between competing placements (or, more simply,
houses). Thorney, for example, never identifies himself by place, in
contrast with Frankford and Mountford. His inheritance achieves no
material reality for us through the theatrical representation of the
Thorney household; rather we see him in another man's house, Sir
Arthur Clarington's. When he marries, he does not establish his own
household; instead he requires his wife to "sojourn" at her uncle's,
where he promises to visit once a month. He refuses the force of Winnifride's conventional argument for cohabitation; still, in denying the

rumor of this marriage to his father, he denies also that he would be so much the atheist as to "make the marriage-bed an inn" (1.2.175). Determined to expatriate with Winnifride, he argues in his turn that "While we together are, we are at home / In any place"; nonetheless, when Susan similarly professes that "I'm there at home, [wherever] thou pleasest to have me," he sends her violently to her "last lodging" (3.2.19–20; 3.3.18–19). Finally, Thorney, who has not known how to reconcile the competing ethical pulls of his master and his father, his first wife and his second, his virtue and his interest, articulates the psychically disintegrative effect of demand and displacement:

> . . . when a man has been an hundred years,
> Hard travelling o'er the tottering bridge of age,
> He's not the thousand part upon his way.
> All life is but a wandering to find home:
> When we are gone, we are there. Happy were man,
> Could here his voyage end; he should not then
> Answer how well or ill he steer'd his soul,
> By heaven's or by hell's compass. . . .
>
>   (4.2.28–35)

This object of desire defeats the strenuous attempts of Old Thorney, Old Carter, Clarington, Winnifride, and Susan to place, house, and therefore lay clear title to him. Old Thorney's epitaph for his son is of an "Untimely lost young man" (5.3.73).[14]

Meanwhile, in *The English Traveller* the competition between Wincott and Old Geraldine for Young Geraldine is also launched in terms of location. Wincott invites Geraldine to "Think this your home, free as your father's house / And to command it, as the Master on't" (p. 10). So frequent is the younger man's resort there that Old Geraldine complains, only half in jest, that his son has been stolen from him. Eventually the father forbids his son to visit Wincott's house, confining him to his own home. A midnight meeting of Wincott and Geraldine thus represents Geraldine's transgression against his father's commands as well as Wincott's infidelity to his wife. In this the title of the play achieves a second significance, for the young gentleman who has been introduced to us as newly returned from a European tour travels throughout the play between the dispositional demands of father and friend. As part of his attempted seduction, Wincott puts in play the

---

14. Granted, Thorney retorts that "He is not lost, / Who bears his peace within him" (5.3.74–90), but Old Carter soon thereafter says to Old Thorney, "we have lost our children, both on'us the wrong way" (5.3.74–75, 146–47).

paradigm of the earlier domestic tragedies: "There's no pleasure that the house can yield, / That can be debarr'd from you" (p. 42). But Geraldine does not construe the invitation as Wendoll did and does not launch a campaign for political control of the household through moral abduction of its mistress. Delavil does take sexual advantage of the proximity that his friendship with Geraldine secures, but his desire does not expand to encompass the house as well. The arrestedness of their ambitions disables Wincott's house of its traditional political meanings and leaves Geraldine untethered by spatial identification and aspiration, compounding his moral ambiguity.

Like *Edward IV*, with its transparent desire to recuperate the monarchy and political obligation, *The English Traveller* makes evident its attempts to manage its economic anxieties. It happily empties its households of women, recastellates residences, and insists that the new commodification of male subjects reconfirms the old orders of privilege and patriarchy. When Mistress Wincott's sexual liaison with Delavil is revealed and results in her convenient death from shame, the way is smoothed for the end of the enforced estrangement of Geraldine and Wincott. The latter will "wear blacks without" as a widower but hold "other thoughts within" in his happy "marriage" with Geraldine. Where Old Geraldine had blocked the liaison with Wincott's wife, he embraces the homosocial bond with Wincott, because by it Geraldine will inherit Wincott's "fair and large estate" and thus increase the Geraldine patrimony. For added emphasis the marriage of men is repeated in the subplot of the play, where a prodigal son abandons another troublesome woman, a prostitute, to "strive to be more dear" to his father instead; again the merchant father's extensive estate is at issue, rather than affect or allegiance. In these ways sons are bound to their fathers by property; women are removed from active agency; and lands and goods perform traditional, conservative cultural functions.[15]

The English Traveller's subplot is borrowed from Plautus's *Mostellaria*, which was known in English as *The Haunted House*. In Heywood's version, the serial self hears its echo in a metamorphic domicile. The riotous Young Lionell is head of household while his merchant father travels. At first the domus is an instrument of his self-fashioning, as he answers his own rhetorical question: "To what may young men best compare themselves?"

> Better to what, than to a house new built?
> The fabric strong, the chambers well contriv'd,

15. A queer reading of this play is equally plausible. My reading is adopted to suit my theme, and I think the generational emphasis (relationships between sons, fathers, and father-figures) does not negate it.

Polished within, without, well beautifi'd;
When all that gaze upon the edifice,
Do not alone commend the workman's craft,
But either make it their fair precedent
By which to build another, or at least,
Wish there to inhabit: Being set to sale,
In comes a slothful tenant, with a family
As lazy and deboshed; Rough tempests rise,
Untile the roof, which by their idleness,
Left unrepaired, the stormy showers beat in,
Rot the main posts and rafters, spoil the rooms,
Deface the ceilings, and in little space,
Bring it to utter ruin, yet the fault,
Not in the architector that first reared it,
But him that should repair it: So it fares
With us young men. . . .
The thrift with which our fathers tiled our roofs,
Submits to every storm and winter's blast.
And yielding place to every riotous sin,
Gives way without, to ruin what's within:
Such is the state I stand in.

(pp. 18–19)

With the state of the fictional household thus linked to the psychic condition of the male protagonist, every turn of this plot then expresses itself through the figuration of the house. From Young Lionell's analogue it becomes the fortress of his clever and presumptuous servant Reignald, a common stews and tavern (in the view of an old and loyal retainer), a storm-tossed ship that must throw off the cargo of its furnishings to remain afloat, a witness to the returned Old Lionell of its recent disorders, an abandoned and haunted house (the site of a fictional murder) to discourage Old Lionell's entry, a structure displaced by its pretended surrogate and next neighbor, sanctuary for the discovered Reignald attempting to escape his master's wrath, and, finally, the residence fancifully restored to its preferred function as the material symbol of the renewed bond of father and son.

The English Traveller is not, properly speaking, a domestic *tragedy*, for Heywood's gynephobic closing fantasy robs it of a formal catastrophe. Through the successive images of an unstable house, however, the subplot emblematizes the oeconomic concerns of the genre. The house serves in *The English Traveller* and in all the domestic tragedies as a symptom of the male subject. It is intimately connected with his political, social, and moral identities and functions. In its early modern economic role the house is also the storehouse of, the mechanism of display for, and the safeguard of his culturally fetishized possessions. As a container for goods it is thus inextricably linked with the semantic twin for goods, the woman. And, to the very extent that goods resist stasis, generate new appetites, and inspire jealousy over their control, to that extent they (like women) unsettle their environment, in yet another way undoing the old chimera of the house-as-castle.

Emblems of the early modern house are many. I have proposed Harington's castle inexpugnable, the Montacute frieze of a skimmington ride, Essex's disordered fortress, the material witness to Thomas Ardern's murder, Frankford's angelic *genius domus*, Michael Sherbrook's totemic door, and Randle Holme's overloaded grid of goods. But the master emblem for the state in which private matters found themselves throughout the post-Reformation period may be Old Lionell's metamorphic house in *The English Traveller*: restless, conflicted, shape-shifting, imperfectly defended and unsusceptible of repose.

BIBLIOGRAPHY OF PUBLISHED SOURCES

Primary Sources

Agrippa, Henricus Cornelius von Nettesheim. *The Commendation of Matrimony* (1526), trans. David Clapham. 1540; STC 201.
———. *De occulta philosophia libri tres.* Antwerp: 1531.
———. *Opera.* 2 vols. ?Strasburg: ?1630.
———. *Three Books of Occult Philosophy*, trans. J. F. 1651; Wing STC A789.
Anglerius, Petrus Martyr. *The Decades of the New World or West India*, trans. Richard Eden. 1555; STC 645.
Anni Regis Henrici Septimi. 1555; STC 9922.
The Apprehension, Arraignment, and Execution of Elizabeth Abbot. 1608; STC 23.
Arden, Thomas. "The Account of Thomas Ardern's Murder from the Wardmote Book of Faversham." In *The Tragedy of Master Arden of Faversham*, ed. M. L. Wine, app. 3, pp. 160–63. The Revels Plays. Manchester: Manchester University Press, 1973.
Arden of Faversham, The Tragedy of Master (1592), ed. M. L. Wine. The Revels Plays. Manchester: Manchester University Press, 1973.
Aristotle. *Aristotle's Politics, or Discourses of Government.* Translated from Greek into French by L. Le Roy; translated from French into English by I. D. 1598; STC 760.
———. *The Ethics of Aristotle*, trans. J. Wylkinson. 1547; STC 754.
———. *The Ethics of Aristotle: The Nicomachean Ethics*, trans. J. A. K. Thomson; rev. Hugh Tredennick. London: Penguin, 1976.
———. *The Politics of Aristotle*, trans. Ernest Barker. Oxford: Clarendon Press, 1946.
[Augustine]. *A Work of the Holy Bishop S. Augustine Concerning Adulterous Marriages.* 1550; STC 955.
Averell, William. *A Marvelous Combat of Contrarities.* 1588; STC 981.

Aylmer, John. *An Harbor for Faithful and True Subjects.* 1559; STC 1005.

Ayrault, Pierre. *A Discourse for Parents' Honor and Authority, Written to Reclaim a Counterfeit Jesuit,* trans. J. Budden. 1614; STC 1012.

Bacon, Francis. *The Essayes or Counsels, Civill and Morall,* ed. Michael Kiernan. Cambridge: Harvard University Press, 1985.

Baker, Richard. *A Chronicle of the Kings of England from the Time of the Roman's Government unto the Reign of our Sovereign Lord King Charles.* 1643; Wing STC B501.

Baldwin, William. *A Treatise of Moral Philosophy, Containing the Sayings of the Wise.* 1547; STC 1253.

Battus, Bartholomaeus. *The Christian Man's Closet,* trans. W. Lowth. 1581; STC 1591.

Bayker, John. Letter to Henry VIII. In *Elizabethan Rogues and Vagabonds,* ed. Frank Aydelotte, app. 3, pp. 145–47. Oxford Historical and Literary Studies, vol. 1. Oxford: Clarendon Press, 1913.

Beard, Thomas. *The Theatre of God's Judgments, or a Collection of Histories.* 1597; STC 1659.

Bernard, Richard. *Joshuah's Godly Resolution in a Conference with Caleb, Touching Household Government.* 2d ed. 1612; STC 1953.

Bilson, Thomas. *The True Difference between Christian Subjection and Unchristian Rebellion.* Oxford: 1585; STC 3071.

The Bloody Book, or the Tragical End of Sir John Fites (alias) Fitz. 1605; STC 10930.

A Bloody New Year's Gift, or a True Declaration of the Murder of Master Robert Heath. 1609; STC 13018.3.

Bodin, Jean. *The Six Bookes of a Commonweale* (1576), trans. Richard Knolles (1606), ed. Kenneth Douglas McRae. Cambridge: Harvard University Press, 1962.

The Book of Common Prayer, 1559, ed. John E. Booty. Washington: Folger Shakespeare Library, 1976.

Bradshaw, William. *A Marriage Feast.* 1620; STC 11680.

Brathwait, Richard. *Some Rules and Orders for the Government of the House of an Earl.* Miscellanea Antiqua Anglicana, vol. 8. London: n.p., 1821.

A Breviat Chronicle Containing all the Kings from Brute to this Day, and Many Notable Acts unto the Year 1552. Canterbury: 1552; STC 9968. Excerpted by Glenn H. Blayney. In "'Arden of Feversham'—An Early Reference." *Notes and Queries* n.s., 2 (August 1955), 336.

The Brideling, Saddling, and Riding of a Rich Churl in Hampshire by one Judith Philips. 1595; STC 19855.

Bullinger, Heinrich. *The Christian State of Matrimony,* trans. Miles Coverdale. Antwerp: 1541 [and London: 1542–75, 6 subsequent editions]; STC 4045.

Bunny, Edmund. *Of Divorce for Adultery, and Marrying Again: That There is No Sufficient Warrant So to Do.* Oxford: 1610; STC 4091.

A Calendar of the White and Black Books of the Cinque Ports, 1432–1955, ed. Felix Hull. Kent Archaeological Society Records, vol. 19, and Joint Publication Series of the Historical Manuscripts Commission, no. 5. London: Her Majesty's Stationery Office, 1966.

Carter, Thomas. *Carter's Christian Commonwealth, or Domestical Duties Deciphered.* 1627; STC 4698.

Cecil, William. "Certain Precepts for the Well Ordering of a Man's Life" (ca. 1584). In *Advice to a Son,* ed. Louis B. Wright, pp. 7–13. Folger Documents of Tudor and Stuart Civilization. Ithaca: Cornell University Press, 1962.

Certain Sermons or Homilies, ed. Mary Ellen Rickey and Thomas B. Stroup. Gainesville: Scholars' Facsimiles and Reprints, 1968.

"Certain Sermons or Homilies" (1547) and "A Homily against Disobedience and Wilful Rebellion" (1570), ed. Ronald B. Bond. Toronto: University of Toronto Press, 1987.

Chamberlain, John. *The Chamberlain Letters: A Selection of the Letters of John Chamberlain Concerning Life in England from 1597 to 1626,* ed. Elizabeth McClure Thomson. London: John Murray, 1965.

Cheke, John. *The Hurt of Sedition How Grievous it is to a Commonwealth.* 1549; STC 5109.

Chester, Robert. *Love's Martyr.* 1601; STC 5119.

Cicero, Marcus Tullius. *Four Several Treatises of M. Tullius Cicero: Containing his Most Learned and Eloquent Discourse of Friendship,* trans. Thomas Newton. 1577; STC 5274.

Cinthio, Giambattista Giraldi. "Cinthio's Narrative," trans. M. R. Ridley. In *Othello,* app. I, pp. 237–46. The Arden Shakespeare. London: Methuen, 1958.

————. Decade Three, Story Seven. *De Gli Hecatommithi,* part 1, sigs. Oo2^r–Pp1^v. Venice: 1565.

————. "From *Gli Hecatommithi*," trans. Geoffrey Bullough. In *Major Tragedies: "Hamlet," "Othello," "King Lear," "Macbeth."* Vol. 7 of *Narrative and Dramatic Sources of Shakespeare.* London: Routledge and Kegan Paul, 1973.

————. *Hecatommithi,* trans. Lawrence Ross. In *Othello,* app. C, pp. 263–71. Indianapolis: Bobbs-Merrill, 1974.

————. *Premier volume des Cent excellentes nouvelles de M. Jean Baptiste Giraldy Cynthien,* trans. Gabriel Chappuys, sigs. Ss3^v–Tt4^v. Paris: 1583.

————. "Prologo." *Altile.* Venice: 1583.

————. "The Story on Which is Founded the *Tragedy of Othello,* from the *Hecatomithi* [sic] of Cinthio," trans. J. Payne Collier. In *Shakespeare's Library,* vol. 2. London: Thomas Rodd, 1850.

Civil and Uncivil Life. A Discourse Where is Disputed What Order of Life Best Beseemeth a Gentleman. 1579; STC 15589.

Coke, Edward. Report on Semayne's Case (1605). In *The Reports of Sir Edward Coke Late Lord Chief-Justice of England* ["The King's Bench Reports"], pp. 453–55. 1658; Wing STC C4944.

————. *The Third Part of the Institutes of the Laws of England: Concerning High Treason, and other Pleas of the Crown, and Criminal Causes* (1628). 1644; Wing STC C4960.

"The Complaint and Lamentation of Mistress Arden of Feversham in Kent" (1633). Excerpted in *The Tragedy of Master Arden of Faversham,* ed. M. L. Wine, app. 4, pp. 164–70. The Revels Plays. Manchester: Manchester University Press, 1973.

Cooke, Richard. *A White Sheet, or A Warning for Whoremongers.* 1629; STC 5676.

The Court of Good Counsel, Wherein is Set Down How a Man Should Choose a Good Wife and a Woman a Good Husband. 1607; STC 5876.

Curio, Caelius Augustinus. *A Notable History of the Saracens*, trans. T. Newton. 1575; STC 6129.

Dalton, Michael. *The Country Justice, Containing the Practice of the Justices of the Peace.* 1618; STC 6205.

Daunce, Edward. *A Brief Discourse of the Spanish State.* 1590; STC 6291.

Dekker, Thomas. *The Shoemaker's Holiday* (1600), ed. R. L. Smallwood and Stanley Wells. The Revels Plays. Manchester: Manchester University Press, 1979.

Dekker, Thomas, John Ford, and William Rowley. *The Witch of Edmonton* (1621), ed. Fredson Bowers, pp. 481–568. In vol. 3 of *The Dramatic Works of Thomas Dekker.* Cambridge: Cambridge University Press, 1958.

————. *The Witch of Edmonton: A Critical Edition*, ed. Etta Soiref Onat. New York: Garland, 1980.

Dering, Edward. *A Brief and Necessary Instruction, Very Needful to Be Known of all Householders.* 1572; STC 6679.

Dillingham, Francis. *A Golden Key [containing] Christian Oeconomy, or Household Government.* 1609; STC 6886.

Dod, John, and Robert Cleaver. *A Godly Form of Household Government.* 1598; STC 5382.

Dodsworth, Roger. *Yorkshire Church Notes, 1619–31*, ed. J. W. Clay. *Yorkshire Archaeological Society Record Series* 34 (1904).

"Domesday Survey," ed. F. W. Ragg. In *The Victoria History of the Counties of England: Kent*, ed. William Page, vol. 3, pp. 177–252. London: St. Catherine Press, 1932.

Donne, John. *Biathanatos: A Declaration of that Paradox, or Thesis, that Self-Homicide is Not so Naturally Sin, That it may Never Be Otherwise* (?1608). 1644; Wing STC D1858.

————. *The Elegies and The Songs and Sonnets*, ed. Helen Gardner. Oxford: Clarendon Press, 1965.

Dorke, Walter. *A Type or Figure of Friendship.* 1589; STC 7060.5.

Dove, John. *Of Divorcement.* 1601; STC 7083.

Elizabeth I. *The Public Speaking of Queen Elizabeth: Selections from her Official Addresses*, ed. George P. Rice, Jr. New York: Columbia University Press, 1951.

Elyot, Thomas. "The Manner to Choose and Cherish a Friend." In *How One May Take Profit of his Enemies, translated out of Plutarch*, sigs. B5ᵛ–B8ʳ. ?1531; STC 20052.

Erasmus, Desiderius. *The Censure and Judgment of . . . Erasmus Whether Divorcement Standeth with the Law of God.* ?1550; STC 10450.

Feltham, Owen. *Resolves Divine, Moral, Political.* 1623; STC 10755.

Fenner, Dudley. *The Arts of Logic and Rhetoric . . . with Examples from the Practice of the Same for Method in the Government of the Family.* 1584; STC 10766.

Filmer, Robert. *Patriarcha, or The Natural Power of Kings.* 1680; Wing STC F922.

Floyd, Thomas. *The Picture of a Perfect Commonwealth.* 1600; STC 11119.

Ford, John. *'Tis Pity She's a Whore* (1633), ed. Brian Morris. The New Mermaids. London: Ernest Benn, 1968.

Gainsford, Thomas. *The Rich Cabinet Furnished with Variety of Excellent Descriptions.* 1616; STC 11522.

Gardiner, Stephen. *De vera obedientia* (1535). In *Obedience in Church and State: Three Political Tracts by Stephen Gardiner,* ed. and trans. Pierre Janelle, pp. 67–171. Cambridge: Cambridge University Press, 1930.

Gataker, Thomas. *Marriage Duties Briefly Couched Together.* 1620; STC 11667.

———. *Two Marriage Sermons: The Former, A Good Wife, God's Gift.* 1620; STC 11680.

Gawdy, Philip. *Letters of Philip Gawdy . . . 1579–1616,* ed. Isaac Herbert Jeayes. London: J. B. Nichols, 1906.

Gerbier, Balthazar. *Counsel and Advice to all Builders.* 1663; Wing STC G552.

Gibbon, Charles. *The Praise of a Good Name.* 1594; STC 11819.

Giorgio, Francesco. *De harmonia mundi totius cantica tria.* Venice: 1525.

Golding, Arthur. *A Brief Discourse of the Late Murder of Master G. Sanders.* 1573; STC 11985. Reprinted in *A Warning for Fair Women: A Critical Edition,* ed. Charles Dale Cannon, app. D, pp. 216–30. The Hague: Mouton, 1975.

Goodcole, Henry. *The Adultress's Funeral Day.* 1635; STC 12009.

———. *A True Declaration of the Happy Conversion of Francis Robinson.* 1618; STC 12013.

———. *The Wonderful Discovery of Elizabeth Sawyer, a Witch* (1621). Reprinted in *The Witch of Edmonton,* ed. Etta Soiref Onat, app. 1, pp. 381–400. New York: Garland, 1980.

Gouge, William. *Of Domestical Duties.* 1622; STC 12119.

Gray, Robert. *An Alarum to England.* 1609; STC 12203.

Greenham, Richard. *The Works of Richard Greenham.* 1599; STC 12312.

Griffith, Matthew. *Bethel, or a Form for Families.* 1633; STC 12368.

Harington, John. "The Praise of Private Life." In *The Letters and Epigrams of Sir John Harington,* ed. Norman Egbert McClure, pp. 323–78. Philadelphia: University of Pennsylvania Press, 1930.

Harrison, William. *The Description of England* (2d ed., 1587), ed. Georges Edelen. Folger Documents of Tudor and Stuart Civilization. Ithaca: Cornell University Press for the Folger Shakespeare Library, 1968.

Heale, William. *An Apology for Women, or an Opposition to Mr. Dr. G. his Assertion that it was Lawful for Husbands to Beat their Wives.* Oxford: 1609; STC 13014.

Hegendorff, Christopher. *Domestical or Household Sermons,* trans. H. Reiginalde. Ipswich: 1548; STC 13021.

Heron, Haly. *A New Discourse of Moral Philosophy Entitled, The Keys of Counsel.* 1579; STC 13228.

Heywood, Thomas. *An Apology for Actors.* 1612; STC 13309.

———. *The Captives, or The Lost Recovered* (1624), ed. Alexander Corbin Judson. New Haven: Yale University Press, 1921.

———. *A Curtain Lecture.* 1637; STC 13312.

———. *The English Traveller* (1625). In *The Dramatic Works of Thomas Heywood,* ed. R. H. Shepherd, vol. 4, pp. 1–95. London: John Pearson, 1874.

———. *The First and Second Parts of King Edward IV* (1599). In *The Dramatic Works of Thomas Heywood,* ed. R. H. Shepherd, vol. 1, pp. 1–187. London: John Pearson, 1874.

————. *Gunaikeion, or Nine Books of Various History Concerning Women, Inscribed by Nine Muses.* 1624; STC 13326.
————. *Thomas Heywood's "The Rape of Lucrece"* (1608), ed. Allan Holaday. Urbana: University of Illinois Press, 1950.
————. *Troia Britannica, or Great Britain's Troy.* 1609; STC 13366.
————. *A True Discourse of the Two Infamous Upstart Prophets, R. Farnham and J. Bull.* 1636; STC 13369.
————. *A Woman Killed with Kindness* (1603), ed. R. W. Van Fossen. The Revels Plays. London: Methuen, 1961.
Holinshed, Raphael. *The Chronicles of England, Scotland, and Ireland.* 2 volumes. 1577; STC 13568.
————. "The Source of *Arden of Faversham* in Holinshed's *Chronicles.*" In *Arden of Faversham,* ed. M. L. Wine, app. 2, pp. 148–59. The Revels Plays. Manchester: Manchester University Press, 1973.
Holme, Randle. *An Academy of Armory, or A Storehouse of Armory and Blazon* (1649), vol. 1. Chester: 1688; Wing STC H2513.
————. *An Academy of Armory, or A Storehouse of Armory and Blazon,* vol. 2, ed. I. H. Jeayes. London: Roxburghe Club, 1905. See also BM Harl. MSS 2026–35.
Holy Bible (1560). Geneva: 1576; STC 2093.
Hooker, Richard. *Of the Laws of Ecclesiastical Polity . . . Books I to IV* (1593), ed. Georges Edelen. Folger Library Edition of the Works of Richard Hooker, vol. 1. Cambridge, Mass.: Belknap Press of Harvard University Press, 1977.
Household and Farm Inventories in Oxfordshire, 1550–1590, ed. M. A. Havinden. Historical Manuscripts Commission, Joint Publication no. 10. London: Her Majesty's Stationery Office, 1965.
Howson, John. *Uxore dimissa propter fornicationem aliam non licet superinducere.* Oxford: 1602; STC 13886.
Index to Testamentary Records in the Commissary Court of London, ed. Marc Fitch. Historical Manuscripts Commission Joint Publication no. 13, vol. 2 (1489–1570). London: Her Majesty's Stationery Office, 1974.
Inedited Tracts, Illustrating the Manners, Opinions, and Occupations of Englishmen during the 16th and 17th Centuries, comp. W[illiam] C[arew] H[azlitt]. N.p.: Roxburghe Library, 1868.
The Institution of a Gentleman. 1555; STC 14104.
"Jacobean Household Inventories," ed. F. G. Emmison. *Publications of the Bedfordshire Historical Record Society* 20 (1938), 1–143.
James VI and I. *Daemonologie* (1597), ed. G. B. Harrison. London: The Bodley Head, 1924.
————. *The Trew Law of Free Monarchies* (1598), ed. Charles Howard McIlwain, pp. 53–70. In *The Political Works of James I* (1616). Cambridge: Harvard University Press, 1918.
Jones, William. *A Brief Exhortation to all Men to Set their Houses in Order.* 1631; STC 14741.
Joye, George. *A Contrary (to a Certain Man's) Consultation, That Adulterers ought to be Punished with Death.* ?1549; STC 14822.
Julius, Philip. "Diary of the Journey of the Most Illustrious Philip Julius, Duke

of Stettin-Pomerania . . . through . . . England, . . . 1602," ed. Gottfried von Bülow. *Transactions of the Royal Historical Society* n.s. [2d ser.], 6 (1892), 1–67.

"Kent Contributors to a Loan to the King, AD 1542," ed. James Greenstreet. *Archaeologia Cantiana* 11 (1877), 398–404.

Kent Obit and Lamp Rents, ed. Arthur Hussey. Kent Archaeological Society Records, vol. 14. Ashford: Headley Brothers for the Records Branch, 1936.

Lambard, William. *Eirenarcha, or of the Office of the Justices of Peace.* 1581; STC 15163.

Lilly, William. *Christian Astrology.* 1647; Wing STC L2215.

List of the Lands of Dissolved Religious Houses. Lists and Indexes. Supplementary Series, no. 3, vol. 2: *Kent—Middlesex.* 1949; rpt. New York: Kraus Reprint, 1964.

Lodge, Thomas. *Wit's Misery, and the World's Madness* (1596). In *The Complete Works of Thomas Lodge*, vol. 4, pp. 1–111. Glasgow: Hunterian Club, 1883.

M.B. *The Trial of True Friendship.* 1596; STC 1053.

Machyn, Henry. *The Diary of Henry Machyn . . . From A.D. 1550 to A.D. 1563*, ed. John Gough Nichols. Camden Society, vol. 42. London: Camden Society, 1848.

Meres, Francis. *Palladis Tamia.* 1598; STC 17834.

Meriton, George. *The Christian Man's Assuring House.* 1614; STC 17837.

Middleton, Thomas, and William Rowley. *A Fair Quarrel* (1617), ed. R. V. Holdsworth. The New Mermaids. London: Ernest Benn, 1974.

A Most Horrible and Detestable Murder Committed at Mayfield in Sussex. 1595; STC 17748.

Mulcaster, Richard. *Positions . . . Necessary for the Training up of Children.* 1581; STC 18253.

Munday, Anthony. *An Advertisement and Defence for Truth against her Backbiters.* 1581; STC 153.7.

———. *A View of Sundry Examples. Reporting Many Strange Murders . . . And all Memorable Murders since the Murder of Master Sanders by George Browne.* 1580; STC 18281.

Newnham, John. *Newnham's Nightcrow . . . Wherein is Remembered that Kindly Regard which Fathers Ought to Have towards their Sons.* 1590; STC 18498.

Niccholes, Alexander. *A Discourse of Marriage and Wiving.* 1615; STC 18514.

Nichols, Josias. *An Order of Household Instruction.* 1596; STC 18540.

North, Dudley. *Some Notes Concerning the Life of Edward Lord North, Baron of Kirtling.* 1682; Wing STC N1286A.

Nowell, Alexander. *A Catechism or First Instruction of Christian Religion*, trans. Thomas Norton. 1570; STC 18708.

Peacham, Henry. *The Complete Gentleman* (1622), ed. Virgil B. Heltzel. Folger Documents of Tudor and Stuart Civilization. Ithaca: Cornell University Press for the Folger Shakespeare Library, 1962.

Percy, Henry. *Advice to his son* (1609), ed. G. B. Harrison. London: Ernest Benn, 1930.

Perkins, William. *Christian Oeconomy* (1609), trans. Thomas Pickering. In *The Work of William Perkins*, ed. Ian Breward, pp. 411–39. Courtenay Library of Reformation Classics, no. 3. Appleton: Sutton Courtenay Press, 1970.

Ponet, John. *A Short Treatise of Politic Power.* Strasburg: 1556; STC 20178.

Ptolemy. *Tetrabiblos*, ed. and trans. F. E. Robbins. Loeb Classical Library. London: William Heinemann, 1948.

Rainolds, John. *A Defence of the Judgment of the Reformed Churches*. Dort: 1609; STC 20607.

A Remonstrance, or Plain Detection of Faults in a Book Entitled, A Demonstration of Discipline. 1590; STC 20881.

Rich, Barnaby. *Faults, Faults, and Nothing Else but Faults*. 1606; STC 20983.

The Second Maiden's Tragedy (1611), ed. Anne Lancashire. The Revels Plays. Manchester: Manchester University Press, 1978.

Segar, William. *Honor Military and Civil*. 1602; STC 22164.

Seneca, Lucius Annaeus. *De beneficiis*, ed. and trans. John W. Basore. Vol. 3 of *Moral Essays*. Loeb Classical Library. London: William Heinemann, 1935.

————. *The Work of the Excellent Philosopher Lucius Annaeus Seneca Concerning Benefitting*, trans. A. Golding. 1578; STC 22215.

————. *The Works of Lucius Annaeus Seneca, both Moral and Natural*, trans. Thomas Lodge (1614). In *Seneca on Benefits Translated by Thomas Lodge*, ed. W. H. D. Rouse. London: J. M. Dent, 1899.

Shakespeare, William. *Othello* (1604), ed. Horace Howard Furness. The New Variorum Shakespeare. Philadelphia: J. B. Lippincott, 1886.

————. *Othello*, ed. M. R. Ridley. The Arden Shakespeare. London: Methuen, 1958.

————. *The Riverside Shakespeare*, ed. G. Blakemore Evans, et al. Boston: Houghton Mifflin, 1974.

————. *The Tragedy of Othello, the Moor of Venice*, ed. Lawrence Ross. Indianapolis: Bobbs-Merrill, 1974.

Sherbrook, Michael. "The Fall of Religious Houses." In *Tudor Treatises*, ed. A. G. Dickens, pp. 89–142. *Yorkshire Archaeological Society Record Series* 125 (1959).

Sidney, Philip. *An Apology for Poetry* (1595), ed. Geoffrey Shepherd. New York: Barnes and Noble, 1973.

Smith, Henry. *A Preparative to Marriage*. 1591; STC 22685.

Smith, Thomas. *De republica anglorum* (1583), ed. Mary Dewar. Cambridge: Cambridge University Press, 1982.

Snawsel, Robert. *A Looking Glass for Married Folks*. 1610; STC 22886.

Southouse, Thomas. *Monasticon favershamiense in agro cantiano*. 1671; Wing STC S4772.

Stanford, William. *Les Pleas del Coron*. 1557; STC 23219.

Stow, John. *The Annals of England*. 1592; STC 23334.

————. *The Chronicles of England*. 1580; STC 23333.

————. *A Summary of English Chronicles*. 1565; STC 23319.

————. *The Summary of English Chronicles*. 1566; STC 23325.4.

————. *Two London Chronicles from the Collections of John Stow*, ed. Charles Lethbridge Kingsford. *Camden Miscellany* 12 (1910), 1–57.

T. E. *The Law's Resolutions of Women's Rights*. 1632; STC 7437.

Tasso, Torquato. *The Householder's Philosophy*, trans. T[homas] K[yd]. 1588; STC 23702.5.

Taylor, John. *Taylor's Travels and Circular Perambulation through, and by more than Thirty Times Twelve Signs of the Zodiac, of the famous Cities of London and Westminster. . . . with an Alphabetical Description of all the Tavern Signs*. 1636; STC 23805.

————. *The Unnatural Father, or the Cruel Murder Committed by one John Rowse*. 1621; STC 23808a. Included in *All the Works of John Taylor the Water Poet*. 1630; STC 23725.

Taylor, Thomas. *The Second Part of the Theatre of God's Judgments.* 1642; Wing STC T570.
Thomas, William. "A Second Discourse . . . for the King's Use: Whether it be Better for a Commonwealth that the Power be in the Nobility or in the Commonalty." In *Historical Memorials, Chiefly Ecclesiastical,* vol. 2, pt. 2 of *Ecclesiastical Memorials, Relating Chiefly to Religion,* ed. John Strype. Oxford: Clarendon Press, 1822.
Tilney, Edmund. *A Brief and Pleasant Discourse of Duties in Marriage, Called the Flower of Friendship.* 1568; STC 24076.
Topsell, Edward. *The History of Four-Footed Beasts.* 1607; STC 24123.
A True Relation of a Barbarous Murder, Committed by Enoch ap Evan, who Cut off his own Natural Mother's Head and his Brother's. 1633; STC 10582.
A True Relation of a Most Desperate Murder, Committed upon Sir John Tindall. 1617; STC 24435.
Tuvill, Daniel. *Essays Politic and Moral and Essays Moral and Theological* (1608–1609), ed. John L. Lievsay. Folger Documents of Tudor and Stuart Civilization 20. Charlottesville: University Press of Virginia for the Folger Shakespeare Library, 1971.
Two Most Unnatural and Bloody Murders. 1605; STC 18288. Excerpted in *A Yorkshire Tragedy,* ed. A. C. Cawley and Barry Gaines, app. A, pp. 94–110. The Revels Plays. Manchester: Manchester University Press, 1986.
Vaughan, William. *The Golden-Grove . . . Necessary for all Such, as Would Know How to Govern themselves, their Houses, or their Country.* 1600; STC 24610.
Vives, Joannes Ludovicus. *Instruction of a Christian Woman,* trans. R. Hyrd. 1529; STC 24856.5.
———. *The Office and Duty of an Husband,* trans. Thomas Paynell. ?1555; STC 24855.
A Warning for Fair Women, ed. Charles Dale Cannon. The Hague: Mouton, 1975.
Watts, Thomas. *The Entry to Christianity, or an Admonition to Householders, for Instruction of their Families.* 1589; STC 25128.
Webbe, George. *The Arraignment of an Unruly Tongue.* 1619; STC 25156.
Weever, John. *Ancient Funeral Monuments within the United Monarchy of Great Britain, Ireland, and the Islands Adjacent.* 1631; STC 25223.
Wentworth, William. "Advice to his son" (1604). In *Wentworth Papers, 1597–1628,* ed. J. P. Cooper. Royal Historical Society, Camden Fourth Series, 12 (1973), pp. 9–24.
Westerman, William. *Two Sermons of Assize: The One Entitled, A Prohibition of Revenge; The Other, A Sword of Maintenance.* 1600; STC 25282.
Whately, William. *A Bride-Bush, or a Wedding Sermon.* 1617; STC 25296.
———. *A Care-Cloth.* 1624; STC 25299.
Whetstone, George. *An Heptameron of Civil Discourses.* 1582; STC 25337.
Whitford, Richard. *A Work for Householders* (1530). 1533; STC 25423.
Willoughby, Cassandra. *The Account of the Willughby's [sic] of Wollaton taken out of the Pedigree, old Letters, and old Books of Accounts in my Brother Sir Thomas Willoughby's study, Dec. A.D. 1702.* Excerpted by Alice T. Friedman in *House and Household in Elizabethan England: Wollaton Hall and the Willoughby Family.* Chicago: University of Chicago Press, 1989.
Wilson, Thomas. *The State of England Anno Dom. 1600,* ed. F. J. Fisher, pp. 1–47. *Camden Miscellany* 16 (1936).
"The Woeful Lamentation of Mistress Anne Sanders, which she wrote with her own

hand, being prisoner in Newgate, justly condemned to death." In *Old English Ballads 1553–1625, Chiefly from Manuscript*, ed. Hyder E. Rollins, pp. 340–48. Cambridge: Cambridge University Press, 1920.

A World of Wonders, A Mass of Murders, A Covy of Cosenages. 1595; STC 14068.5.

Wright, Leonard. *Display of Duty.* 1589; STC 26025.

Wright, Thomas. *The Passions of the Mind in General* (1601), ed. Thomas O. Sloan. Urbana: University of Illinois Press, 1971.

Yarington, Robert. *Two Lamentable Tragedies* (1601). Students' Facsimile Edition 153. Amersham: John S. Farmer, 1913.

A Yorkshire Tragedy (1605), ed. A. C. Cawley and Barry Gaines. The Revels Plays. Manchester: Manchester University Press, 1986.

Secondary Sources

Adams, Henry Hitch. *English Domestic or, Homiletic Tragedy 1575 to 1642*. New York: Columbia University Press, 1943.

Adams, Simon. "Eliza Enthroned? The Court and Its Politics." In *The Reign of Elizabeth I*, ed. Christopher Haigh, pp. 55–77. Athens: University of Georgia Press, 1987.

Adamson, W. D. "Unpinned or Undone? Desdemona's Critics and the Problem of Sexual Innocence." *Shakespeare Studies* 13 (1980), 169–86.

Agnew, Jean-Christophe. *Worlds Apart: The Market and the Theater in Anglo-American Thought, 1550–1750*. Cambridge: Cambridge University Press, 1986.

Alexander, Bonnie L. "Cracks in the Pedestal: A Reading of *A Woman Killed with Kindness*." *Massachusetts Studies in English* 7, no. 1 (1978), 1–11.

Amussen, Susan D. "Gender, Family, and the Social Order, 1560–1725." In *Order and Disorder in Early Modern England*, ed. Anthony Fletcher and John Stevenson, pp. 196–217. Cambridge: Cambridge University Press, 1985.

———. *An Ordered Society: Gender and Class in Early Modern England*. Oxford: Basil Blackwell, 1988.

Ariès, Philippe. Introduction to *Passions of the Renaissance*, ed. Roger Chartier, trans. Arthur Goldhammer. Vol. 3 of *A History of Private Life*, ed. Ariès et al. 1986; Cambridge: Belknap Press of Harvard University Press, 1989.

Axton, Marie. *The Queen's Two Bodies: Drama and the Elizabethan Succession*. London: Royal Historical Society, 1977.

Bailey, F. G. *Gifts and Poisons: The Politics of Reputation*. Oxford: Basil Blackwell, 1971.

———. *Stratagems and Spoils: A Social Anthropology of Politics*. Oxford: Basil Blackwell, 1969.

Barley, Maurice W. *The English Farmhouse and Cottage*. London: Routledge and Kegan Paul, 1961.

———. *Houses and History*. London: Faber and Faber, 1986.

Barthes, Roland. *Mythologies*, trans. Annette Lavers. New York: Hill and Wang, 1972.

Batho, Gordon. "Landlords in England: Noblemen, Gentlemen, and Yeomen." In *The Agrarian History of England and Wales*, ed. H. P. R. Finberg, vol. 4, *1500–1640*, ed. Joan Thirsk, pp. 276–306. Cambridge: Cambridge University Press, 1967.

Beier, A. L. *Masterless Men: The Vagrancy Problem in England, 1560–1640.* London: Methuen, 1985.

Beith-Halahmi, Esther Yael. *Angell Fayre or Strumpet Lewd: Jane Shore as an Example of Erring Beauty in Sixteenth-Century Literature.* Salzburg Studies in English Literature, dir. Erwin A. Stürzl. Elizabethan and Renaissance Studies, ed. James Hogg. Salzburg: Institut für Englische Sprache und Literatur, Universität Salzburg, 1974.

Bellamy, John. *The Tudor Law of Treason.* London: Routledge and Kegan Paul, 1979.

Belsey, Catherine. "Alice Arden's Crime." *Renaissance Drama* n.s., 13 (1982), 83–102.

———. *The Subject of Tragedy: Identity and Difference in Renaissance Drama.* London: Methuen, 1985.

Berry, Lloyd E. "A Note on Heywood's *A Woman Killed with Kindness.*" *Modern Language Review* 58 (January 1963), 64–65.

Bescou, Yves. "Thomas Heywood et le problème de l'adultère dans *Une femme tuée par la bonté.*" *Revue Anglo Américaine* 9 (1931).

Bethell, S. L. "Shakespeare's Imagery: The Diabolic Images in *Othello.*" *Shakespeare Survey* 5 (1952), 62–80.

Bevington, David. *Tudor Drama and Politics: A Critical Approach to Topical Meaning.* Cambridge: Harvard University Press, 1968.

Blayney, Glenn H. "Massinger's Reference to the Calverley Story." *Notes and Queries* n.s., 1 (January 1954), 17–18.

Bluestone, Max. *From Story to Stage: The Dramatic Adaptation of Prose Fiction in the Period of Shakespeare and His Contemporaries.* The Hague: Mouton, 1974.

———. "The Imagery of Tragic Melodrama in *Arden of Feversham.*" *Drama Survey* 5 (Summer 1966), 171–81.

Boase, T. S. R. "Illustrations of Shakespeare's Plays in the Seventeenth and Eighteenth Centuries." *Journal of the Warburg and Courtauld Institutes* 10 (1947), 83–108.

Boose, Lynda E. "Othello's Handkerchief: 'The Recognizance and Pledge of Love.'" *English Literary Renaissance* 5 (Autumn 1975), 360–74.

Bowers, Fredson. *Elizabethan Revenge Tragedy, 1587–1642.* Princeton: Princeton University Press, 1940.

Bowers, Rick. "*A Woman Killed with Kindness*: Plausibility on a Smaller Scale." *SEL* 24 (Spring 1984), 293–306.

Bradbrook, M. C. *Themes and Conventions of Elizabethan Tragedy.* Cambridge: Cambridge University Press, 1969.

———. "Thomas Heywood, Shakespeare's Shadow." In *Aspects of Dramatic Form in the English and Irish Renaissance*, pp. 112–28. Vol. 3 of *The Collected Papers of Muriel Bradbrook.* Sussex: Harvester Press, 1983.

Braddock, Robert C. "The Rewards of Office-holding in Tudor England." *JBS* 14 (May 1975), 29–47.

Bradley, A. C. *Shakespearean Tragedy: Lectures on "Hamlet," "Othello," "King Lear," "Macbeth."* 1904; rpt. London: Macmillan, 1967.

Bristol, Michael D. *Carnival and Theater: Plebeian Culture and the Structure of Authority in Renaissance England.* New York: Methuen, 1985.

Brodwin, Leonora Leet. "The Domestic Tragedy of Frank Thorney in *The Witch of Edmonton.*" *SEL* 7 (Spring 1967), 311–28.

———. *Elizabethan Love Tragedy, 1587–1625.* New York: New York University Press, 1971.

Bromley, Laura G. "Domestic Conduct in *A Woman Killed with Kindness*." *SEL* 26 (1986), 259–76.

Brooks, E. St. John. "A Pamphlet by Arthur Golding: The Murder of George Saunders." *Notes and Queries* 174 (12 March 1938), 182–84.

Brown, Arthur. "Citizen Comedy and Domestic Drama." In *Jacobean Theater*, ed. John Russell Brown and Bernard Harris, pp. 62–83. London: Edward Arnold, 1960.

———. "Thomas Heywood's Dramatic Art." In *Essays on Shakespeare and Elizabethan Drama in Honor of Hardin Craig*, ed. Richard Hosley, pp. 327–39. Columbia: University of Missouri Press, 1962.

Bryan, Margaret B. "Food Symbolism in *A Woman Killed with Kindness*." *Renaissance Papers* (1974), 9–17.

Bullen, A. H. Introduction to *Arden of Feversham, A Tragedy*. London: J. W. Jarvis, 1887.

Bullough, Geoffrey. Introduction to *Othello, the Moor of Venice*. In *Major Tragedies: "Hamlet," "Othello," "King Lear," "Macbeth."* Vol. 7 of *Narrative and Dramatic Sources of Shakespeare*. London: Routledge and Kegan Paul, 1973.

Burke, Kenneth. "*Othello*: An Essay to Illustrate a Method." *Hudson Review* 4 (Summer 1951), 165–203.

Burnett, David. *Longleat: The Story of an English Country House*. London: Collins, 1978.

Bushby, Lady Frances. *Three Men of the Tudor Time*. London: David Nutt, 1911.

Camden, Carroll. *The Elizabethan Woman*. Houston: Elsevier Press, 1952.

Cannon, Charles Dale. Introduction to *A Warning for Fair Women*. The Hague: Mouton, 1975.

Canuteson, John. "The Theme of Forgiveness in the Plot and Subplot of *A Woman Killed with Kindness*." *Renaissance Drama* n.s., 2 (1969), 123–41.

Capp, Bernard. *English Almanacs, 1500–1800: Astrology and the Popular Press*. Ithaca: Cornell University Press, 1979.

Cary, Cecile Williamson. "'Go Breake This Lute': Music in Heywood's *A Woman Killed with Kindness*." *Huntington Library Quarterly* 37 (February 1974), 111–22.

Cassirer, Ernst. *Mythical Thought*. Vol. 2 of *The Philosophy of Symbolic Forms*, trans. Ralph Manheim. New Haven: Yale University Press, 1955.

Cavell, Stanley. "Othello and the Stake of the Other." In *Disowning Knowledge in Six Plays of Shakespeare*, pp. 125–42. Cambridge: Cambridge University Press, 1987.

Cawley, A. C. *English Domestic Drama: A Yorkshire Tragedy*. An Inaugural Lecture. [Cambridge]: Leeds University Press, 1966.

———. "*A Yorkshire Tragedy* and *Two Most Vnnaturall and Bloodie Murthers*." In *The Morality of Art: Essays Presented to G. Wilson Knight by his Colleagues and Friends*, ed. D. W. Jefferson, pp. 102–18. London: Routledge and Kegan Paul, 1969.

Cawley, A. C., and Barry Gaines. Preface and Introduction to *A Yorkshire Tragedy*. The Revels Plays. Manchester: Manchester University Press, 1986.

Chambers, E. K. *The Elizabethan Stage*. 4 vols. Oxford: Clarendon Press, 1923.

Chapman, Raymond. "*Arden of Faversham*: Its Interest Today." *English* 11 (Spring 1956), 15–17.

Clark, Andrew. "An Annotated List of Lost Domestic Plays, 1578–1624." *Research Opportunities in Renaissance Drama* 18 (1975), 29–44.

_____. "An Annotated List of Sources and Related Material for Elizabethan Domestic Tragedy, 1591–1625." *Research Opportunities in Renaissance Drama* 17 (1974), 25–33.

_____. *Domestic Drama: A Survey of the Origins, Antecedents, and Nature of the Domestic Play in England, 1500–1640.* 2 vols. Salzburg Studies in English Literature, dir. Erwin A. Stürzl. Jacobean Drama Studies, ed. James Hogg. Salzburg: Institut für Englische Sprache und Literatur, Universität Salzburg, 1975.

Clark, Arthur Melville. *Thomas Heywood: Playwright and Miscellanist.* Oxford: Basil Blackwell, 1931.

Clark, Peter. *English Provincial Society from the Reformation to the Revolution: Religion, Politics, and Society in Kent, 1500–1640.* Hassocks: Harvest Press, 1977.

_____. Introduction to *The European Crisis of the 1590s.* London: George Allen and Unwin, 1985.

_____. "The Migrant in Kentish Towns, 1580–1640." In *Crisis and Order in English Towns, 1500–1700: Essays in Urban History,* pp. 117–63. London: Routledge and Kegan Paul, 1972.

_____. "Reformation and Radicalism in Kentish Towns c. 1500–1553." In *Stadtbürgertum und Adel in der Reformation,* ed. Wolfgang J. Mommsen et al., pp. 107–27. Publications of the German Historical Institute, London, vol. 5. Stuttgart: Ernest Klett, 1979.

Clark, Peter, and Paul Slack. *English Towns in Transition, 1500–1700.* Oxford: Oxford University Press, 1976.

_____. Introduction to *Crisis and Order in English Towns, 1500–1700: Essays in Urban History.* London: Routledge and Kegan Paul, 1972.

Colie, Rosalie L. *The Resources of Kind: Genre-Theory in the Renaissance,* ed. Barbara K. Lewalski. Berkeley: University of California Press, 1973.

Collier, John Payne. *The History of English Dramatic Poetry to the Time of Shakespeare.* London: J. Murray, 1831.

Comensoli, Viviana. "Witchcraft and Domestic Tragedy in *The Witch of Edmonton.*" In *The Politics of Gender in Early Modern Europe,* ed. Jean R. Brink, Allison P. Coudert, and Maryanne C. Horowitz, pp. 43–59. Sixteenth-Century Essays and Studies, vol. 12. Kirksville, Mo.: Sixteenth-Century Journal Publishers, 1989.

Cook, Ann Jennalie. "The Design of Desdemona: Doubt Raised and Resolved." *Shakespeare Studies* 13 (1980), 187–96.

_____. *The Privileged Playgoers of Shakespeare's London, 1576–1642.* Princeton: Princeton University Press, 1981.

Cook, David. "*A Woman Killed with Kindness*: An Unshakespearian Tragedy." *English Studies* 45 (October 1964), 353–72.

Copley, Frank W. "*Arden of Feversham,* A Play Published in 1592 A.D. and Based on the Pressing Iron Murder Case." Paper delivered at the Literary Clinic of Buffalo, N.Y. on 12 November 1951. Buffalo: n.p., 1951.

Coppinger, Abel H. "Alice Arden, Murderess." In *Twelve Bad Women,* ed. Arthur Vincent, pp. 32–46. London: T. Fisher Unwin, 1897.

Corbin, Peter and Douglas Sedge. Introduction to *Three Jacobean Witchcraft Plays.* The Revels Plays Companion Library. Manchester: Manchester University Press, 1986.

Coursen, Herbert R., Jr. "The Subplot of *A Woman Killed with Kindness.*" *English Language Notes* 2 (March 1965), 180–85.

Cressy, David. "Describing the Social Order of Elizabethan and Stuart England." *Literature and History*, no. 3 (March 1976), 29–44.
_____. *Literacy and the Social Order: Reading and Writing in Tudor and Stuart England.* Cambridge: Cambridge University Press, 1980.
Cromwell, Otelia. *Thomas Heywood: A Study in the Elizabethan Drama of Everyday Life.* New Haven: Yale University Press, 1928.
Cunningham, J. V. *Woe or Wonder: The Emotional Effect of Shakespearean Tragedy.* 1951; rpt. Denver: Alan Swallow, 1964.
Curry, Patrick. "Astrology in Early Modern England: The Making of a Vulgar Knowledge." In *Science, Culture, and Popular Belief in Renaissance Europe*, ed. Stephen Pumfrey, Paolo L. Rossi, and Maurice Slawinski, pp. 274–91. Manchester: Manchester University Press, 1991.
Cushman, Robert. "Kings and Drag Queens." Review of RSC production of *Arden of Feversham. The Observer*, 21 August 1983, p. 25.
Cust, Lionel. "Arden of Feversham." *Archaeologia Cantiana* 34 (1920), 101–38.
Dane, Herbert. "The Story of a Thousand Years: A Chronology of Faversham's History from the Earliest Times to 1968." *Faversham Papers*, no. 5 (1968).
Davidson, Diane. *Feversham.* New York: Crown, 1969.
Davies, Kathleen M. "Continuity and Change in Literary Advice on Marriage." In *Marriage and Society: Studies in the Social History of Marriage*, ed. R. B. Outhwaite, pp. 58–80. London: Europa, 1981.
_____. "The Sacred Condition of Equality—How Original Were Puritan Doctrines of Marriage?" *Social History* 5 (May 1977), 563–80.
Davis, Natalie Zemon. *Fiction in the Archives: Pardon Tales and Their Tellers in Sixteenth-Century France.* Stanford: Stanford University Press, 1987.
_____. "The Reasons of Misrule." In *Society and Culture in Early Modern France*, pp. 97–123. 1971; Stanford: Stanford University Press, 1975.
_____. "Women on Top." In *Society and Culture in Early Modern France*, pp. 124–51. Stanford: Stanford University Press, 1975.
Davison, Peter. *Othello.* The Critics Debate, series ed. Michael Scott. Houndmills: Macmillan, 1988.
Dawson, Anthony B. "Witchcraft/Bigamy: Cultural Conflict in *The Witch of Edmonton.*" *Renaissance Drama* n.s., 20 (1989), 77–98.
de Iongh, Jane. *Mary of Hungary, Second Regent of the Netherlands*, trans. M. D. Herter Norton. New York: Norton, 1958.
de Mendonça, Barbara Heliodora C. "*Othello*: A Tragedy Built on a Comic Structure." *Shakespeare Survey* 21 (1968), 31–38.
Dessen, Alan C. *Elizabethan Drama and the Viewer's Eye.* Chapel Hill: University of North Carolina Press, 1977.
_____. *Elizabethan Stage Conventions and Modern Interpreters.* Cambridge: Cambridge University Press, 1984.
_____. "Recovering Shakespeare's Images." *Word and Image* 4 (July–December 1988), 618–25.
_____. *Shakespeare and the Late Moral Plays.* Lincoln: University of Nebraska Press, 1986.
Diderot, Denis. "Second Entretien sur le *Fils Naturel*" (1757). In *Oeuvres Esthétiques*, ed. Paul Vernière, pp. 97–134. Paris: Garnier Frères, 1968.
Dolan, Frances E. *Dangerous Familiars: Representations of Domestic Crime in England, 1550–1700.* Ithaca: Cornell University Press, 1994.

_____. "Gender, Moral Agency, and Dramatic Form in *A Warning for Fair Women*." *SEL* 29 (Spring 1989), 201–18.

Dollimore, Jonathan. *Radical Tragedy: Religion, Ideology, and Power in the Drama of Shakespeare and His Contemporaries*. Brighton: Harvester Press, 1984.

Donne, C. E. *An Essay on the Tragedy of "Arden of Feversham."* Paper delivered to the Kent Archaeological Society, Faversham, in July 1872. London: R. Smith, 1873.

Doran, Madeleine. "Good Name in *Othello*." *SEL* 7 (Spring 1967), 195–217.

Douglas, Mary. *Purity and Danger: An Analysis of Concepts of Pollution and Taboo*. 1966; rpt. London: Routledge, 1991.

Dusinberre, Juliet. *Shakespeare and the Nature of Women*. New York: Macmillan, 1975.

Elliott, Martin. *Shakespeare's Invention of Othello: A Study in Early Modern English*. Houndmills: Macmillan, 1988.

Elton, G. R. "The Divine Right of Kings." In *Parliament/Political Thought*, pp. 193–214. Vol. 2 of *Studies in Tudor and Stuart Politics and Government, Papers and Reviews 1946–72*. Cambridge: Cambridge University Press, 1974.

_____. *Policy and Police: The Enforcement of the Reformation in the Age of Thomas Cromwell*. Cambridge: Cambridge University Press, 1972.

Emmison, Frederick George. *Elizabethan Life: Morals and the Church Courts*. Essex Record Office Publications, no. 63. Chelmsfeld: Essex County Council, 1973.

"English Drama from the Mid-Sixteenth to the Later Eighteenth Century." Exhibition Catalogue. Pierpont Morgan Library, New York City, 22 October 1945–2 March 1946.

Erickson, Peter. *Patriarchal Structures in Shakespeare's Drama*. Berkeley: University of California Press, 1985.

Everett, Barbara. *Young Hamlet: Essays on Shakespeare's Tragedies*. Oxford: Clarendon Press, 1989.

Ezell, Margaret J. M. *The Patriarch's Wife: Literary Evidence and the History of the Family*. Chapel Hill: University of North Carolina Press, 1987.

Fabre, Daniel. "Families: Privacy versus Custom." In *Passions of the Renaissance*, ed. Roger Chartier, trans. Arthur Goldhammer, pp. 531–69. Vol. 3 of *A History of Private Life*, ed. Ariès et al. 1986; Cambridge: Belknap Press of Harvard University Press, 1989.

Fenton, James. "The Thinking Man's Macbeth." Review of RSC production of *Arden of Feversham*. *The Sunday Times*, 4 April 1982, p. 12.

Fitz, Linda T. "'What Says the Married Woman?': Marriage Theory and Feminism in the English Renaissance." *Mosaic* 13 (1980), 1–22.

Fletcher, Anthony. *Tudor Rebellions*, 3d ed. Seminar Studies in History. London: Longman, 1983.

Friedlaender, Marc. "Some Problems of *A Yorkshire Tragedy*." *Studies in Philology* 35 (April 1938), 238–53.

Friedman, Alice T. *House and Household in Elizabethan England: Wollaton Hall and the Willoughby Family*. Chicago: University of Chicago Press, 1989.

Frye, Northrop. *The Secular Scripture: A Study of the Structure of Romance*. Cambridge: Harvard University Press, 1976.

Gardner, Helen. "*Othello*: A Retrospect, 1900–67." *Shakespeare Survey* 21 (1968), 1–11.

Geertz, Clifford. *The Interpretation of Cultures: Selected Essays*. New York: Basic Books, 1973.

_____. *Local Knowledge: Further Essays in Interpretive Anthropology*. New York: Basic Books, 1983.

Gilbert, Allan H. "Thomas Heywood's Debt to Plautus." *Journal of English and Germanic Philologies* 12 (October 1913), 593–611.

Gillet, Louis. "*Arden of Feversham*" (1940), trans. Max Bluestone. In *Shakespeare's Contemporaries*, ed. Max Bluestone and Norman Rabkin, pp. 149–56. Englewood Cliffs: Prentice-Hall, 1961.

Gillis, John R. *For Better, For Worse: British Marriages, 1600 to the Present*. Oxford: Oxford University Press, 1985.

Girard, René. *The Scapegoat*, trans. Yvonne Freccero. 1982; Baltimore: Johns Hopkins University Press, 1986.

Giraud, Francis F. "On the Parish Clerks and Sexton of Faversham, A.D. 1506–1593." *Archaeologia Cantiana* 20 (1893), 203–10.

Giraud, Francis F., and Charles E. Donne. *A Visitor's Guide to Faversham, Containing a Concise History of the Town*. 1876; rpt. Faversham Reprints no. 3, 1988.

Girouard, Mark. *Robert Smythson and the Elizabethan Country House*. New Haven: Yale University Press, 1983.

Godelier, Maurice. *The Mental and the Material: Thought, Economy, and Society*, trans. Martin Thom. 1984; London: Verso, 1986.

Golding, Louis Thorn. *An Elizabethan Puritan: Arthur Golding the Translator of Ovid's "Metamorphoses" and also of John Calvin's "Sermons."* New York: Richard R. Smith, 1937.

Gras, Norman Scott Brien. *The Early English Customs System*. Cambridge: Harvard University Press, 1918.

Greenblatt, Stephen. *Renaissance Self-Fashioning from More to Shakespeare*. Chicago: University of Chicago Press, 1980.

_____. *Shakespearean Negotiations: The Circulation of Social Energy in Renaissance England*. Berkeley: University of California Press, 1988.

Gregson, J. M. *Public and Private Man in Shakespeare*. London: Croom Helm, 1983.

Grivelet, Michel. "The Simplicity of Thomas Heywood." *Shakespeare Survey* 14 (1961), 56–65.

_____. *Thomas Heywood et le drame domestique Elizabéthain*. Paris: Didier, 1957.

Gutierrez, Nancy A. "The Irresolution of Melodrama: The Meaning of Adultery in *A Woman Killed with Kindness*." *Exemplaria* 1 (October 1989), 265–91.

Guy, John. *Tudor England*. Oxford: Oxford University Press, 1988.

Haller, William and Malleville. "The Puritan Art of Love." *Huntington Library Quarterly* 5 (January 1942), 235–72.

Hansen, Abby Jane Dubman. "Shakespeare's *Othello*." *Explicator* 35 (Summer 1977), 4–6.

Harrison, G. B. *A Last Elizabethan Journal, Being a Record of Those Things Most Talked of During the Years 1599–1603*. London: Constable, 1933.

Harrison, Molly. *People and Furniture: A Social Background to the English Home*. London: Ernest Benn, 1971.

Hasted, Edward. *The History and Topographical Survey of the County of Kent*. 4 vols. Canterbury: Simmons and Kirkby, 1778–99.

_____. "The Parish and Town of Faversham by Edward Hasted." *Faversham Papers*, no. 6 (1969).

Heilman, Robert Bechtold. *Tragedy and Melodrama*. Seattle: University of Washington Press, 1968.

Heinemann, Margot. *Puritanism and Theatre: Thomas Middleton and Opposition Drama under the Early Stuarts.* Past and Present Publications. Cambridge: Cambridge University Press, 1980.

Henderson, Diana E. "Many Mansions: Reconstructing *A Woman Killed with Kindness.*" *SEL* 26 (Spring 1986), 277–94.

Henderson, Katherine Usher, and Barbara F. McManus, eds. *Half Humankind: Contexts and Texts of the Controversy about Women in England, 1540–1640.* Urbana: University of Illinois Press, 1985.

Herndl, George C. *The High Design: English Renaissance Tragedy and the Natural Law.* Lexington: University Press of Kentucky, 1970.

Hibbard, G. R. "*Othello* and the Pattern of Shakespearian Tragedy." *Shakespeare Survey* 21 (1968), 39–46.

Holdsworth, W. S. *A History of English Law.* 17 vols. 3d ed. London: Methuen, 1922–72.

Holt, Anita. "*Arden of Feversham*: A Study of the Play First Published in 1592." *Faversham Papers* 7 (1970).

Hooper, Gifford. "Heywood's *A Woman Killed with Kindness,* Scene XIV: Sir Charles's Plan." *English Language Notes* 11 (March 1974), 181–88.

Hopkinson, A. F. Introduction to *Arden of Feversham.* Shakespeare's Doubtful Plays. London: M. E. Sims, 1898.

———. Introduction to *A Warning for Fair Women.* London: M. E. Sims, 1893.

———. *Play Sources: The Original Stories on Which were Founded the Tragedies of "Arden of Feversham" and "A Warning for Fair Women," to which is added Thomas Kyd's Pamphlet "The Murder of John Brewen."* London: M. E. Sims, 1913.

Hoskins, W. G. *The Age of Plunder: King Henry's England, 1500–1547.* Social and Economic History of England. London: Longman, 1976.

———. "The Rebuilding of Rural England, 1570–1640." *Past and Present,* no. 4 (November 1953), 44–59. Reprinted in W. G. Hoskins, *Provincial England: Essays in Social and Economic History,* pp. 131–48. London: Macmillan, 1963.

Houlbrooke, Ralph A. *The English Family, 1450–1700.* Themes in British Social History. London: Longman, 1984.

———, ed. *English Family Life, 1576–1716: An Anthology from Diaries.* Oxford: Basil Blackwell, 1988.

Howard, Jean E. "The New Historicism in Renaissance Studies." *English Literary Renaissance* 16 (Winter 1986), 13–43.

———. "Scripts and/versus Playhouses: Ideological Production and the Renaissance Public Stage." *Renaissance Drama* 20 (1989), 31–49.

Howard, Maurice. *The Early Tudor Country House: Architecture and Politics, 1490–1550.* London: George Philip, 1987.

Hoy, Cyrus. Introduction and Commentary to *The Witch of Edmonton.* In vol. 3 of *The Dramatic Works of Thomas Dekker,* ed. Fredson Bowers, pp. 233–68. Cambridge: Cambridge University Press, 1980.

Hudson, Winthrop S. *John Ponet (1516?-1556), Advocate of Limited Monarchy.* Chicago: University of Chicago Press, 1942.

Hunter, G. K. "*Henry IV* and the Elizabethan Two-Part Play." In *Dramatic Identities and Cultural Tradition: Studies in Shakespeare and His Contemporaries,* pp. 303–18. Liverpool: Liverpool University Press, 1978.

Hussey, Arthur, ed. *Kent Chantries.* Kent Archaeological Society Records, vol. 12. Ashford: Headley Brothers for the Records Branch, 1936.

Hussey, Christopher. "The Setting of a Notorious Murder." *Country Life*, 13 January 1966, 76–79.

Hyde, Lewis. *The Gift: Imagination and the Erotic Life of Property*. New York: Vintage Books, 1979.

Hyde, P. G. M. "Henry Hatch and the Battle over His Will." *Archaeologia Cantiana* 102 (1985), 111–28.

Ingram, Martin. *Church Courts, Sex, and Marriage in England, 1570–1640*. Past and Present Publications. Cambridge: Cambridge University Press, 1987.

Jacob, Edward. *The History of the Town and Port of Faversham, in the County of Kent*. London: J. March, 1774.

Jardine, Lisa. *Still Harping on Daughters: Women and Drama in the Age of Shakespeare*. New York: Harvester Wheatsheaf, 1983.

Jed, Stephanie H. *Chaste Thinking: The Rape of Lucretia and the Birth of Humanism*. Bloomington: Indiana University Press, 1989.

Jessup, Frank W. *A History of Kent*. London: Darwen Finlayson, 1958.

Johnson, Marilyn L. *Images of Women in the Works of Thomas Heywood*. Salzburg Studies in English Literature, dir. Erwin A. Stürzl. Jacobean Drama Studies, ed. James Hogg. Salzburg: Institut für Englische Sprache und Literatur, Universität Salzburg, 1974.

Johnston, George Burke. "The Lute Speech in *A Woman Killed with Kindness*." *Notes and Queries* n.s., 5 (December 1958), 525–26.

Jones, W. R. D. *The Tudor Commonwealth, 1529–1559*. London: Athlone Press, 1970.

Jordan, W. K. *Edward VI: The Young King*. Cambridge: Belknap Press of Harvard University Press, 1968.

————. *Philanthropy in England, 1480–1660: A Study of the Changing Pattern of English Social Aspirations*. London: George Allen and Unwin, 1959.

————. *Social Institutions in Kent, 1480–1660: A Study of the Changing Pattern of Social Aspirations*. Archaeologia Cantiana 75 (1961).

Kantorowicz, Ernst H. *The King's Two Bodies: A Study in Mediaeval Political Theology*. Princeton: Princeton University Press, 1957.

Kelley, Donald R. *The Human Measure: Social Thought in the Western Legal Tradition*. Cambridge: Harvard University Press, 1990.

————. "Ideas of Resistance before Elizabeth." In *The Historical Renaissance: New Essays on Tudor and Stuart Literature and Culture*, ed. Heather Dubrow and Richard Strier, pp. 48–76. Chicago: University of Chicago Press, 1988.

Kendrick, T. D. *St. James in Spain*. London: Methuen, 1960.

Kermode, Frank. Introduction to *Othello, the Moor of Venice*. In *The Riverside Shakespeare*, ed. G. Blakemore Evans et al., pp. 1198–1202. Boston: Houghton Mifflin, 1974.

Kiefer, Frederick. "Heywood as Moralist in *A Woman Killed with Kindness*." *Medieval and Renaissance Drama in England* 3 (1986), 83–99.

Kiernan, V. G. "Private Property in History." In *Family and Inheritance: Rural Society in Western Europe, 1200–1800*, ed. Jack Goody, Joan Thirsk, and E. P. Thompson, pp. 361–98. Past and Present Publications. Cambridge: Cambridge University Press, 1976.

Knight, G. Wilson. *The Wheel of Fire: Interpretations of Shakespearian Tragedy with Three New Essays*. 1930; 4th ed. London: Methuen, 1949.

Kraye, Jill. "Moral Philosophy." In *The Cambridge History of Renaissance Philosophy*, ed.

Quentin Skinner and Eckhard Kessler, pp. 303–86. Cambridge: Cambridge University Press, 1988.

Larwood, Jacob, and John Camden Hotten. *English Inn Signs*. Rev. ed. of *History of Signboards* (1866). London: Chatto and Windus, 1951.

Laslett, Peter. *The World We Have Lost—Further Explored*. 3d ed. London: Methuen, 1983.

Laslett, Peter, and Richard Wall, eds. *Household and Family in Past Time*. Cambridge: Cambridge University Press, 1972.

Latham, Agnes M. C. "Sir Walter Ralegh's *Instructions to his Son*." In *Elizabethan and Jacobean Studies Presented to Frank Percy Wilson*, ed. Herbert Davis and Helen Gardner, pp. 199–218. Oxford: Clarendon Press, 1959.

Lee, Dal. *Dictionary of Astrology*. New York: Coronet Communications and Constellation International, 1968.

Lee, Sidney L. "The Topical Side of the Elizabethan Drama." In *Transactions of the New Shakspere Society, 1887–92*, pp. 1–36. London: Kegan Paul for the New Shakspere Society, 1887.

Lefebvre, Henri. *The Production of Space*, trans. Donald Nicholson-Smith. 1974; Oxford: Basil Blackwell, 1991.

Leggatt, Alexander. "*Arden of Faversham*." *Shakespeare Survey* 36 (1983), 121–33.

Lehmberg, Stanford E. *The Reformation Parliament, 1529–1536*. Cambridge: Cambridge University Press, 1970.

Leites, Edmund. "The Duty to Desire: Love, Friendship, and Sexuality in Some Puritan Theories of Marriage." *Journal of Social History* 15 (Spring 1982), 383–408.

———. *The Puritan Conscience and Modern Sexuality*. New Haven: Yale University Press, 1986.

Levin, Richard. "The Double Plot of *The Second Maiden's Tragedy*." *SEL* 3 (Spring 1963), 219–31.

———. *The Multiple Plot in English Renaissance Drama*. Chicago: University of Chicago Press, 1971.

Lévi-Strauss, Claude. *The Elementary Structures of Kinship*, trans. James Harle Bell, John Richard von Sturmer, and Rodney Needham. 1949; rev. ed. London: Eyre and Spottiswoode, 1969.

Lieblein, Leanore. "The Context of Murder in English Domestic Plays, 1590–1610." *SEL* 23 (Spring 1983), 181–96.

Lockyer, Roger. *The Early Stuarts: A Political History of England, 1603–1642*. London: Longman, 1989.

Loomba, Ania. *Gender, Race, Renaissance Drama*. Manchester: Manchester University Press, 1989.

Lomax, Derek W. *The Reconquest of Spain*. London: Longman, 1978.

Lucas, R. Valerie. "Puritan Preaching and the Politics of the Family." In *The Renaissance Englishwoman in Print: Counterbalancing the Canon*, ed. Anne M. Haselkorn and Betty S. Travitsky, pp. 224–40. Amherst: University of Massachusetts Press, 1990.

McAlindon, T. *Shakespeare and Decorum*. London: Macmillan, 1973.

MacCaffrey, Wallace T. "Place and Patronage in Elizabethan Politics." In *Elizabethan Government and Society: Essays Presented to Sir John Neale*, ed. S. T. Bindoff, J. Hurstfield, and C. H. Williams, pp. 95–126. London: Athlone Press, 1961.

MacCary, W. Thomas. *Friends and Lovers: The Phenomenology of Desire in Shakespearean Comedy.* New York: Columbia University Press, 1985.

McCutchan, J. Wilson. "Justice and Equity in the English Morality Play." *Journal of the History of Ideas* 19 (June 1958), 405–10.

McDermott, John J. "Henryson's *Testament of Cresseid* and Heywood's *A Woman Killed with Kindness.*" *Renaissance Quarterly* 20 (Spring 1967), 16–21.

Macfarlane, Alan. *The Family Life of Ralph Josselin: A Seventeenth-Century Clergyman.* Cambridge: Cambridge University Press, 1970.

———. *Marriage and Love in England: Modes of Reproduction, 1300–1840.* Oxford: Basil Blackwell, 1986.

Machin, R. "The Great Rebuilding: A Reassessment." *Past and Present* 77 (November 1977), 33–56.

McLuskie, Kathleen. "The Patriarchal Bard: Feminist Criticism and Shakespeare: *King Lear* and *Measure for Measure.*" *Political Shakespeare: New Essays in Cultural Materialism,* ed. Jonathan Dollimore and Alan Sinfield, pp. 88–108. Ithaca: Cornell University Press, 1985.

———. "'Tis but a Woman's Jar': Family and Kinship in Elizabethan Domestic Drama." *Literature and History* 9 (Autumn 1983), 228–39.

McNeir, Waldo F. "Heywood's Sources for the Main Plot of *A Woman Killed with Kindness.*" In *Studies in the English Renaissance Drama,* ed. Josephine Waters Bennett, Oscar Cargill, and Vernon Hall, Jr., pp. 189–211. New York: New York University Press, 1959.

Marshburn, Joseph H. "'A Cruell Murder Donne in Kent' and Its Literary Manifestations." *Studies in Philology* 46 (April 1949), 131–40.

Marshburn, Joseph H., and Alan R. Velie, eds. *Blood and Knavery: A Collection of English Renaissance Pamphlets and Ballads of Crime and Sin.* Rutherford, N.J.: Fairleigh Dickinson University Press, 1973.

Martin, Robert Grant. "A Critical Study of Thomas Heywood's *Gunaikeion.*" *Studies in Philology* 20 (April 1923), 160–83.

Mauss, Marcel. *The Gift: Forms and Functions of Exchange in Archaic Societies,* trans. Ian Cunnison. 1925; New York: Norton, 1967.

Maxwell, Baldwin. *Studies in the Shakespeare Apocrypha.* New York: King's Crown Press of Columbia University, 1956.

Mehl, Dieter. *The Elizabethan Dumb Show.* 1964; London: Methuen, 1966.

Mercer, E. "The Houses of the Gentry." *Past and Present* 5 (May 1954), 11–32.

Mills, Laurens J. *One Soul in Bodies Twain: Friendship in Tudor Literature and Stuart Drama.* Bloomington, Ind.: Principia Press, 1937.

Morgan, Arthur Eustace. "English Domestic Drama." Paper delivered 22 May 1912. *Transactions of the Royal Society of Literature of the United Kingdom* 2d ser., 31, pt. 3 (1912), 175–207.

Mukerji, Chandra. *From Graven Images: Patterns of Modern Materialism.* New York: Columbia University Press, 1983.

Murphy, G. N. "A Note on Iago's Name." In *Literature and Society,* ed. Bernice Slote, pp. 38–43. Lincoln: University of Nebraska Press, 1964.

Murray, K. M. E. *The Constitutional History of the Cinque Ports.* Manchester: Manchester University Press, 1935.

Murray, Timothy. "*Othello's* Foul Generic Thoughts and Methods." In *Persons in Groups: Social Behavior as Identity Formation in Medieval and Renaissance Europe,* ed.

Richard C. Trexler, pp. 67–77. Binghamton, N.Y.: Medieval and Renaissance Texts and Studies, 1985.

Nauert, Charles Garfield, Jr. *Agrippa and the Crisis of Renaissance Thought*. Illinois Studies in the Social Sciences 55. Urbana: University of Illinois Press, 1965.

Neely, Carol Thomas. "Women and Men in *Othello*: 'What should such a fool / Do with so good a woman?'" *Shakespeare Studies* 10 (1977), 133–58.

Neill, Michael. "Changing Places in *Othello*." *Shakespeare Survey* 37 (1984), 115–31.

Nelson, Benjamin. *The Idea of Usury: From Tribal Brotherhood to Universal Otherhood*. 2d ed. Chicago: University of Chicago Press, 1969.

Nelson, T. G. A., and Charles Haines. "Othello's Unconsummated Marriage." *Essays in Criticism* 33 (January 1983), 1–18.

Nethercot, Arthur H., Charles R. Baskervill, and Virgil B. Heltzel, eds. *Elizabethan Plays*. Rev. ed. New York: Holt, Rinehart, and Winston, 1971.

Neumann, Erich. "The Scapegoat Psychology." Excerpted in *The Scapegoat: Ritual and Literature*, ed. John B. Vickery and J'nan M. Sellery, pp. 43–51. 1969; rpt. Boston: Houghton Mifflin, 1972.

Newman, Karen. "Portia's Ring: Unruly Women and Structures of Exchange in *The Merchant of Venice*." *Shakespeare Quarterly* 38 (Spring 1987), 19–33.

——. "Renaissance Family Politics and Shakespeare's *The Taming of the Shrew*." *English Literary Renaissance* 16 (Winter 1986), 86–100.

Nosworthy, J. M. "The Southouse Text of *Arden of Feversham*." *Library* 5th ser., 5 (September 1950), 113–29.

Notestein, Wallace. "The English Woman, 1580–1650." *Studies in Social History, A Tribute to G. M. Trevelyan*, ed. J. H. Plumb, pp. 69–107. London: Longman, 1955.

O'Connell, Laura Stevenson. "The Elizabethan Bourgeois Hero-Tale: Aspects of an Adolescent Social Consciousness." In *After the Reformation: Essays in Honor of J. H. Hexter*, ed. Barbara C. Malament, pp. 267–90. Philadelphia: University of Pennsylvania Press, 1980.

Oliphant, E. H. C. *Shakespeare and His Fellow Dramatists*. New York: Prentice-Hall, 1929.

Oman, Charles W. C. *Castles*. 1926; rpt. New York: Beekman House, 1978.

Onat, Etta Soiref. Introduction to *The Witch of Edmonton: A Critical Edition*. New York: Garland Publishing, 1980.

Orlin, Lena Cowen. "'The Causes and Reasons of All Artificial Things' in the Elizabethan Domestic Environment." *Medieval and Renaissance Drama in England* 7 (1994).

——. "Desdemona's Disposition." In *Shakespearean Tragedy and Gender*, ed. Shirley Nelson Garner and Madelon Gohlke Sprengnether. Bloomington: University of Indiana Press, forthcoming 1995.

——. "Man's House as His Castle in *Arden of Feversham*." *Medieval and Renaissance Drama in England* 2 (1985), 57–89.

——. "The Performance of Things in *The Taming of the Shrew*." *Yearbook of English Studies* 23 (1993), 167–88.

Ornstein, Robert. "Bourgeois Morality and Dramatic Convention in *A Woman Killed with Kindness*." In *English Renaissance Drama: Essays in Honor of Madeleine Doran and Mark Eccles*, ed. Standish Henning, Robert Kimbrough, and Richard Knowles, pp. 128–41. Carbondale: Southern Illinois University Press, 1976.

Ortner, Sherry B. "Gender and Sexuality in Hierarchical Societies: The Case of Polynesia and Some Comparative Implications." In *Sexual Meanings: The Cultural Construction of Gender and Sexuality*, ed. Sherry B. Ortner and Harriet Whitehead, pp. 359–409. Cambridge: Cambridge University Press, 1981.

Palliser, D. M. *The Age of Elizabeth: England under the Later Tudors, 1547–1603*. Social and Economic History of England. London: Longman, 1983.

Parker, Patricia. "Shakespeare and Rhetoric: 'Dilation' and 'delation' in *Othello*." In *Shakespeare and the Question of Theory*, ed. Patricia Parker and Geoffrey Hartman, pp. 54–74. New York: Methuen, 1985.

Percival, Arthur. *Faversham, Kent: The Official Guide*. Faversham: Borough Council, ?1971.

Philp, Brian. *Excavations at Faversham, 1965*. First Research Report of the Kent Archaeological Research Groups' Council. Crawley: Boscobel Press, 1968.

Pocock, J. G. A. "Texts as Events: Reflections on the History of Political Thought." In *Politics of Discourse: The Literature and History of Seventeenth-Century England*, ed. Kevin Sharpe and Steven N. Zwicker, pp. 21–34. Berkeley: University of California Press, 1987.

Pollard, A. F. *England under Protector Somerset*. London: Kegan Paul, 1900.

Powell, Chilton Latham. *English Domestic Relations, 1487–1653*. New York: Columbia University Press, 1917.

Price, A. W. *Love and Friendship in Plato and Aristotle*. Oxford: Clarendon Press, 1989.

Rabkin, Norman. "The Double Plot: Notes on the History of a Convention." *Renaissance Drama* 7 (1964), 55–69.

———. "Dramatic Deception in Heywood's *The English Traveller*." *SEL* 1 (Spring 1961), 1–16.

Ranald, Margaret Loftus. "The Indiscretions of Desdemona." *Shakespeare Quarterly* 14 (Spring 1963), 127–39.

Rao, G. Nageswara. *The Domestic Drama*. Tirupati: Sri Venkateswara University Press, [1978].

Rauchbauer, Otto. "Visual and Rhetorical Imagery in Th[omas] Heywood's *A Woman Killed with Kindness*." *English Studies* 57 (June 1976), 200–210.

Reay, Barry, ed. *Popular Culture in Seventeenth-Century England*. 1985; rpt. London: Routledge, 1988.

Reiss, Timothy J. *Tragedy and Truth: Studies in the Development of a Renaissance and Neoclassical Discourse*. New Haven: Yale University Press, 1980.

Ribner, Irving. *The English History Play in the Age of Shakespeare*. Princeton: Princeton University Press, 1957.

———. *Jacobean Tragedy: The Quest for Moral Order*. London: Methuen, 1962.

Richardson, Walter C. *History of the Court of Augmentations, 1536–1554*. Baton Rouge: Louisiana State University Press, 1961.

Ridley, M. R. Introduction to *Othello*. The Arden Shakespeare. London: Methuen, 1958.

Rosaldo, Michelle Zimbalist. "Woman, Culture, and Society: A Theoretical Overview." *Woman, Culture, and Society*, ed. Michelle Zimbalist Rosaldo and Louise Lamphere, pp. 17–42. Stanford: Stanford University Press, 1974.

Ross, Lawrence. Introduction to *The Tragedy of Othello, the Moor of Venice*. Indianapolis: Bobbs-Merrill, 1974.

Rubin, Gayle. "The Traffic in Women: Notes on the 'Political Economy' of Sex." In

Toward an Anthropology of Women, ed. Rayna R. Reiter, pp. 157–210. New York: Monthly Review Press, 1975.

Rudnytsky, Peter L. "*A Woman Killed with Kindness* as Subtext for *Othello*." *Renaissance Drama* n.s., 14 (1983), 103–24.

Ruoff, James. "*Othello*." In *The Major Shakespearean Tragedies: A Critical Bibliography*, ed. Edward Quinn, James Ruoff, and Joseph Grennen. New York: Free Press, 1973.

Rutton, W. L. "Cheney of Shurland, Kent, and of Toddington, Bed[ford]s[hire]." *Archaeologia Cantiana* 24 (1900), 122–27.

Sanders, Norman. Introduction to *Othello*. The New Cambridge Shakespeare. Cambridge: Cambridge University Press, 1984.

Schelling, Felix E. *The English Chronicle Play: A Study in the Popular Historical Literature Environing Shakespeare*. New York: Macmillan, 1902.

Schochet, Gordon J. *Patriarchalism in Political Thought: The Authoritarian Family and Political Speculation and Attitudes Especially in Seventeenth-Century England*. New York: Basic Books, 1975.

––––––. "Patriarchalism, Politics, and Mass Attitudes in Stuart England." *Historical Journal* 12, no. 3 (1969), 413–41.

Scobie, Brian W. M. Introduction to *A Woman Killed with Kindness*. The New Mermaids. London: A. and C. Black, 1985.

Seaver, Paul S. *Wallington's World: A Puritan Artisan in Seventeenth-Century London*. Stanford: Stanford University Press, 1985.

Sedgwick, Eve Kosofsky. *Between Men: English Literature and Male Homosocial Desire*. New York: Columbia University Press, 1985.

Shanley, Mary Lyndon. "Marriage Contract and Social Contract in Seventeenth-Century English Political Thought." *Western Political Quarterly* 32 (March 1979), 79–91.

Sharp, Buchanan. *In Contempt of All Authority: Rural Artisans and Riot in the West of England, 1586–1660*. Berkeley: University of California Press, 1980.

Sharpe, J. A. *Crime in Early Modern England, 1550–1750*. Themes in British Social History. London: Longman, 1984.

––––––. "Domestic Homicide in Early Modern England." *Historical Journal* 24 (1981), 29–48.

––––––. "'Last Dying Speeches': Religion, Ideology, and Public Execution in Seventeenth-Century England." *Past and Present*, no. 107 (May 1985), 144–67.

Sharpe, Robert Boies. "The Domestic Crime Play, 1594–1603." In *The Real War of the Theater: Shakespeare's Fellows in Rivalry with the Admiral's Men, 1594–1603—Repertories, Devices, and Types*, pp. 125–30. New York: Modern Language Association, 1935.

Simpson, Alan. *The Wealth of the Gentry, 1540–1660*. East Anglian Studies. Cambridge: Cambridge University Press, 1961.

Simpson, Richard. Introduction to *A Warning for Fair Women*. Vol. 2 of *The School of Shakspere*. New York: J. W. Bouton, 1878.

Sinfield, Alan. *Faultlines: Cultural Materialism and the Politics of Dissident Reading*. Berkeley: University of California Press, 1992.

––––––. *Literature in Protestant England, 1560–1660*. London: Croom Helm, 1983.

Skipp, Victor. *Crisis and Development: An Ecological Case Study of the Forest of Arden, 1570–1674*. Cambridge: Cambridge University Press, 1978.

Slack, Paul. *Poverty and Policy in Tudor and Stuart England.* Themes in British Social History. London: Longman, 1988.
————. "Vagrants and Vagrancy in England, 1598–1664." *Economic History Review* 2d ser., 27 (August 1974), 360–79.
Smith, Hallett D. "*A Woman Killed with Kindness.*" *PMLA* 53 (March 1938), 138–47.
Smith, John Hazel. *Shakespeare's "Othello": A Bibliography.* New York: AMS Press, 1988.
Smith, Robert Metcalf. "The Nature of Domestic Tragedy." In *Types of Domestic Tragedy,* pp. 1–6. New York: Prentice-Hall, 1928.
Snow, Edward A. "Sexual Anxiety and the Male Order of Things in *Othello.*" *English Literary Renaissance* 10 (Autumn 1980), 384–412.
Snyder, Susan. "*Othello*: A Modern Perspective." In *Othello,* ed. Barbara Mowat and Paul Werstine, pp. 287–98. The New Folger Library Shakespeare. New York: Washington Square Press, 1993.
————. "*Othello* and the Conventions of Romantic Comedy." *Renaissance Drama* n.s., 5 (1972), 123–41.
————, ed. "*Othello*": *Critical Essays.* New York: Garland, 1988.
Sommerville, J. P. *Politics and Ideology in England, 1603–1640.* London: Longman, 1986.
Spacks, Patricia Meyer. "Honor and Perception in *A Woman Killed with Kindness.*" *Modern Language Quarterly* 20 (December 1959), 321–32.
Speaight, Robert. *William Poel and the Elizabethan Revival.* London: William Heinemann, 1954.
Sper, Felix. "The Germ of the Domestic Drama." *Poet Lore* 40 (Winter 1929), 544–51.
Spring, Eileen. "Law and the Theory of the Affective Family." *Albion* 16 (Spring 1984), 1–20.
Spufford, Margaret. *Small Books and Pleasant Histories: Popular Fiction and its Readership in Seventeenth-Century England.* Past and Present Publications. Cambridge: Cambridge University Press, 1981.
Spurgeon, Caroline F. E. *Shakespeare's Imagery and What It Tells Us.* Cambridge: Cambridge University Press, 1935.
Stallybrass, Peter. "Patriarchal Territories: The Body Enclosed." In *Rewriting the Renaissance: The Discourses of Sexual Difference in Early Modern Europe,* ed. Margaret W. Ferguson, Maureen Quilligan, and Nancy J. Vickers, pp. 123–42. Chicago: University of Chicago Press, 1986.
Stallybrass, Peter, and Allon White. *The Politics and Poetics of Transgression.* Ithaca: Cornell University Press, 1986.
Stapleton, Henry. *Memorials of Calverley Parish Church and its Forty-One Vicars with some account of the Old Hall, Calverley.* Leeds: Richard Jackson, n.d.
Starkey, David. Introduction to *The English Court: From the Wars of the Roses to the Civil War,* ed. David Starkey. London: Longman, 1987.
Stevenson, Laura Caroline. *Praise and Paradox: Merchants and Craftsmen in Elizabethan Popular Literature.* Cambridge: Cambridge University Press, 1984.
Stewart, Bain Tate. "The Misunderstood Dreams in the Plays of Shakespeare and His Contemporaries." In *Essays in Honor of Walter Clyde Curry,* pp. 197–206. Vanderbilt University Studies in the Humanities 2. Nashville: Vanderbilt University Press, 1954.

Stilling, Roger. *Love and Death in Renaissance Tragedy.* Baton Rouge: Louisiana State University Press, 1976.

Stone, James S. *The Cult of Santiago: Traditions, Myths, and Pilgrimages.* New York: Longman, 1927.

Stone, Lawrence. *The Crisis of the Aristocracy, 1558–1641.* Oxford: Clarendon Press, 1965.

_____. *The Family, Sex, and Marriage in England, 1500–1800.* New York: Harper and Row, 1977.

_____, ed. *Social Change and Revolution in England, 1540–1640.* London: Longman, 1965.

Sturgess, Keith. "The Early Quartos of Heywood's *A Woman Killed with Kindness.*" *Library* 5th ser., 25 (June 1970), 93–104.

_____. Introduction to *Three Elizabethan Domestic Tragedies.* Baltimore: Penguin Books, 1969.

Swaine, Anthony. *Faversham: Its History, Its Present Role, and the Pattern for Its Future.* Maidstone: Kent County Council and Faversham Borough Council, 1970.

Sykes, H. Dugdale. *Sidelights on Shakespeare.* Stratford-upon-Avon: Shakespeare Head Press, 1919.

Symonds, John Addington. *Shakspere's Predecessors in the English Drama.* London: Smith, Elder, 1884.

Telfer, Canon W. "Faversham Abbey and Its Last Abbot, John Caslock." *Faversham Papers,* no. 2 (1965).

_____. "Faversham's Court of Orphans." *Archaeologia Cantiana* 81 (1966), 191–202.

Thirsk, Joan. *Economic Policy and Projects: The Development of a Consumer Society in Early Modern England.* Oxford: Clarendon Press, 1978.

Thomas, Keith. "The Double Standard." *Journal of the History of Ideas* 20 (April 1959), 195–216.

Thompson, E. P. "Rough Music: 'Le Charivari Anglais.'" *Annales, Economies, Sociétés, Civilisations* 27 (1972), 285–312.

Thomson, Gladys Scott. *Two Centuries of Family History: A Study in Social Development.* London: Longman, 1930.

Thorp, Willard. *The Triumph of Realism in Elizabethan Drama, 1558–1612.* Princeton: Princeton University Press, 1928.

Todd, Margo. "Humanists, Puritans, and the Spiritualized Household." *Church History* 49 (1980), 18–34.

Townsend, Freda L. "The Artistry of Thomas Heywood's Double Plots." *Philological Quarterly* 25 (April 1946), 97–119.

"A tragic fact, of 1550." [Untitled collection of tales.] London: J. Roe, 1804.

Truchet, Sybil. "Alice Arden and the Religion of Love." *Caliban* 17, no. 1 (1980), 39–44.

Trussler, Simon. Commentary in *The Witch of Edmonton.* Methuen Student Editions. London: Methuen, 1983.

Tyack, Geoffrey. *The Making of the Warwickshire Country House, 1500–1650.* Warwickshire Local History Society Occasional Paper, no. 4 (July 1982).

Ulrici, Hermann. *Shakespeare's Dramatic Art,* trans. A.J.W.M. London: Chapman Brothers, 1846.

Underdown, David. *Revel, Riot, and Rebellion: Popular Politics and Culture in England, 1603–1660.* Oxford: Oxford University Press, 1985.

Ure, Peter. "Marriage and the Domestic Drama in Heywood and Ford." *Elizabethan and Jacobean Drama: Critical Essays by Peter Ure*, ed. J. C. Maxwell, pp. 145–65. 1951; rpt. Liverpool: Liverpool University Press, 1974.

Van Fossen, R. W. Introduction to *A Woman Killed with Kindness*. The Revels Plays. London: Methuen, 1961.

van Gennep, Arnold. *The Rites of Passage*, trans. Monika B. Vizedom and Gabrielle L. Caffee. 1908; Chicago: University of Chicago Press, 1960.

Velte, Mowbray. *The Bourgeois Elements in the Dramas of Thomas Heywood*. Ph.D. dissertation, Princeton University (Mysore City: Wesleyan Mission Press, 1922).

Vickers, Brian. Introduction to *Occult and Scientific Mentalities in the Renaissance*. Cambridge: Cambridge University Press, 1984.

Walker, D. P. *Spiritual and Demonic Magic from Ficino to Campanella*. London: Warburg Institute, University of London, 1958.

Wall, Stephen. "Black Will and Shakebag." Review of RSC production of *Arden of Feversham*. *Times Literary Supplement*, 16 April 1982, p. 19.

Wallace, John M. "*Timon of Athens* and the Three Graces: Shakespeare's Senecan Study." *Modern Philology* 83 (May 1986), 349–63.

Warnke, Karl, and Ludwig Proescholdt, eds. Introduction to *Arden of Feversham*. Pseudo-Shakespearian Plays 5. Halle: Max Niemeyer, 1888.

"Was *Arden of Feversham* Written by Shakespeare?" *Monthly Journal of the Faversham Institute* 8 (July 1881), 291–94.

Weinberg, Bernard. *A History of Literary Criticism in the Italian Renaissance*. 2 vols. Chicago: University of Chicago Press, 1961.

West, Edward Sackville. "The Significance of *The Witch of Edmonton*." *Criterion* 17 (October 1937), 23–32.

West, Trudy. *The Timber-Frame House in England*. Newton Abbot: David and Charles, 1971.

Whitaker, Thomas Dunham. *Loidis and Elmete*. Leeds and Wakefield, 1816.

White, Hayden. "The Value of Narrativity in the Representation of Reality." In *On Narrative*, ed. W. J. T. Mitchell, pp. 1–23. Chicago: University of Chicago Press, 1981.

White, Martin. Introduction to *Arden of Faversham*. The New Mermaids. London: Ernest Benn, 1982.

Whiting, Bartlett Jere, with Helen Wescott Whiting. *Proverbs, Sentences, and Proverbial Phrases from English Writing Mainly before 1500*. Cambridge: Belknap Press of Harvard University Press, 1968.

Wiffen, J. H. *Historical Memoirs of the House of Russell*. 2 vols. London: Longman, 1833.

Willen, Diane. *John Russell, First Earl of Bedford*. London: Royal Historical Society, 1981.

Wiltenburg, Joy. *Disorderly Women and Female Power in the Street Literature of Early Modern England and Germany*. Charlottesville: University of Virginia Press, 1992.

Wine, M. L. Introduction to *Arden of Faversham*. The Revels Plays. Manchester: Manchester University Press, 1973.

Wood, Margaret. *The English Mediaeval House*. 1965; rpt. New York: Harper Colophon, 1983.

Woodbridge, Linda. *Women and the English Renaissance: Literature and the Nature of Womankind, 1540–1620*. Urbana: University of Illinois Press, 1984.

Wright, Louis B. "Heywood and the Popularizing of History." *Modern Language Notes* 43 (May 1928), 287–93.

————. "The Male-Friendship Cult in Thomas Heywood's Plays." *Modern Language Notes* 42 (December 1927), 510–14.

————. *Middle-Class Culture in Elizabethan England*. Chapel Hill: University of North Carolina Press, 1935.

Wrightson, Keith. *English Society, 1580–1680*. London: Hutchinson, 1982.

————. "The Social Order of Early Modern England: Three Approaches." *The World We Have Gained: Histories of Population and Social Structure, Essays Presented to Peter Laslett on His Seventieth Birthday*, ed. Lloyd Bonfield, Richard M. Smith, and Keith Wrightson, pp. 177–202. Oxford: Basil Blackwell, 1986.

Yost, John. "The Value of Married Life for the Social Order in the Early English Renaissance." *Societas* 6 (Winter 1976), 25–39.

Youings, Joyce. *The Dissolution of the Monasteries*. London: George Allen and Unwin, 1971.

————. *Sixteenth-Century England*. The Pelican Social History of Britain, ed. J. H. Plumb. Harmondsworth: Penguin Books, 1984.

Youngblood, Sarah. "Theme and Imagery in *Arden of Feversham*," *SEL* 3 (Spring 1963), 207–18.

Zeldin, Theodore. "Personal History and the History of the Emotions." *Journal of Social History* 15 (Spring 1982), 339–47.

Zell, Michael L. "The Mid-Tudor Market in Crown Land in Kent," *Archaeologia Cantiana* 97 (1981), 53–70.

INDEX

Absolutism, 11, 89–90, 125, 126–27. *See also* Divine right; Kingship; Monarchy
Academy of Armory, An (Holme), 256–59, 269
Adams, Henry Hitch, 9–10, 91n.12, 97n.24, 108n.51, 112, 117n.69, 121n.73, 140n.7, 144n.14, 159n.43, 246–47
Adultery, 81, 92, 147–51, 152–53, 167–68, 179–80. *See also* Cuckoldry
Adultress's Funeral Day, The (Goodcole), 16, 65n.106, 69, 71, 77n.124
Advertisement . . . for Truth against her Backbiters, An (Munday), 87–88
Advice to his son (Percy), 151n.25, 165
"Advice to his son" (Wentworth), 44, 155, 164–65, 169, 186
Agnew, Jean-Christophe, 172, 187, 263
Agrippa von Nettesheim, Henricus Cornelius. *See Commendation of Matrimony, The*; *De occulta philosophia*
Alarum to England, An (Gray), 93n.16
Alberti, Leon Battista, 187n.10
"Alice Arden's crime," 18, 64, 71, 73, 76, 80, 237
Allestree, Richard, 197
All's Well That Ends Well (Shakespeare), 202, 206–7
Almanacs, 196–98
Altile (Cinthio), 75–76, 77–78, 238–39
Amussen, Susan D., 10n.13, 73n.117, 101n.36, 127n.85
Analogy. *See* Thought: analogical
Ancient and Memorable History of Lord Cheyne, The, 58–61
Ancient Funeral Monuments (Weever), 62
Angels, 153–54, 181

Anglerius, Petrus Martyr, 202n.24
Annals of England, The (Stow), 64n.106, 106, 233
Anne of Cleves, 26
Antony and Cleopatra (Shakespeare), 202, 206
Apology for Actors, An (Heywood), 129–30, 181
Apology for Poetry, An (Sidney), 75
Apology for Women, An (Heale), 180n.93
Apprehension . . . of Elizabeth Abbot, 186
Architecture, domestic, 2–3, 34–40, 63, 70, 230–33. *See also* Household: spaces
Archives, 19–20; and fiction, 10, 40, 137; fiction as, 10, 131, 137, 158; and women in, 20, 39, 62, 79–84, 261
Arden of Feversham, 8–9, 11, 15, 17, 19, 67, 72, 74–76, 90–91, 91–98, 103, 104–5, 108, 113, 133, 167, 171, 179, 184, 246n.1, 247, 249, 252, 260; and Thomas Ardern, 43, 54, 57, 61, 63–64, 69, 79
Ardern, Alyce: Ardern's wife and murderer, 15, 18, 24, 40, 51, 53, 61, 65, 66, 72, 89, 104; North's stepdaughter, 24, 53–54; raped, 80–84; and women in archives, 20, 39, 62, 79–84, 261
Ardern, Margaret (Ardern's heir), 24n.14, 39n.56, 42, 43, 62, 261
Ardern, Thomas, 15–78, 182, 229, 238, 243–44, 261, 262, 269; and the "Arden" of *Arden of Feversham*, 17, 43, 54, 61, 63–64, 67, 72; and the "Arden" of the chronicles, 18, 20, 21, 40–41, 42, 45–46, 47, 64, 66–68, 71, 72; and the "Arden" of other redactions, 60, 65–69, 73, 76–78, 237–38; and Aucher, 47–48; and

Ardern, Thomas (cont.)
  Auncell, 49, 261; birth of, 21; charged by
    Morleyn, 54–55; and Cheyney, 21–22,
    25–28, 33, 54–55, 56, 58–62; as church
    warden, 33, 35n.49; compared to Thynne,
    69–71; as comptroller of Sandwich, 28,
    30, 33, 40; as customer of Faversham, 27–
    28, 40, 49–50, 261; daughter of, 24n.14,
    39n.56, 42, 43, 62, 261; disenfranchise-
    ment of, 41–43, 54, 73; distrust of, in Fa-
    versham, 43–47, 50–51, 61–62; and
    Dunkyn, 31, 41, 42–43, 50; establishment
    of, 21–40, 46–47; in Faversham town
    government, 31–35, 40, 41, 47; and
    Fowle, 43, 52–53; house of, 17–18, 34–
    40, 65, 232; as householder, 17–18, 40,
    71–73, 86, 243–44; as king's man, 31, 48;
    as landlord, 35, 44–46; land transactions
    of, 25, 28–31; marriage of, 24, 39–40,
    53–54; as mayor, 33–35, 43, 261; as mid-
    dleman, 50, 53; mother of, 66; murder
    of, 15–16, 18, 19–20, 22, 50–62, 65–67;
    as negotiator of Faversham charter of in-
    corporation, 31–33, 42, 50; as "new"
    man, 22, 28, 37, 229; and North, 21–22,
    23–25, 33, 53–54; and Norton, 44, 48–
    49, 50, 53; notoriety of, 15–16, 62–63,
    67–68, 71, 76–78, 79; offices of, 21, 24–
    25, 27–28, 40; reactions to the murder
    of, in Faversham, 51, 62, 74, 81–82; re-
    wards of, 24–25, 30; as steward, 25, 40,
    54–55; and the Valentine's Day fair-
    grounds, 30–31, 41–42, 66; wealth of,
    30; will of, 42, 43, 47, 62
Ariès, Philippe, 1, 182–83
Aristotle, 11, 76, 85, 99n.28, 126, 139. See
  also Nicomachean Ethics, The; Oeconomics,
  The; Politics, The
Aristotle's Politics (I.D.), 126
Arraignment, Condemnation, and Execution of
  Master Calverley, The, 233
Arraignment of an Unruly Tongue, The
  (Webbe), 197–99, 200
Arrows, 197–201, 206
Ars Grammatica (Diomedes), 75, 76
Astrology, 196, 201–2, 207–12. See also Oc-
  cult sciences
Aucher, Sir Anthony, 30, 45–46, 47–48,
  50–51, 52, 56
Audley, Sir Thomas, 24
Auncell, Simon, 33, 44, 46n.72, 49
Authority, 87, 90, 92–94, 120–21, 129, 193.
  See also Government
Averell, William, 201
Aylmer, John, 85n.1, 89
Ayrault, Pierre, 73n.117

Bacon, Sir Francis, 140n.5
Bailey, F. G., 43–45, 50, 53, 166, 177

Baker, Richard, 65n.106, 68
Baldwin, William. See Mirror for Magistrates,
  A; Treatise of Moral Philosophy, A
"Ballad of Lamentable Murder Done in
  Yorkshire, A," 233
Barthes, Roland, 237
Batho, Gordon, 27n.26, 30n.38, 46n.73,
  48n.77
Battus, Bartholomaeus, 180–81
Bayker, John, 46n.73
Beard, Thomas, 65n.106, 67, 71
Bellamy, John, 57n.96, 106n.47
Belsey, Catherine, 18, 92n.13, 101n.36,
  247n.3. See also "Alice Arden's crime"
Benefice: in practice, 170–72, 173, 176–77,
  180; in theory, 13, 139, 157, 158–66,
  177–78
Bernard, Richard, 87, 98
Bethel (Griffith), 101, 102n.37, 103
Biathanatos (Donne), 180n.93
Bilson, Thomas, 73, 98, 99, 126–27
Blackwyll, 51, 52, 57–62, 65, 67
Bloody Book, The, 195, 239–43, 245
Bloody New Year's Gift, A, 153
Bodin, Jean, 73n.115, 99n.31, 126, 193–94,
  236–37, 244
Boleyn, Anne, 53, 55, 248–49
Boleyn, George, Viscount Rochford, 25
Book of Common Prayer, The, 99, 139
Boulogne, siege of, 52, 61, 62
Bowers, Rick, 169n.64
Braddock, Robert C., 23n.13, 28n.32,
  30n.38
Bradford, John, 131–32n.1
Bradshaw, George, 51, 52, 61, 62, 65, 74
Bradshaw, William, 142
Brathwait, Richard, 183–84, 186–87
Bretnor, Thomas, 198
Breviat Chronicle, A, 64n.106, 65–66
Bride-Bush, A (Whately), 86, 98, 100, 101,
  102, 112, 150, 180n.93, 188, 220, 236n.82
Brideling, Saddling, and Riding . . . by one
  Judith Philips, The, 110n.53
Brief and Necessary Instruction, Very Needful to
  be Known of all Householders, A (Dering),
  87n.4
Brief Discourse of the Late Murder of Master G.
  Sanders, A (Golding), 106, 182–83, 188
Brief Discourse of the Spanish State, A
  (Daunce), 204, 212, 229
Brief Exhortation to all Men to Set their Houses
  in Order, A (Jones), 98n.27
Bristol, Michael D., 5n.6, 142n.9, 159n.41
Bromley, Laura G., 166n.57, 171n.68
Brooke, Christopher, 130
Bryan, Margaret B., 157n.38
Bullinger, Heinrich, 99, 116
Bunny, Edmund, 180n.93
Burke, Kenneth, 200n.17, 218n.48

Caba (or Cava) of Spain, 83, 203–4, 248
Cacanus (in Ponet), 80–81, 83–84
Calverley, Walter, 229–33, 237–38, 239–40, 261, 262
Cannon, Charles Dale, 108n.51, 112n.56, 118n.71
Canterbury Tales, The, 103
Canuteson, John, 158n.39, 171n.69
Captives, The (Heywood), 9
Care-Cloth, A (Whately), 172, 180n.93
Carter, Thomas, 100, 103n.39, 112
Carter's Christian Commonwealth (Carter), 100, 103n.39, 112
Caslock, John, 32, 35, 44, 50n.81
Cassirer, Ernst, 192–94, 244, 262
Castles, 2–11, 102–3, 244–45, 267–68, 269. *See also* House, meanings of
"Cautions in Friendship" (Tuvill), 163
Cavendish, Richard, 56, 61
Cawley, A. C., 229n.72, 233n.77, 237n.85, 238n.86, 253, 254n.3
Caxton, William, 159n.42
Cecil, William, Lord Burghley, 135, 164
Centaurs, 196, 201–2, 206–7, 213, 214, 217
Center and locality, 48, 49–50, 53, 56, 63
"Certain Precepts for the Well Ordering of a Man's Life" (Cecil), 164
Certain Sermons or Homilies, 88. *See also* "Exhortation to Obedience"; "Homily Against Disobedience and Willful Rebellion, The"; "Homily of the State of Matrimony, The"
Chamberlain, John, 135–36
Chantries Act, 49
Chappuys, Gabriel, 215–16n.44
Chastity (female), 82–83, 105, 129–30, 154, 175, 227–28. *See also* Adultery; Virginity
Cheke, Sir John, 88, 128n.87
Cheyney, John, 55–56
Cheyney, Sir Thomas, 21–22, 25–28, 29, 33, 40, 45, 49, 53, 54–62, 67, 79
Christian Astrology (Lilly), 206n.32
Christian Man's Assuring House, The (Meriton), 96
Christian Man's Closet, The (Battus), 180–81
Christian Oeconomy (Perkins), 86, 99n.31, 100, 102, 109, 113n.58, 125, 150n.22, 179, 215n.43, 221
Christian State of Matrimony, The (Bullinger), 99, 116
Chronicle of the Kings of England, A (Baker), 65n.106, 68
Chronicles of England, The (Stow), 64n.106, 233
Chronicles of England, Scotland, and Ireland, The (Holinshed), 15, 16, 20, 21, 22n.11, 40–42, 43n.64, 45, 47, 52, 53n.88, 57, 61, 64, 67–68, 69, 71, 72, 74, 77, 79, 89, 94n.17, 97, 106

Cicero, Marcus Tullius, 99n.28. *See also De amicitia*
Cinque Ports, 25, 26, 32, 55. *See also* Faversham; Sandwich
Cinthio, Giraldi. *See Altile*; *Hecatommithi*
City comedy, 244
Civil and Uncivil Life, 146, 167
Clapham, David, 139n.3, 180n.93. *See also Commendation of Matrimony, The*
Clark, Andrew, 91n.12, 247n.3
Clark, Arthur Melville, 130n.91, 158n.40, 177n.84
Clark, Peter, 21n.7, 27n.26, 31, 33n.48, 47, 48, 53n.88, 90n.10, 113n.58
Classes. *See* Social rank
Cleaver, Robert. *See Godly Form of Household Government, A*
Clytemnestra, 68–69
Cohabitation, 133–34, 193–94, 215–16, 265–66. *See also* Divorce (separation)
Coke, Sir Edward. *See* Semayne's Case; *Third Part of the Institutes, The*
Cole, James, 132–33
Colie, Rosalie L., 74, 76
Collier, John Payne, 9, 75n.122, 199n.15, 205n.29
Collins, Richard, 255
Colwell, Robert, 44, 45
Comedy of Errors, The (Shakespeare), 196, 206, 220n.54, 223
Commendation of Matrimony, The (Agrippa), 73, 139–40, 145, 150–51, 180n.93, 207n.34, 219, 223, 244
"Complaint and Lamentation of Mistress Arden, The," 64–65n.106, 69
Complete Gentleman, The (Peacham), 164
Conflict of authorities, 91, 100–102, 110–11, 112, 116–17, 120–22, 129, 134. *See also* Ideals, obsolescence of; Ideology: ambiguities, contestations, and failures of
Conscience, 91, 114–16, 122, 124, 226–28
Cook, Ann Jennalie, 186n.9, 228–29n.69
Cooke, Richard, 74, 81
Corruption (political), 23–24, 28, 40, 47, 50, 63
Cosmic space, 192–93, 207
Counsel and Advice to all Builders (Gerbier), 192, 244
Country Justice, The (Dalton), 186n.9
Court cases, 7, 48–49, 51, 54–55, 131, 133–34, 237–38. *See also* Justice: civic; Thought: legal
Court of Augmentations, 22, 23, 24–25, 28, 32–33, 46, 47, 52
Court of Good Counsel, The, 167
Cranmer, Thomas, 48n.79, 56
Cromwell, Thomas, 22, 24–25, 30n.38, 32, 47, 48, 54–55, 56, 70

Cuckoldry, 71–73, 152, 173–74. *See also* Adultery
Curio, Caelius Augustinus, 202–5
Curtain Lecture, A (Heywood), 140, 145, 176n.81, 177n.84, 185
Cust, Lionel, 21n.5, 27n.25, 27n.28, 31n.40, 39n.55, 62n.101, 69n.109

Daemonologie (James), 239n.88
Dalton, Michael, 186n.9
Dane, Herbert, 26n.23, 27n.26, 32n.44, 33n.47
Daunce, Edward, 204, 212, 229
Davies, Kathleen M., 139n.2, 178–79
Davis, Natalie Zemon, 5n.6, 10, 18n.3, 104
De amicitia (Cicero), 105, 138, 159–63, 166, 171, 172, 179
De beneficiis (Seneca), 138, 159–63, 166, 170n.67, 172, 173, 177, 180
Debt, 132–33, 154–57, 170–71
Decades of the New World (Anglerius), 202n.24
Decorum (literary), 16, 20, 68, 74–76, 247. *See also* Impertinence (literary)
Defence of the Judgment of the Reformed Churches, A (Rainolds), 64–65n.106, 68–69, 71, 76, 100–101, 180n.93
De harmonia mundi totius (Giorgio), 207n.34
Deianira, 202
Dekker, Thomas. *See Page of Plymouth*; *Shoemaker's Holiday, The*; *Witch of Edmonton, The*
De occulta philosophia (Agrippa), 207–11, 239n.88
De republica anglorum (Thomas Smith), 85n.1, 101, 102, 126, 138
Dering, Edward, 87n.4
De sacramento matrimonii (Agrippa). *See Commendation of Matrimony, The*
Descartes, René, 188–89
Description of England, The (Harrison), 2, 7, 8, 11, 46, 63–64, 147, 255, 261
Dessen, Alan C., 108n.51, 145n.17, 153
De vera obedientia (Gardiner), 99n.28, 128n.87
Devereux, Robert, Earl of Essex, 7–8, 11, 242, 269
De vita solitaria (Petrarch), 4
Diaries, 1, 131, 182–83. *See also* Machyn, Henry
Diderot, Denis, 9
Dillingham, Francis, 220n.54
Diomedes, 75, 76
Discourse for Parents' Honor, A (Ayrault), 73n.117
Discourse of Marriage, A (Niccholes), 170
Display of Duty (Wright), 105n.45
Dissolution of the monasteries, 2, 17, 20, 23–24, 27, 28, 63, 191, 230, 232
Divine right, 16, 126–27

Divorce (separation), 134–36, 149–51, 179–80, 242–43. *See also* Cohabitation
Dod, John, 132. *See also Godly Form of Household Government, A*
Dodsworth, Roger, 229, 233
Dollimore, Jonathan, 130n.92
Domestical or Household Sermons (Hegendorff), 87, 98
Domestic conduct books. *See* Oeconomic tracts
Domestic crime, 8–9, 105–7, 111, 113–14, 194, 225, 228, 229, 233, 236–38, 241. *See also* Ardern, Thomas: murder of; Infanticide
Domestic disorder, 5, 8–9, 13, 16, 18, 19, 63, 66, 68, 71–72, 77, 91–94, 97–98, 113, 132–36, 215–23, 234–37, 238–39, 240, 242–43, 247, 269. *See also* Ideology: domestic
Domestic ethic, 9, 11, 76, 138, 166–67, 180–81
Domestic tragedy. *See* Tragedy: domestic
Donne, C. E., 21n.5, 26n.20, 26n.23, 32n.44, 33n.46, 35n.52, 42n.61
Donne, John, 138, 151–53, 180n.93
Dorke, Walter, 163–64, 201n.19
Douglas, Mary, 97n.24, 103–4
Dove, John, 99, 100n.32, 150, 180n.93
Drama, cultural functions of, 4, 8–9, 10, 13, 19, 90–91, 107–8, 128–30, 137–38, 140–41, 172, 179–81, 238–39, 245, 247, 253, 263
Dunkyn, Thomas, 31, 41, 42–43, 50
Duty, 97–98, 102, 111, 128, 132–36, 141, 142–43, 178–79, 180–81, 217–20, 236, 244

Economy: cash, 20, 23–24, 28, 263–65; merchant, 2–3, 27, 63, 254–55. *See also* Goods; Men: exchange of; Women: exchange of
Eden, Richard, 202n.24
Edward IV (Heywood), 91, 105, 107–8, 118–25, 128–30, 134, 135, 136, 167n.61, 173, 243–44, 246, 249, 260, 261, 267
Edward VI of England, 22, 26, 28n.30, 47, 49
Eirenarcha (Lambard), 102
Elizabeth I of England, 7–8, 22, 26, 45, 70, 89, 90, 113, 135, 165
Elliott, Martin, 196n.12, 200n.17, 219n.52, 220n.53, 224n.63
Ellwood, Thomas, 186
Elton, G. R., 25n.16, 55
Elyot, Thomas, 163–64
Emmison, Frederick George, 49n.80, 133n.5, 150n.22
English Traveller, The (Heywood), 246n.1, 251–52, 263, 264–65, 266–69

Entry to Christianity, The (Watts), 98n.27, 125
Erasmus, Desiderius, 138, 162, 180n.93
Essayes, The (Bacon), 140n.5
Everett, Barbara, 205
"Exhortation to Obedience," 88, 116n.66, 117

Fair Maid of Bristow, The, 75n.122
Fair Quarrel, A (Middleton and Rowley), 114n.59
"Fall of Religious Houses, The" (Sherbrook), 191–92, 269
Faults, Faults (Rich), 124n.76, 164
Faversham, Kent, 26–27, 43–45, 46–47, 48–50, 61–62, 261; and charter of incorporation, 31–33, 42, 50; town government, 31, 33–35, 41–43, 54; Wardmote (record) Book, 15, 18, 30, 31, 33–35, 41, 42, 43, 51n.84, 52, 57, 61–62, 65–66, 67, 71–72, 80
Faversham Abbey, 27, 29, 30, 32, 34–37, 43–45
Feltham, Owen, 163, 164, 170, 178, 201n.20
Fetherstone, John, 256
Filmer, Robert, 129
Finche, Edmund, 56
Fites, John, 239–43, 261
Flower of Friendship, The (Tilney), 104, 105n.45, 128n.88, 151n.25, 166, 176n.82, 178, 220, 236
Floyd, Thomas, 71, 88
Flushing, Flanders, 57–61, 261
Ford, John. See *'Tis Pity She's a Whore*; *Witch of Edmonton, The*
Fowle, Adam, 43, 52–53
Friedman, Alice T., 134n.6, 135, 188
Friendship: in practice, 155–56, 163–67, 170–73, 260, 261; in theory, 12–13, 137–38, 158–63, 177–79
Frye, Northrop, 157

Gaines, Barry, 229n.72, 233n.77, 237n.85, 238n.86, 253, 254n.3
Gainsford, Thomas, 101, 167, 169, 220n.54
Gardiner, Stephen, 48, 87, 99n.28, 128n.87
Gataker, Thomas. See *Good Wife, God's Gift, A*; *Marriage Duties*
Gawdy, Philip, 77, 106–7
Geertz, Clifford, 19, 127, 129, 192, 207
Gender hierarchy, 5, 82–84, 92, 99–101, 104, 114, 134–36, 141, 173–79, 222, 227–28, 242–43, 262–63
Genius domus, 151–54
Gentili, Alberico, 163, 173, 261
Gerbier, Balthazar, 192, 244
Ghost of Richard III, The (Brooke), 130
Gibbon, Charles, 51
Gifts, 62, 260; gift theory, 170–71; women as gifts, 176–77

Gillet, Louis, 69n.109, 92n.14, 97n.24
Gillis, John R., 133, 141–42, 143n.11
Giorgio, Francesco, 207n.34
Giraud, Francis F., 26n.20, 26n.23, 32n.44, 33n.46, 35n.49, 35n.52, 42n.51
God and the King (Mocket), 127
Godelier, Maurice, 262
Godly Form of Household Government, A (Dod and Cleaver), 71n.113, 85, 93n.17, 94n.18, 97, 99n.31, 100, 101, 102, 103, 109, 116, 125, 126, 128–29n.88, 133, 135, 151, 167, 169–70, 215–16, 220n.54, 220-21n.55, 224, 244, 245
Godly Meditations upon the Lord's Prayer (Bradford), 131–32n.1
Godolphin, Sir William, 57–58
Golden Key, A (Dillingham), 220n.54
Golding, Arthur, 106, 159, 182–83, 188
Goodcole, Henry, 16, 65n.106, 69, 71, 77n.124, 93n.16
Goods, 1, 2–3, 27, 35, 39, 49, 55, 61–62, 63, 80, 108–9, 135, 137, 146, 172–73, 180, 186, 188–89, 203, 204, 225, 232, 244, 254–63, 269
Good Wife, God's Gift, A (Gataker), 77, 176
Gouge, William, 125, 132, 215n.43, 227n.65
Government: church, 20, 32, 33–34, 48–49, 63; household, 11, 17, 71–73, 85–86, 97–98, 98–104, 108–9, 126, 128, 134–36, 139–41, 171–72, 193–94, 218–20, 242–43, 244 (see also Household); local, 31–35, 63 (see also Faversham); national, 7–8, 16–17, 20, 57 (see also Household: Royal; Privy Council)
Gray, Robert, 93n.16
Greene, John, 45–46, 47, 51, 52, 61, 62
Greenham, Richard, 178
Greville, Sir Fulke, 134
Grey, Lady Jane, 22
Griffith, Matthew, 101, 102n.37, 103
Grivelet, Michel, 151n.26, 247n.3
Gunaikeion (Heywood), 175, 177n.84
Gutierrez, Nancy A., 147n.19, 161n.47, 161n.48, 172n.71, 177n.85
Guy, John, 25n.16, 28n.32, 99n.28
Gyll, Thomas, 255–56

Hall, John, 187
Harbor for Faithful and True Subjects, An (Aylmer), 85n.1, 89
Harington, Sir John, 4, 8, 11, 159n.42, 239, 269
Harrison, William. See *Description of England, The*
Hasted, Edward, 26n.20, 26n.23, 27n.24, 44n.67, 45n.69
Heale, William, 180n.93
Hecatommithi, Gli (Cinthio), 199, 205, 212, 215–16, 220n.53, 223, 228

Hegendorff, Christopher, 87, 98
Henry II of England, 7, 41
Henry IV, Part One (Shakespeare), 103
Henry VIII of England, 23, 25, 26, 28, 35,
    49, 55, 69–70, 248–49
Henslowe, Philip, 91n.12
Heptameron of Civil Discourses, An (Whet-
    stone), 85n.1, 97, 133–34
Hercules, 202
Heron, Haly, 164, 165
Heywood, Thomas. See Apology for Actors,
    An; Captives, The; Curtain Lecture, A; Ed-
    ward IV; English Traveller, The; Gunaikeion;
    Philocothonista; Rape of Lucrece, The; Troia
    Britannica; True Discourse of the Two Infa-
    mous Upstart Prophets, A; Woman Killed with
    Kindness, A
Hicks, Sir Michael, 135, 136
"History of a Most Horrible Murder Com-
    mitted at Feversham, The" (Stow), 21, 40–
    42, 43n.64, 45, 47, 52–53, 57, 64n.106,
    65, 66, 67–68, 71, 72
History of Four-Footed Beasts, The (Topsell),
    202n.22
Hobbes, Thomas, 263
Hoby, Sir Philip, 57–59
Holdsworth, W. S., 51n.85
Holinshed, Raphael. See Chronicles of En-
    gland, Scotland, and Ireland, The
Holme, Randle, 256–59, 269
Holt, Anita, 41n.59
Holy Bible, The, 139, 200
"Homily Against Disobedience and Willful
    Rebellion, The," 88, 124
"Homily of the State of Matrimony, The,"
    100, 101, 102n.37, 112, 138–39, 178
Honor (male), 151, 157, 180–81, 202
Honor Military and Civil (Segar), 138, 262
Hooker, Richard, 100n.33, 125
Hoskins, W. G., 27n.26, 63
Hospitality, 137, 139, 148, 173, 224
Hothfield Manor, 25, 40, 54–55
House, meanings of, 2–11, 18, 40, 139–40,
    146, 150–53, 154–56, 173, 191–92, 252,
    267–69
Household: as commonwealth, 72–73, 85,
    92, 97, 101, 123, 133–34, 242; for de-
    fense and repose, 2, 5, 103, 148, 269;
    economic role of, 13, 101, 128–29, 192;
    government of, as aristocracy, 87, 100,
    102, 242–43; hierarchy of, 86, 92–94,
    109, 118, 133, 134–35, 171–72, 179, 219;
    as man's castle, 2, 4, 102–3, 148, 244–45,
    267–69; as patrimony, 155–56, 234n.80;
    political structure of, 11–13, 85–86, 192;
    Royal, 17, 25–26, 55, 69–70, 185; ser-
    vants of, 86, 108–9, 145–48, 150, 152–
    53, 171–72, 173, 186, 188, 224–25, 254–
    55; social role of, 3, 8, 10–11, 17, 19, 72–

73, 86, 88–89, 128, 135–36, 139, 180–81,
    191–92, 217, 245; spaces, 37–38, 134,
    145–49, 182–89, 193–94, 231–32, 256;
    as woman's place, 102–3, 117, 220, 226–
    28, 244–45, 252
Householder's Philosophy, The (Tasso), 13, 100
Household manuals. See Oeconomic tracts
Howson, John, 180n.93
Hurt of Sedition How Grievous it is to a Com-
    monwealth, The (Cheke), 88, 128n.87
Hyde, Lewis, 170, 173, 176–77
Hyde, P. G. M., 21, 30n.37, 44n.67

Ideals, obsolescence of, 137–38, 140–41,
    158, 159, 165–66, 172, 180–81. See also
    Ideology: ambiguities, contestations, and
    failures of
Ideology, 86–91; ambiguities, contestations,
    and failures of, 8, 13, 76, 87, 89–90, 91,
    101, 102–5, 107–8, 112, 113, 128–30,
    223, 226–28, 235–36, 237, 238–39, 242–
    43, 247; domestic, 3, 215–16, 219–22;
    political, 11–12, 85–90, 126–28; popular
    understandings of, 129–30, 131–36. See
    also Patriarchalism
Impertinence (literary), 16, 75–76, 90, 179,
    247
Infanticide, 229, 236–37, 245
Inns, 196, 266; "strangers in," 150–51, 219
Institution of a Gentleman, The, 46
Instruction of a Christian Woman (Vives), 176–
    77
Instructions to his son (Raleigh), 165, 173

Jacob, Edward, 35n.49, 39n.55, 44n.67
James VI and I of Britain, 117n.67, 239,
    241. See also Daemonologie; Trew Law of
    Free Monarchies, The
"Jealousy" (Donne), 138, 151–53
Jed, Stephanie H., 187n.10, 202
Jew of Malta, The (Marlowe), 184n.4
Jones, W. R. D., 46n.74, 52n.86, 59n.97
Jones, William, 98n.27
Jonson, Ben, 91
Joshuah's Godly Resolution (Bernard), 87, 98
Josselin, Ralph, 165
Jourdain, M., 93n.17
Joye, George, 180n.93
Julian, Earl of Cepta, 83, 203–4, 261–62
Julius, Philip, Duke of Stettin-Pomerania,
    2n.3, 5–7, 133
Justice, 83–84, 228; civic, 51–53, 61, 74, 81,
    82, 105–6, 133–34, 154, 241; private,
    149–51, 153–54, 187–89. See also Court
    cases; Revenge

Kelley, Donald R., 1, 262
Kempsale, Edward, 255–56
Kermode, Frank, 206

Killingworth, Mistress, 186
Kindness, 158–59, 172
King Lear (Shakespeare), 202n.22
Kingship, 80, 87, 98, 123–25, 126–27. *See also* Absolutism; Divine right; Monarchy
King's two bodies, 90, 111
Knight, G. Wilson, 217n.46, 247
Kristeva, Julia, 177, 250
Kyd, Thomas, 13, 100n.33

Lambard, William, 27, 102
Laslett, Peter, 215n.43
Latham, Agnes M. C., 164, 165
Latimer, Hugh, 117
Law's Resolutions of Women's Rights, The (T. E.), 106, 108
Lefebvre, Henri, 193
Lehmberg, Stanford E., 24n.15, 25n.16, 27n.25
Leites, Edmund, 139n.2, 173n.74, 177–78
Levin, Richard, 158n.39, 166n.57, 168n.62
Lévi-Strauss, Claude, 176–77
Lieblein, Leanore, 161n.47, 170n.67, 174n.78
Lievsay, John L., 164n.53
Lilly, William, 206n.32
Littleton, Elizabeth, Lady Willoughby, 134–46, 261
Lodge, Thomas, 106, 159
Long, Sir Richard, 28–29
Looking Glass for Married Folks, A (Snawsel), 235–36
Losebagg, George, 51
Luborsky, Ruth Samson, 196
Lucrece, 168–69, 202, 248

McAlindon, T., 201, 217n.46, 222n.57
MacCaffrey, Wallace T., 40
Macfarlane, Alan, 165
Machyn, Henry, 57, 64n.106, 66–67, 71, 106
"Manner to Choose and Cherish a Friend, The" (Elyot), 163–64
Marguerite of Navarre, 140
Marlowe, Christopher, 184n.4
Marriage, 137–41, 144–45, 177–79, 194–95, 221–22, 261; advancement through, 22–24, 70–71, 138; ceremony, 141–44; companionate, 137–38, 177–79; and inauguration of household, 138–40, 141–45, 150–51, 191–92, 193–94, 215–16, 219–20, 223–25, 265–66; and initiation of male anxieties, 132–33, 143–44, 167–68, 194–95, 224–26, 234; as male rite of passage, 138–40, 142–43, 222; social functions of, 83, 138, 139–40, 141–43, 180–81, 191–92, 242–43; as woman's punishment, 100. *See also* Cohabitation, Divorce (separation)

Marriage Duties (Gataker), 99, 116, 127, 166
Marriage Feast, A (Bradshaw), 142
Marshall, William, 44, 51
Marvelous Combat of Contrarities, A (Averell), 201
Mary of Hungary, 57
Mary of Scotland, 165n.56
Mary I of England, 22, 26, 56
Massi, J. M., 235n.81
Mauss, Marcel, 177
Maxwell, Baldwin, 234n.79
Men: comprehensive household responsibilities of, 3–4, 97, 133, 169–70, 194–95, 238–39; contestatory nature of, 165–66, 177; exchange of, 263–67; and homosocial relations, 141, 159–66, 173, 251–52, 267; household authority of, 3, 19, 40, 86–87, 91–94, 98–100, 102, 103, 116, 126, 138, 171–72, 193–95; householding by, and self-authorization, 4–5, 138–40, 145, 149, 151, 181, 187–89; household mismanagement by, 71–73, 94–98, 108–9, 113, 132–33, 194–95, 219–23, 234–35, 238–39, 240–41; social role of, 3, 138, 142–43, 148. *See also* Honor (male); Virginity
Meres, Francis, 143, 201
Meriton, George, 96
Middleton, Thomas, 114n.59
Midsummer Night's Dream, A (Shakespeare), 202, 206
Mills, Laurens J., 159n.42, 163n.51
Mirror for Magistrates, A (Baldwin), 59n.97
Miseries of Enforced Marriage, The, 246n.1
Misrule, rites of, 5, 6, 81–82. *See also* Marriage: ceremony
Mocket, Richard, 127
Monarchy, 86–87, 89–90, 98–99. *See also* Absolutism; Divine right; Kingship
Montacute House, 5, 6, 8, 11, 133, 269
Moral philosophy, 137–41, 158–66, 172–73, 180–81
Morison, Richard, 87
Morleyn, Walter, 54–55
Morsby, Thomas, 15, 51, 53–54, 62, 65, 66, 72
Mostellaria (Plautus), 267
Most Horrible and Detestable Murder, A, 77, 237–38
Moyle, Sir Thomas, 52–53
Mulcaster, Richard, 88–89, 102
Munday, Anthony, 87–88, 106
Murfyn, Alice, 22, 23, 53–54
Murphy, G. N., 205
Murray, K. M. E., 26n.20, 32n.44, 54n.90

Naming, 205–12
Nationalization, 2, 3, 16–17, 44n.65, 63
Natural law, 86, 115, 212, 229, 237

Neely, Carol Thomas, 227n.66, 228–29n.69
Neill, Michael, 214n.38, 214n.42
Nelson, Benjamin, 163n.51, 173n.74
Nessus, 202, 206, 207, 213
Neumann, Erich, 82
New Almanac and Prognostication for the Year of our Lord God 1615, A (Bretnor), 198
New Discourse of Moral Philosophy, A (Heron), 164, 165
Newman, Karen, 5n.6, 177n.85
Newnham, John, 156n.36
Newnham's Nightcrow (Newnham), 156n.36
Newton, Thomas, 159n.42, 171n.70
Niccholes, Alexander, 170
Nicomachean Ethics, The (Aristotle), 72–73, 85, 98, 100, 128, 138, 139, 159–63
Nissen, Heinrich, 192–93, 244
North, Sir Dudley, 22n.8, 54n.89
North, Sir Edward, 21–25, 26, 27, 28, 33, 39, 49, 53–54, 56, 57, 72
Norton, Clement, 44, 48–49, 50, 53, 56
Norwich, 21, 66
Notable History of the Saracens, A (Curio), 202–5

Obedience, 87–89, 91, 99–101, 104, 111, 115–17, 124, 193, 218–19, 226–28
Obligation, 11–12, 86–87, 98–99, 111, 124, 126–29, 193
Occult sciences, 194, 206, 207–12
Oeconomics, The (pseudo-Aristotle), 139
Oeconomic tracts, 11, 18–19, 86–87, 97, 102, 103, 131, 166–67, 215–16, 223
"Of Company and Fellowship" (Heron), 164, 165
Of Divorce for Adultery (Bunny), 180n.93
Of Divorcement (Dove), 99, 100n.32, 150
Of Domestical Duties (Gouge), 125, 132, 215n.43, 227n.65
Office, 23–24, 25–26, 27–28, 70, 244. *See also* Professions
Office and Duty of an Husband, The (Vives), 83
Of the Laws of Ecclesiastical Polity (Hooker), 100n.33, 125
Ortner, Sherry B., 101
Othello (Shakespeare), 192–228, 234, 238–39, 243–45, 246–50, 261

Page of Plymouth (Jonson and Dekker), 69, 91
Paget, William, 48, 70
Painter, William, 177
Palace of Pleasure, The (Painter), 177
Palladis Tamia (Meres), 143, 201
Parliament, 22, 24, 70, 165
Passions of the Mind in General, The (Wright), 166, 201n.20
Patriarcha (Filmer), 129

Patriarchalism, 11–12, 85–136, 176–77, 178–79, 194–95, 236; domestic, 3, 17, 19, 86, 98–104, 138, 140–41, 242–43; political, 86, 89, 116–17, 125–30
Peacham, Henry, 164
Pelagius of Spain, 204, 261
Percival, Arthur, 21n.5, 27n.25, 31n.40, 41, 42n.63, 43n.64, 45n.70, 46n.71, 62n.102
Percy, Henry, 151n.25, 165
Perkins, William, 132. *See also Christian Oeconomy*
Petrarch, Francesco, 4
Petty treason, 51, 86, 89, 106, 186n.9
Philip II of Spain, 22
Philocothonista (Heywood), 233
Picture of a Perfect Commonwealth, The (Floyd), 71, 88
Piers Plowman, 103
Plato, 159n.42
Plautus, 267
Pleas del Coron, Les (Stanford), 102
Plutarch, 23, 162
Pocock, J. G. A., 13, 205–6n.30
Political constitution, 72–73, 86–87, 202. *See also* Monarchy
Politics, The (Aristotle), 87, 126, 139, 202, 213, 214
Ponder, Cislye, 51, 62, 65, 66
Ponet, John, 80–84, 261
Poor relief, 17, 47, 63
Pope, Sir Thomas, 23, 24, 25
Positions (Mulcaster), 88–89, 102
Praise of a Good Name, The (Gibbon), 51
Praise of Private Life, The (Harington), 4, 8, 11, 269
Preparative to Marriage, A (Henry Smith), 98, 99, 101, 103n.39, 112, 116, 133, 150, 153–54, 179, 215n.43, 220n.54, 222, 226–27, 236n.82, 236n.83
Print culture, 17, 76
Privacy, 1, 185–89; suspicion of, 7–8
Private matters, 4, 16, 18–19, 20, 62–66, 71–78, 91, 131, 246
Privilege, 155, 229–34, 237, 240–41, 256, 262
Privy Council, 22, 23, 26, 49–50, 51, 52, 53, 55–56, 57, 69, 70, 71, 106
Professions, 20, 63, 243–44, 248–49. *See also* Office
Prognostication for this Present Year of Grace 1623, A (Allestree), 197
Prohibition of Revenge, A (Westerman), 124
Property: and anxieties of ownership, 1, 83, 137, 141, 172–74, 183–86, 191–92, 225–26, 234, 261–62; English investment in, 1, 10, 137–38, 180–81; and private matters, 1, 3, 182–89, 193
Ptolemy, 207, 212
Public, definition of, 150

Public and private spheres: analogies between, 72–73, 76, 80, 85–89, 90–91, 92, 98–99, 213–14, 247; distinctions between, 87, 118–20, 125–26, 129; hierarchy of, 11–12, 16, 82, 83–84, 86, 89, 125–26; unstable boundaries of, 71–74, 89, 243–45
Public culture, 12–13, 15–16, 19, 20, 71–78, 131–36, 238–39. See also Drama, cultural functions of; Ideology: popular understandings of

Race, 201–4, 237, 245, 249
Rainolds, John. See Defence of the Judgment of the Reformed Churches, A
Raleigh, Sir Walter, 165, 173
Ramiro I of Spain, 204–5
Rape, 79–84, 168–70, 202–5, 206, 213–15, 248–49
Rape of Lucrece, The (Heywood), 167–69, 170, 172, 174n.77
Rastell, William, 159n.42
Rauchbauer, Otto, 145n.15, 147n.19, 151n.26, 169n.64
Rebellion: domestic, 92–94, 104, 171; political, 7, 88, 119–20, 202
Reformation, consequences of, 1–3, 16–18, 48–49, 82, 87–88, 248–49
Remonstrance, or Plain Detection of Faults, A, 128
Reports of Sir Edward Coke, The, 2, 11, 103, 148
Resistance, 80, 118, 122, 202–5, 227–28
Resolves Divine, Moral, Political (Feltham), 163, 164, 170, 178, 201n.20
Revenge, 153, 179–80, 203, 241. See also Justice: private
Rich, Barnaby, 124n.76, 164
Rich, Sir Richard, 22n.9, 23, 24, 25, 32
Rich Cabinet, The (Gainsford), 101, 167, 169, 220n.54
Richardson, Walter C., 22n.9, 22n.10, 23n.13, 24n.15, 25n.16, 48n.77, 48n.78
Ridley, M. R., 195n.9, 199n.15, 215n.44, 219n.52, 220n.53, 220n.55, 225, 248n.4
Roche Abbey, 191–92
Roderick of Spain, 203–5
Romilda (in Ponet), 80–81, 83, 261
Ross, Lawrence, 195n.9, 196n.12, 199n.15, 200, 215n.44, 217n.47, 219n.52, 224n.62, 228n.68
Rowley, William, 114n.59, 246n.1, 250–52, 263–66
Rubin, Gayle, 177
Russell, Sir John, 55
Ryle, Gilbert, 19

Sagittarius, 196–98, 207–12, 228
Sagittar/y, 194–201, 206–13, 216–26

St. Augustine, 180n.93
St. James the Apostle, 204–12
Sanders, George, 105–6, 182–84, 188, 244, 261
Sanders, Norman, 248n.4
Sandwich, Kent, 28, 30, 33, 40
Santiago Matamoros, 204–5
Saunderson, Mighell, 51, 65
Scacie, John, 186
Scapegoat psychology, 82
Schelling, Felix E., 69n.109, 91n.12
Schochet, Gordon J., 73n.117, 87n.4, 99n.28, 114n.60, 127–28
Scobie, Brian W. M., 149n.21, 151n.26
Seaver, Paul S., 132–33
Second Maiden's Tragedy, The, 167–69, 170, 172
Segar, William, 138, 262
Semayne's Case (Coke), 2, 11, 103, 148
Seneca, Lucius Annaeus. See De beneficiis
Sethe, John, 33, 44
Seymour, Edward, Duke of Somerset, 22, 46n.74, 69–70
Shakespeare, William, 201n.19, 248. See also All's Well That Ends Well; Antony and Cleopatra; Comedy of Errors, The; Henry IV, Part One; King Lear; Midsummer Night's Dream, A; Othello; Taming of the Shrew, The; Tempest, The; Timon of Athens; Titus Andronicus; Troilus and Cressida
Sherbrook, Michael, 191–92, 269
Shoemaker's Holiday, The (Dekker), 244
Short Treatise of Politic Power, A (Ponet), 80–84, 261
Sidney, Sir Philip, 75
Sims, John, 255
Sinfield, Alan, 205n.29, 250n.6
Six Bookes of a Commonweale, The (Bodin), 73n.115, 126, 193–94, 236–37, 244
Skimmington Ride, 5, 6, 133, 269
Skipp, Victor, 256
Slack, Paul, 27n.26, 31, 90n.10, 113n.58
Slavery, 156–57
Smith, Henry. See Preparative to Marriage, A
Smith, M. G., 104n.43
Smith, Thomas, 85n.1, 101, 102, 126, 138
Snawsel, Robert, 235–36
Snyder, Susan, 195–96n.9, 214n.41, 227, 248n.5
Social rank, 5, 9–10, 17, 26, 43, 63–64, 138, 146–47, 155–56, 173, 229, 233, 240–41, 255–56, 262
Social regulation, 3, 5–7, 86–87, 88, 245, 262. See also Ideology
Socrates, 85n.1, 105, 139–40, 143n.13, 157
Some Rules and Orders for the Government of the House of an Earl (Brathwait), 183–84, 186–87

Sommerville, J. P., 99n.28, 115n.62, 117n.67, 194n.8
Southhouse, Thomas, 39
Space. See Cosmic space; Household: spaces
Spacks, Patricia Meyer, 156, 158n.39, 159n.43, 169n.63, 171n.69
Spain, 201–5, 207, 212–13, 239, 248
Speaight, Robert, 95n.19
Spurgeon, Caroline F. E., 214n.40
Stafford, Elsabeth, 51, 65
Stallybrass, Peter, 217n.46, 227n.66, 229n.70
Stanford, Sir William, 102
Starkey, Thomas, 87
Stephen of England, 7, 27, 32, 39
Stevenson, Laura Caroline, 123n.74
Stone, Lawrence, 7, 177–78
Stow, John. See Annals of England, The; Chronicles of England, The; "History of a Most Horrible Murder Committed at Feversham, The"; Summary of English Chronicles, A; Summary of English Chronicles, The; Two London Chronicles
Strype, John, 23
Studies, 134, 182–89. See also Household: spaces
Sturgess, Keith, 246
Subjectivity, 182–89, 262. See also Men: householding by, and self-authorization
Suicide, 174–75, 179–80, 241, 245
Summary of English Chronicles, A (Stow), 22n.11, 64n.106
Summary of English Chronicles, The (Stow), 64n.106
Sword of Maintenance, A (Westerman), 2n.3, 177
Symonds, John Addington, 69n.109, 75n.122, 92n.14, 97n.24, 254

Taming of the Shrew, The (Shakespeare), 158
Tasso, Torquato, 13, 100
Taylor, Edward Ayers, 95n.20, 247n.3
Taylor, John, 65n.106, 69, 71, 196, 200
Taylor, Thomas, 64–65n.106, 69, 71
Taylor's Travels (John Taylor), 196, 200
Telfer, Canon W., 24n.14, 27n.25, 27n.28, 32n.44, 35n.50, 35n.52, 42n.61, 45n.69, 62n.101
Tempest, The (Shakespeare), 75n.120
Tetrabiblos (Ptolemy), 207, 212
Theatre of God's Judgments, The (Beard), 65n.106, 67, 71
Theatre of God's Judgments, The Second Part of the (Thomas Taylor), 65n.106, 69, 71
Thick description, 19
Third Part of the Institutes, The (Coke), 102, 245
Thomas, Keith, 82
Thomas, William, 92–93, 133
Thomson, Gladys Scott, 55n.93

Thought: abstract, 84, 87, 112; analogical, 10–12, 85–91, 98–99, 125, 128, 242, 247; legal, 1, 2, 82–83, 102–3 (see also Court cases; Justice; Petty treason); mythical, 192–94 (see also Occult sciences)
Three Books of Occult Philosophy (Agrippa). See De occulta philosophia
Thynne, Sir John, 69–71
Tilney, Edmund. See Flower of Friendship, The
Timon of Athens (Shakespeare), 138, 180
Tiptoft, John, 159n.42
'Tis Pity She's a Whore (Ford), 99n.29
Titus Andronicus (Shakespeare), 202, 206
Todd, Margo, 139n.2, 178n.88, 180
Tongue, 197–201
Topsell, Edward, 202n.22
Townsend, Freda L., 154n.32, 157n.38, 175n.79
Tragedy, domestic, 8–10, 12, 76, 90–91, 119, 140, 238, 246–52, 268–69; inauguration of, 19, 74–76; political structure of, 12, 90, 91–98, 253
Tragedy, orthodox, 9, 12, 75, 247
Treatise of Moral Philosophy, A (Baldwin), 105n.45, 140n.5, 143, 171n.70
Trew Law of Free Monarchies, The (James), 89–90, 94, 126–27
Trial of True Friendship, The (M. B.), 68–69
Troia Britannica (Heywood), 65n.106, 69, 71
Troilus and Cressida (Shakespeare), 221
True Declaration of the Happy Conversion of Francis Robinson, A (Goodcole), 93n.16
True Difference between Christian Subjection and Unchristian Rebellion, The (Bilson), 73, 98, 99, 126–27
True Discourse of the Two Infamous Upstart Prophets, A (Heywood), 47
True Relation of a Barbarous Murder Committed by Enoch ap Evan, A, 233
True Relation of a Most Desperate Murder, A, 77n.124
Tuvill, Daniel, 163
Two Lamentable Tragedies (Yarington), 9, 75n.122, 91, 93n.17, 105, 106–8, 113–18, 120, 123, 128–30, 132, 171, 246n.1, 260, 261
Two London Chronicles (Stow), 64n.106
Two Marriage Sermons (Gataker), 77, 176
Two Most Unnatural and Bloody Murders, 233, 234n.78, 235, 239
Tyack, Geoffrey, 256
Type or Figure of Friendship, A (Dorke), 163–64, 201n.19
Tyranny, 90, 117, 124, 202

Unnatural Father, The (John Taylor), 65n.106, 69, 71
Ure, Peter, 140n.7, 156n.35, 158n.39, 175n.79, 247n.3

Van Fossen, R. W., 140n.7, 144n.14, 157n.37, 158, 161n.47, 161n.48, 169n.64, 174, 177n.84
van Gennep, Arnold, 143
Vickers, Brian, 194
View of Sundry Examples Reporting Many Strange Murders, A (Munday), 106
Virginity, 156–57, 204–5
Vives, Joannes Ludovicus, 83, 138, 176
Volpone (Marlowe), 184n.4

Wallace, John M., 180
Wallington, Nehemiah, 132–33
Warning for Fair Women, A, 9, 75n.122, 91, 105–6, 107–12, 113, 118, 120–21, 123, 128–30, 131–32n.1, 132, 135, 167n.61, 173, 182, 246n.1, 249, 260, 261
Watts, Thomas, 98n.27, 125
Webbe, George, 197–99, 200
Weber, Max, 104n.43
Weever, John, 62
Weinberg, Bernard, 75–78
Wentworth, Sir William, 44, 155, 164–65, 169, 186
Westerman, William, 2n.3, 124, 177
Whately, William. *See Bride-Bush, A; Care-Cloth, A*
Whetstone, George, 85n.1, 97, 133–34
White, Hayden, 10
White Sheet, or A Warning for Whoremongers, A (Cooke), 74, 81
Whitford, Richard, 100–101, 104–5
Wilkins, George, 246n.1
Willoughby, Cassandra, 134–36, 188
Willoughby, Sir Francis, 134–36
Wiltenburg, Joy, 238
Wine, M. L., 21n.5, 41n.60, 61n.99, 65n.107, 69n.110, 93n.17, 95n.19
Witch of Edmonton, The (Dekker, Ford, and Rowley), 75n.122, 246n.1, 250–52, 263–66
Wit's Misery (Lodge), 106
"Woeful Lamentation of Mistress Anne Sanders, The," 106
Wolsey, Thomas, 35, 55, 56

Woman Killed with Kindness, A (Heywood), 75n.122, 137–81, 183–89, 191–92, 201n.19, 241, 246n.1, 249, 250, 260–61, 269
Women: and ambiguous political role in household, 100–102, 103–4, 107–8, 112, 128, 242–43; characterologic substance of, in drama, 173–74, 250; and economic role in household, 101, 128–29, 135–36; and ethical role in household, 140, 150–51, 228, 242–43; exchange of, 142, 176–77, 263; and male anxieties of title, 137, 141, 191–92, 202, 217–19, 224–26, 234, 237–38, 262, 269; place of, in history, 20, 78–79, 242; place of, in Renaissance culture, 79–80, 82–84, 90, 99–100, 101–4, 134–36, 139–40, 150–51, 176–77, 178–79, 242–43; political subjection of, 99–101, 104, 114, 133, 135, 140, 142–43, 179; as property, 82–83, 173–74, 176–77, 217–18, 269; as threat, 18, 68, 103–4, 105, 242–43, 267; understood nature of, 111–12
Work for Householders, A (Whitford), 100–101, 104–5
Work of the Holy Bishop S. Augustine, A, 180n.93
World of Wonders, A Mass of Murders, A, 64–65n.106, 69, 106, 107
Wright, Leonard, 105n.45
Wright, Louis B., 161n.48, 163n.51, 177–78
Wright, Thomas, 166, 201n.20

Xenophon, 85n.1

Yarington, Robert. *See Two Lamentable Tragedies*
Yorkshire Tragedy, A, 75n.122, 194–95, 228–29, 233–37, 239, 245, 246n.1, 249, 250, 253–55, 259, 262–63
Youings, Joyce, 25n.17, 28n.31, 28n.32, 29n.33, 29n.35, 30n.38, 46n.73
Youngblood, Sarah, 97n.24

Zell, Michael L., 26n.22, 28n.31
Zodiacal man, 196–98, 213

GENERAL THEOLOGICAL SEMINARY
NEW YORK

DATE DUE

			Printed in USA